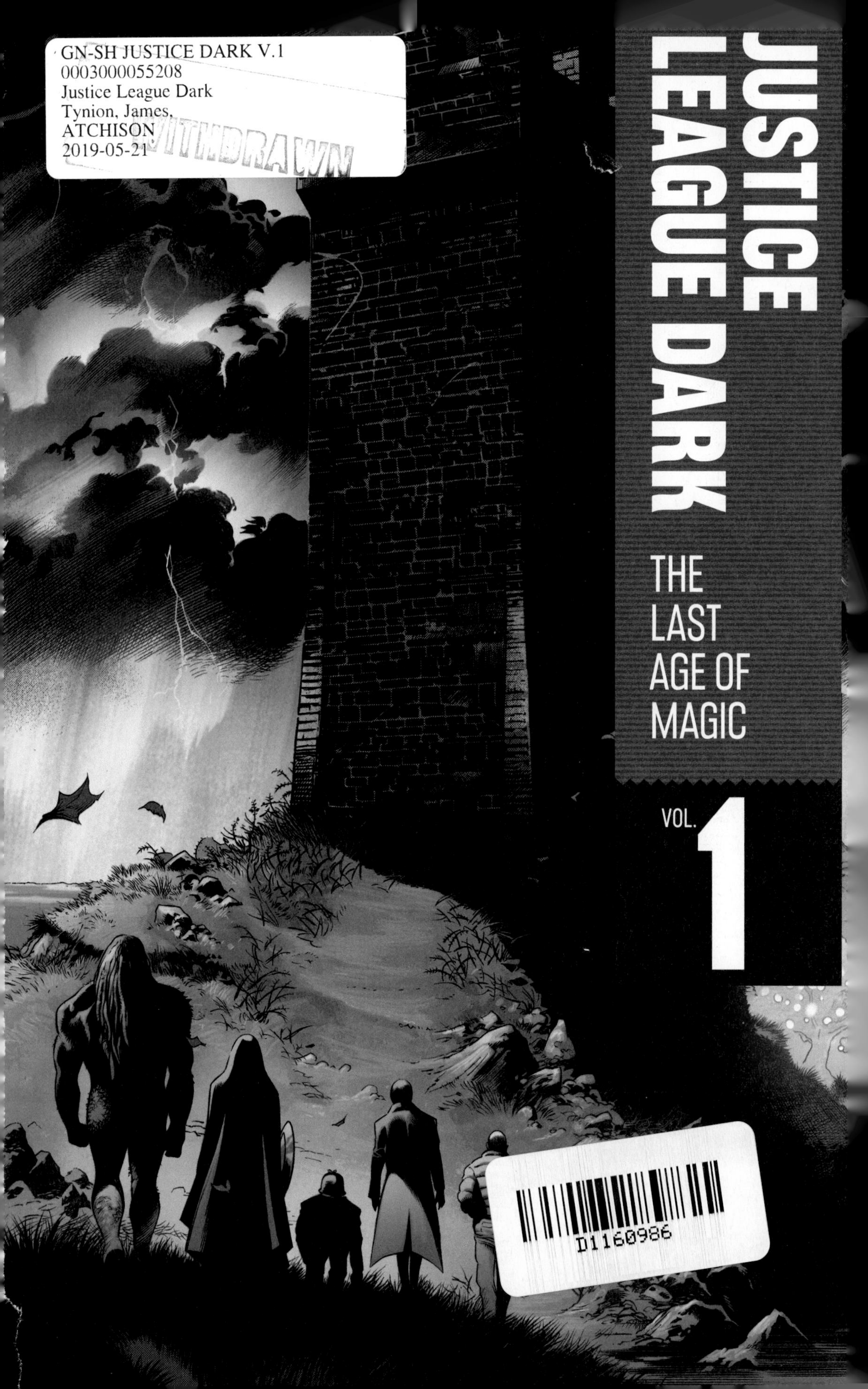

JUSTICE LEAGUE DARK

THE LAST AGE OF MAGIC

VOL. 1

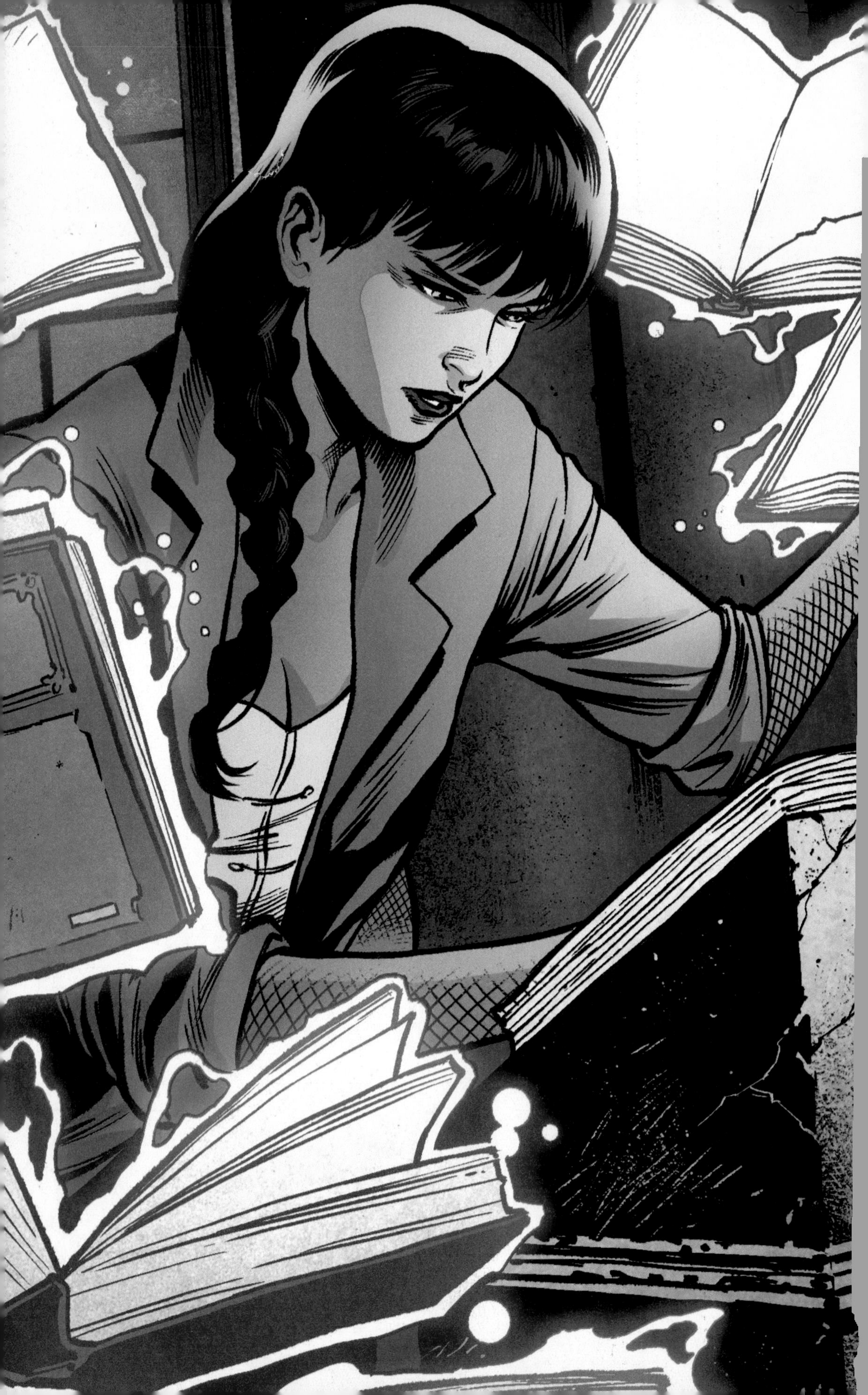

JUSTICE LEAGUE DARK

THE LAST AGE OF MAGIC

writer
JAMES TYNION IV

pencillers
ALVARO MARTÍNEZ BUENO
DANIEL SAMPERE

inkers
RAUL FERNANDEZ
JUAN ALBARRAN

colorists
BRAD ANDERSON
ADRIANO LUCAS

letterer
ROB LEIGH

collection cover artists
GREG CAPULLO
JONATHAN GLAPION
and FCO PLASCENCIA

VOL.

1

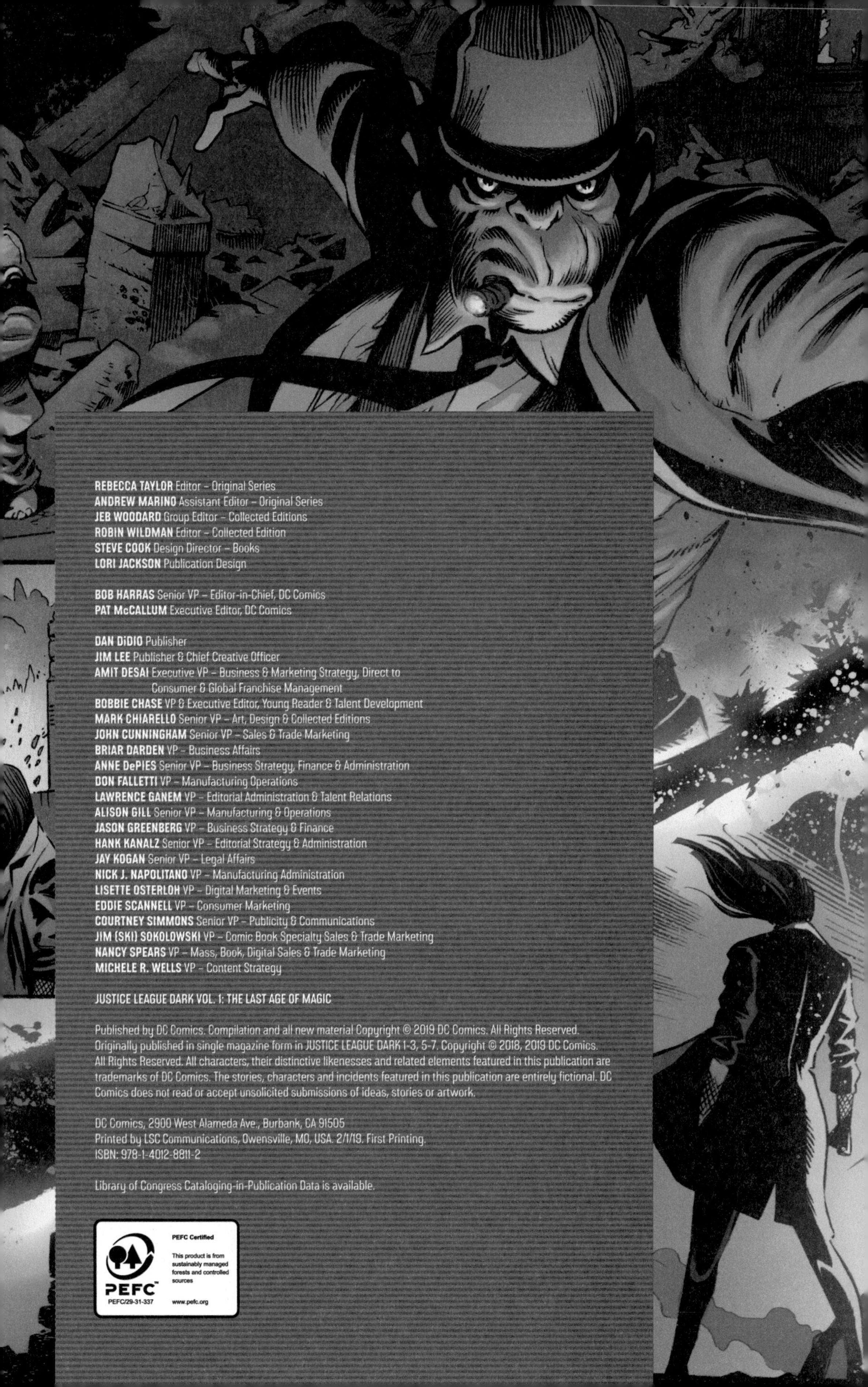

REBECCA TAYLOR Editor – Original Series
ANDREW MARINO Assistant Editor – Original Series
JEB WOODARD Group Editor – Collected Editions
ROBIN WILDMAN Editor – Collected Edition
STEVE COOK Design Director – Books
LORI JACKSON Publication Design

BOB HARRAS Senior VP – Editor-in-Chief, DC Comics
PAT McCALLUM Executive Editor, DC Comics

DAN DiDIO Publisher
JIM LEE Publisher & Chief Creative Officer
AMIT DESAI Executive VP – Business & Marketing Strategy, Direct to Consumer & Global Franchise Management
BOBBIE CHASE VP & Executive Editor, Young Reader & Talent Development
MARK CHIARELLO Senior VP – Art, Design & Collected Editions
JOHN CUNNINGHAM Senior VP – Sales & Trade Marketing
BRIAR DARDEN VP – Business Affairs
ANNE DePIES Senior VP – Business Strategy, Finance & Administration
DON FALLETTI VP – Manufacturing Operations
LAWRENCE GANEM VP – Editorial Administration & Talent Relations
ALISON GILL Senior VP – Manufacturing & Operations
JASON GREENBERG VP – Business Strategy & Finance
HANK KANALZ Senior VP – Editorial Strategy & Administration
JAY KOGAN Senior VP – Legal Affairs
NICK J. NAPOLITANO VP – Manufacturing Administration
LISETTE OSTERLOH VP – Digital Marketing & Events
EDDIE SCANNELL VP – Consumer Marketing
COURTNEY SIMMONS Senior VP – Publicity & Communications
JIM (SKI) SOKOLOWSKI VP – Comic Book Specialty Sales & Trade Marketing
NANCY SPEARS VP – Mass, Book, Digital Sales & Trade Marketing
MICHELE R. WELLS VP – Content Strategy

JUSTICE LEAGUE DARK VOL. 1: THE LAST AGE OF MAGIC

DC Comics, 2900 West Alameda Ave., Burbank, CA 91505
Printed by LSC Communications, Owensville, MO, USA. 2/1/19. First Printing.
ISBN: 978-1-4012-8811-2

Library of Congress Cataloging-in-Publication Data is available.

PEFC Certified
This product is from sustainably managed forests and controlled sources
PEFC
PEFC/29-31-337
www.pefc.org

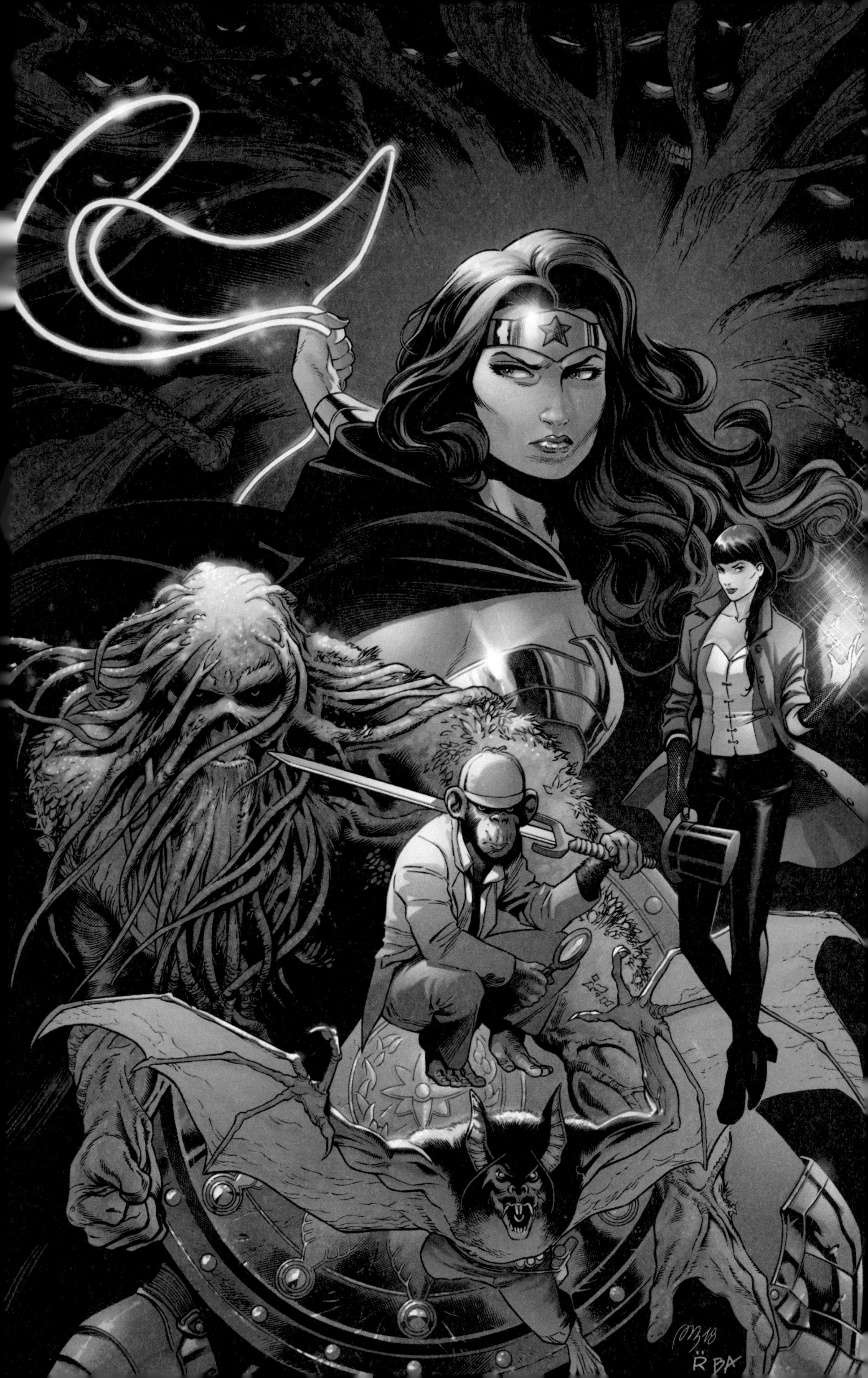

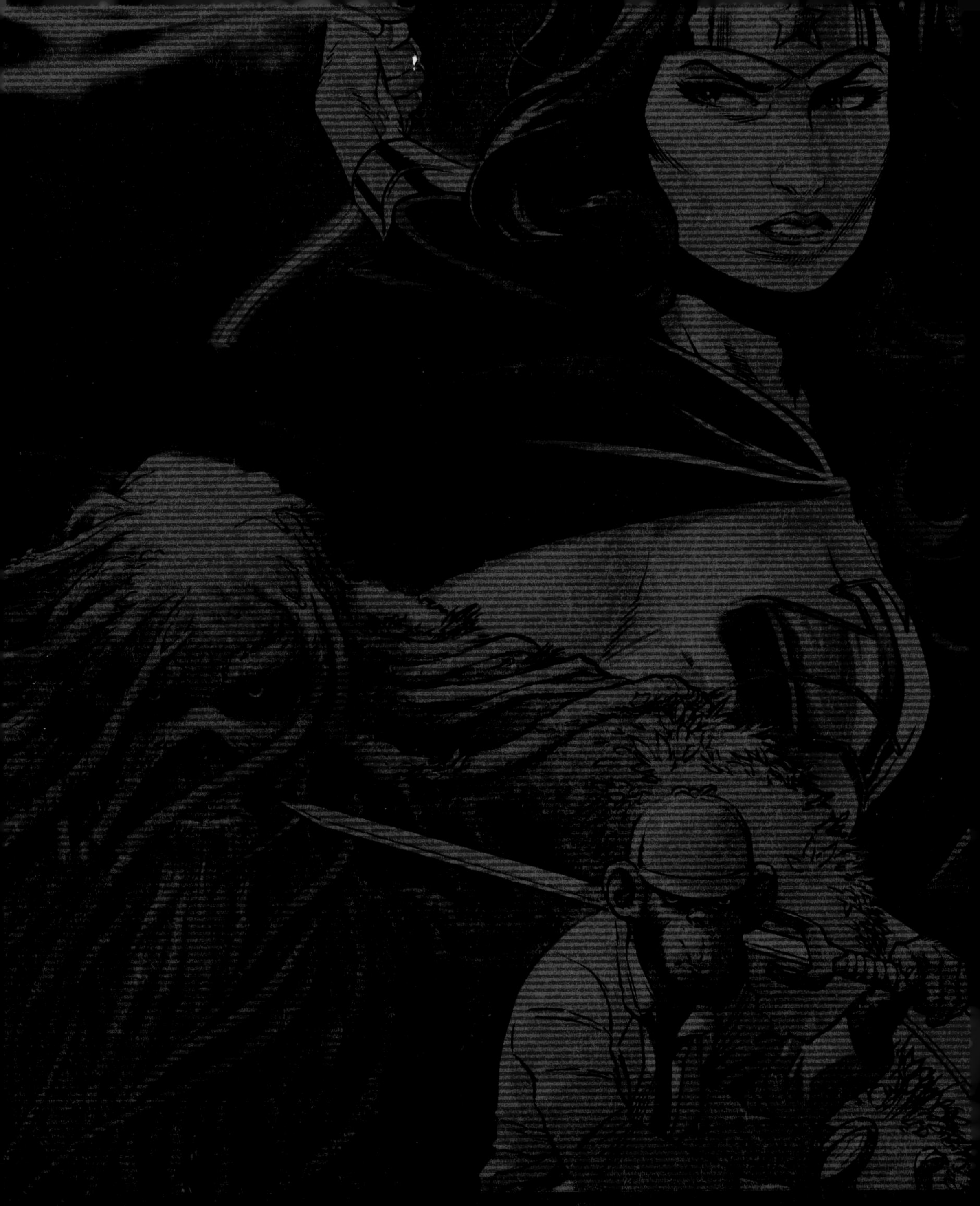

JUSTICE LEAGUE DARK

#1

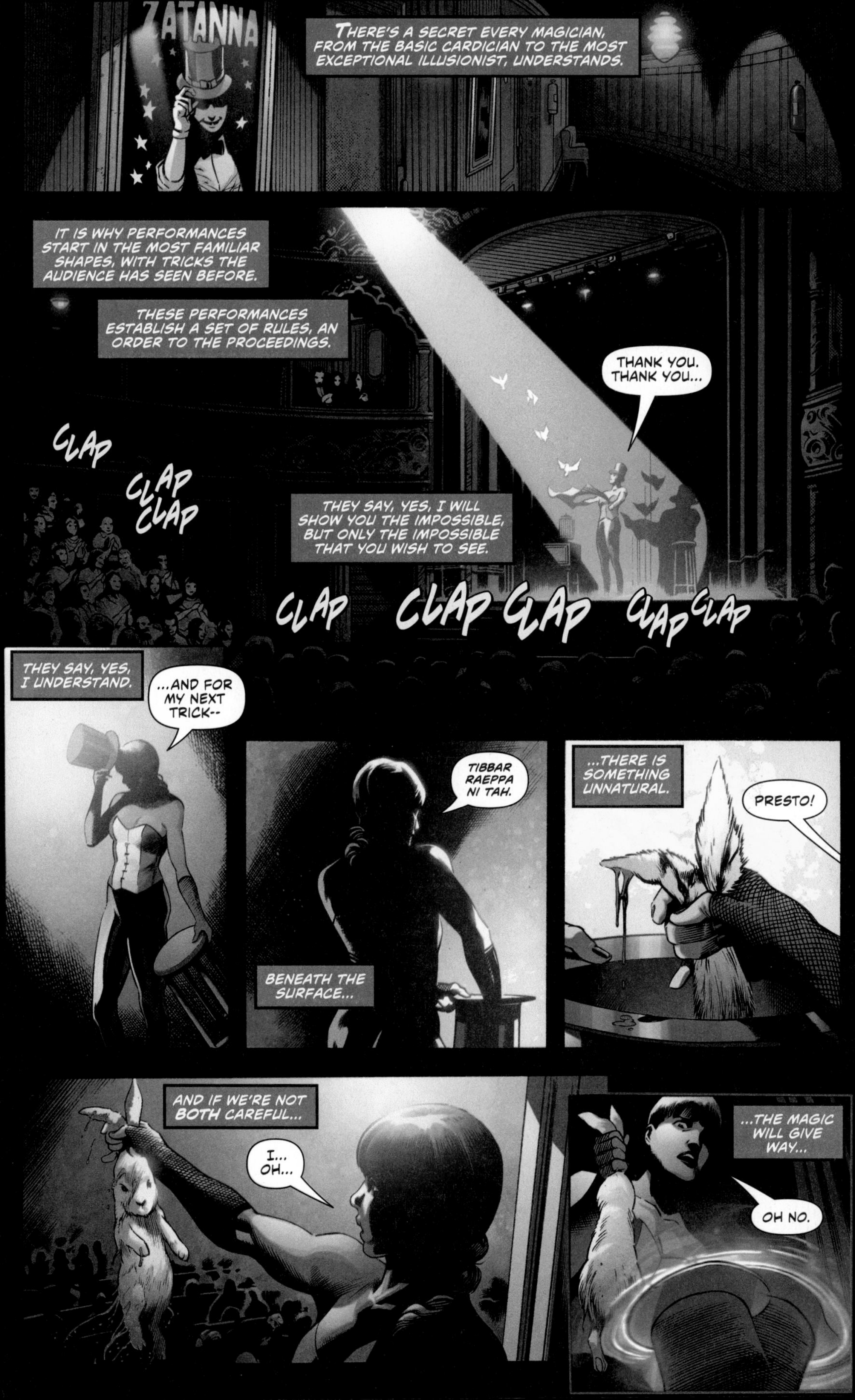
ZATANNA
THERE'S A SECRET EVERY MAGICIAN, FROM THE BASIC CARDICIAN TO THE MOST EXCEPTIONAL ILLUSIONIST, UNDERSTANDS.
IT IS WHY PERFORMANCES START IN THE MOST FAMILIAR SHAPES, WITH TRICKS THE AUDIENCE HAS SEEN BEFORE.
THESE PERFORMANCES ESTABLISH A SET OF RULES, AN ORDER TO THE PROCEEDINGS.
THANK YOU. THANK YOU...
CLAP
CLAP CLAP
THEY SAY, YES, I WILL SHOW YOU THE IMPOSSIBLE, BUT ONLY THE IMPOSSIBLE THAT YOU WISH TO SEE.
CLAP CLAP CLAP CLAP CLAP
THEY SAY, YES, I UNDERSTAND.
...AND FOR MY NEXT TRICK--
TIBBAR RAEPPA NI TAH.
BENEATH THE SURFACE...
...THERE IS SOMETHING UNNATURAL.
PRESTO!
AND IF WE'RE NOT BOTH CAREFUL...
I... OH...
...THE MAGIC WILL GIVE WAY...
OH NO.

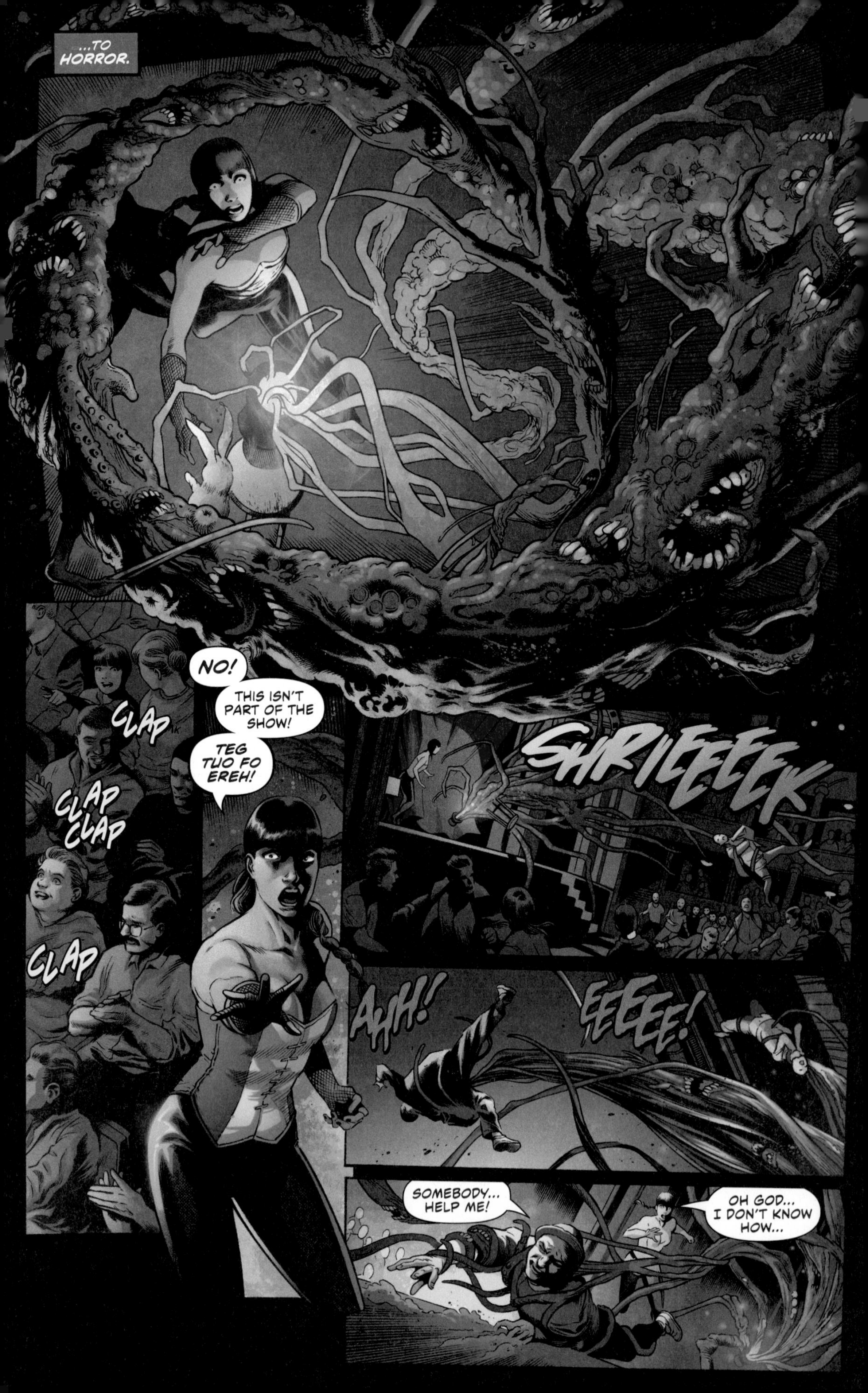
...TO HORROR.
NO!
THIS ISN'T PART OF THE SHOW!
TEG TUO FO EREH!
CLAP
CLAP CLAP
CLAP
SHRIEEEEK
AHH!
EEEEE!
SOMEBODY... HELP ME!
OH GOD... I DON'T KNOW HOW...

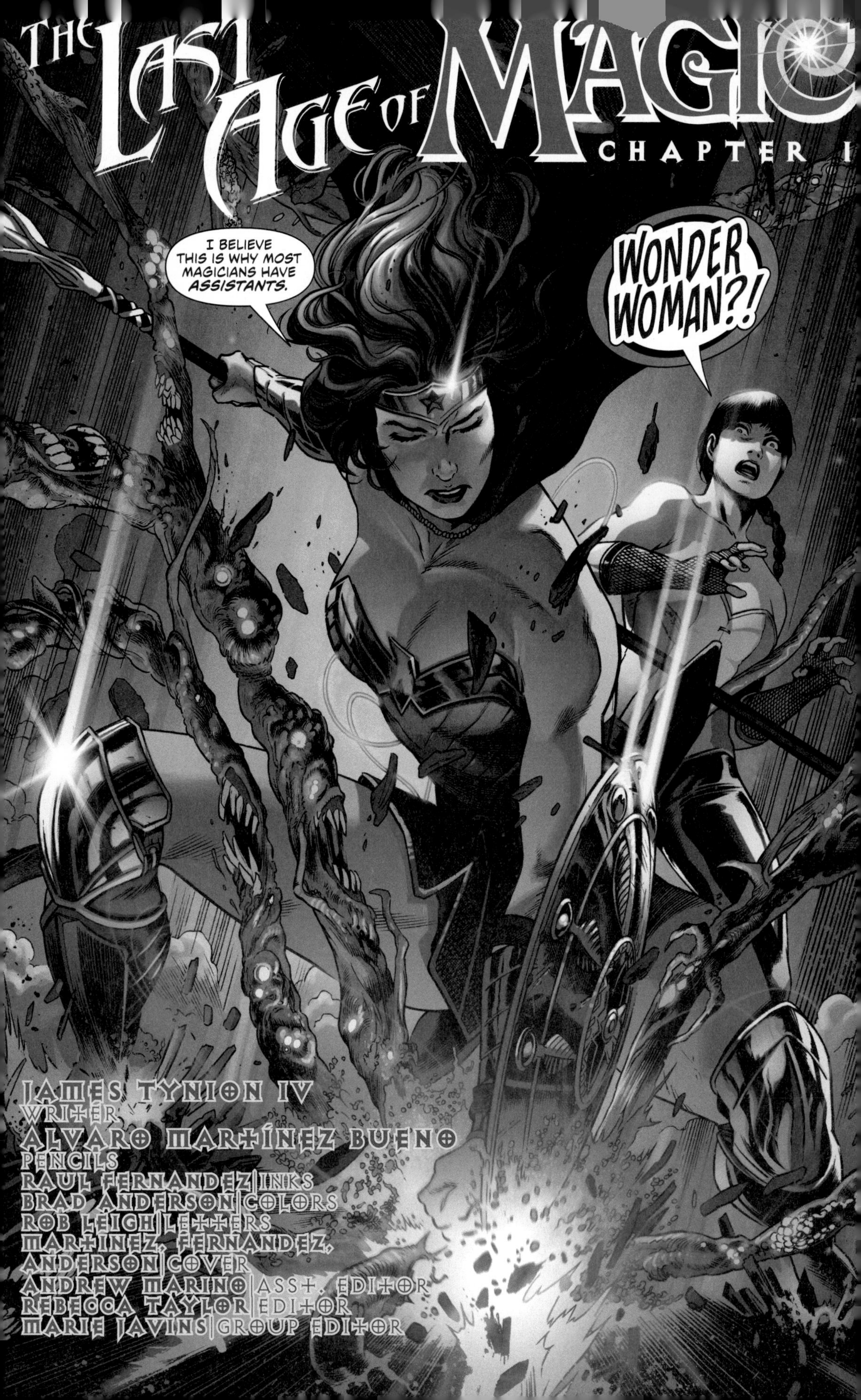
THE LAST AGE OF MAGIC
CHAPTER I
I BELIEVE THIS IS WHY MOST MAGICIANS HAVE ASSISTANTS.
WONDER WOMAN?!
JAMES TYNION IV
WRITER
ALVARO MARTÍNEZ BUENO
PENCILS
RAUL FERNANDEZ|INKS
BRAD ANDERSON|COLORS
ROB LEIGH|LETTERS
MARTINEZ, FERNANDEZ, ANDERSON|COVER
ANDREW MARINO|ASST. EDITOR
REBECCA TAYLOR|EDITOR
MARIE JAVINS|GROUP EDITOR

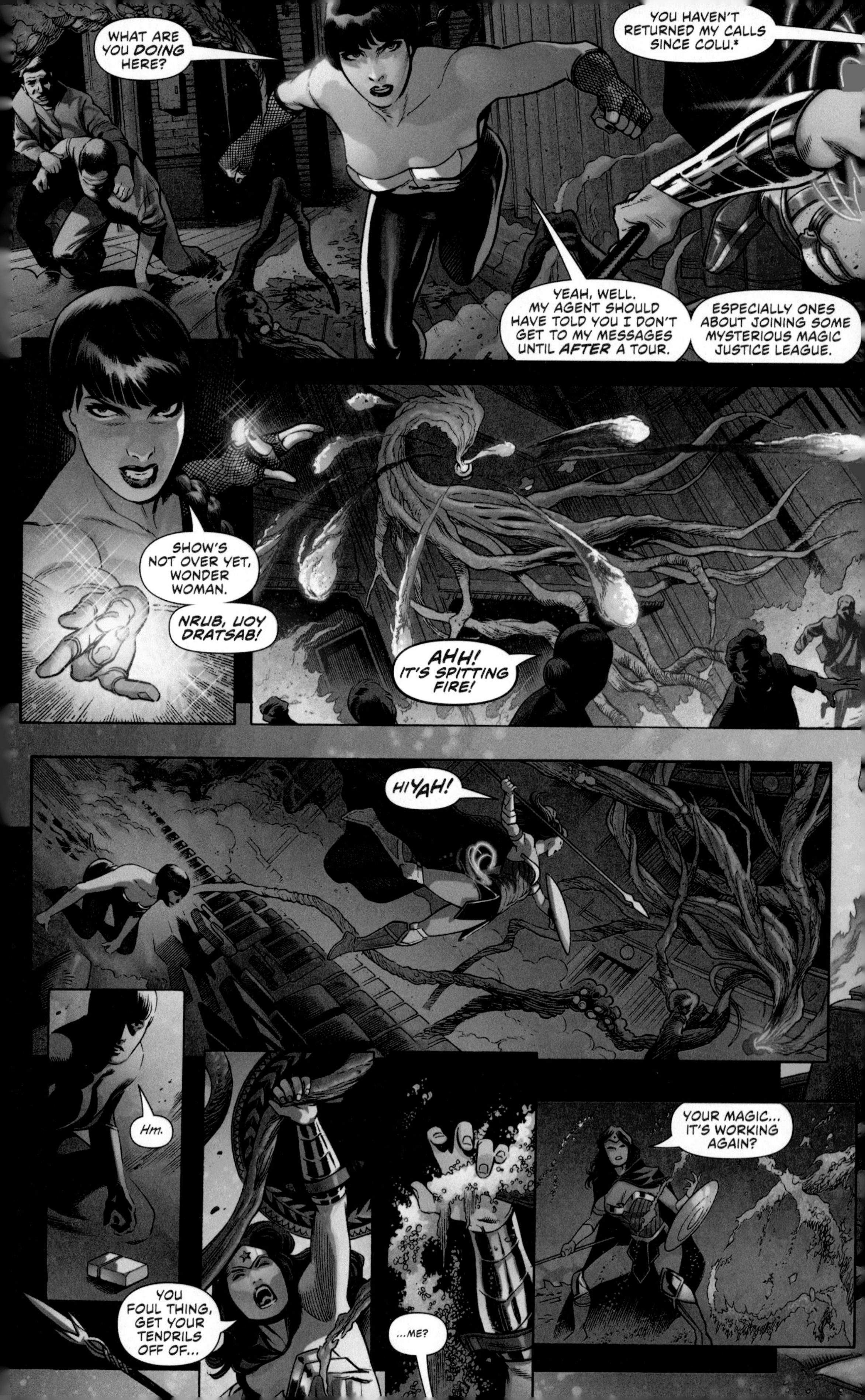
WHAT ARE YOU DOING HERE?
YOU HAVEN'T RETURNED MY CALLS SINCE COLU.*
YEAH, WELL. MY AGENT SHOULD HAVE TOLD YOU I DON'T GET TO MY MESSAGES UNTIL AFTER A TOUR.
ESPECIALLY ONES ABOUT JOINING SOME MYSTERIOUS MAGIC JUSTICE LEAGUE.
SHOW'S NOT OVER YET, WONDER WOMAN.
NRUB, UOY DRATSAB!
AHH! IT'S SPITTING FIRE!
HIYAH!
Hm.
YOU FOUL THING, GET YOUR TENDRILS OFF OF...
...ME?
YOUR MAGIC... IT'S WORKING AGAIN?

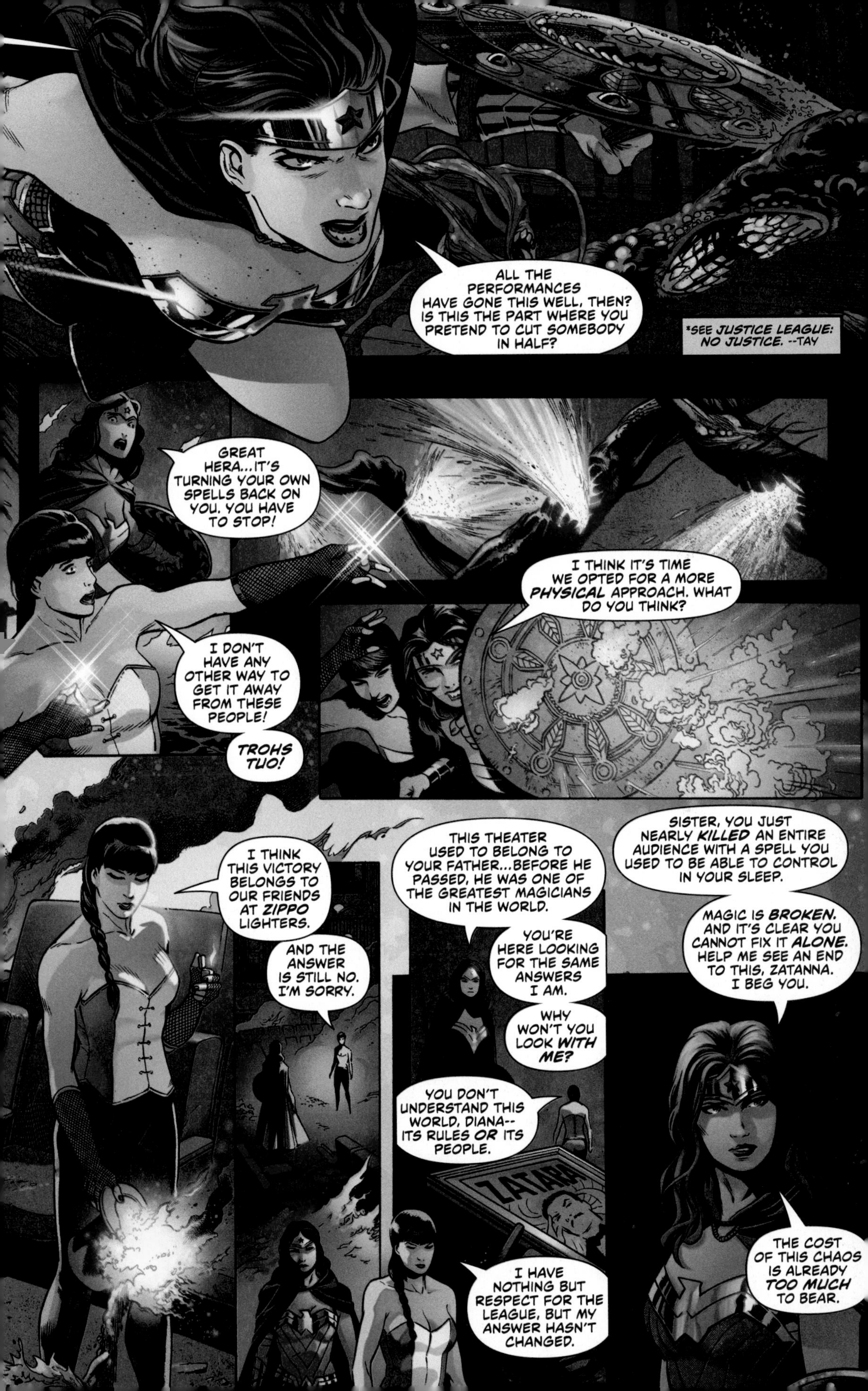

ALL THE PERFORMANCES HAVE GONE THIS WELL, THEN? IS THIS THE PART WHERE YOU PRETEND TO CUT SOMEBODY IN HALF?
*SEE JUSTICE LEAGUE: NO JUSTICE. --TAY
GREAT HERA...IT'S TURNING YOUR OWN SPELLS BACK ON YOU. YOU HAVE TO STOP!
I DON'T HAVE ANY OTHER WAY TO GET IT AWAY FROM THESE PEOPLE!
TROHS TUO!
I THINK IT'S TIME WE OPTED FOR A MORE PHYSICAL APPROACH. WHAT DO YOU THINK?
I THINK THIS VICTORY BELONGS TO OUR FRIENDS AT ZIPPO LIGHTERS.
AND THE ANSWER IS STILL NO. I'M SORRY.
THIS THEATER USED TO BELONG TO YOUR FATHER...BEFORE HE PASSED, HE WAS ONE OF THE GREATEST MAGICIANS IN THE WORLD.
YOU'RE HERE LOOKING FOR THE SAME ANSWERS I AM.
WHY WON'T YOU LOOK WITH ME?
YOU DON'T UNDERSTAND THIS WORLD, DIANA-- ITS RULES OR ITS PEOPLE.
ZATARA
I HAVE NOTHING BUT RESPECT FOR THE LEAGUE, BUT MY ANSWER HASN'T CHANGED.
SISTER, YOU JUST NEARLY KILLED AN ENTIRE AUDIENCE WITH A SPELL YOU USED TO BE ABLE TO CONTROL IN YOUR SLEEP.
MAGIC IS BROKEN. AND IT'S CLEAR YOU CANNOT FIX IT ALONE. HELP ME SEE AN END TO THIS, ZATANNA. I BEG YOU.
THE COST OF THIS CHAOS IS ALREADY TOO MUCH TO BEAR.

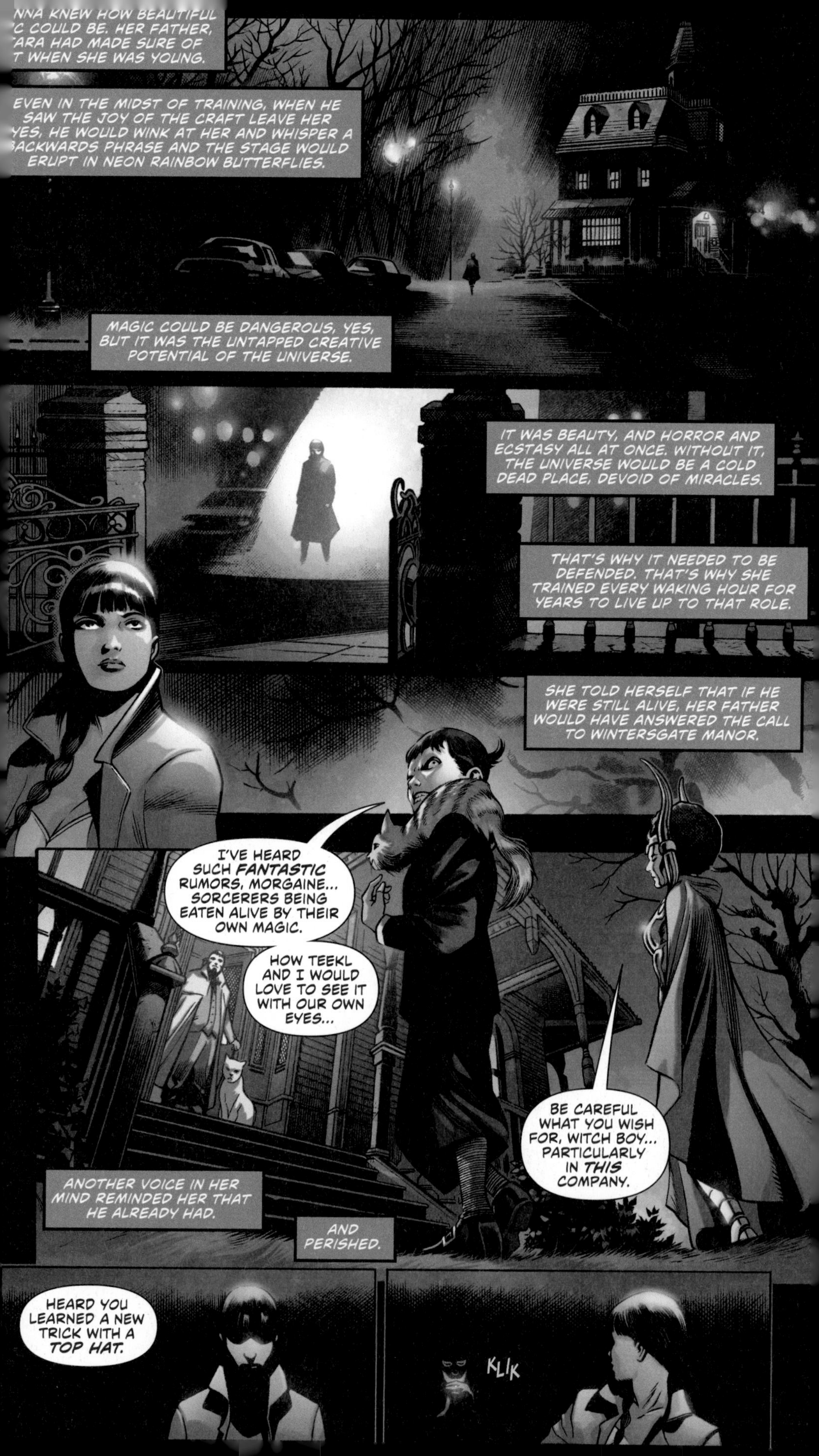

NNA KNEW HOW BEAUTIFUL
C COULD BE. HER FATHER,
ARA HAD MADE SURE OF
T WHEN SHE WAS YOUNG.
EVEN IN THE MIDST OF TRAINING, WHEN HE SAW THE JOY OF THE CRAFT LEAVE HER YES, HE WOULD WINK AT HER AND WHISPER A ACKWARDS PHRASE AND THE STAGE WOULD ERUPT IN NEON RAINBOW BUTTERFLIES.
MAGIC COULD BE DANGEROUS, YES, BUT IT WAS THE UNTAPPED CREATIVE POTENTIAL OF THE UNIVERSE.
IT WAS BEAUTY, AND HORROR AND ECSTASY ALL AT ONCE. WITHOUT IT, THE UNIVERSE WOULD BE A COLD DEAD PLACE, DEVOID OF MIRACLES.
THAT'S WHY IT NEEDED TO BE DEFENDED. THAT'S WHY SHE TRAINED EVERY WAKING HOUR FOR YEARS TO LIVE UP TO THAT ROLE.
SHE TOLD HERSELF THAT IF HE WERE STILL ALIVE, HER FATHER WOULD HAVE ANSWERED THE CALL TO WINTERSGATE MANOR.
I'VE HEARD SUCH FANTASTIC RUMORS, MORGAINE... SORCERERS BEING EATEN ALIVE BY THEIR OWN MAGIC.
HOW TEEKL AND I WOULD LOVE TO SEE IT WITH OUR OWN EYES...
BE CAREFUL WHAT YOU WISH FOR, WITCH BOY... PARTICULARLY IN THIS COMPANY.
ANOTHER VOICE IN HER MIND REMINDED HER THAT HE ALREADY HAD.
AND PERISHED.
HEARD YOU LEARNED A NEW TRICK WITH A TOP HAT.
KLIK

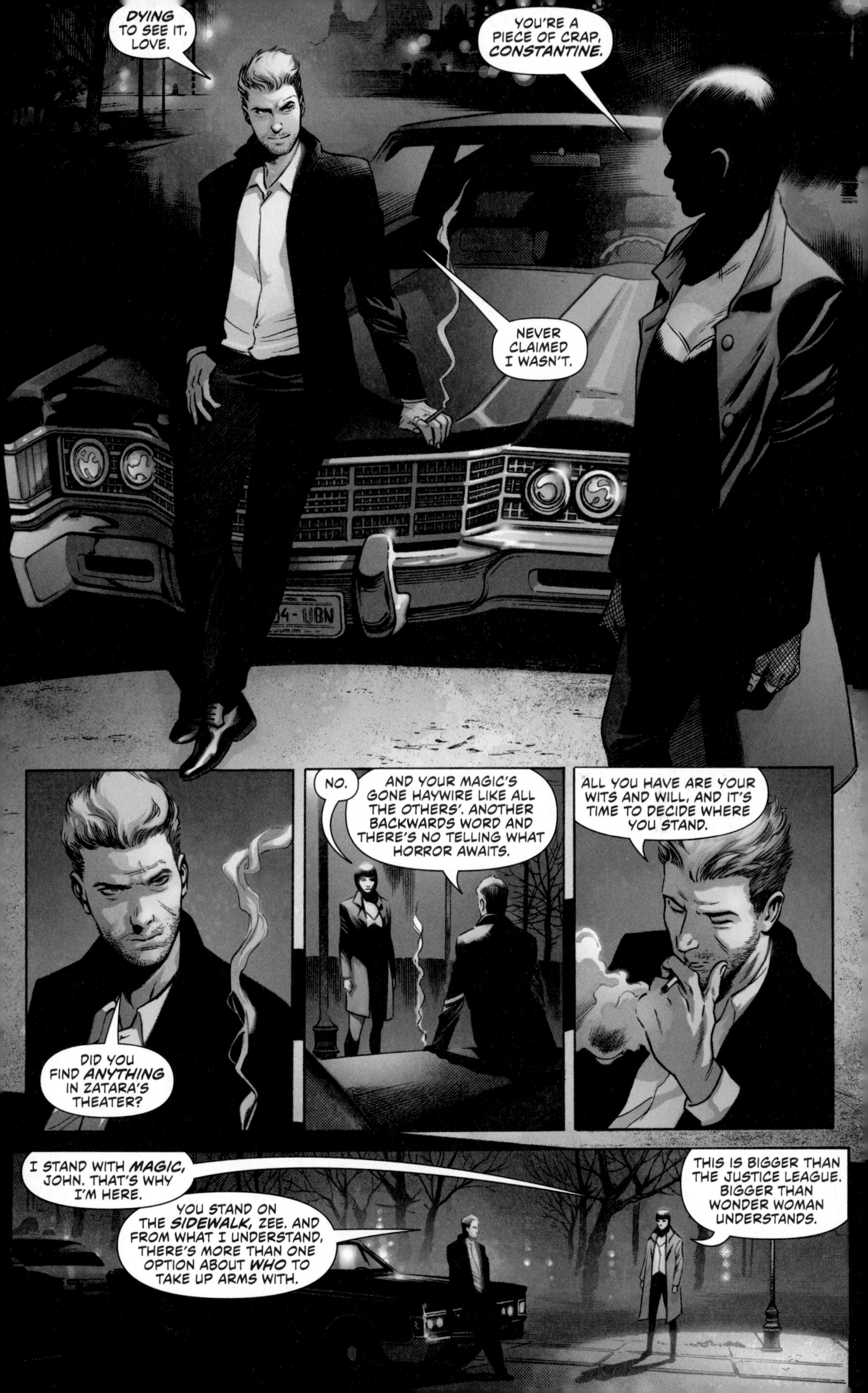
DYING TO SEE IT, LOVE.
YOU'RE A PIECE OF CRAP, CONSTANTINE.
NEVER CLAIMED I WASN'T.
DID YOU FIND ANYTHING IN ZATARA'S THEATER?
NO.
AND YOUR MAGIC'S GONE HAYWIRE LIKE ALL THE OTHERS'. ANOTHER BACKWARDS WORD AND THERE'S NO TELLING WHAT HORROR AWAITS.
ALL YOU HAVE ARE YOUR WITS AND WILL, AND IT'S TIME TO DECIDE WHERE YOU STAND.
I STAND WITH MAGIC, JOHN. THAT'S WHY I'M HERE.
YOU STAND ON THE SIDEWALK, ZEE. AND FROM WHAT I UNDERSTAND, THERE'S MORE THAN ONE OPTION ABOUT WHO TO TAKE UP ARMS WITH.
THIS IS BIGGER THAN THE JUSTICE LEAGUE. BIGGER THAN WONDER WOMAN UNDERSTANDS.

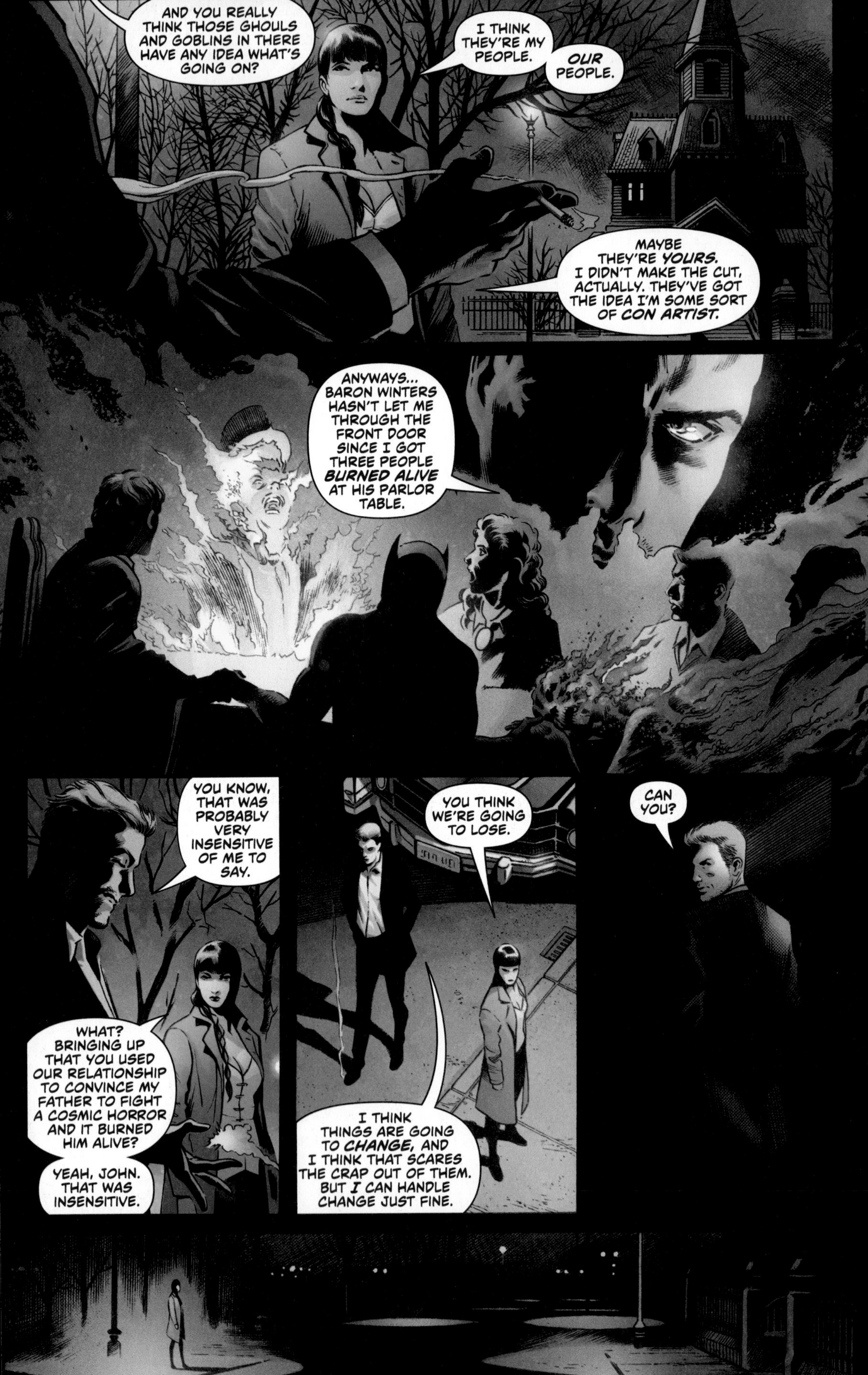
AND YOU REALLY THINK THOSE GHOULS AND GOBLINS IN THERE HAVE ANY IDEA WHAT'S GOING ON?
I THINK THEY'RE MY PEOPLE.
OUR PEOPLE.
MAYBE THEY'RE YOURS. I DIDN'T MAKE THE CUT, ACTUALLY. THEY'VE GOT THE IDEA I'M SOME SORT OF CON ARTIST.
ANYWAYS... BARON WINTERS HASN'T LET ME THROUGH THE FRONT DOOR SINCE I GOT THREE PEOPLE BURNED ALIVE AT HIS PARLOR TABLE.
YOU KNOW, THAT WAS PROBABLY VERY INSENSITIVE OF ME TO SAY.
WHAT? BRINGING UP THAT YOU USED OUR RELATIONSHIP TO CONVINCE MY FATHER TO FIGHT A COSMIC HORROR AND IT BURNED HIM ALIVE?
YEAH, JOHN. THAT WAS INSENSITIVE.
YOU THINK WE'RE GOING TO LOSE.
I THINK THINGS ARE GOING TO CHANGE, AND I THINK THAT SCARES THE CRAP OUT OF THEM. BUT I CAN HANDLE CHANGE JUST FINE.
CAN YOU?

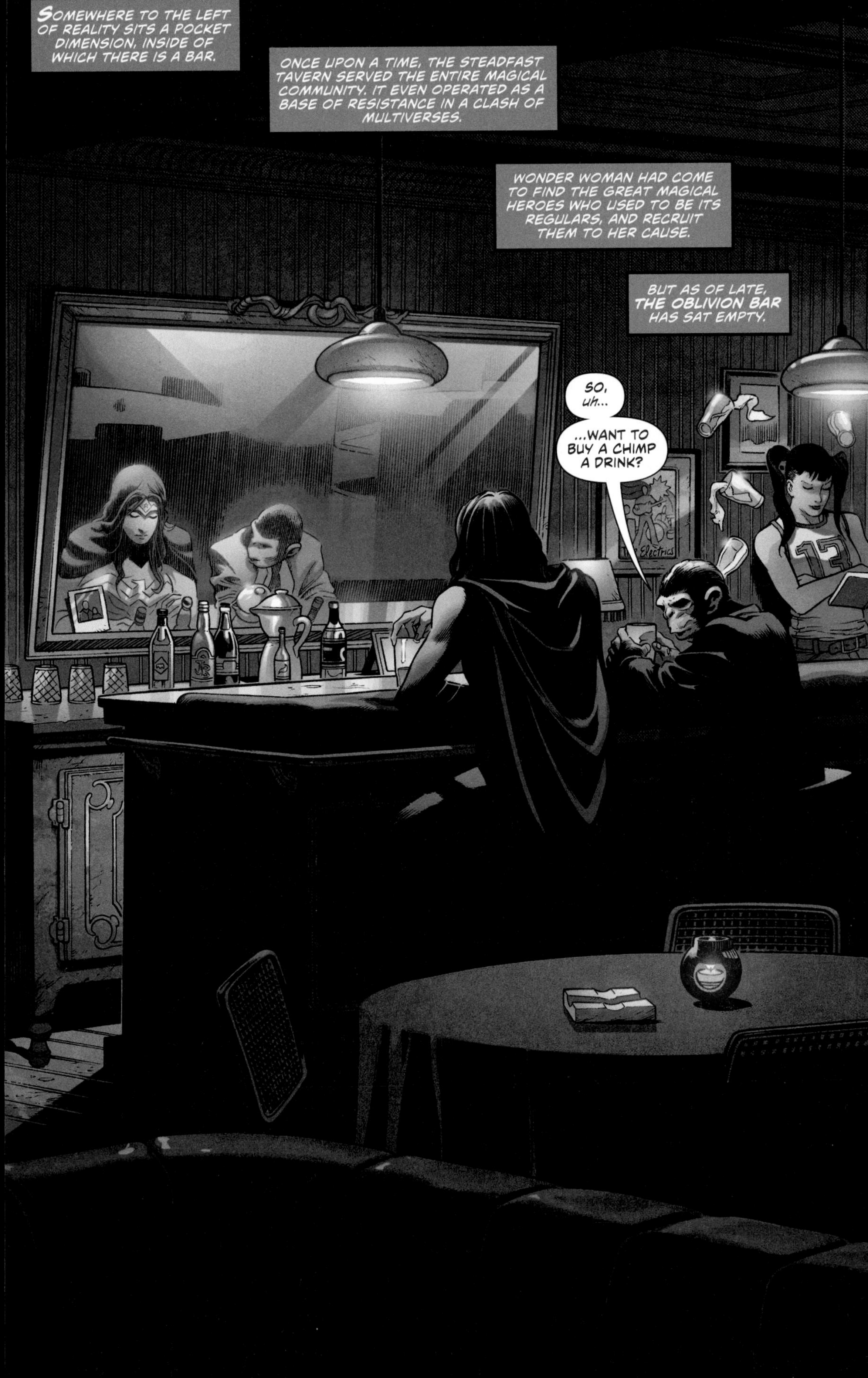
SOMEWHERE TO THE LEFT OF REALITY SITS A POCKET DIMENSION, INSIDE OF WHICH THERE IS A BAR.
ONCE UPON A TIME, THE STEADFAST TAVERN SERVED THE ENTIRE MAGICAL COMMUNITY. IT EVEN OPERATED AS A BASE OF RESISTANCE IN A CLASH OF MULTIVERSES.
WONDER WOMAN HAD COME TO FIND THE GREAT MAGICAL HEROES WHO USED TO BE ITS REGULARS, AND RECRUIT THEM TO HER CAUSE.
BUT AS OF LATE, THE OBLIVION BAR HAS SAT EMPTY.
SO, uh...
...WANT TO BUY A CHIMP A DRINK?

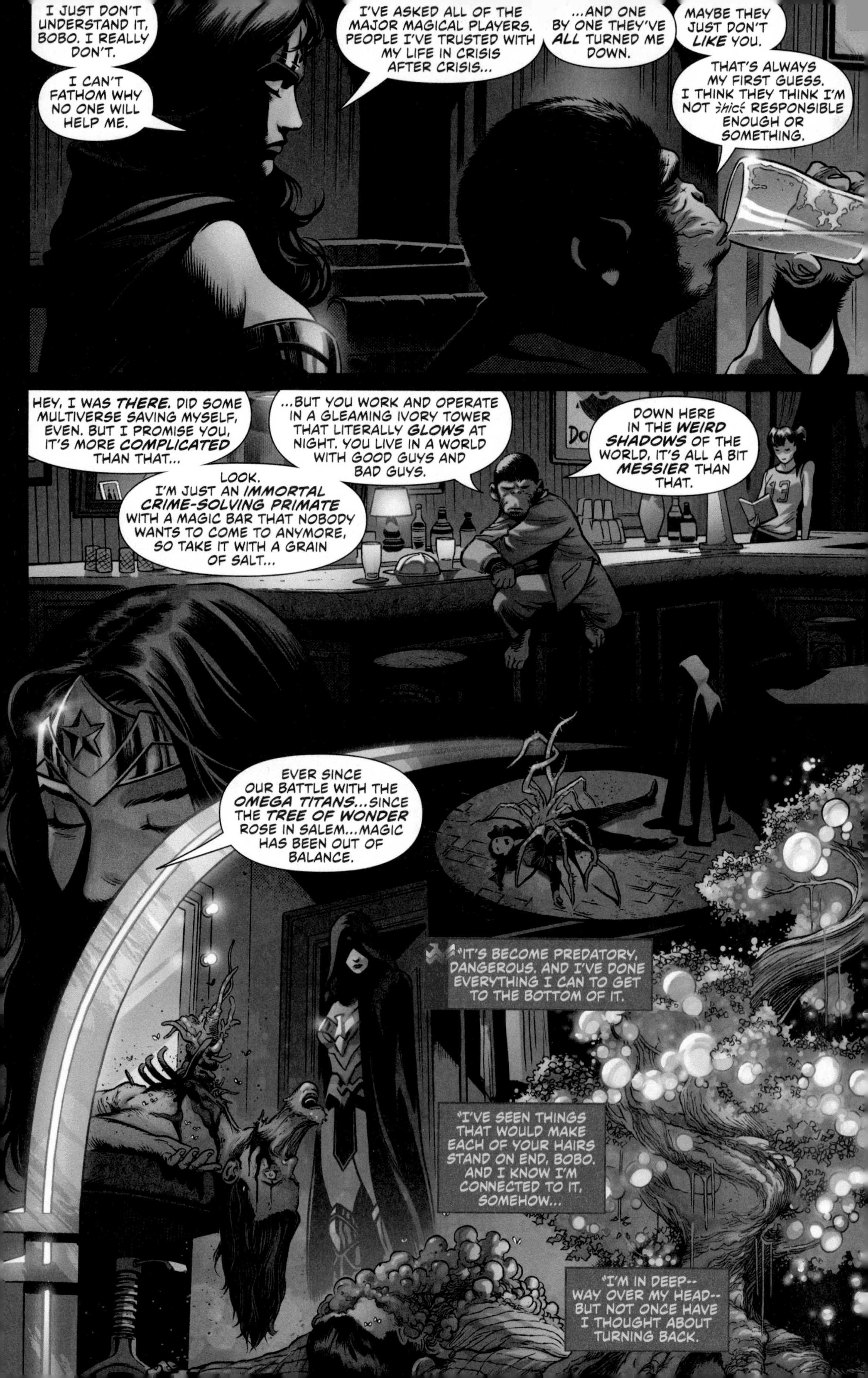
I JUST DON'T UNDERSTAND IT, BOBO. I REALLY DON'T.
I CAN'T FATHOM WHY NO ONE WILL HELP ME.
I'VE ASKED ALL OF THE MAJOR MAGICAL PLAYERS. PEOPLE I'VE TRUSTED WITH MY LIFE IN CRISIS AFTER CRISIS...
...AND ONE BY ONE THEY'VE ALL TURNED ME DOWN.
MAYBE THEY JUST DON'T LIKE YOU.
THAT'S ALWAYS MY FIRST GUESS. I THINK THEY THINK I'M NOT *HIC* RESPONSIBLE ENOUGH OR SOMETHING.
HEY, I WAS THERE. DID SOME MULTIVERSE SAVING MYSELF, EVEN. BUT I PROMISE YOU, IT'S MORE COMPLICATED THAN THAT...
...BUT YOU WORK AND OPERATE IN A GLEAMING IVORY TOWER THAT LITERALLY GLOWS AT NIGHT. YOU LIVE IN A WORLD WITH GOOD GUYS AND BAD GUYS.
DOWN HERE IN THE WEIRD SHADOWS OF THE WORLD, IT'S ALL A BIT MESSIER THAN THAT.
LOOK. I'M JUST AN IMMORTAL CRIME-SOLVING PRIMATE WITH A MAGIC BAR THAT NOBODY WANTS TO COME TO ANYMORE, SO TAKE IT WITH A GRAIN OF SALT...
EVER SINCE OUR BATTLE WITH THE OMEGA TITANS...SINCE THE TREE OF WONDER ROSE IN SALEM...MAGIC HAS BEEN OUT OF BALANCE.
"IT'S BECOME PREDATORY, DANGEROUS. AND I'VE DONE EVERYTHING I CAN TO GET TO THE BOTTOM OF IT.
"I'VE SEEN THINGS THAT WOULD MAKE EACH OF YOUR HAIRS STAND ON END, BOBO. AND I KNOW I'M CONNECTED TO IT, SOMEHOW...
"I'M IN DEEP--WAY OVER MY HEAD--BUT NOT ONCE HAVE I THOUGHT ABOUT TURNING BACK.

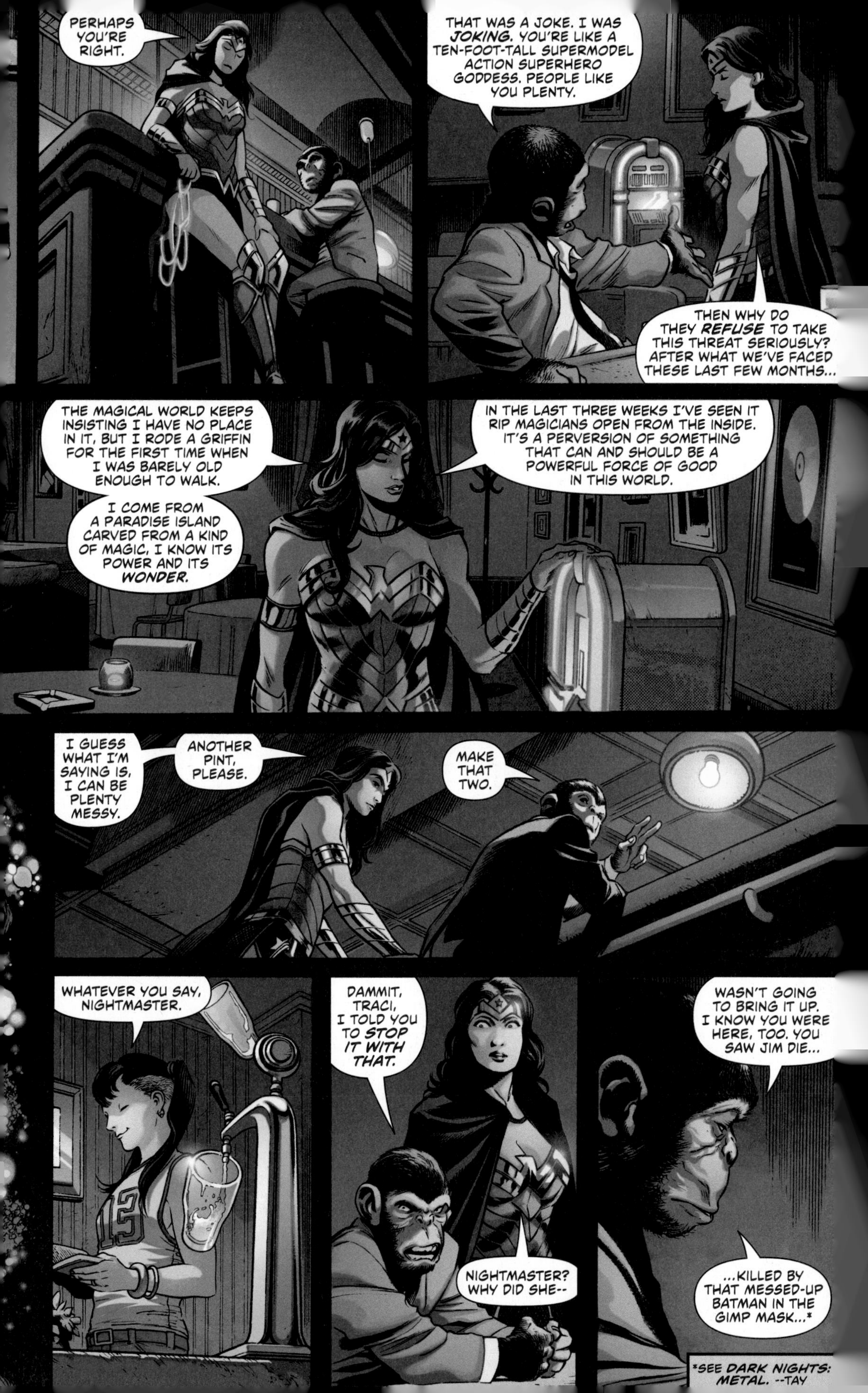
PERHAPS YOU'RE RIGHT.
THAT WAS A JOKE. I WAS JOKING. YOU'RE LIKE A TEN-FOOT-TALL SUPERMODEL ACTION SUPERHERO GODDESS. PEOPLE LIKE YOU PLENTY.
THEN WHY DO THEY REFUSE TO TAKE THIS THREAT SERIOUSLY? AFTER WHAT WE'VE FACED THESE LAST FEW MONTHS...
THE MAGICAL WORLD KEEPS INSISTING I HAVE NO PLACE IN IT, BUT I RODE A GRIFFIN FOR THE FIRST TIME WHEN I WAS BARELY OLD ENOUGH TO WALK.
I COME FROM A PARADISE ISLAND CARVED FROM A KIND OF MAGIC. I KNOW ITS POWER AND ITS WONDER.
IN THE LAST THREE WEEKS I'VE SEEN IT RIP MAGICIANS OPEN FROM THE INSIDE. IT'S A PERVERSION OF SOMETHING THAT CAN AND SHOULD BE A POWERFUL FORCE OF GOOD IN THIS WORLD.
I GUESS WHAT I'M SAYING IS, I CAN BE PLENTY MESSY.
ANOTHER PINT, PLEASE.
MAKE THAT TWO.
WHATEVER YOU SAY, NIGHTMASTER.
DAMMIT, TRACI, I TOLD YOU TO STOP IT WITH THAT.
NIGHTMASTER? WHY DID SHE--
WASN'T GOING TO BRING IT UP. I KNOW YOU WERE HERE, TOO. YOU SAW JIM DIE...
...KILLED BY THAT MESSED-UP BATMAN IN THE GIMP MASK...*
*SEE DARK NIGHTS: METAL. --TAY

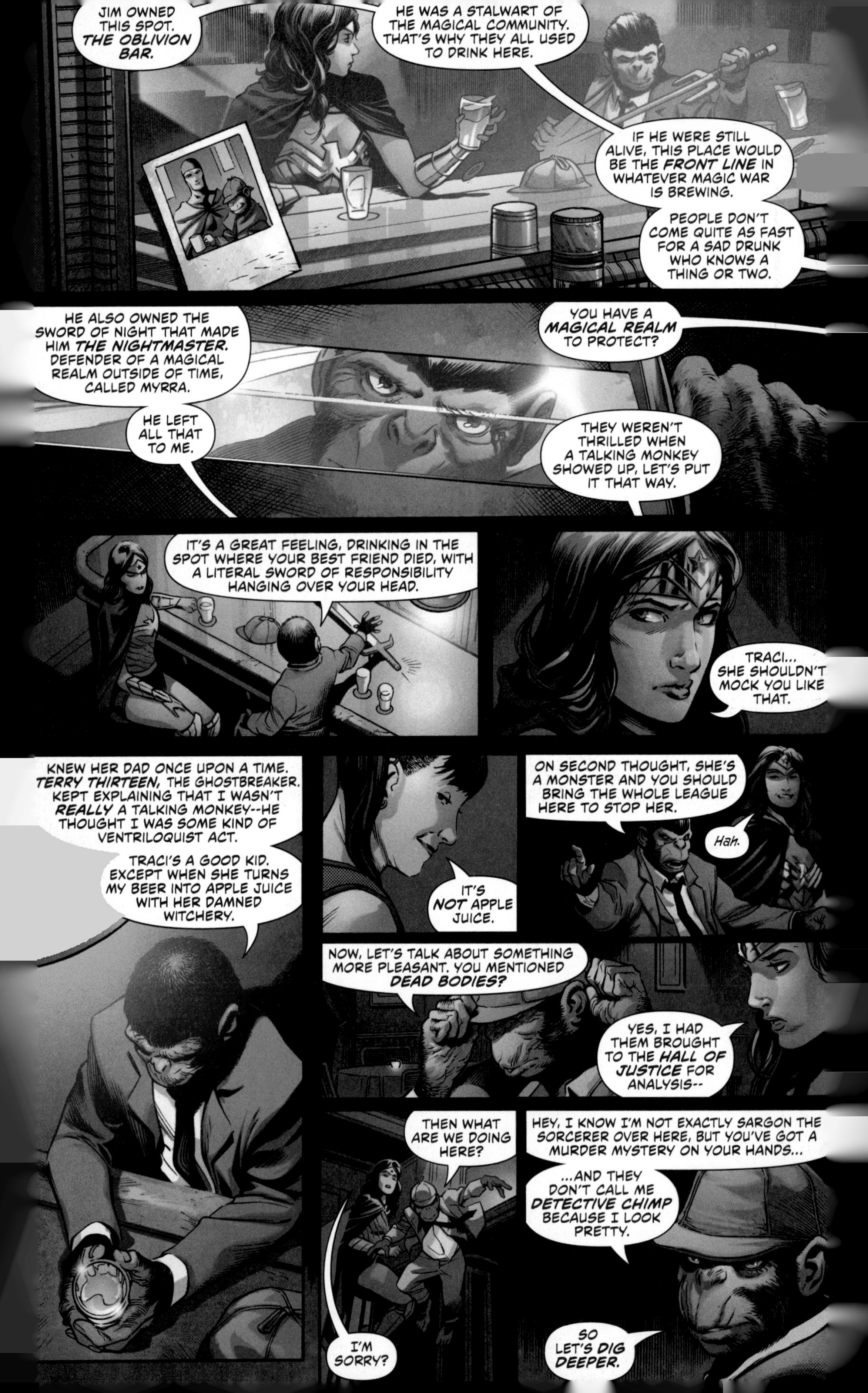
JIM OWNED THIS SPOT. THE OBLIVION BAR.
HE WAS A STALWART OF THE MAGICAL COMMUNITY. THAT'S WHY THEY ALL USED TO DRINK HERE.
IF HE WERE STILL ALIVE, THIS PLACE WOULD BE THE FRONT LINE IN WHATEVER MAGIC WAR IS BREWING.
PEOPLE DON'T COME QUITE AS FAST FOR A SAD DRUNK WHO KNOWS A THING OR TWO.
HE ALSO OWNED THE SWORD OF NIGHT THAT MADE HIM THE NIGHTMASTER. DEFENDER OF A MAGICAL REALM OUTSIDE OF TIME, CALLED MYRRA.
HE LEFT ALL THAT TO ME.
YOU HAVE A MAGICAL REALM TO PROTECT?
THEY WEREN'T THRILLED WHEN A TALKING MONKEY SHOWED UP, LET'S PUT IT THAT WAY.
IT'S A GREAT FEELING, DRINKING IN THE SPOT WHERE YOUR BEST FRIEND DIED, WITH A LITERAL SWORD OF RESPONSIBILITY HANGING OVER YOUR HEAD.
TRACI... SHE SHOULDN'T MOCK YOU LIKE THAT.
KNEW HER DAD ONCE UPON A TIME. TERRY THIRTEEN, THE GHOSTBREAKER. KEPT EXPLAINING THAT I WASN'T REALLY A TALKING MONKEY--HE THOUGHT I WAS SOME KIND OF VENTRILOQUIST ACT.
TRACI'S A GOOD KID. EXCEPT WHEN SHE TURNS MY BEER INTO APPLE JUICE WITH HER DAMNED WITCHERY.
IT'S NOT APPLE JUICE.
ON SECOND THOUGHT, SHE'S A MONSTER AND YOU SHOULD BRING THE WHOLE LEAGUE HERE TO STOP HER.
Hah.
NOW, LET'S TALK ABOUT SOMETHING MORE PLEASANT. YOU MENTIONED DEAD BODIES?
YES, I HAD THEM BROUGHT TO THE HALL OF JUSTICE FOR ANALYSIS--
THEN WHAT ARE WE DOING HERE?
I'M SORRY?
HEY, I KNOW I'M NOT EXACTLY SARGON THE SORCERER OVER HERE, BUT YOU'VE GOT A MURDER MYSTERY ON YOUR HANDS...
...AND THEY DON'T CALL ME DETECTIVE CHIMP BECAUSE I LOOK PRETTY.
SO LET'S DIG DEEPER.

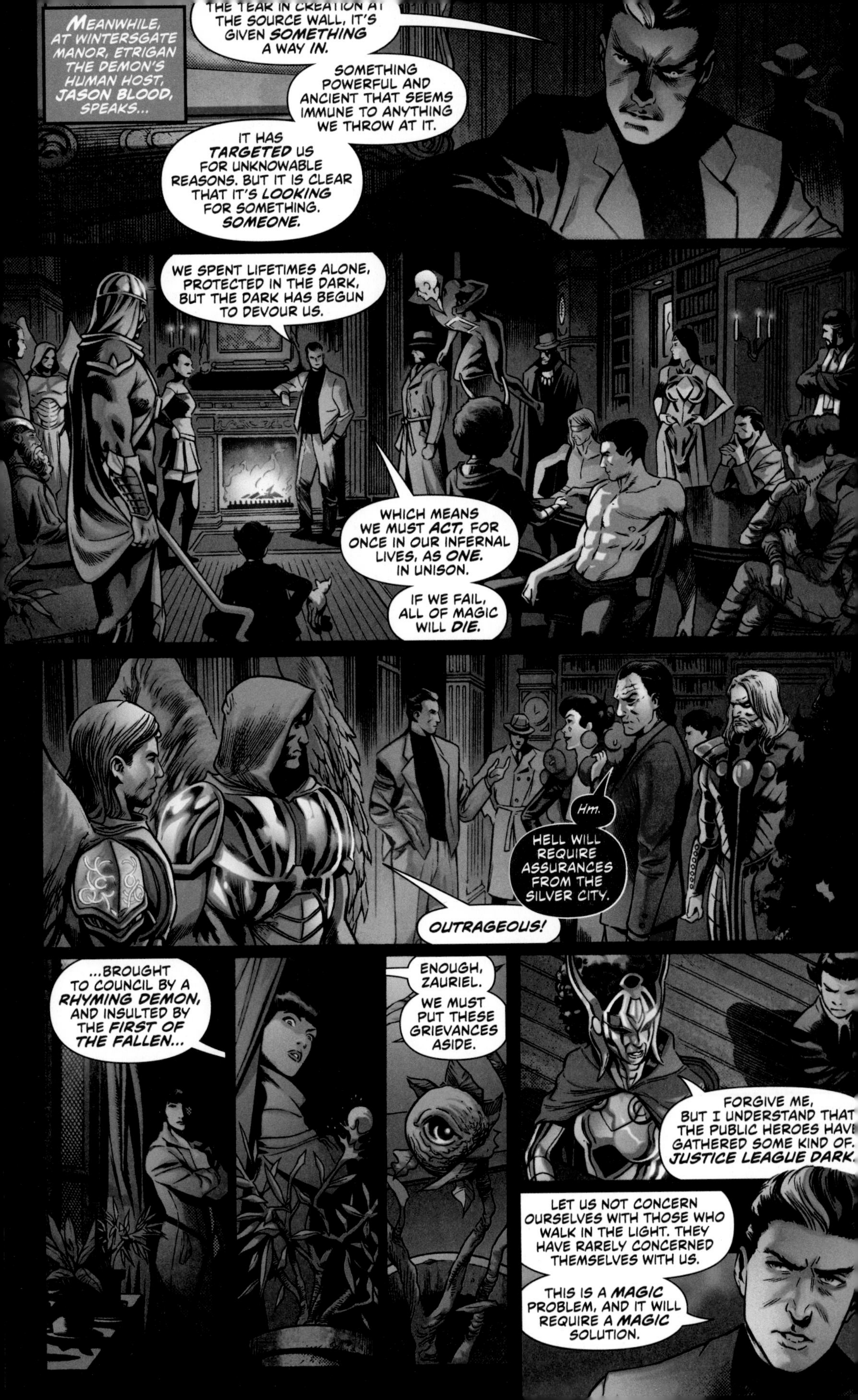
MEANWHILE, AT WINTERSGATE MANOR, ETRIGAN THE DEMON'S HUMAN HOST, JASON BLOOD, SPEAKS...
THE TEAR IN CREATION AT THE SOURCE WALL, IT'S GIVEN SOMETHING A WAY IN.
SOMETHING POWERFUL AND ANCIENT THAT SEEMS IMMUNE TO ANYTHING WE THROW AT IT.
IT HAS TARGETED US FOR UNKNOWABLE REASONS. BUT IT IS CLEAR THAT IT'S LOOKING FOR SOMETHING. SOMEONE.
WE SPENT LIFETIMES ALONE, PROTECTED IN THE DARK, BUT THE DARK HAS BEGUN TO DEVOUR US.
WHICH MEANS WE MUST ACT, FOR ONCE IN OUR INFERNAL LIVES, AS ONE. IN UNISON.
IF WE FAIL, ALL OF MAGIC WILL DIE.
Hm.
HELL WILL REQUIRE ASSURANCES FROM THE SILVER CITY.
OUTRAGEOUS!
...BROUGHT TO COUNCIL BY A RHYMING DEMON, AND INSULTED BY THE FIRST OF THE FALLEN...
ENOUGH, ZAURIEL.
WE MUST PUT THESE GRIEVANCES ASIDE.
FORGIVE ME, BUT I UNDERSTAND THAT THE PUBLIC HEROES HAVE GATHERED SOME KIND OF... JUSTICE LEAGUE DARK.
LET US NOT CONCERN OURSELVES WITH THOSE WHO WALK IN THE LIGHT. THEY HAVE RARELY CONCERNED THEMSELVES WITH US.
THIS IS A MAGIC PROBLEM, AND IT WILL REQUIRE A MAGIC SOLUTION.

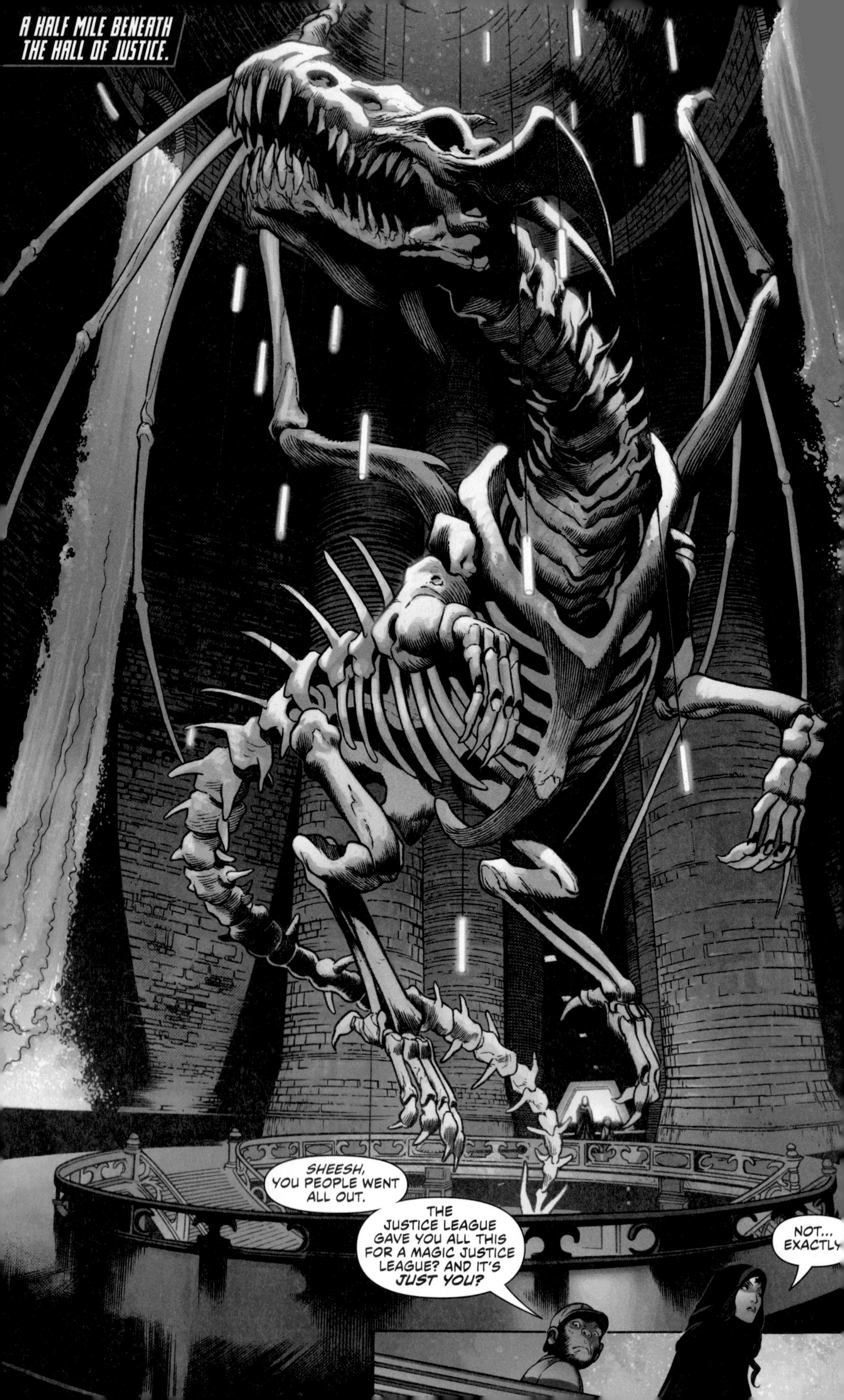
A HALF MILE BENEATH THE HALL OF JUSTICE.
SHEESH, YOU PEOPLE WENT ALL OUT.
THE JUSTICE LEAGUE GAVE YOU ALL THIS FOR A MAGIC JUSTICE LEAGUE? AND IT'S JUST YOU?
NOT... EXACTLY

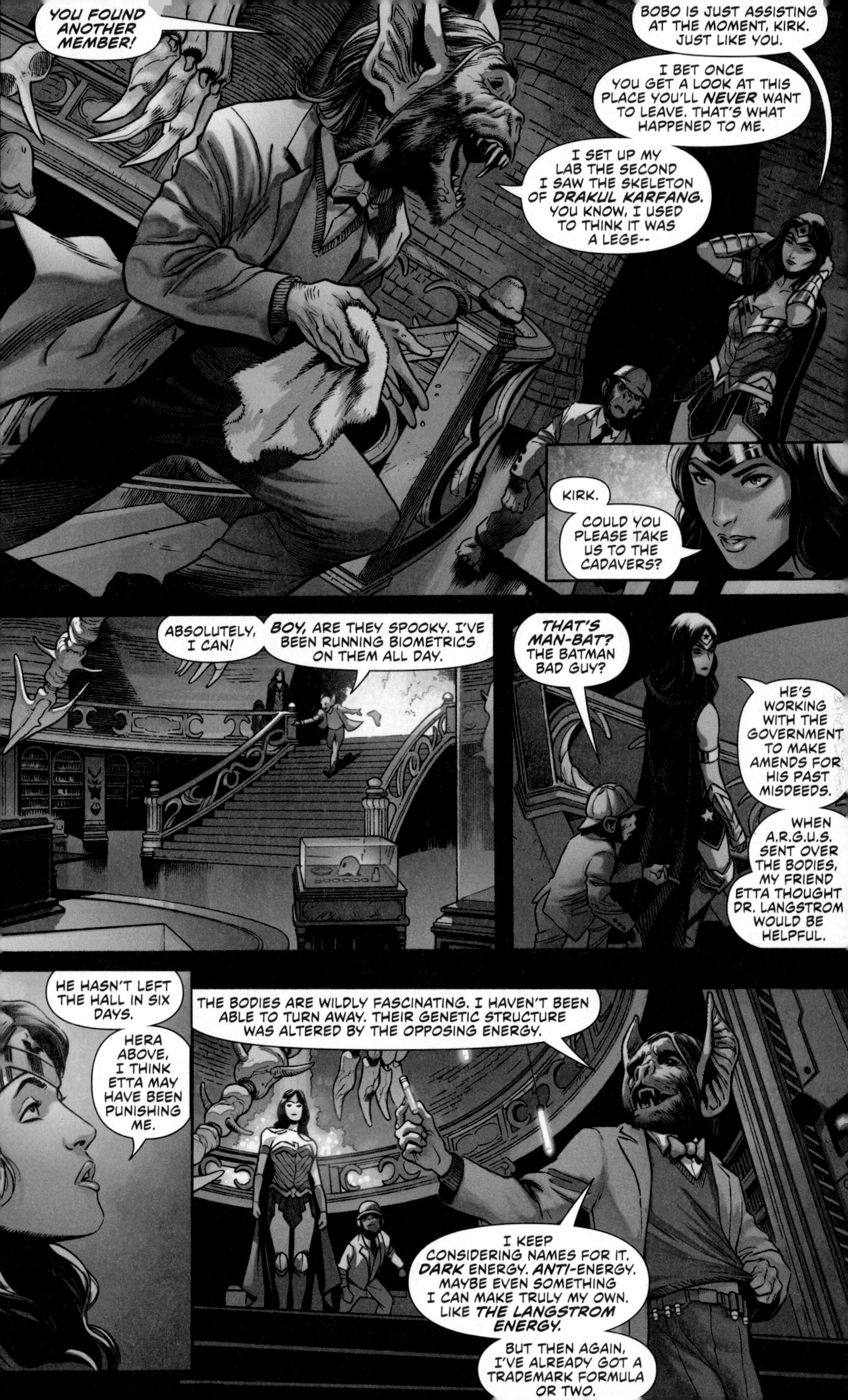
YOU FOUND ANOTHER MEMBER!
BOBO IS JUST ASSISTING AT THE MOMENT, KIRK. JUST LIKE YOU.
I BET ONCE YOU GET A LOOK AT THIS PLACE YOU'LL NEVER WANT TO LEAVE. THAT'S WHAT HAPPENED TO ME.
I SET UP MY LAB THE SECOND I SAW THE SKELETON OF DRAKUL KARFANG. YOU KNOW, I USED TO THINK IT WAS A LEGE--
KIRK.
COULD YOU PLEASE TAKE US TO THE CADAVERS?
ABSOLUTELY, I CAN!
BOY, ARE THEY SPOOKY. I'VE BEEN RUNNING BIOMETRICS ON THEM ALL DAY.
THAT'S MAN-BAT? THE BATMAN BAD GUY?
HE'S WORKING WITH THE GOVERNMENT TO MAKE AMENDS FOR HIS PAST MISDEEDS.
WHEN A.R.G.U.S. SENT OVER THE BODIES, MY FRIEND ETTA THOUGHT DR. LANGSTROM WOULD BE HELPFUL.
HE HASN'T LEFT THE HALL IN SIX DAYS.
HERA ABOVE, I THINK ETTA MAY HAVE BEEN PUNISHING ME.
THE BODIES ARE WILDLY FASCINATING. I HAVEN'T BEEN ABLE TO TURN AWAY. THEIR GENETIC STRUCTURE WAS ALTERED BY THE OPPOSING ENERGY.
I KEEP CONSIDERING NAMES FOR IT. DARK ENERGY. ANTI-ENERGY. MAYBE EVEN SOMETHING I CAN MAKE TRULY MY OWN. LIKE THE LANGSTROM ENERGY.
BUT THEN AGAIN, I'VE ALREADY GOT A TRADEMARK FORMULA OR TWO.

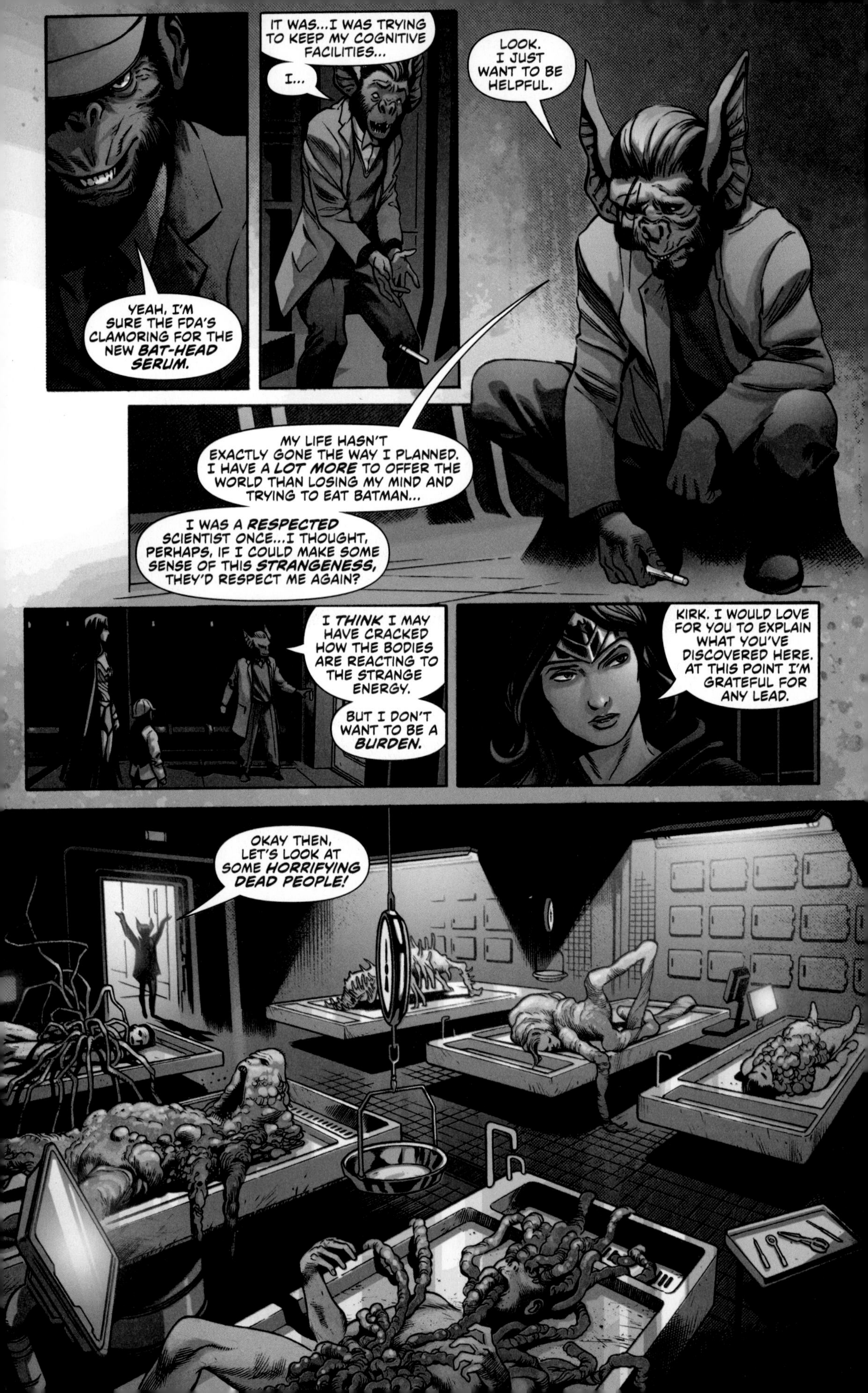
YEAH, I'M SURE THE FDA'S CLAMORING FOR THE NEW BAT-HEAD SERUM.
IT WAS...I WAS TRYING TO KEEP MY COGNITIVE FACILITIES...
I...
LOOK. I JUST WANT TO BE HELPFUL.
MY LIFE HASN'T EXACTLY GONE THE WAY I PLANNED. I HAVE A LOT MORE TO OFFER THE WORLD THAN LOSING MY MIND AND TRYING TO EAT BATMAN...
I WAS A RESPECTED SCIENTIST ONCE...I THOUGHT, PERHAPS, IF I COULD MAKE SOME SENSE OF THIS STRANGENESS, THEY'D RESPECT ME AGAIN?
I THINK I MAY HAVE CRACKED HOW THE BODIES ARE REACTING TO THE STRANGE ENERGY.
BUT I DON'T WANT TO BE A BURDEN.
KIRK. I WOULD LOVE FOR YOU TO EXPLAIN WHAT YOU'VE DISCOVERED HERE. AT THIS POINT I'M GRATEFUL FOR ANY LEAD.
OKAY THEN, LET'S LOOK AT SOME HORRIFYING DEAD PEOPLE!

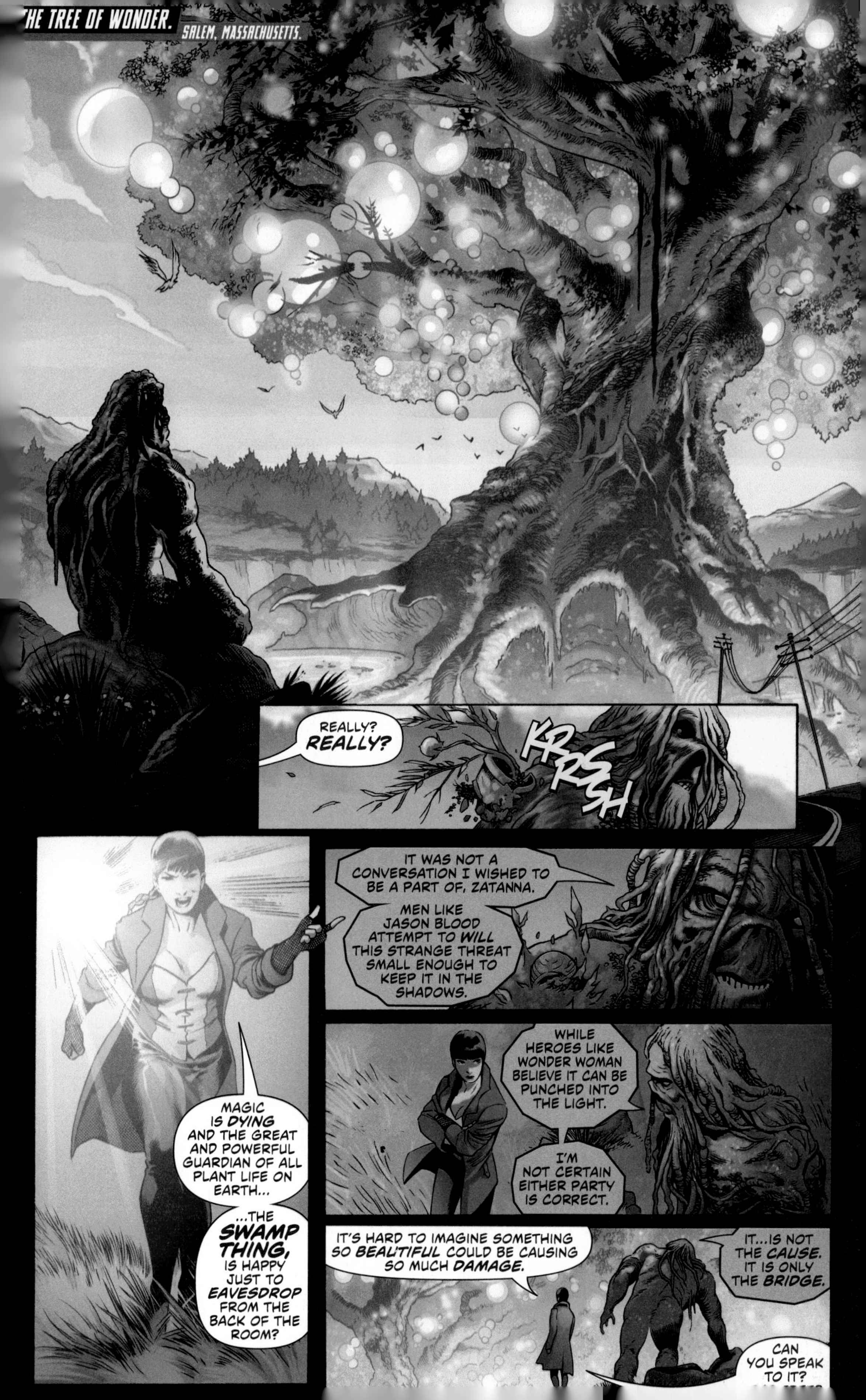

THE TREE OF WONDER.
SALEM, MASSACHUSETTS.
REALLY? REALLY?
KRRSSH
IT WAS NOT A CONVERSATION I WISHED TO BE A PART OF, ZATANNA.
MEN LIKE JASON BLOOD ATTEMPT TO WILL THIS STRANGE THREAT SMALL ENOUGH TO KEEP IT IN THE SHADOWS.
MAGIC IS DYING AND THE GREAT AND POWERFUL GUARDIAN OF ALL PLANT LIFE ON EARTH...
...THE SWAMP THING, IS HAPPY JUST TO EAVESDROP FROM THE BACK OF THE ROOM?
WHILE HEROES LIKE WONDER WOMAN BELIEVE IT CAN BE PUNCHED INTO THE LIGHT.
I'M NOT CERTAIN EITHER PARTY IS CORRECT.
IT'S HARD TO IMAGINE SOMETHING SO BEAUTIFUL COULD BE CAUSING SO MUCH DAMAGE.
IT...IS NOT THE CAUSE. IT IS ONLY THE BRIDGE.
CAN YOU SPEAK TO IT?

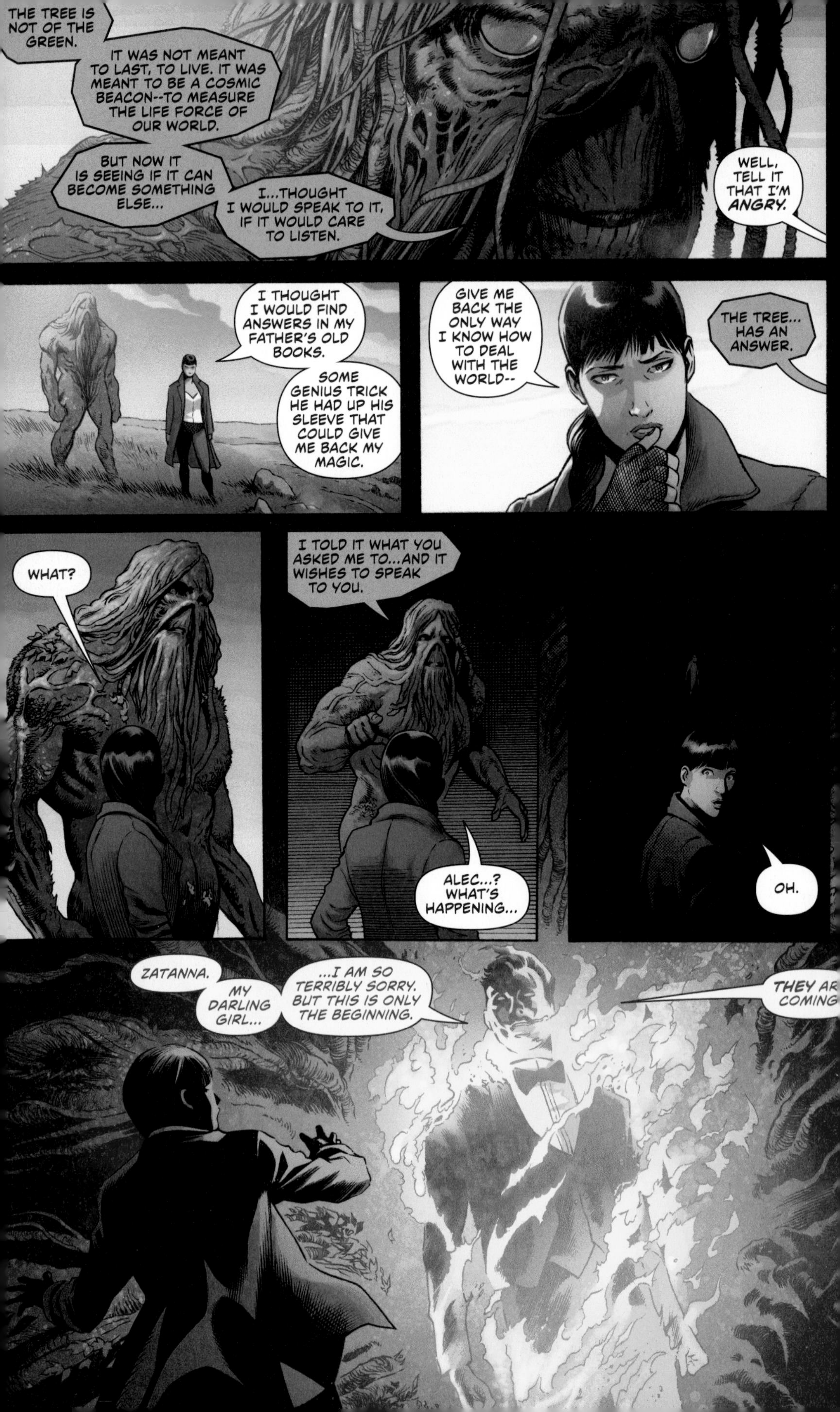
THE TREE IS NOT OF THE GREEN.
IT WAS NOT MEANT TO LAST, TO LIVE. IT WAS MEANT TO BE A COSMIC BEACON--TO MEASURE THE LIFE FORCE OF OUR WORLD.
BUT NOW IT IS SEEING IF IT CAN BECOME SOMETHING ELSE...
I...THOUGHT I WOULD SPEAK TO IT, IF IT WOULD CARE TO LISTEN.
WELL, TELL IT THAT I'M *ANGRY.*
I THOUGHT I WOULD FIND ANSWERS IN MY FATHER'S OLD BOOKS.
SOME GENIUS TRICK HE HAD UP HIS SLEEVE THAT COULD GIVE ME BACK MY MAGIC.
GIVE ME BACK THE ONLY WAY I KNOW HOW TO DEAL WITH THE WORLD--
THE TREE... HAS AN ANSWER.
WHAT?
I TOLD IT WHAT YOU ASKED ME TO...AND IT WISHES TO SPEAK TO YOU.
ALEC...? WHAT'S HAPPENING...
OH.
ZATANNA.
MY DARLING GIRL...
...I AM SO TERRIBLY SORRY. BUT THIS IS ONLY THE BEGINNING.

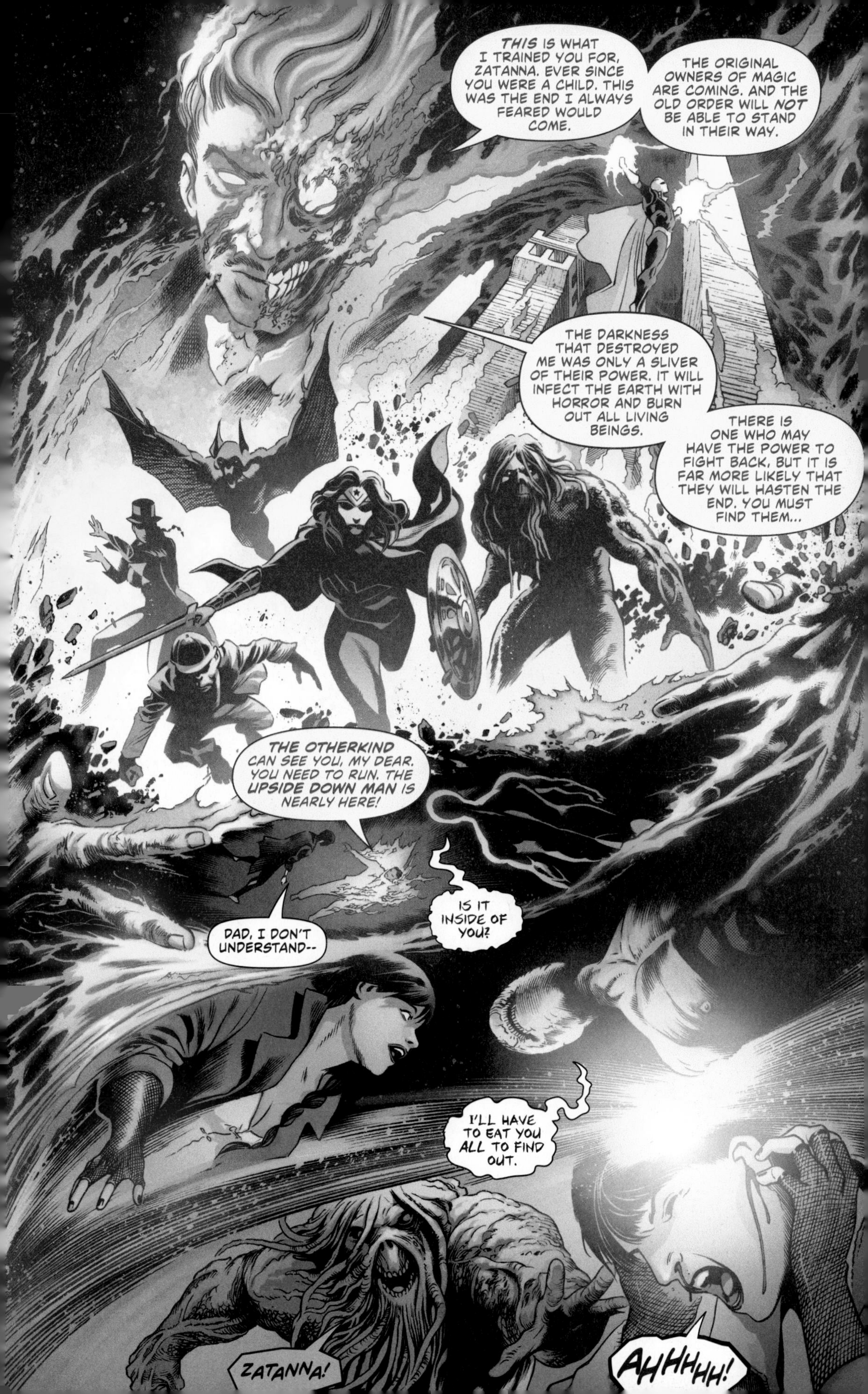
THIS IS WHAT I TRAINED YOU FOR, ZATANNA. EVER SINCE YOU WERE A CHILD. THIS WAS THE END I ALWAYS FEARED WOULD COME.
THE ORIGINAL OWNERS OF MAGIC ARE COMING. AND THE OLD ORDER WILL NOT BE ABLE TO STAND IN THEIR WAY.
THE DARKNESS THAT DESTROYED ME WAS ONLY A SLIVER OF THEIR POWER. IT WILL INFECT THE EARTH WITH HORROR AND BURN OUT ALL LIVING BEINGS.
THERE IS ONE WHO MAY HAVE THE POWER TO FIGHT BACK, BUT IT IS FAR MORE LIKELY THAT THEY WILL HASTEN THE END. YOU MUST FIND THEM...
THE OTHERKIND CAN SEE YOU, MY DEAR. YOU NEED TO RUN. THE UPSIDE DOWN MAN IS NEARLY HERE!
DAD, I DON'T UNDERSTAND--
IS IT INSIDE OF YOU?
I'LL HAVE TO EAT YOU ALL TO FIND OUT.
ZATANNA!
AHHHHH!

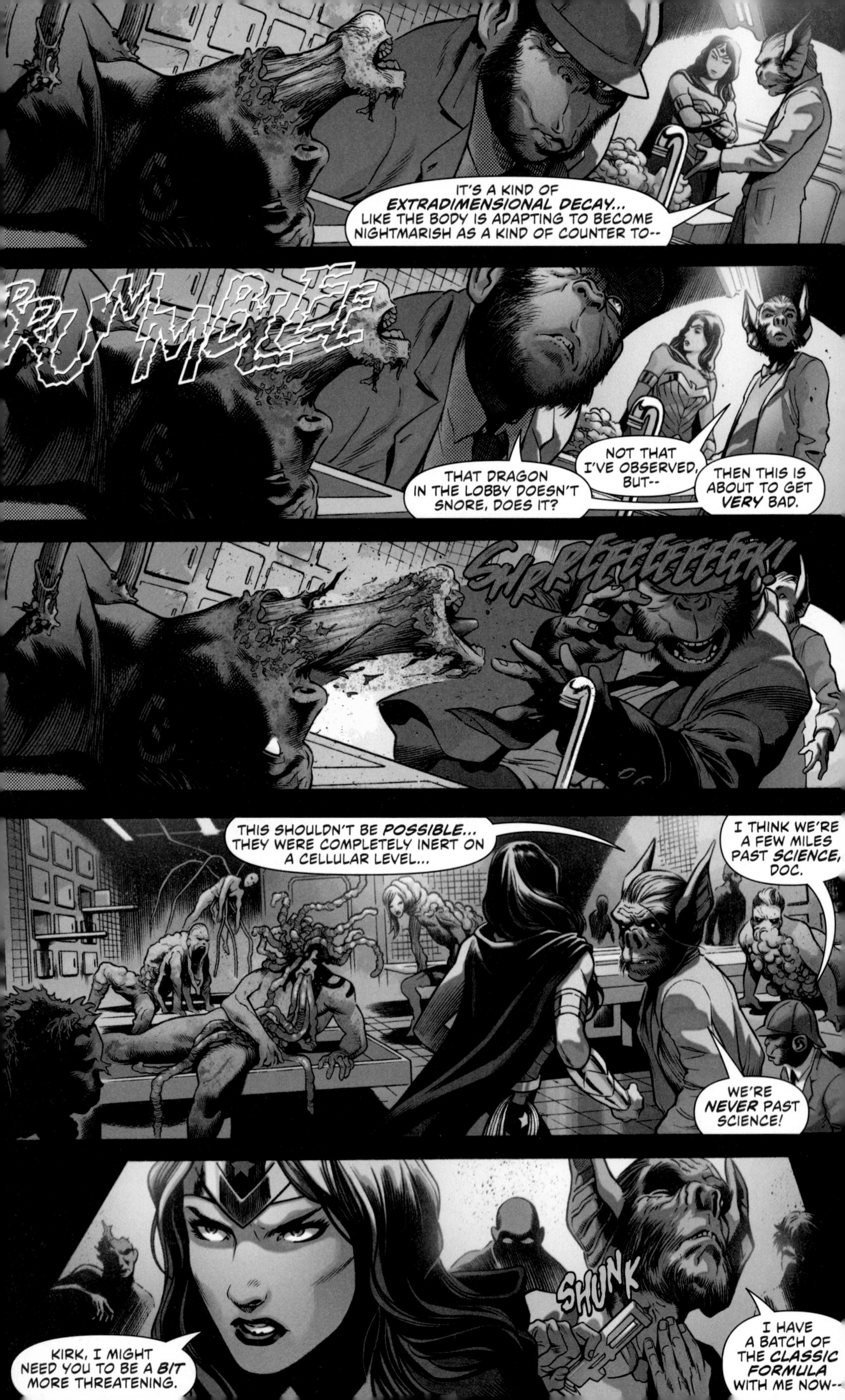
IT'S A KIND OF EXTRADIMENSIONAL DECAY... LIKE THE BODY IS ADAPTING TO BECOME NIGHTMARISH AS A KIND OF COUNTER TO--
RUMBLE
THAT DRAGON IN THE LOBBY DOESN'T SNORE, DOES IT?
NOT THAT I'VE OBSERVED, BUT--
THEN THIS IS ABOUT TO GET VERY BAD.
THIS SHOULDN'T BE POSSIBLE... THEY WERE COMPLETELY INERT ON A CELLULAR LEVEL...
I THINK WE'RE A FEW MILES PAST SCIENCE, DOC.
WE'RE NEVER PAST SCIENCE!
SHUNK
KIRK, I MIGHT NEED YOU TO BE A BIT MORE THREATENING.
I HAVE A BATCH OF THE CLASSIC FORMULA WITH ME NOW--

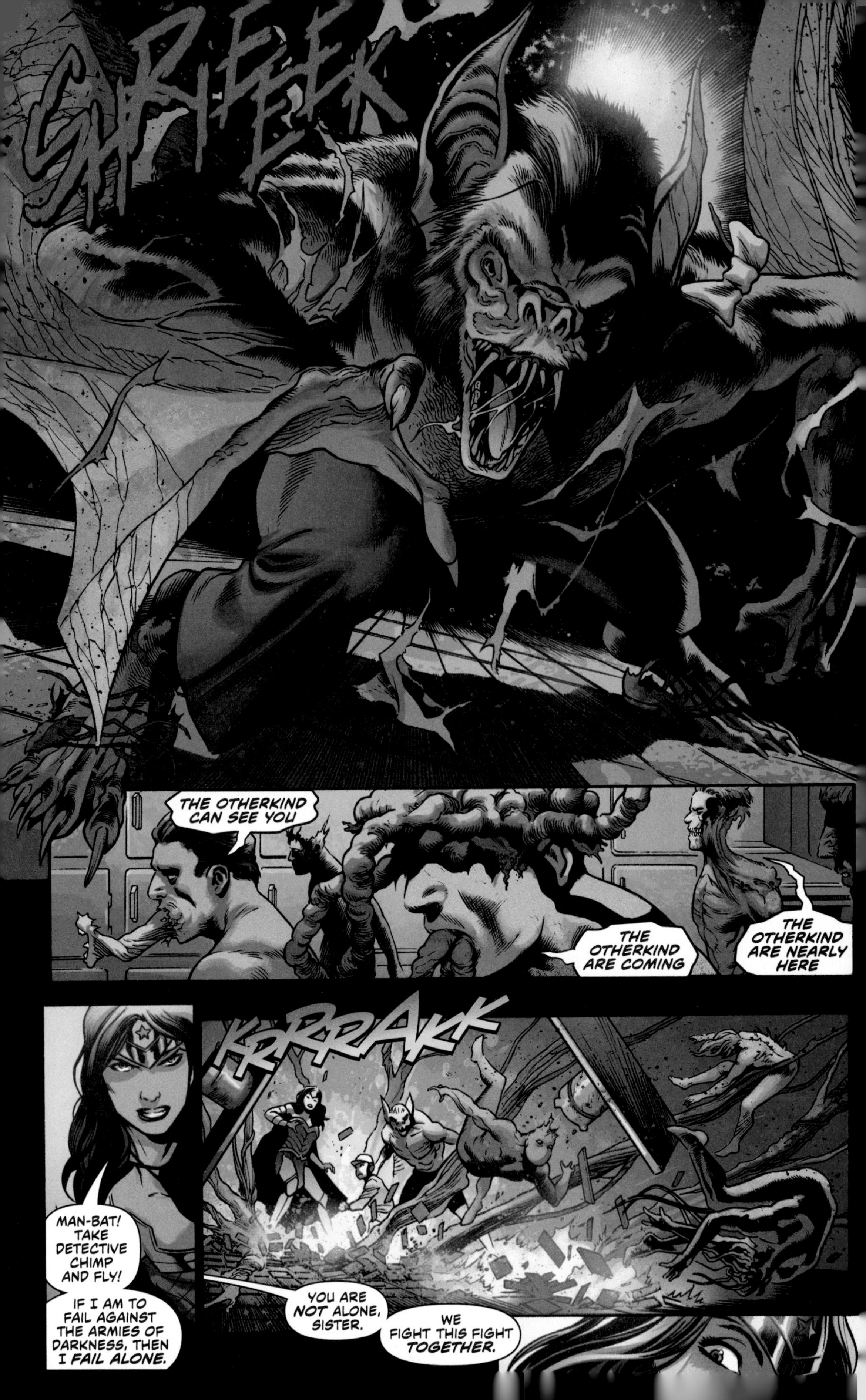
SHRIEEEK
THE OTHERKIND CAN SEE YOU
THE OTHERKIND ARE COMING
THE OTHERKIND ARE NEARLY HERE
KRRRAKK
MAN-BAT! TAKE DETECTIVE CHIMP AND FLY!
IF I AM TO FAIL AGAINST THE ARMIES OF DARKNESS, THEN I FAIL ALONE.
YOU ARE NOT ALONE, SISTER.
WE FIGHT THIS FIGHT TOGETHER.

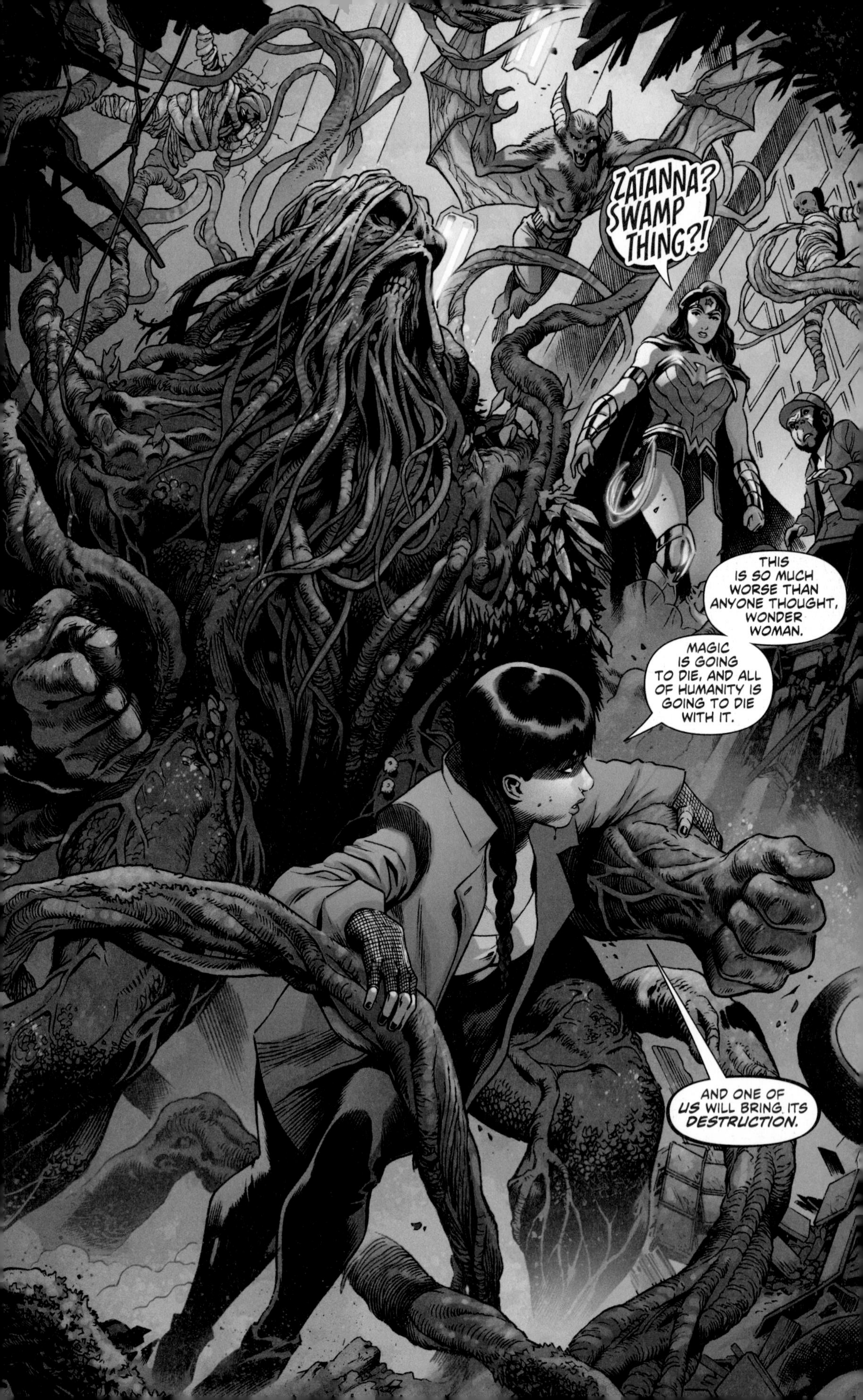
ZATANNA? SWAMP THING?!
THIS IS SO MUCH WORSE THAN ANYONE THOUGHT, WONDER WOMAN.
MAGIC IS GOING TO DIE, AND ALL OF HUMANITY IS GOING TO DIE WITH IT.
AND ONE OF US WILL BRING ITS DESTRUCTION.

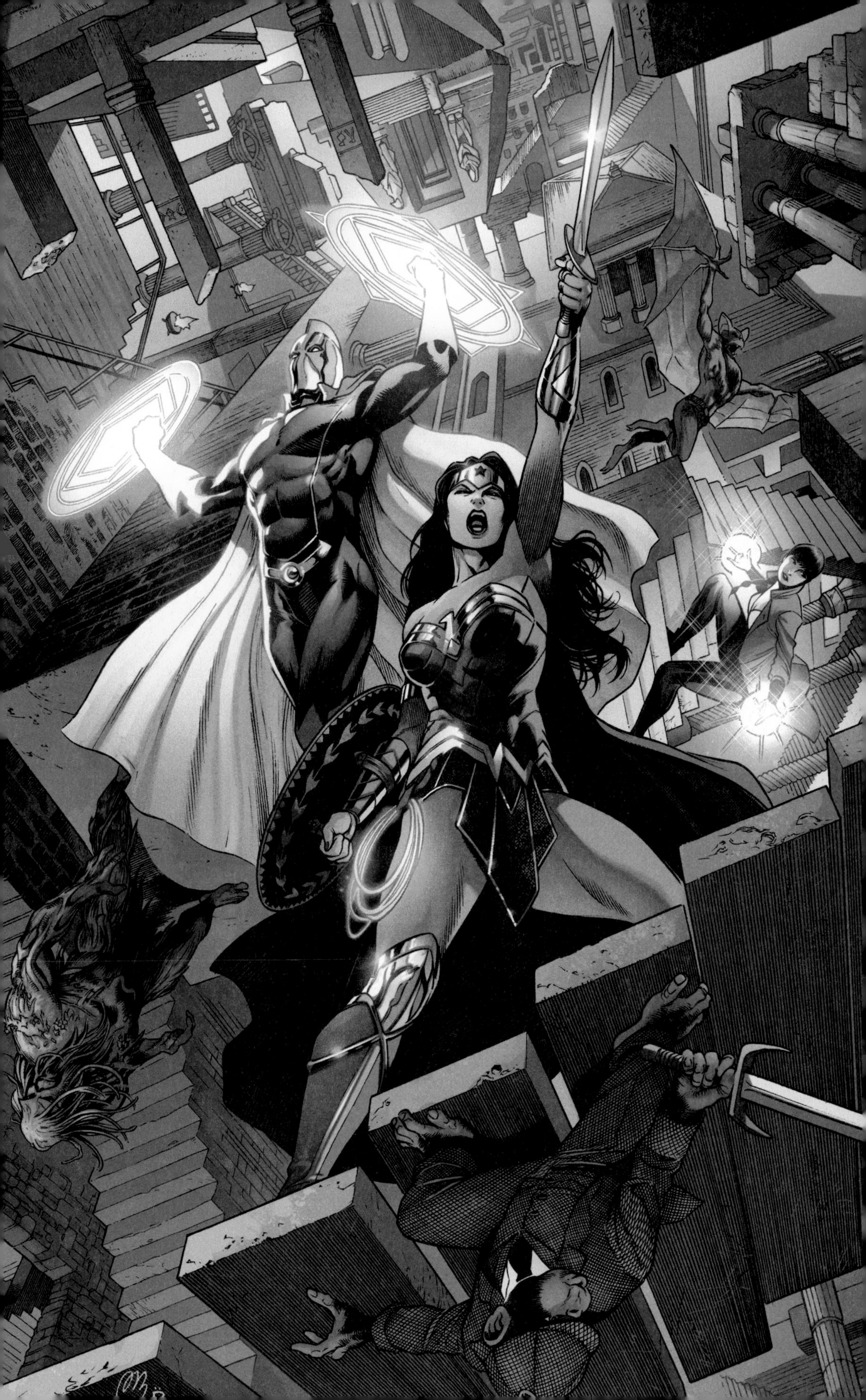

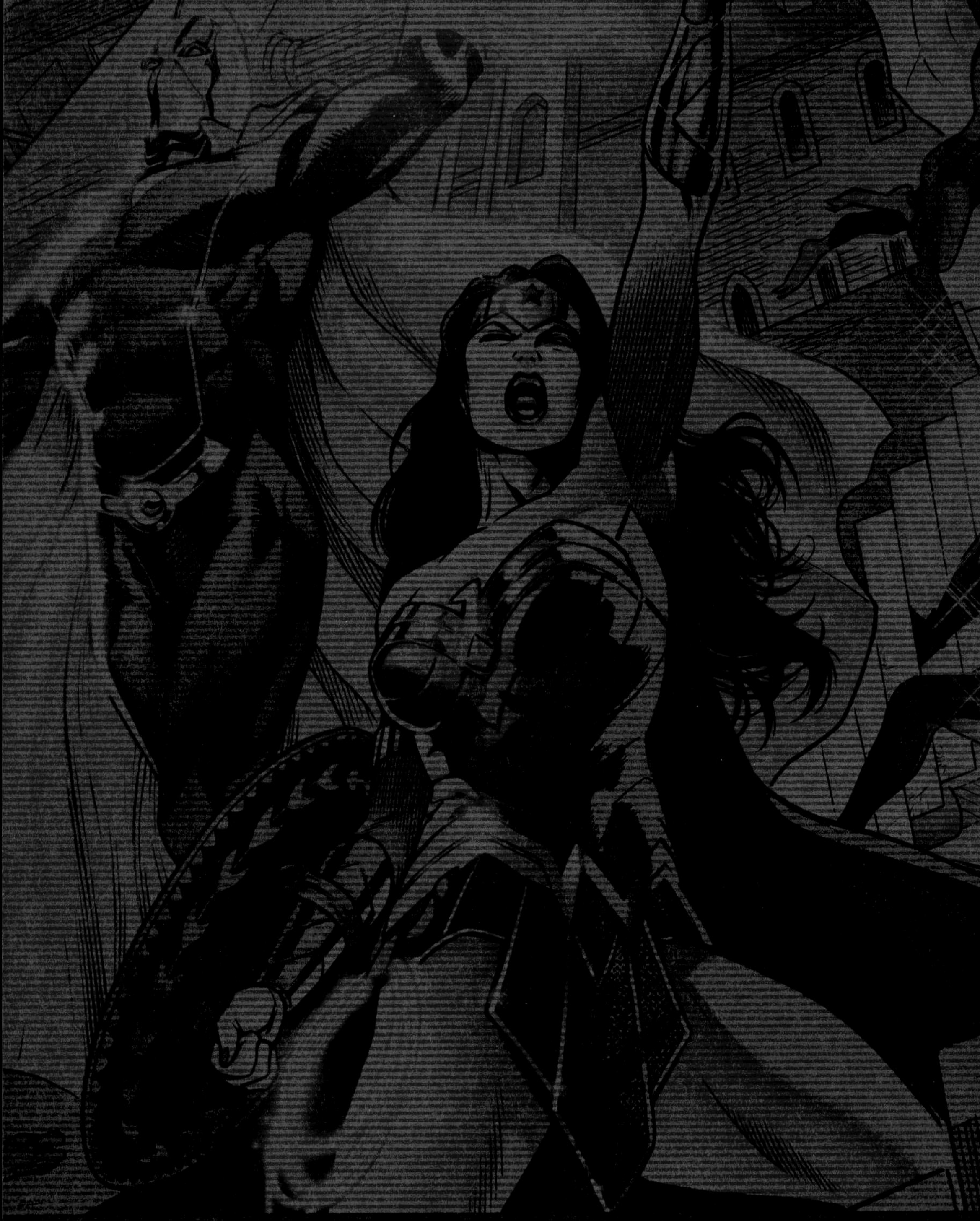

JUSTICE LEAGUE DARK
#2

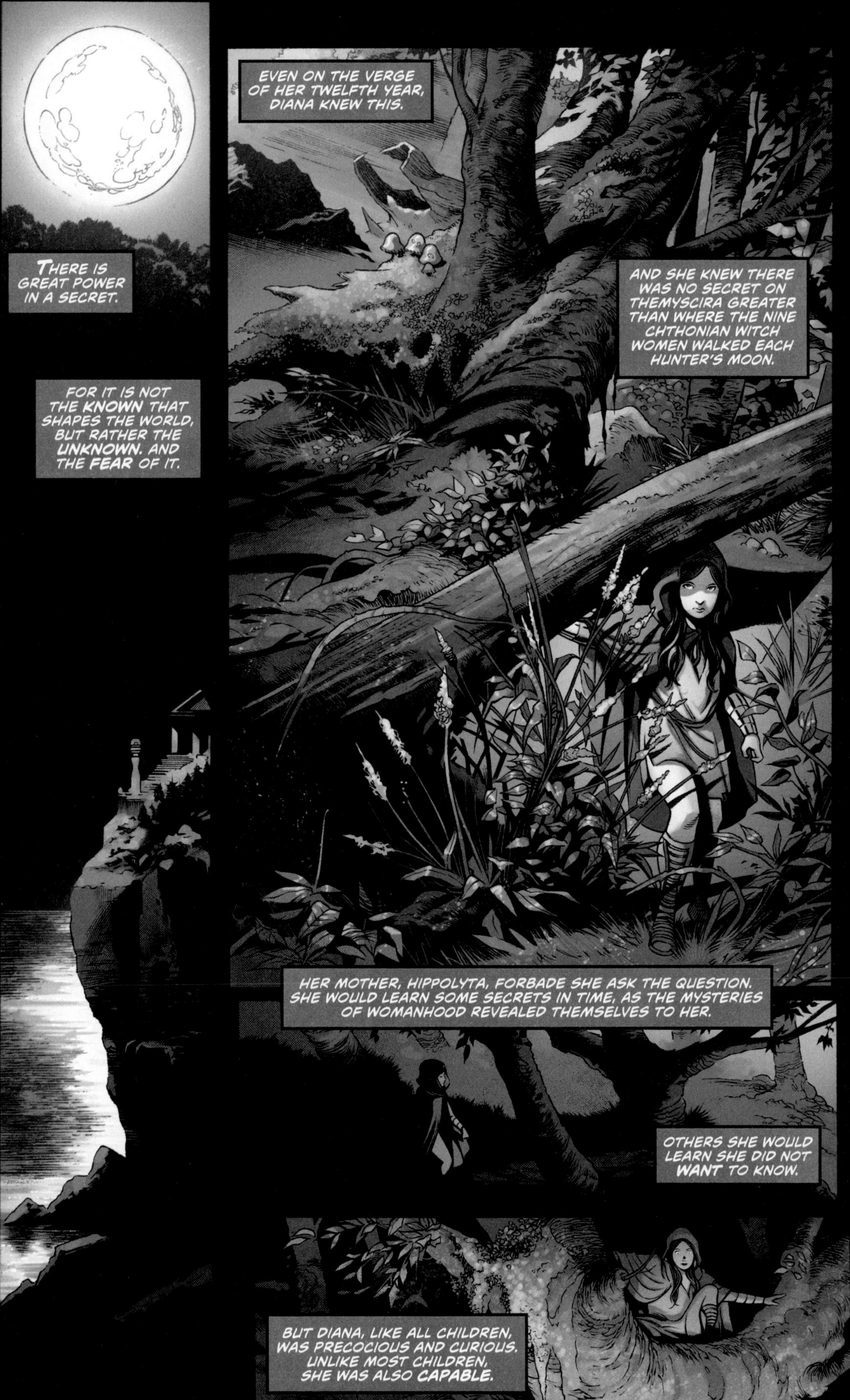
THERE IS GREAT POWER IN A SECRET.
FOR IT IS NOT THE KNOWN THAT SHAPES THE WORLD, BUT RATHER THE UNKNOWN. AND THE FEAR OF IT.
EVEN ON THE VERGE OF HER TWELFTH YEAR, DIANA KNEW THIS.
AND SHE KNEW THERE WAS NO SECRET ON THEMYSCIRA GREATER THAN WHERE THE NINE CHTHONIAN WITCH WOMEN WALKED EACH HUNTER'S MOON.
HER MOTHER, HIPPOLYTA, FORBADE SHE ASK THE QUESTION. SHE WOULD LEARN SOME SECRETS IN TIME, AS THE MYSTERIES OF WOMANHOOD REVEALED THEMSELVES TO HER.
OTHERS SHE WOULD LEARN SHE DID NOT WANT TO KNOW.
BUT DIANA, LIKE ALL CHILDREN, WAS PRECOCIOUS AND CURIOUS. UNLIKE MOST CHILDREN, SHE WAS ALSO CAPABLE.

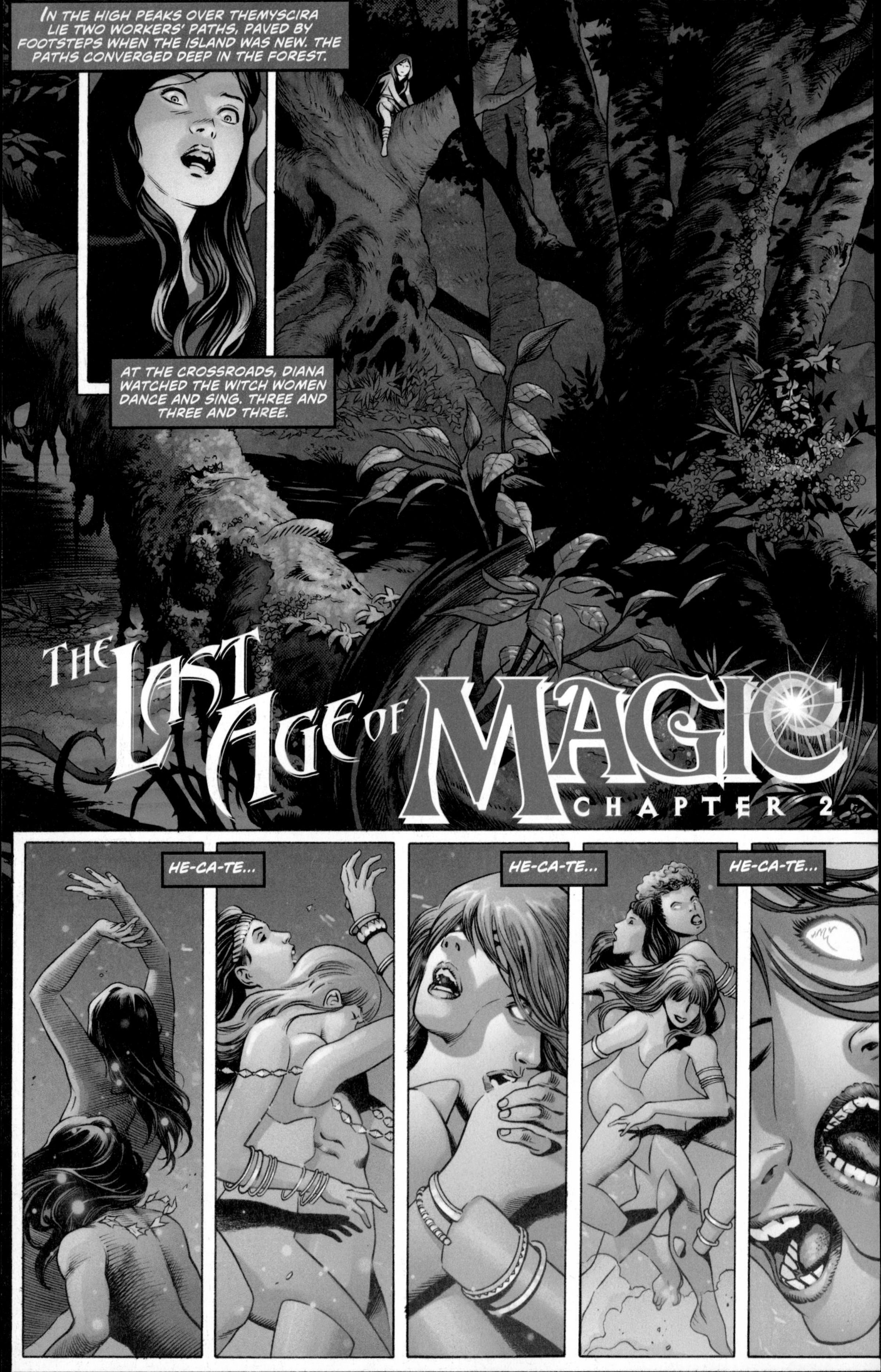
IN THE HIGH PEAKS OVER THEMYSCIRA LIE TWO WORKERS' PATHS, PAVED BY FOOTSTEPS WHEN THE ISLAND WAS NEW. THE PATHS CONVERGED DEEP IN THE FOREST.
AT THE CROSSROADS, DIANA WATCHED THE WITCH WOMEN DANCE AND SING. THREE AND THREE AND THREE.
THE LAST AGE OF MAGIC
CHAPTER 2
HE-CA-TE...
HE-CA-TE...
HE-CA-TE...

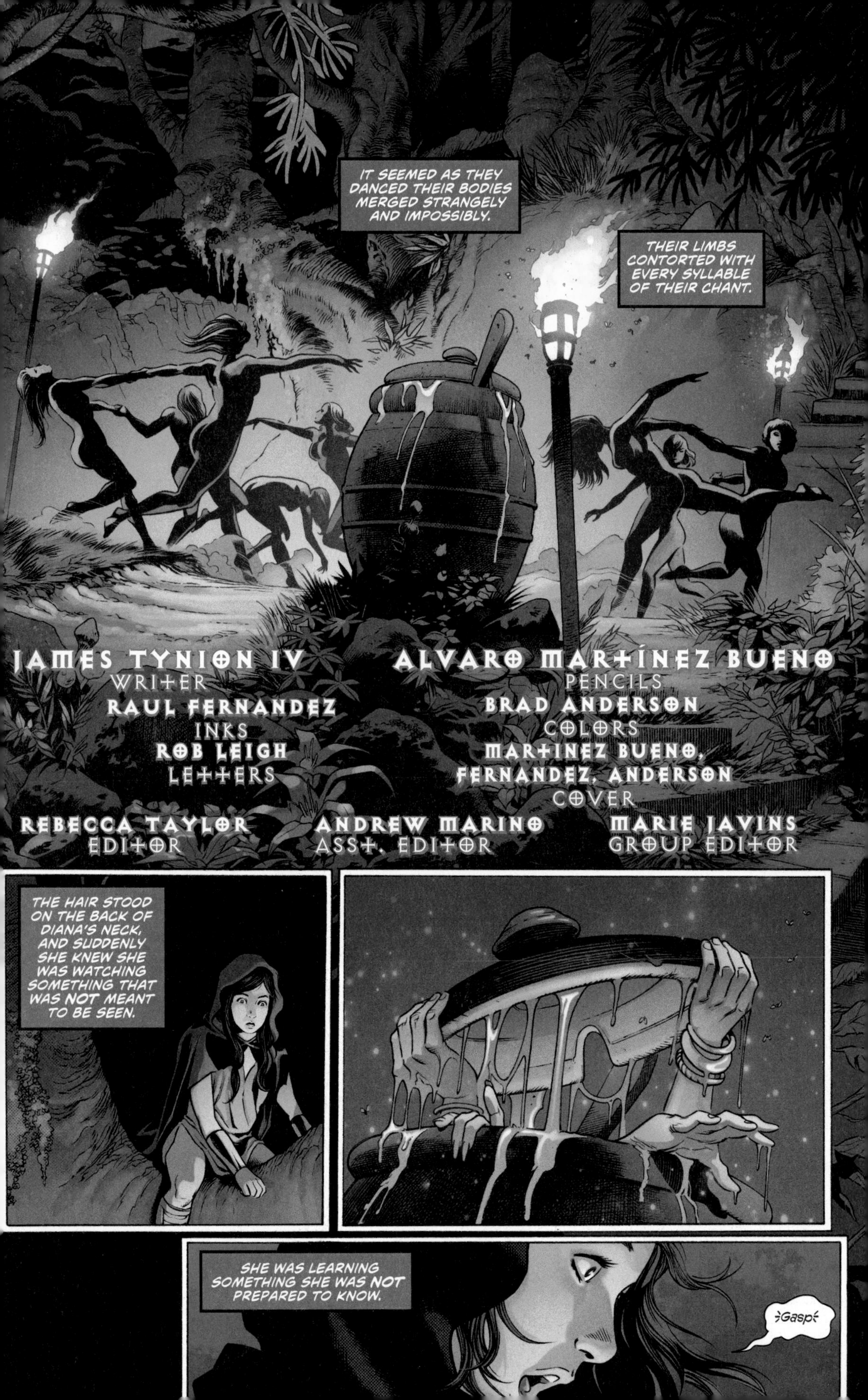
IT SEEMED AS THEY DANCED THEIR BODIES MERGED STRANGELY AND IMPOSSIBLY.
THEIR LIMBS CONTORTED WITH EVERY SYLLABLE OF THEIR CHANT.
JAMES TYNION IV WRITER
ALVARO MARTÍNEZ BUENO PENCILS
RAUL FERNANDEZ INKS
BRAD ANDERSON COLORS
ROB LEIGH LETTERS
MARTINEZ BUENO, FERNANDEZ, ANDERSON COVER
REBECCA TAYLOR EDITOR
ANDREW MARINO ASST. EDITOR
MARIE JAVINS GROUP EDITOR
THE HAIR STOOD ON THE BACK OF DIANA'S NECK, AND SUDDENLY SHE KNEW SHE WAS WATCHING SOMETHING THAT WAS NOT MEANT TO BE SEEN.
SHE WAS LEARNING SOMETHING SHE WAS NOT PREPARED TO KNOW.
Gasp

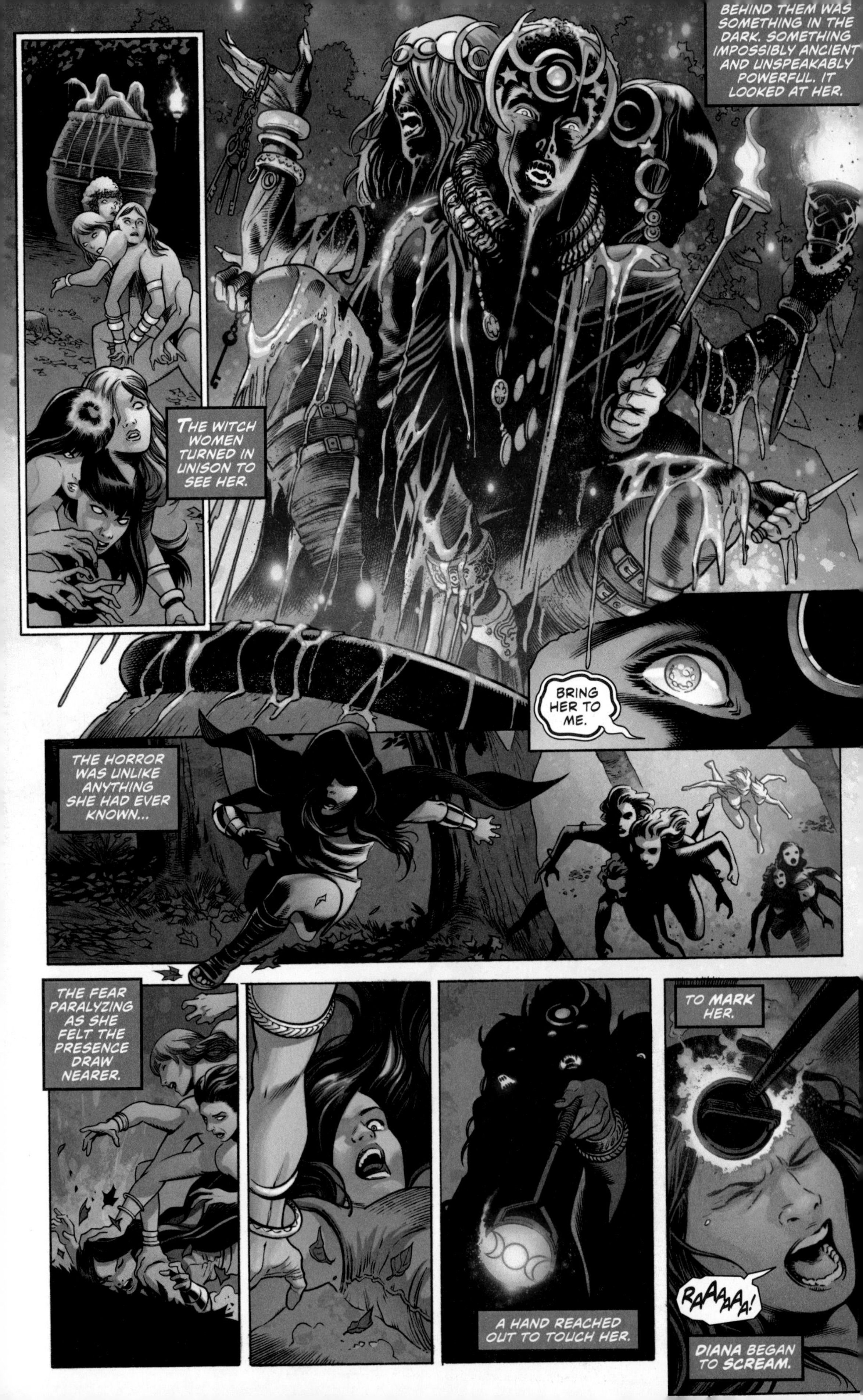
BEHIND THEM WAS SOMETHING IN THE DARK. SOMETHING IMPOSSIBLY ANCIENT AND UNSPEAKABLY POWERFUL. IT LOOKED AT HER.
THE WITCH WOMEN TURNED IN UNISON TO SEE HER.
BRING HER TO ME.
THE HORROR WAS UNLIKE ANYTHING SHE HAD EVER KNOWN...
THE FEAR PARALYZING AS SHE FELT THE PRESENCE DRAW NEARER.
A HAND REACHED OUT TO TOUCH HER.
TO MARK HER.
RAAAAAA!
DIANA BEGAN TO SCREAM.

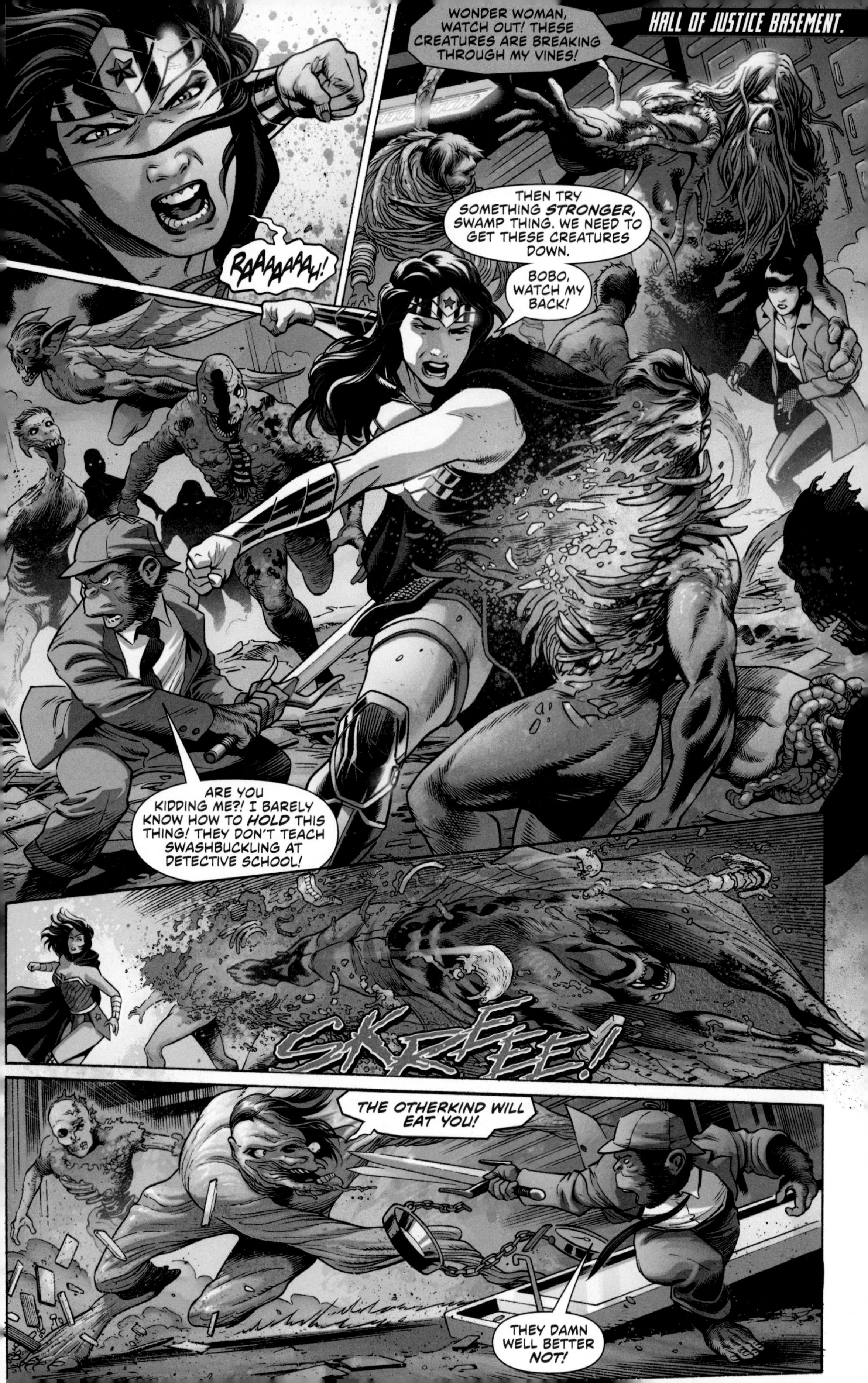

HALL OF JUSTICE BASEMENT.
WONDER WOMAN, WATCH OUT! THESE CREATURES ARE BREAKING THROUGH MY VINES!
RAAAAAAAH!
THEN TRY SOMETHING STRONGER, SWAMP THING. WE NEED TO GET THESE CREATURES DOWN.
BOBO, WATCH MY BACK!
ARE YOU KIDDING ME?! I BARELY KNOW HOW TO HOLD THIS THING! THEY DON'T TEACH SWASHBUCKLING AT DETECTIVE SCHOOL!
SKREEE!
THE OTHERKIND WILL EAT YOU!
THEY DAMN WELL BETTER NOT!

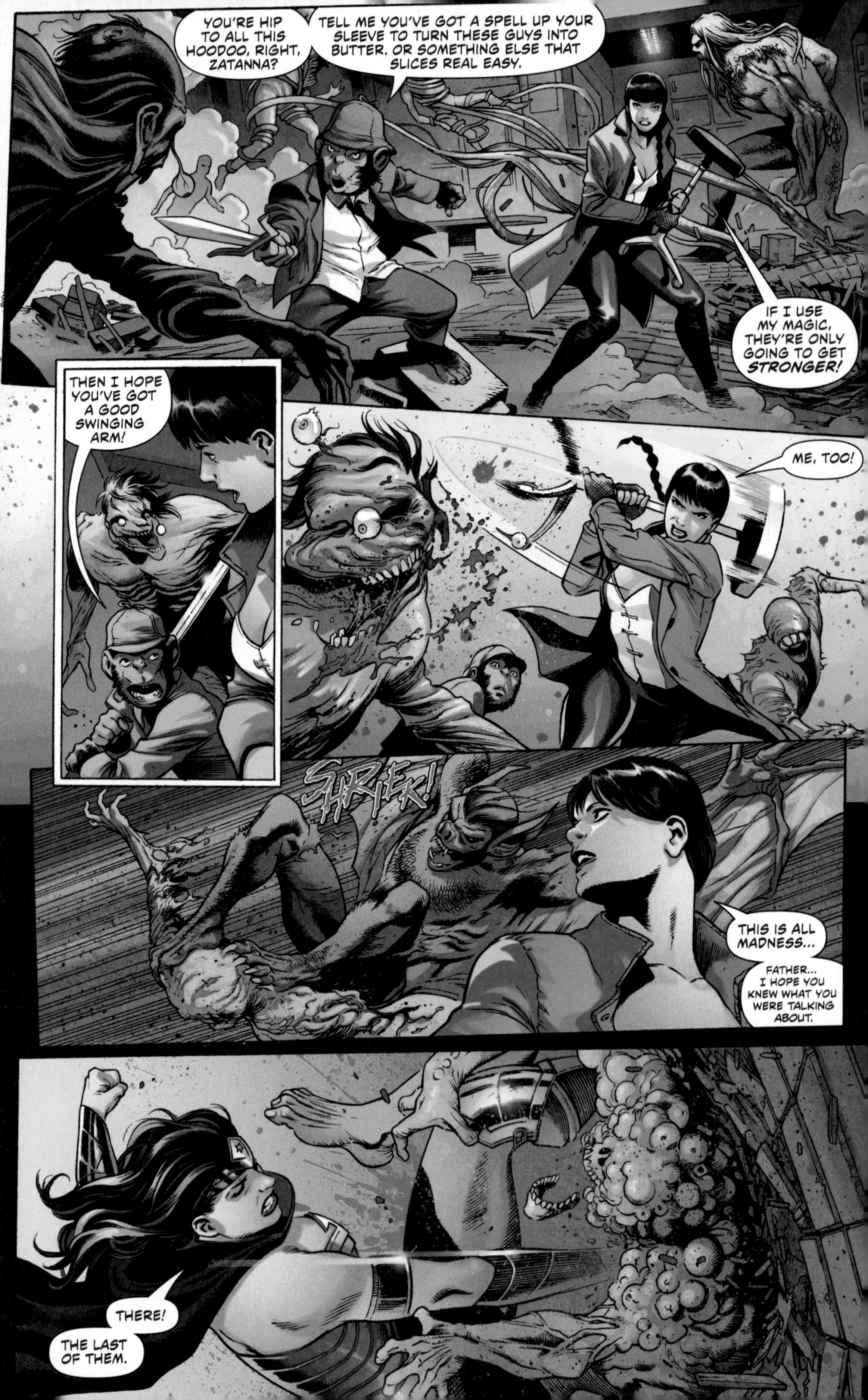
YOU'RE HIP TO ALL THIS HOODOO, RIGHT, ZATANNA?
TELL ME YOU'VE GOT A SPELL UP YOUR SLEEVE TO TURN THESE GUYS INTO BUTTER. OR SOMETHING ELSE THAT SLICES REAL EASY.
IF I USE MY MAGIC, THEY'RE ONLY GOING TO GET STRONGER!
THEN I HOPE YOU'VE GOT A GOOD SWINGING ARM!
ME, TOO!
SHRIEK!
THIS IS ALL MADNESS...
FATHER... I HOPE YOU KNEW WHAT YOU WERE TALKING ABOUT.
THERE!
THE LAST OF THEM.

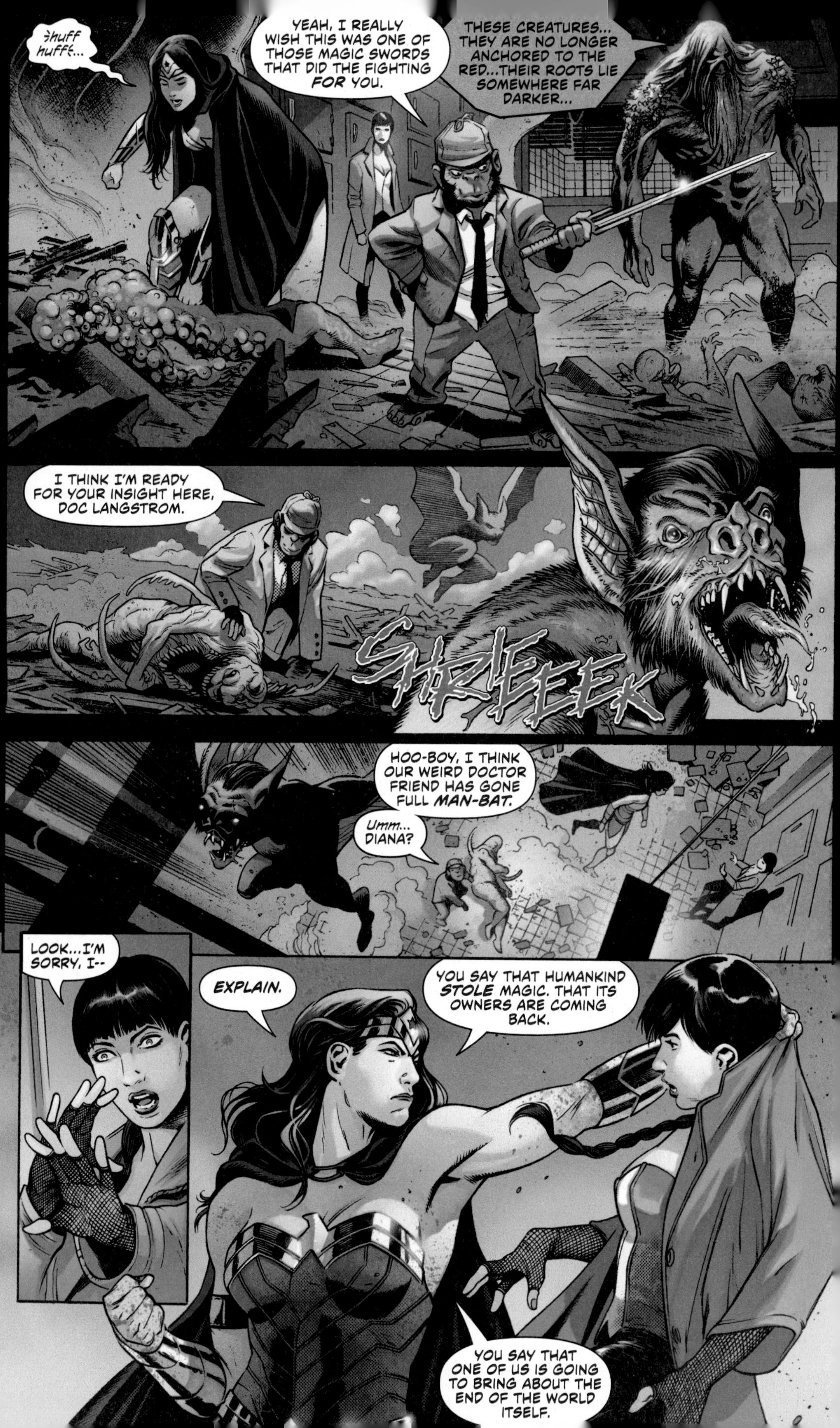
shuff huff...
YEAH, I REALLY WISH THIS WAS ONE OF THOSE MAGIC SWORDS THAT DID THE FIGHTING FOR YOU.
THESE CREATURES... THEY ARE NO LONGER ANCHORED TO THE RED...THEIR ROOTS LIE SOMEWHERE FAR DARKER...
I THINK I'M READY FOR YOUR INSIGHT HERE, DOC LANGSTROM.
SHRIEEEK
HOO-BOY, I THINK OUR WEIRD DOCTOR FRIEND HAS GONE FULL MAN-BAT.
Umm... DIANA?
LOOK...I'M SORRY, I--
EXPLAIN.
YOU SAY THAT HUMANKIND STOLE MAGIC. THAT ITS OWNERS ARE COMING BACK.
YOU SAY THAT ONE OF US IS GOING TO BRING ABOUT THE END OF THE WORLD ITSELF.

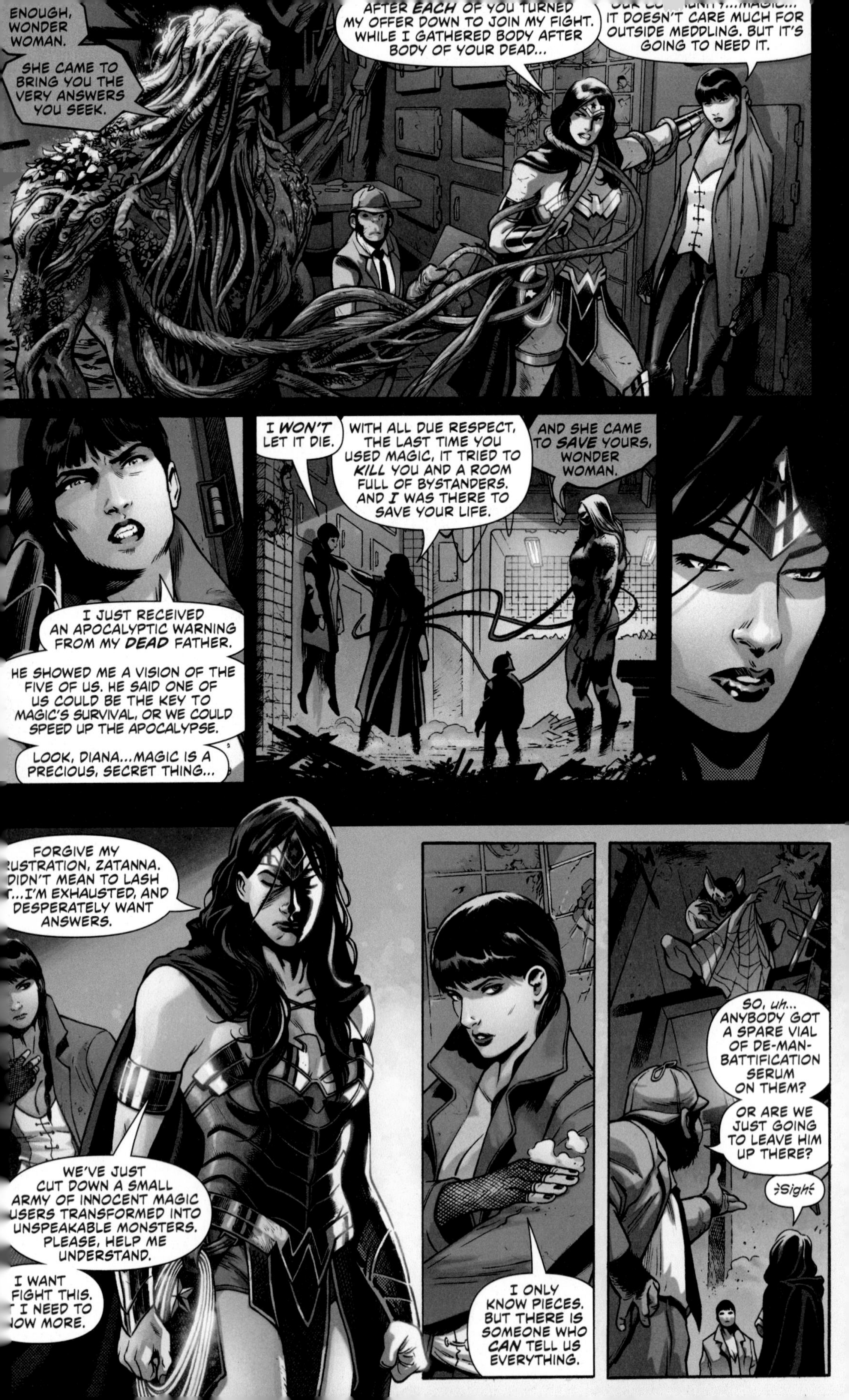

ENOUGH, WONDER WOMAN.
SHE CAME TO BRING YOU THE VERY ANSWERS YOU SEEK.
AFTER EACH OF YOU TURNED MY OFFER DOWN TO JOIN MY FIGHT. WHILE I GATHERED BODY AFTER BODY OF YOUR DEAD...
IT DOESN'T CARE MUCH FOR OUTSIDE MEDDLING. BUT IT'S GOING TO NEED IT.
I JUST RECEIVED AN APOCALYPTIC WARNING FROM MY DEAD FATHER.
HE SHOWED ME A VISION OF THE FIVE OF US. HE SAID ONE OF US COULD BE THE KEY TO MAGIC'S SURVIVAL, OR WE COULD SPEED UP THE APOCALYPSE.
LOOK, DIANA...MAGIC IS A PRECIOUS, SECRET THING...
I WON'T LET IT DIE.
WITH ALL DUE RESPECT, THE LAST TIME YOU USED MAGIC, IT TRIED TO KILL YOU AND A ROOM FULL OF BYSTANDERS. AND I WAS THERE TO SAVE YOUR LIFE.
AND SHE CAME TO SAVE YOURS, WONDER WOMAN.
FORGIVE MY RUSTRATION, ZATANNA. DIDN'T MEAN TO LASH ...I'M EXHAUSTED, AND DESPERATELY WANT ANSWERS.
WE'VE JUST CUT DOWN A SMALL ARMY OF INNOCENT MAGIC USERS TRANSFORMED INTO UNSPEAKABLE MONSTERS. PLEASE, HELP ME UNDERSTAND.
I WANT FIGHT THIS. I NEED TO OW MORE.
I ONLY KNOW PIECES. BUT THERE IS SOMEONE WHO CAN TELL US EVERYTHING.
SO, uh... ANYBODY GOT A SPARE VIAL OF DE-MAN-BATTIFICATION SERUM ON THEM?
OR ARE WE JUST GOING TO LEAVE HIM UP THERE?
Sigh

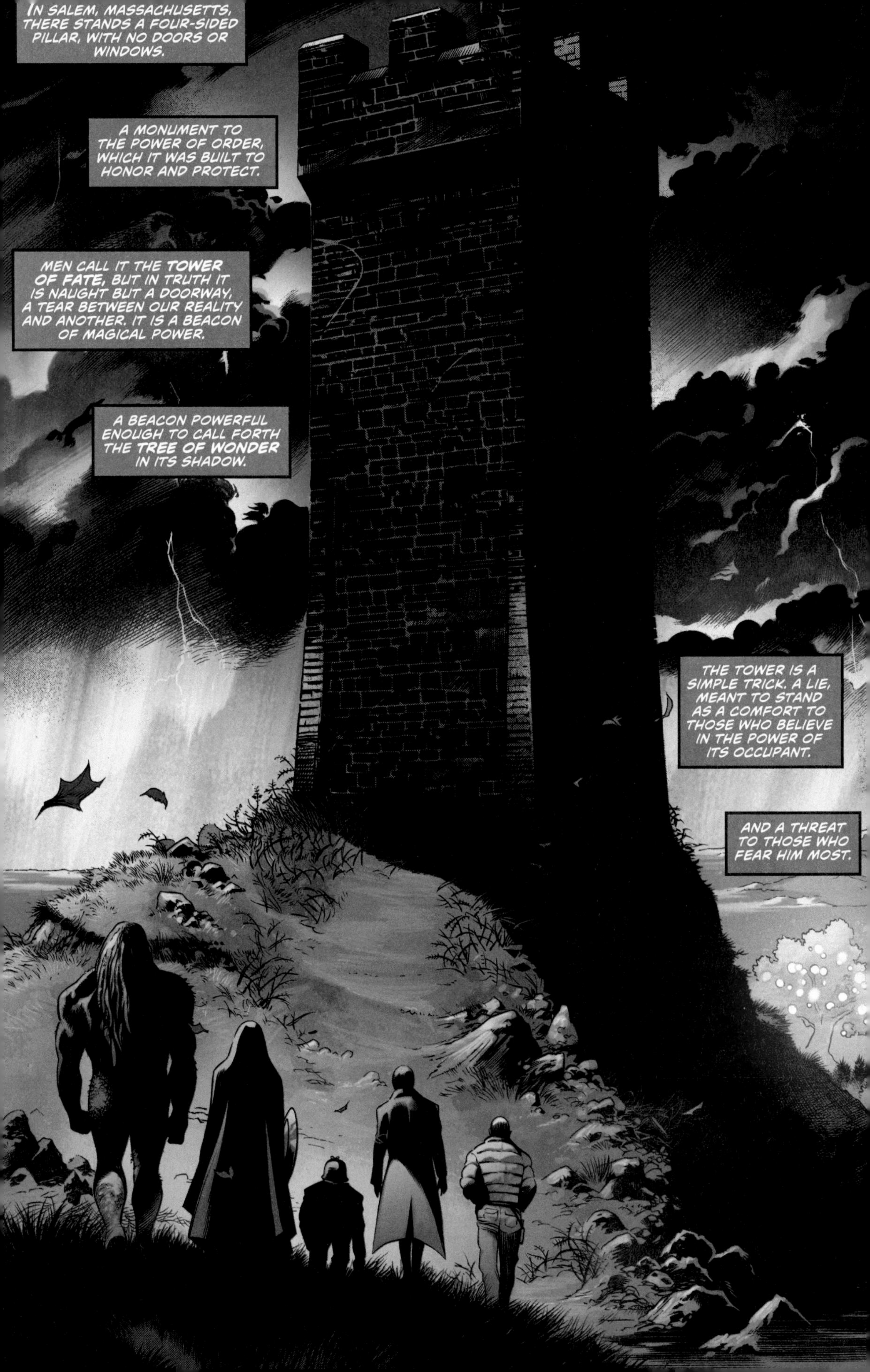
IN SALEM, MASSACHUSETTS, THERE STANDS A FOUR-SIDED PILLAR, WITH NO DOORS OR WINDOWS.
A MONUMENT TO THE POWER OF ORDER, WHICH IT WAS BUILT TO HONOR AND PROTECT.
MEN CALL IT THE TOWER OF FATE, BUT IN TRUTH IT IS NAUGHT BUT A DOORWAY, A TEAR BETWEEN OUR REALITY AND ANOTHER. IT IS A BEACON OF MAGICAL POWER.
A BEACON POWERFUL ENOUGH TO CALL FORTH THE TREE OF WONDER IN ITS SHADOW.
THE TOWER IS A SIMPLE TRICK. A LIE, MEANT TO STAND AS A COMFORT TO THOSE WHO BELIEVE IN THE POWER OF ITS OCCUPANT.
AND A THREAT TO THOSE WHO FEAR HIM MOST.

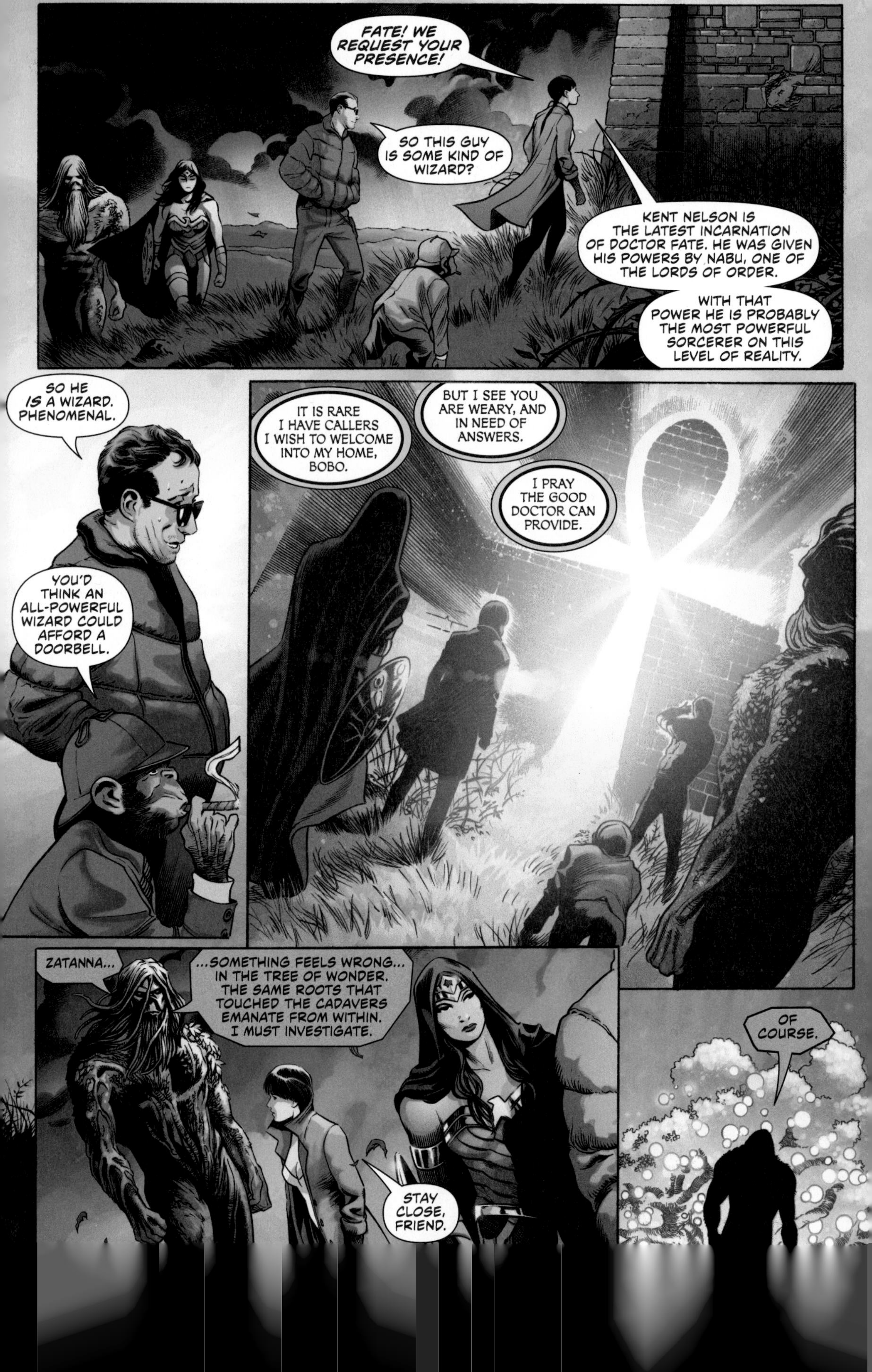
FATE! WE REQUEST YOUR PRESENCE!
SO THIS GUY IS SOME KIND OF WIZARD?
KENT NELSON IS THE LATEST INCARNATION OF DOCTOR FATE. HE WAS GIVEN HIS POWERS BY NABU, ONE OF THE LORDS OF ORDER.
WITH THAT POWER HE IS PROBABLY THE MOST POWERFUL SORCERER ON THIS LEVEL OF REALITY.
SO HE IS A WIZARD. PHENOMENAL.
YOU'D THINK AN ALL-POWERFUL WIZARD COULD AFFORD A DOORBELL.
IT IS RARE I HAVE CALLERS I WISH TO WELCOME INTO MY HOME, BOBO.
BUT I SEE YOU ARE WEARY, AND IN NEED OF ANSWERS.
I PRAY THE GOOD DOCTOR CAN PROVIDE.
ZATANNA...
...SOMETHING FEELS WRONG... IN THE TREE OF WONDER. THE SAME ROOTS THAT TOUCHED THE CADAVERS EMANATE FROM WITHIN. I MUST INVESTIGATE.
STAY CLOSE, FRIEND.
OF COURSE.

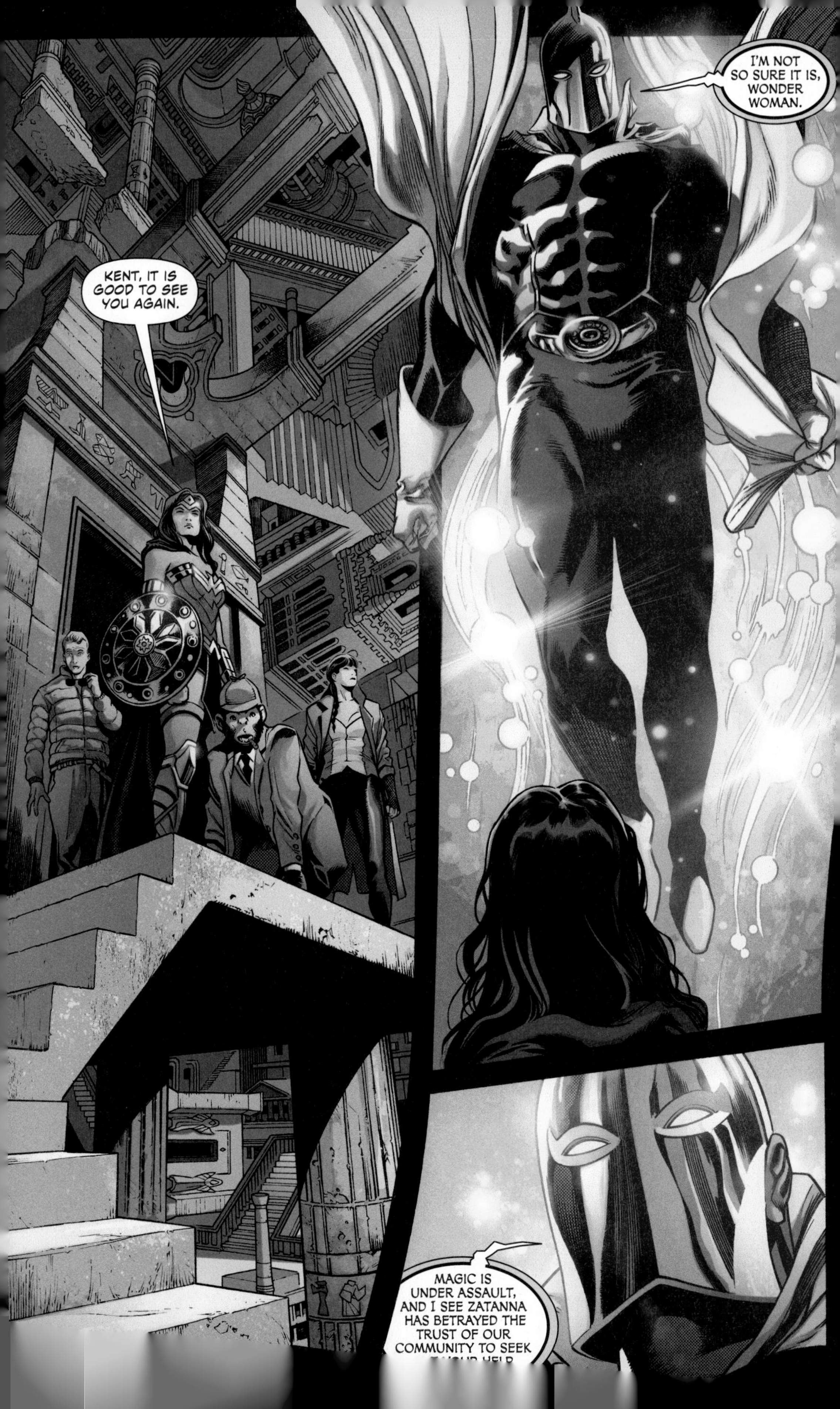
KENT, IT IS GOOD TO SEE YOU AGAIN.
I'M NOT SO SURE IT IS, WONDER WOMAN.
MAGIC IS UNDER ASSAULT, AND I SEE ZATANNA HAS BETRAYED THE TRUST OF OUR COMMUNITY TO SEEK

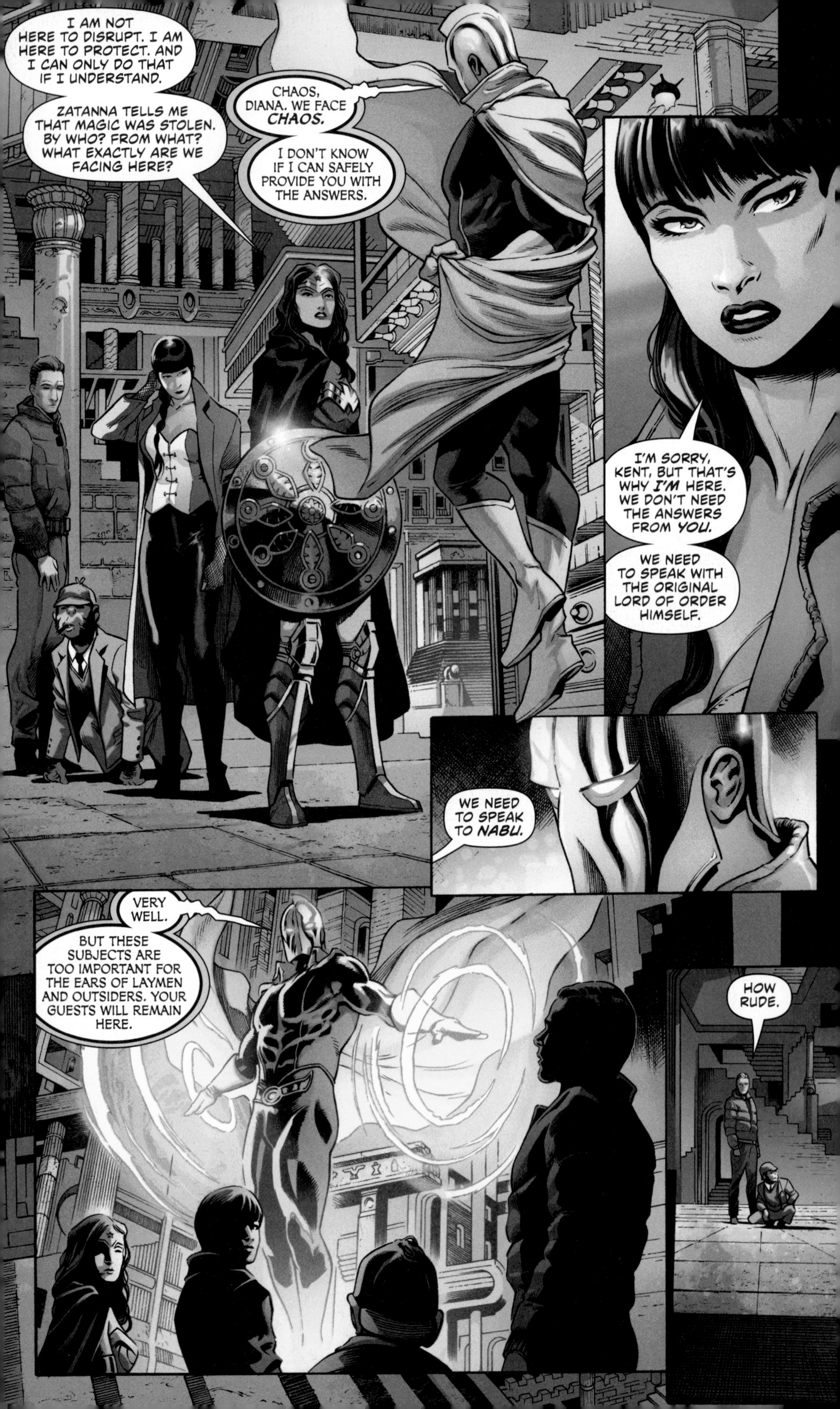

I AM NOT HERE TO DISRUPT. I AM HERE TO PROTECT. AND I CAN ONLY DO THAT IF I UNDERSTAND.
ZATANNA TELLS ME THAT MAGIC WAS STOLEN. BY WHO? FROM WHAT? WHAT EXACTLY ARE WE FACING HERE?
CHAOS, DIANA. WE FACE CHAOS.
I DON'T KNOW IF I CAN SAFELY PROVIDE YOU WITH THE ANSWERS.
I'M SORRY, KENT, BUT THAT'S WHY I'M HERE. WE DON'T NEED THE ANSWERS FROM YOU.
WE NEED TO SPEAK WITH THE ORIGINAL LORD OF ORDER HIMSELF.
WE NEED TO SPEAK TO NABU.
VERY WELL.
BUT THESE SUBJECTS ARE TOO IMPORTANT FOR THE EARS OF LAYMEN AND OUTSIDERS. YOUR GUESTS WILL REMAIN HERE.
HOW RUDE.

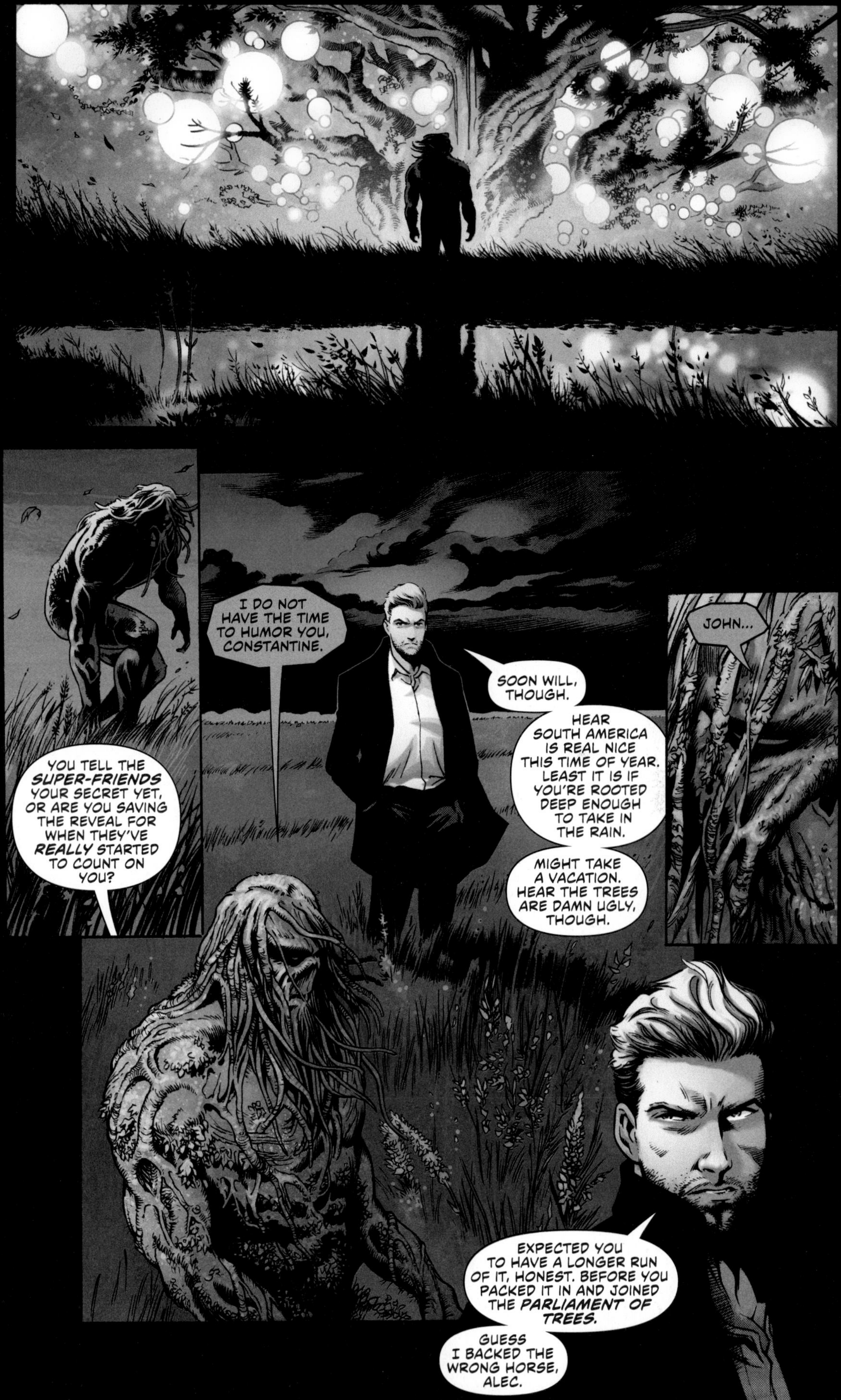
YOU TELL THE SUPER-FRIENDS YOUR SECRET YET, OR ARE YOU SAVING THE REVEAL FOR WHEN THEY'VE REALLY STARTED TO COUNT ON YOU?
I DO NOT HAVE THE TIME TO HUMOR YOU, CONSTANTINE.
SOON WILL, THOUGH.
HEAR SOUTH AMERICA IS REAL NICE THIS TIME OF YEAR. LEAST IT IS IF YOU'RE ROOTED DEEP ENOUGH TO TAKE IN THE RAIN.
MIGHT TAKE A VACATION. HEAR THE TREES ARE DAMN UGLY, THOUGH.
JOHN...
EXPECTED YOU TO HAVE A LONGER RUN OF IT, HONEST. BEFORE YOU PACKED IT IN AND JOINED THE PARLIAMENT OF TREES.
GUESS I BACKED THE WRONG HORSE, ALEC.

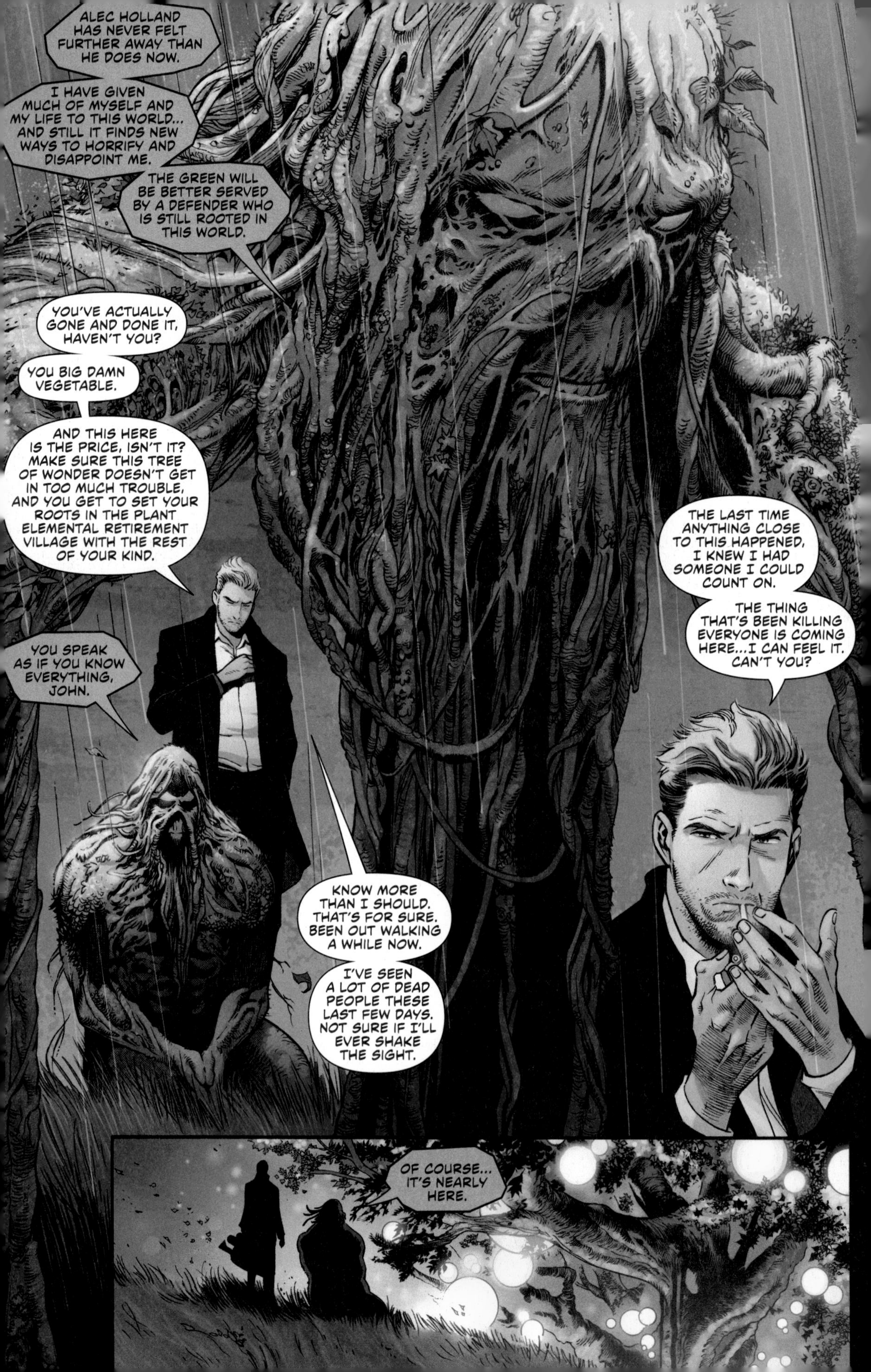

ALEC HOLLAND HAS NEVER FELT FURTHER AWAY THAN HE DOES NOW.
I HAVE GIVEN MUCH OF MYSELF AND MY LIFE TO THIS WORLD... AND STILL IT FINDS NEW WAYS TO HORRIFY AND DISAPPOINT ME.
THE GREEN WILL BE BETTER SERVED BY A DEFENDER WHO IS STILL ROOTED IN THIS WORLD.
YOU'VE ACTUALLY GONE AND DONE IT, HAVEN'T YOU?
YOU BIG DAMN VEGETABLE.
AND THIS HERE IS THE PRICE, ISN'T IT? MAKE SURE THIS TREE OF WONDER DOESN'T GET IN TOO MUCH TROUBLE, AND YOU GET TO SET YOUR ROOTS IN THE PLANT ELEMENTAL RETIREMENT VILLAGE WITH THE REST OF YOUR KIND.
YOU SPEAK AS IF YOU KNOW EVERYTHING, JOHN.
KNOW MORE THAN I SHOULD. THAT'S FOR SURE. BEEN OUT WALKING A WHILE NOW.
I'VE SEEN A LOT OF DEAD PEOPLE THESE LAST FEW DAYS. NOT SURE IF I'LL EVER SHAKE THE SIGHT.
THE LAST TIME ANYTHING CLOSE TO THIS HAPPENED, I KNEW I HAD SOMEONE I COULD COUNT ON.
THE THING THAT'S BEEN KILLING EVERYONE IS COMING HERE...I CAN FEEL IT. CAN'T YOU?
OF COURSE... IT'S NEARLY HERE.

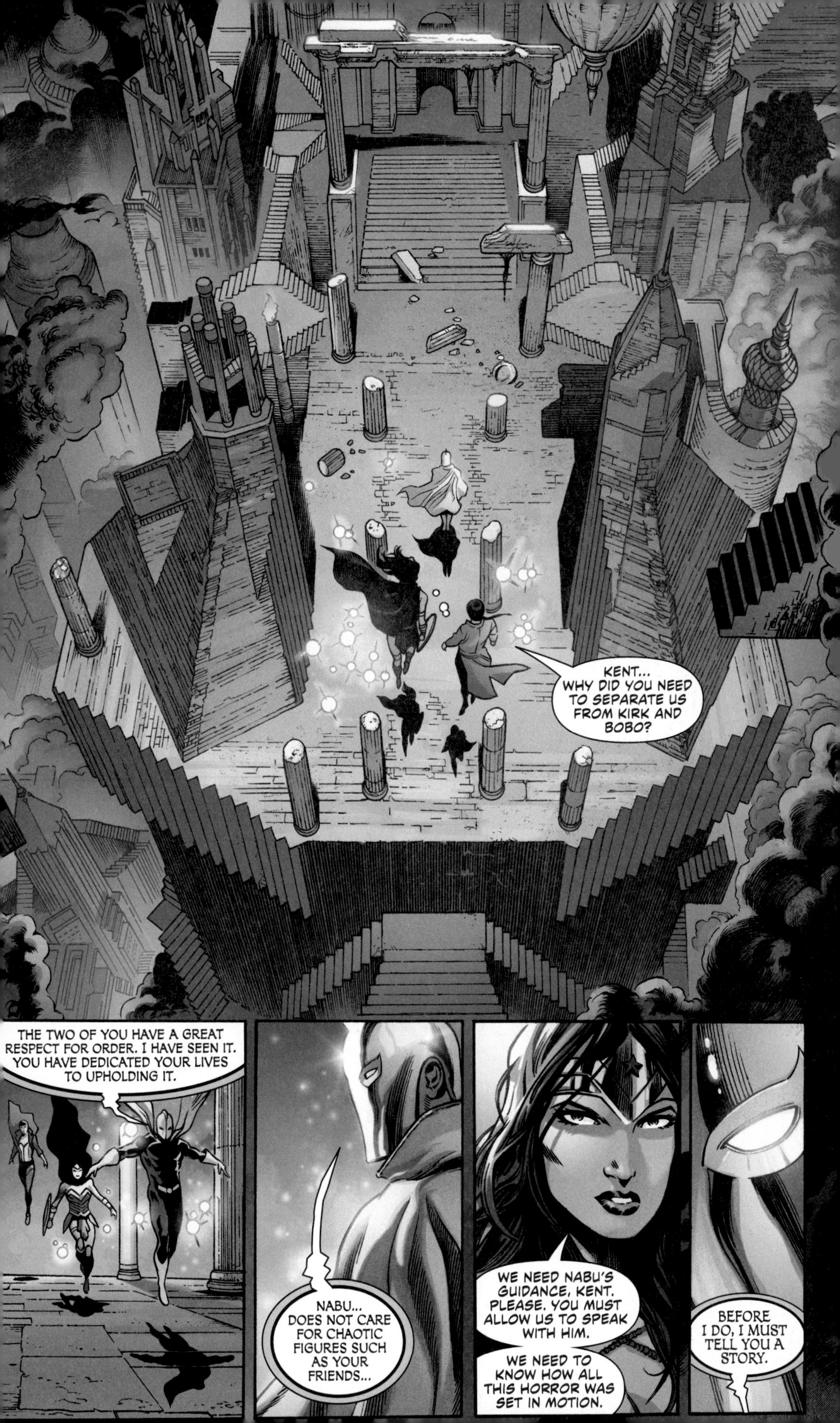
KENT... WHY DID YOU NEED TO SEPARATE US FROM KIRK AND BOBO?
THE TWO OF YOU HAVE A GREAT RESPECT FOR ORDER. I HAVE SEEN IT. YOU HAVE DEDICATED YOUR LIVES TO UPHOLDING IT.
NABU... DOES NOT CARE FOR CHAOTIC FIGURES SUCH AS YOUR FRIENDS...
WE NEED NABU'S GUIDANCE, KENT. PLEASE. YOU MUST ALLOW US TO SPEAK WITH HIM.
WE NEED TO KNOW HOW ALL THIS HORROR WAS SET IN MOTION.
BEFORE I DO, I MUST TELL YOU A STORY.

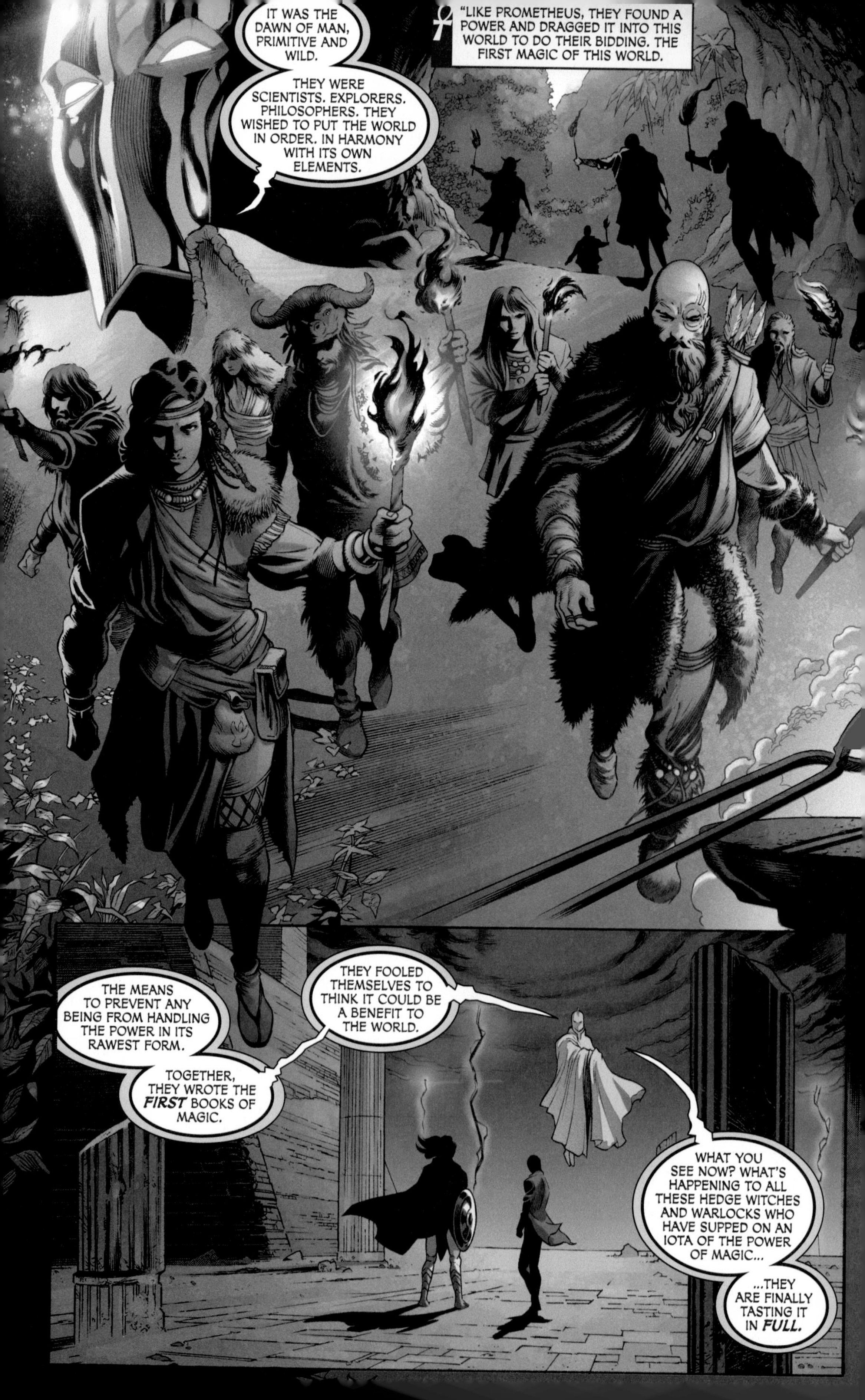
IT WAS THE DAWN OF MAN, PRIMITIVE AND WILD.
THEY WERE SCIENTISTS. EXPLORERS. PHILOSOPHERS. THEY WISHED TO PUT THE WORLD IN ORDER. IN HARMONY WITH ITS OWN ELEMENTS.
"LIKE PROMETHEUS, THEY FOUND A POWER AND DRAGGED IT INTO THIS WORLD TO DO THEIR BIDDING. THE FIRST MAGIC OF THIS WORLD.
THE MEANS TO PREVENT ANY BEING FROM HANDLING THE POWER IN ITS RAWEST FORM.
TOGETHER, THEY WROTE THE *FIRST* BOOKS OF MAGIC.
THEY FOOLED THEMSELVES TO THINK IT COULD BE A BENEFIT TO THE WORLD.
WHAT YOU SEE NOW? WHAT'S HAPPENING TO ALL THESE HEDGE WITCHES AND WARLOCKS WHO HAVE SUPPED ON AN IOTA OF THE POWER OF MAGIC...
...THEY ARE FINALLY TASTING IT IN *FULL.*

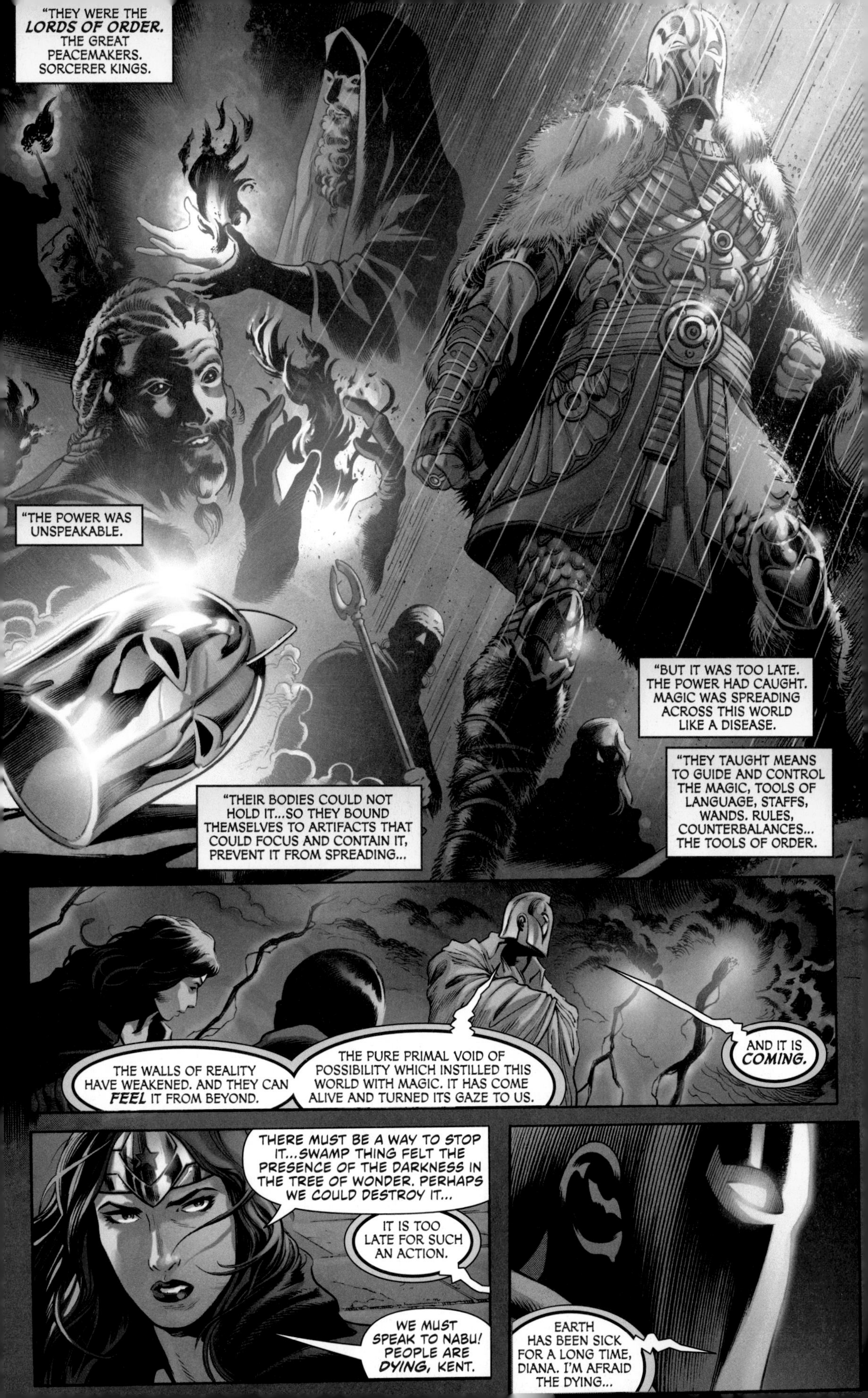
"THEY WERE THE LORDS OF ORDER. THE GREAT PEACEMAKERS. SORCERER KINGS.
"THE POWER WAS UNSPEAKABLE.
"THEIR BODIES COULD NOT HOLD IT...SO THEY BOUND THEMSELVES TO ARTIFACTS THAT COULD FOCUS AND CONTAIN IT, PREVENT IT FROM SPREADING...
"BUT IT WAS TOO LATE. THE POWER HAD CAUGHT. MAGIC WAS SPREADING ACROSS THIS WORLD LIKE A DISEASE.
"THEY TAUGHT MEANS TO GUIDE AND CONTROL THE MAGIC, TOOLS OF LANGUAGE, STAFFS, WANDS. RULES, COUNTERBALANCES... THE TOOLS OF ORDER.
THE WALLS OF REALITY HAVE WEAKENED. AND THEY CAN FEEL IT FROM BEYOND.
THE PURE PRIMAL VOID OF POSSIBILITY WHICH INSTILLED THIS WORLD WITH MAGIC. IT HAS COME ALIVE AND TURNED ITS GAZE TO US.
AND IT IS COMING.
THERE MUST BE A WAY TO STOP IT...SWAMP THING FELT THE PRESENCE OF THE DARKNESS IN THE TREE OF WONDER. PERHAPS WE COULD DESTROY IT...
IT IS TOO LATE FOR SUCH AN ACTION.
WE MUST SPEAK TO NABU! PEOPLE ARE DYING, KENT.
EARTH HAS BEEN SICK FOR A LONG TIME, DIANA. I'M AFRAID THE DYING...

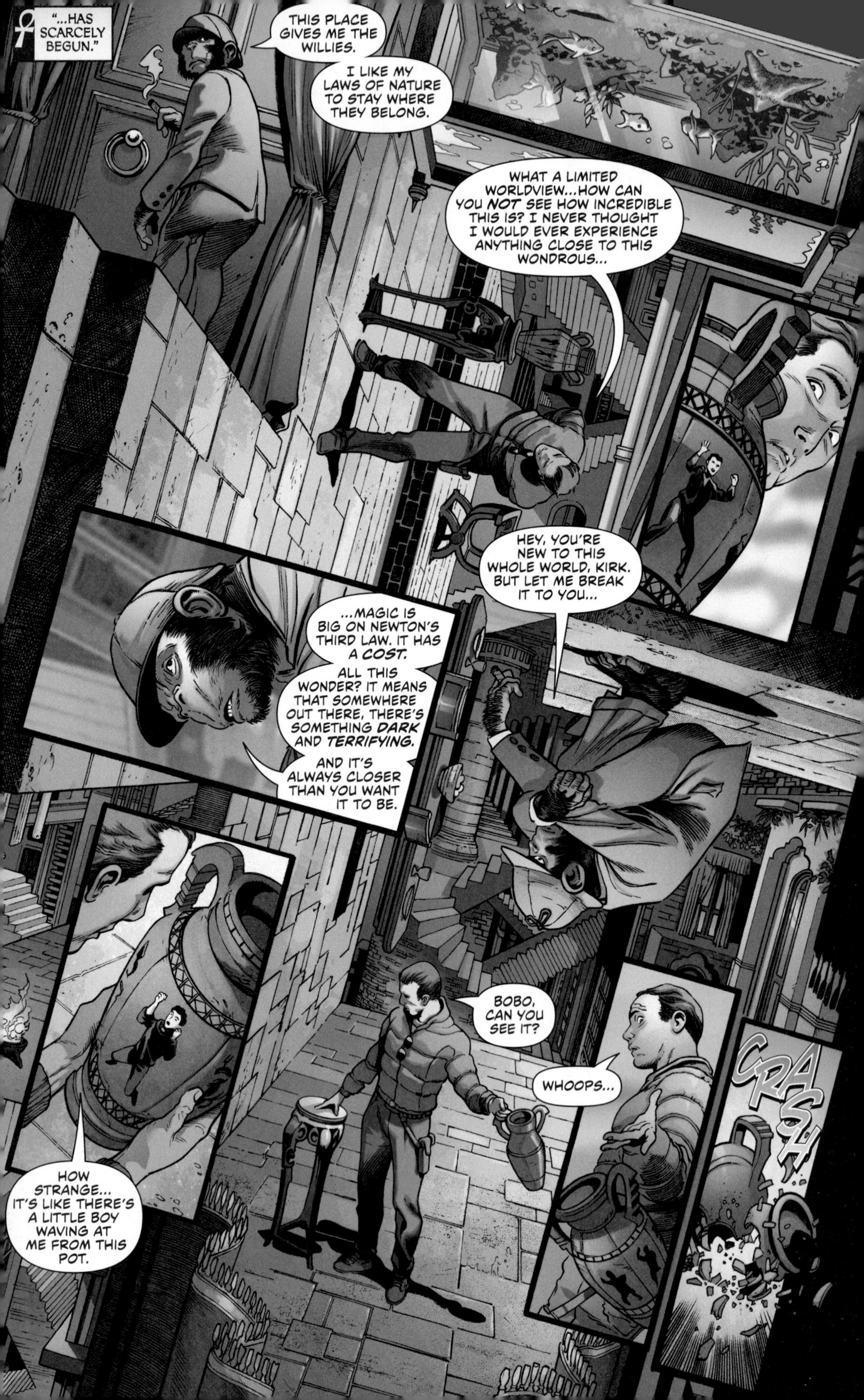
"...HAS SCARCELY BEGUN."
THIS PLACE GIVES ME THE WILLIES.
I LIKE MY LAWS OF NATURE TO STAY WHERE THEY BELONG.
WHAT A LIMITED WORLDVIEW...HOW CAN YOU NOT SEE HOW INCREDIBLE THIS IS? I NEVER THOUGHT I WOULD EVER EXPERIENCE ANYTHING CLOSE TO THIS WONDROUS...
HEY, YOU'RE NEW TO THIS WHOLE WORLD, KIRK. BUT LET ME BREAK IT TO YOU...
...MAGIC IS BIG ON NEWTON'S THIRD LAW. IT HAS A COST.
ALL THIS WONDER? IT MEANS THAT SOMEWHERE OUT THERE, THERE'S SOMETHING DARK AND TERRIFYING.
AND IT'S ALWAYS CLOSER THAN YOU WANT IT TO BE.
HOW STRANGE... IT'S LIKE THERE'S A LITTLE BOY WAVING AT ME FROM THIS POT.
BOBO, CAN YOU SEE IT?
WHOOPS...
CRASH

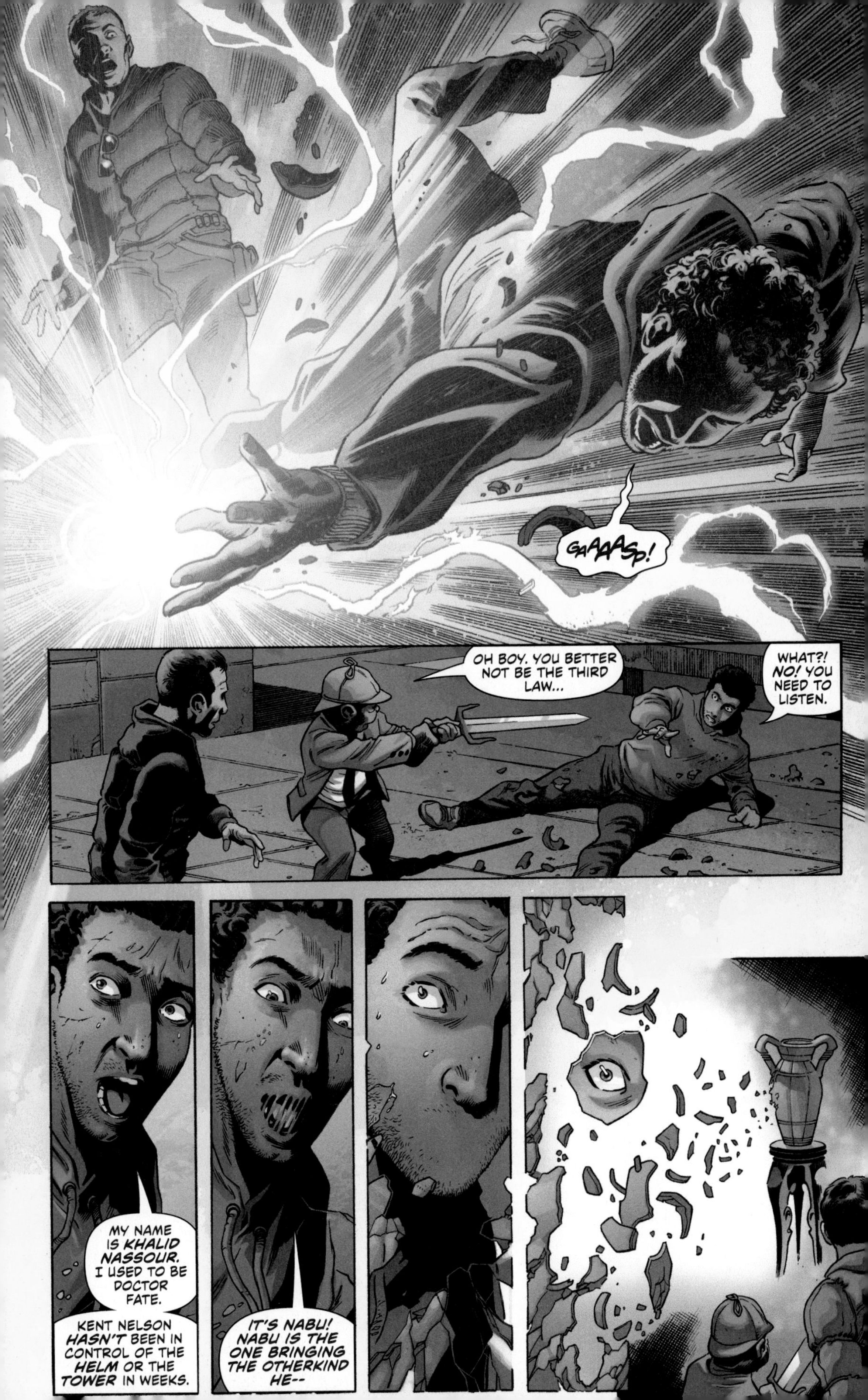
GAAAASP!
OH BOY. YOU BETTER NOT BE THE THIRD LAW...
WHAT?! NO! YOU NEED TO LISTEN.
MY NAME IS KHALID NASSOUR. I USED TO BE DOCTOR FATE.
KENT NELSON HASN'T BEEN IN CONTROL OF THE HELM OR THE TOWER IN WEEKS.
IT'S NABU! NABU IS THE ONE BRINGING THE OTHERKIND HE--

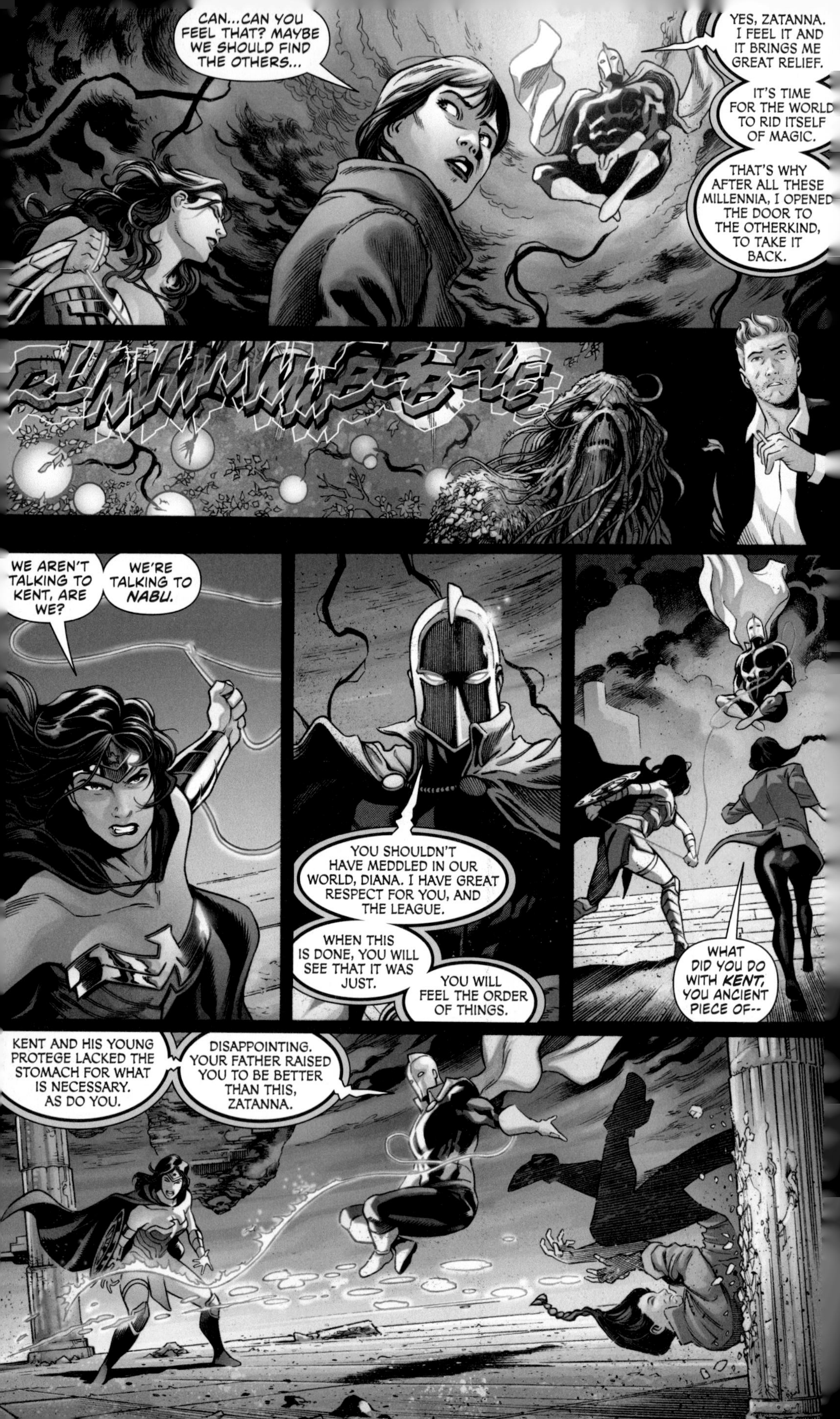
CAN...CAN YOU FEEL THAT? MAYBE WE SHOULD FIND THE OTHERS...
YES, ZATANNA. I FEEL IT AND IT BRINGS ME GREAT RELIEF.
IT'S TIME FOR THE WORLD TO RID ITSELF OF MAGIC.
THAT'S WHY AFTER ALL THESE MILLENNIA, I OPENED THE DOOR TO THE OTHERKIND, TO TAKE IT BACK.
WE AREN'T TALKING TO KENT, ARE WE?
WE'RE TALKING TO *NABU.*
YOU SHOULDN'T HAVE MEDDLED IN OUR WORLD, DIANA. I HAVE GREAT RESPECT FOR YOU, AND THE LEAGUE.
WHEN THIS IS DONE, YOU WILL SEE THAT IT WAS JUST.
YOU WILL FEEL THE ORDER OF THINGS.
WHAT DID YOU DO WITH *KENT,* YOU ANCIENT PIECE OF--
KENT AND HIS YOUNG PROTEGE LACKED THE STOMACH FOR WHAT IS NECESSARY. AS DO YOU.
DISAPPOINTING. YOUR FATHER RAISED YOU TO BE BETTER THAN THIS, ZATANNA.

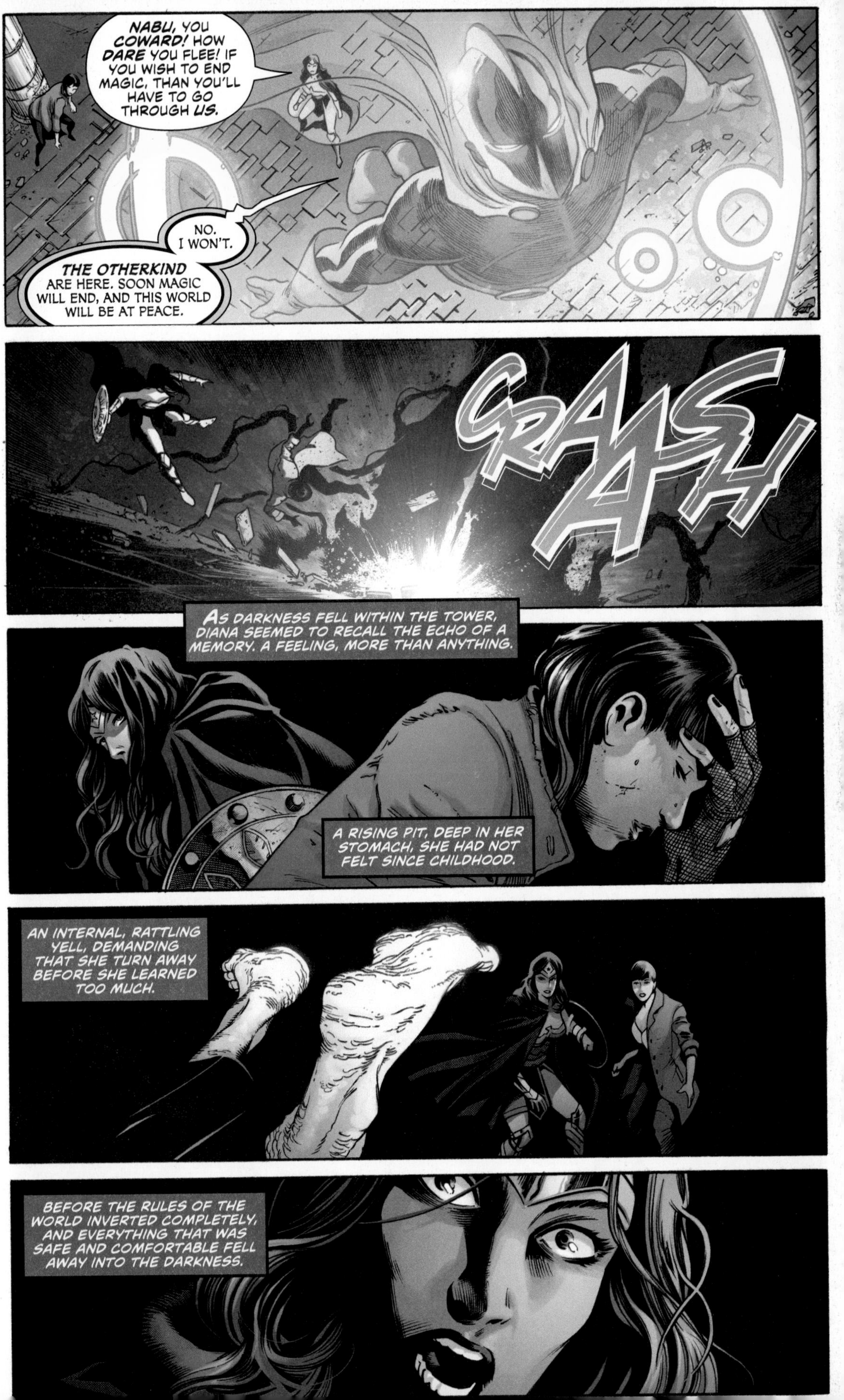
NABU, YOU COWARD! HOW DARE YOU FLEE! IF YOU WISH TO END MAGIC, THAN YOU'LL HAVE TO GO THROUGH US.
NO. I WON'T.
THE OTHERKIND ARE HERE. SOON MAGIC WILL END, AND THIS WORLD WILL BE AT PEACE.
CRAASH
AS DARKNESS FELL WITHIN THE TOWER, DIANA SEEMED TO RECALL THE ECHO OF A MEMORY. A FEELING, MORE THAN ANYTHING.
A RISING PIT, DEEP IN HER STOMACH, SHE HAD NOT FELT SINCE CHILDHOOD.
AN INTERNAL, RATTLING YELL, DEMANDING THAT SHE TURN AWAY BEFORE SHE LEARNED TOO MUCH.
BEFORE THE RULES OF THE WORLD INVERTED COMPLETELY, AND EVERYTHING THAT WAS SAFE AND COMFORTABLE FELL AWAY INTO THE DARKNESS.

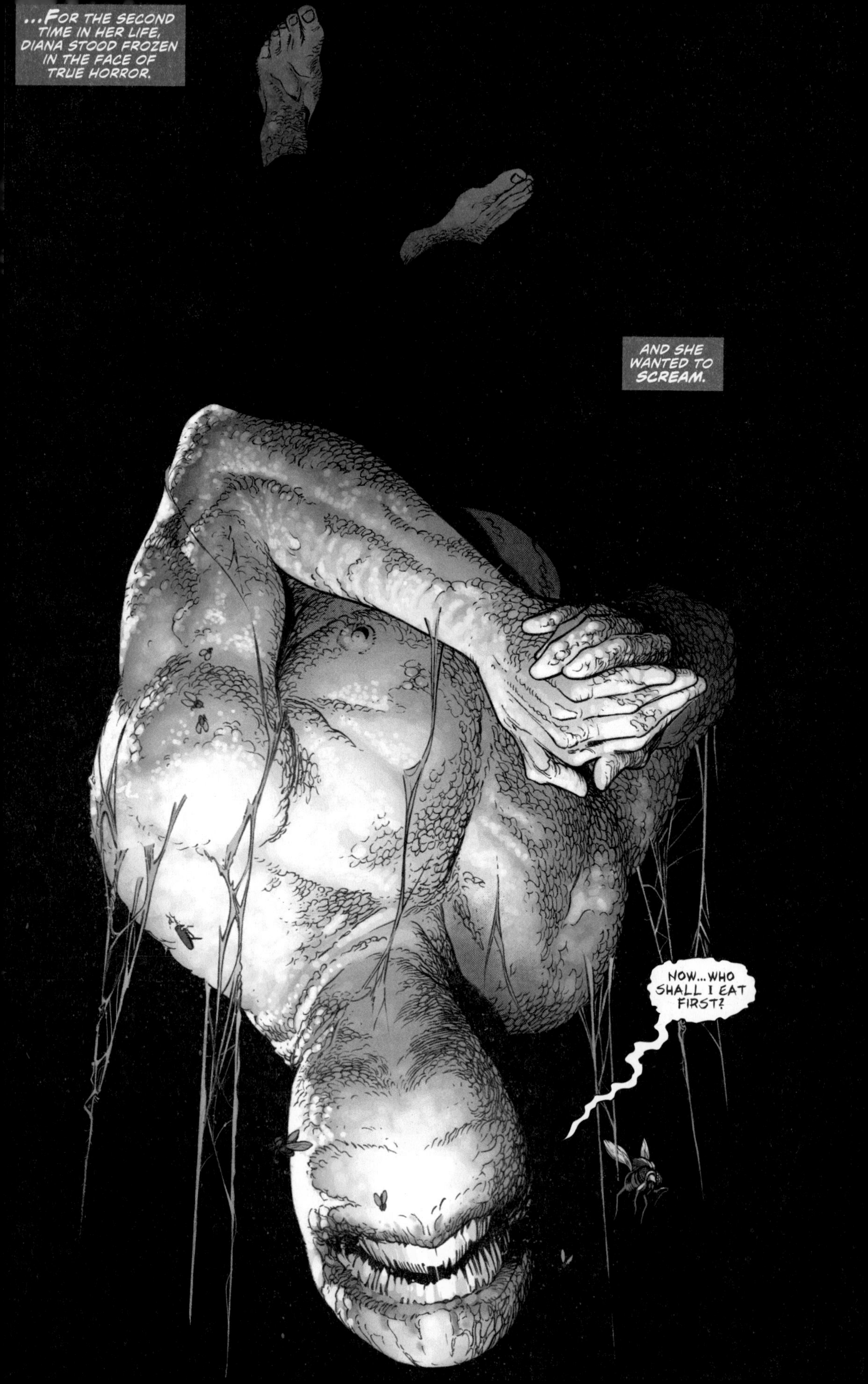
...FOR THE SECOND TIME IN HER LIFE, DIANA STOOD FROZEN IN THE FACE OF TRUE HORROR.
AND SHE WANTED TO SCREAM.
NOW...WHO SHALL I EAT FIRST?

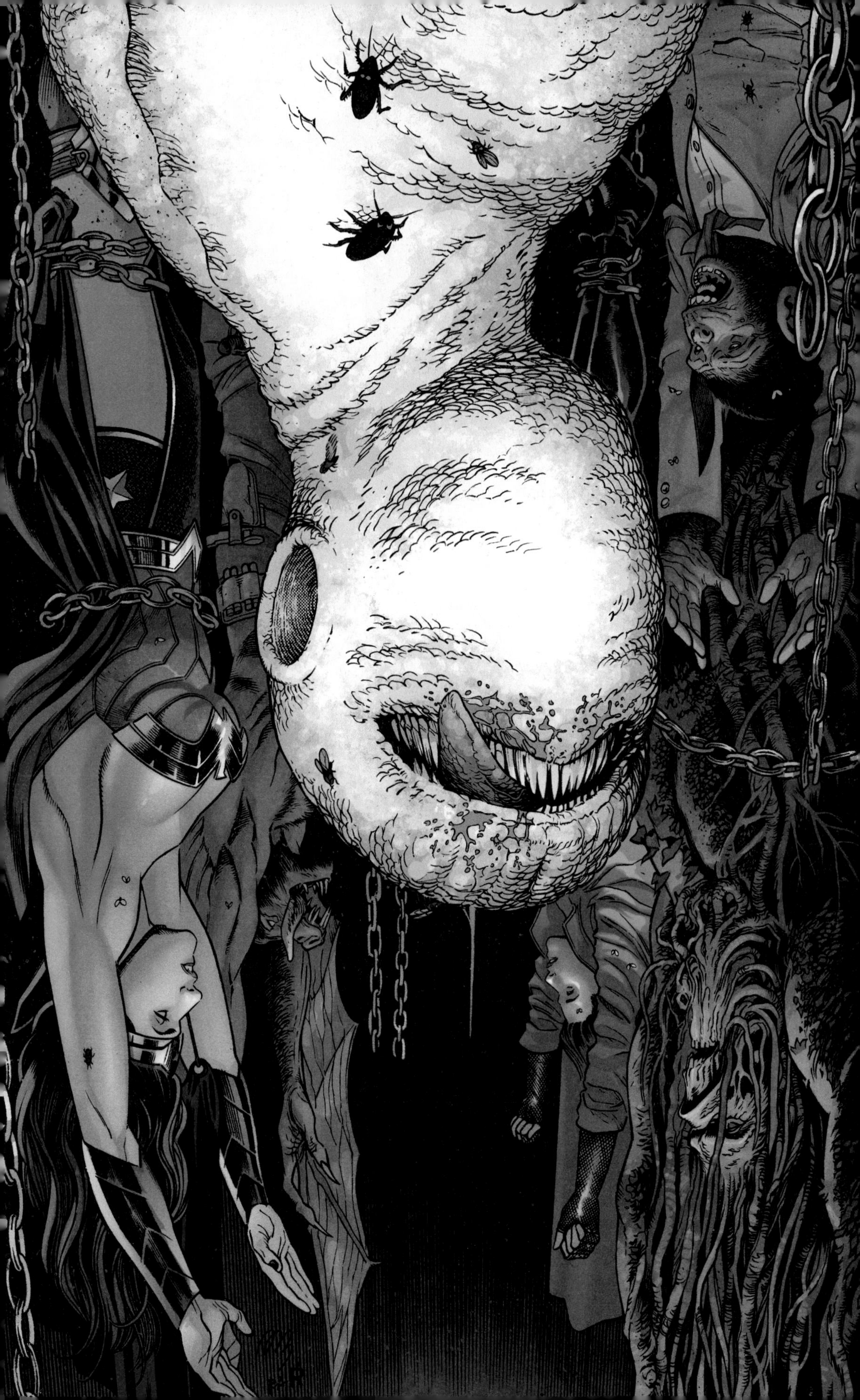

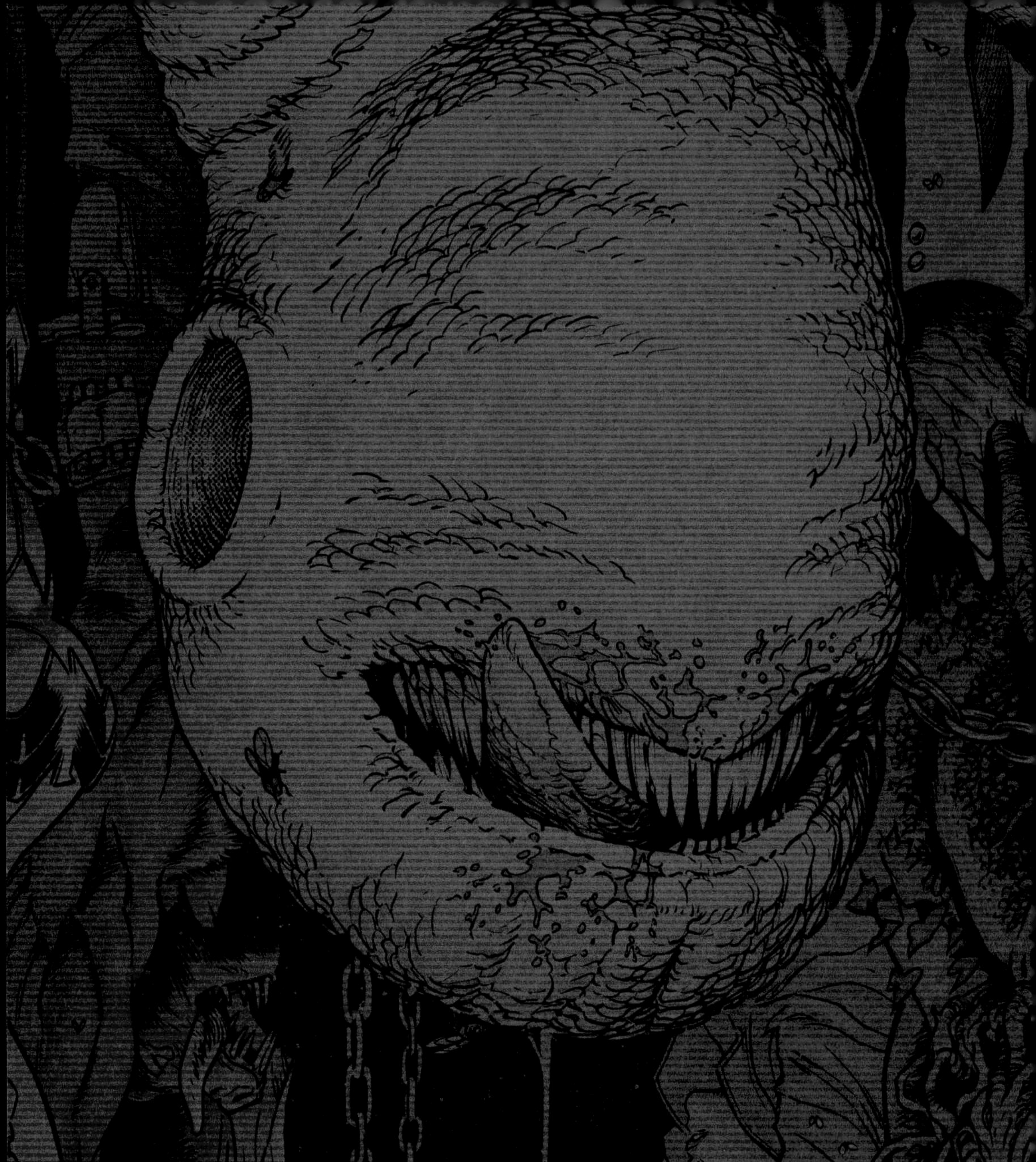

JUSTICE LEAGUE DARK
#3

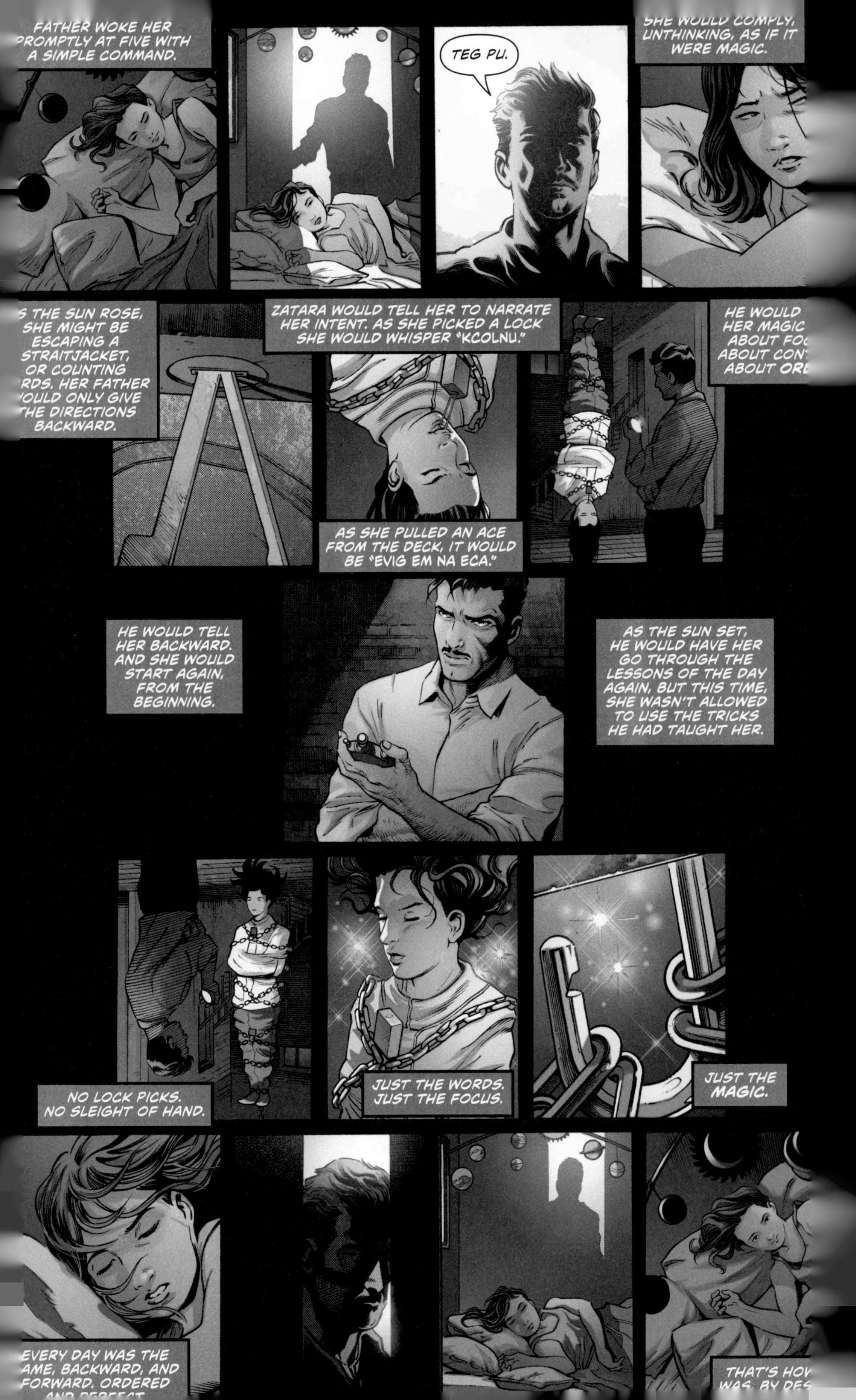
FATHER WOKE HER PROMPTLY AT FIVE WITH A SIMPLE COMMAND.
TEG PU.
SHE WOULD COMPLY, UNTHINKING, AS IF IT WERE MAGIC.
S THE SUN ROSE, SHE MIGHT BE ESCAPING A STRAITJACKET, OR COUNTING RDS. HER FATHER OULD ONLY GIVE THE DIRECTIONS BACKWARD.
ZATARA WOULD TELL HER TO NARRATE HER INTENT. AS SHE PICKED A LOCK SHE WOULD WHISPER "KCOLNU."
AS SHE PULLED AN ACE FROM THE DECK, IT WOULD BE "EVIG EM NA ECA."
HE WOULD HER MAGIC ABOUT FO ABOUT CON ABOUT ORD
HE WOULD TELL HER BACKWARD. AND SHE WOULD START AGAIN, FROM THE BEGINNING.
AS THE SUN SET, HE WOULD HAVE HER GO THROUGH THE LESSONS OF THE DAY AGAIN, BUT THIS TIME, SHE WASN'T ALLOWED TO USE THE TRICKS HE HAD TAUGHT HER.
NO LOCK PICKS. NO SLEIGHT OF HAND.
JUST THE WORDS. JUST THE FOCUS.
JUST THE MAGIC.
EVERY DAY WAS THE AME, BACKWARD, AND FORWARD. ORDERED
THAT'S HOW WAS. BY DES

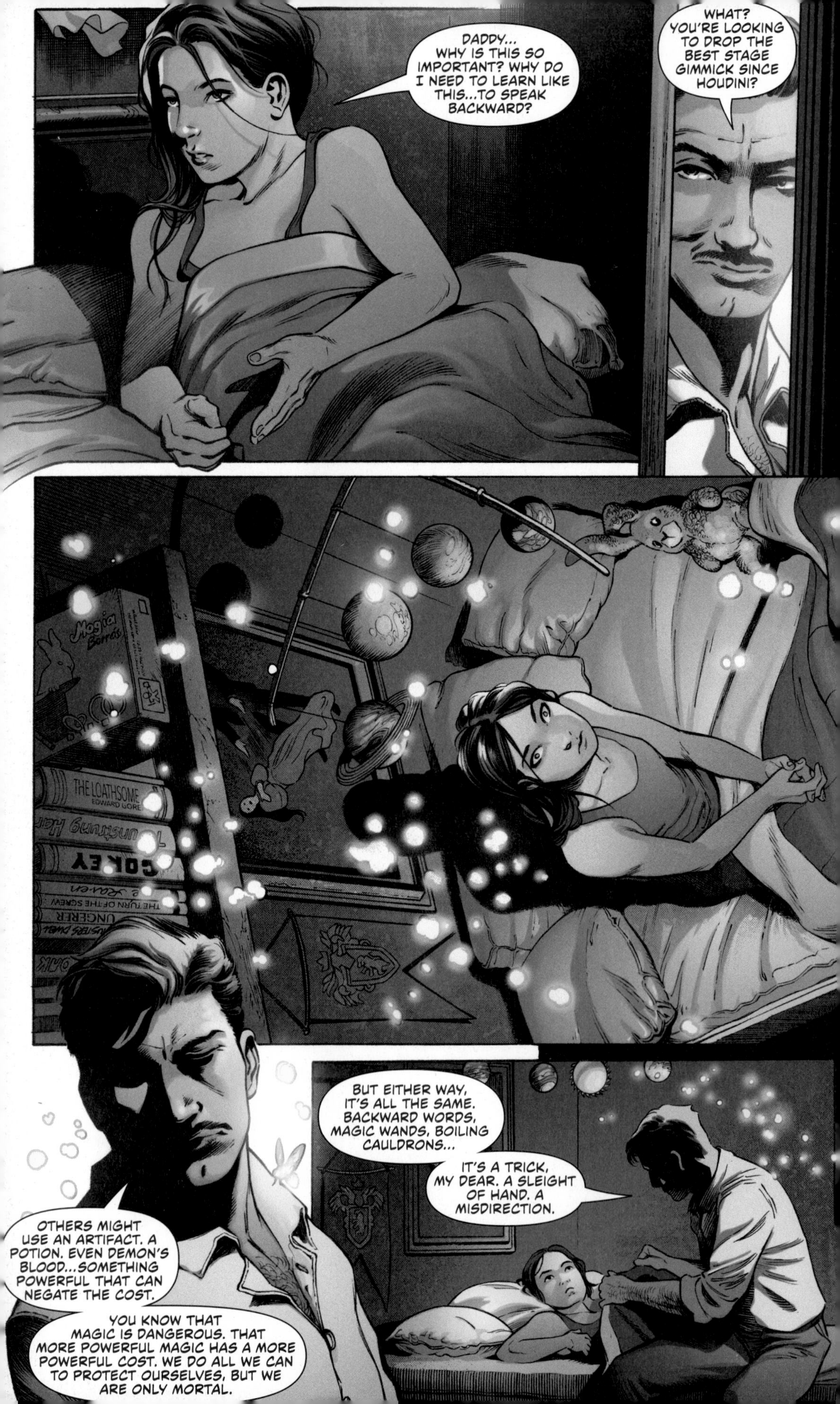
DADDY... WHY IS THIS SO IMPORTANT? WHY DO I NEED TO LEARN LIKE THIS...TO SPEAK BACKWARD?
WHAT? YOU'RE LOOKING TO DROP THE BEST STAGE GIMMICK SINCE HOUDINI?
Magia Borrás
THE LOATHSOME
OTHERS MIGHT USE AN ARTIFACT. A POTION. EVEN DEMON'S BLOOD...SOMETHING POWERFUL THAT CAN NEGATE THE COST.
YOU KNOW THAT MAGIC IS DANGEROUS. THAT MORE POWERFUL MAGIC HAS A MORE POWERFUL COST. WE DO ALL WE CAN TO PROTECT OURSELVES, BUT WE ARE ONLY MORTAL.
BUT EITHER WAY, IT'S ALL THE SAME. BACKWARD WORDS, MAGIC WANDS, BOILING CAULDRONS...
IT'S A TRICK, MY DEAR. A SLEIGHT OF HAND. A MISDIRECTION.

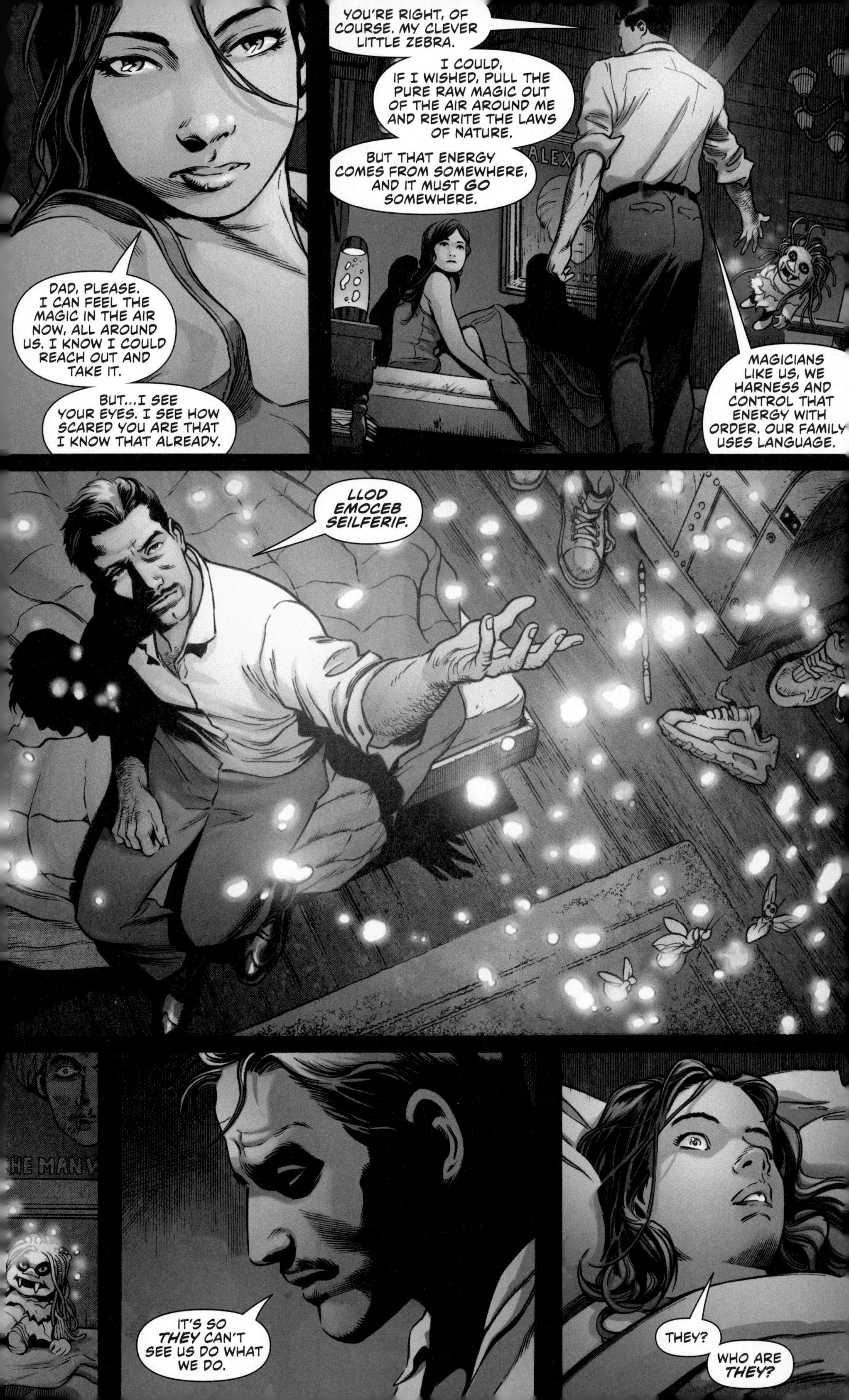
DAD, PLEASE. I CAN FEEL THE MAGIC IN THE AIR NOW, ALL AROUND US. I KNOW I COULD REACH OUT AND TAKE IT.
BUT...I SEE YOUR EYES. I SEE HOW SCARED YOU ARE THAT I KNOW THAT ALREADY.
YOU'RE RIGHT, OF COURSE. MY CLEVER LITTLE ZEBRA.
I COULD, IF I WISHED, PULL THE PURE RAW MAGIC OUT OF THE AIR AROUND ME AND REWRITE THE LAWS OF NATURE.
BUT THAT ENERGY COMES FROM SOMEWHERE, AND IT MUST GO SOMEWHERE.
ALEX
MAGICIANS LIKE US, WE HARNESS AND CONTROL THAT ENERGY WITH ORDER. OUR FAMILY USES LANGUAGE.
LLOD EMOCEB SEILFERIF.
HE MAN W
IT'S SO THEY CAN'T SEE US DO WHAT WE DO.
THEY?
WHO ARE THEY?

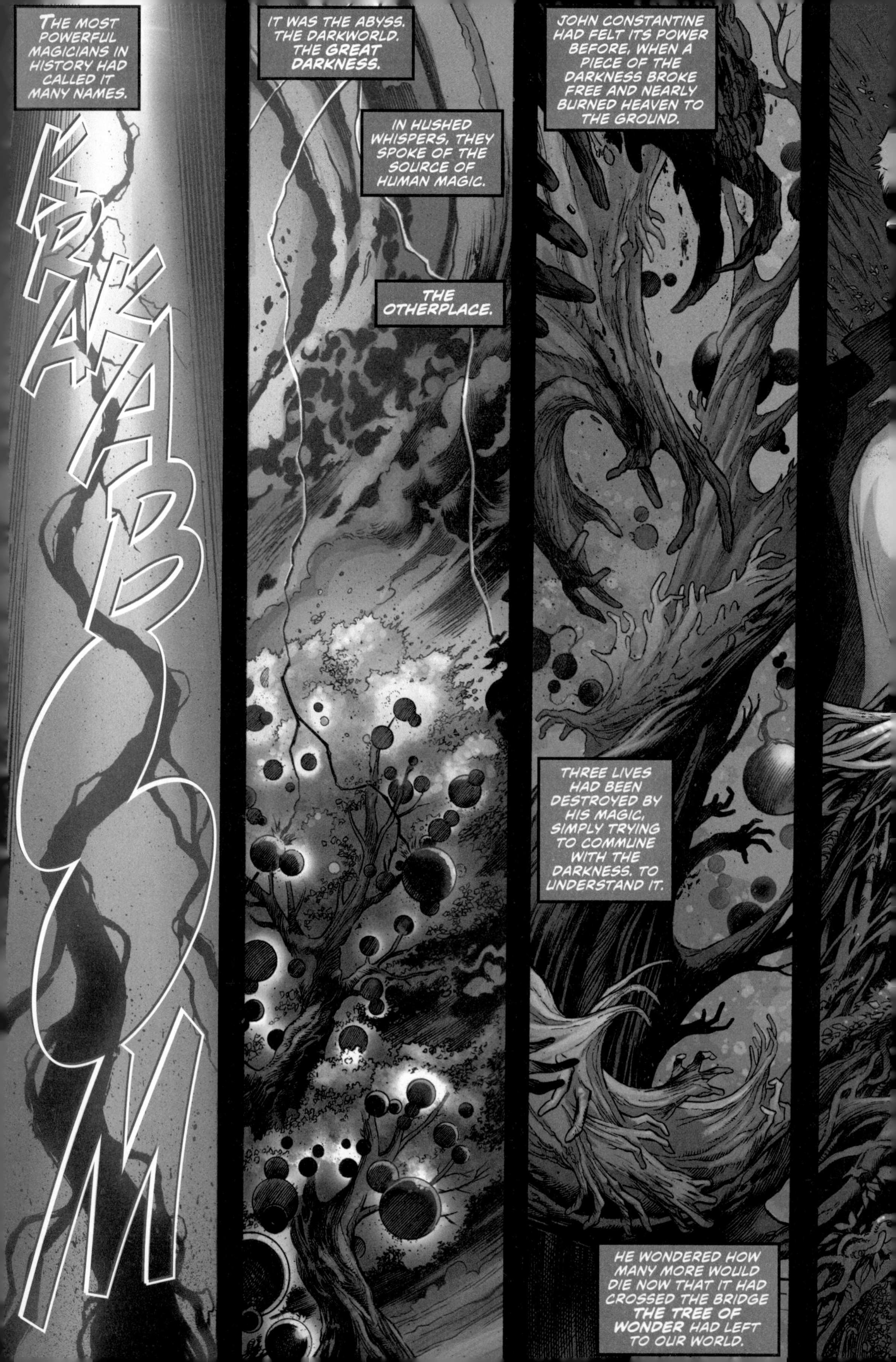
THE MOST POWERFUL MAGICIANS IN HISTORY HAD CALLED IT MANY NAMES.
KRAKABOOM
IT WAS THE ABYSS. THE DARKWORLD. THE GREAT DARKNESS.
IN HUSHED WHISPERS, THEY SPOKE OF THE SOURCE OF HUMAN MAGIC.
THE OTHERPLACE.
JOHN CONSTANTINE HAD FELT ITS POWER BEFORE, WHEN A PIECE OF THE DARKNESS BROKE FREE AND NEARLY BURNED HEAVEN TO THE GROUND.
THREE LIVES HAD BEEN DESTROYED BY HIS MAGIC, SIMPLY TRYING TO COMMUNE WITH THE DARKNESS. TO UNDERSTAND IT.
HE WONDERED HOW MANY MORE WOULD DIE NOW THAT IT HAD CROSSED THE BRIDGE THE TREE OF WONDER HAD LEFT TO OUR WORLD.

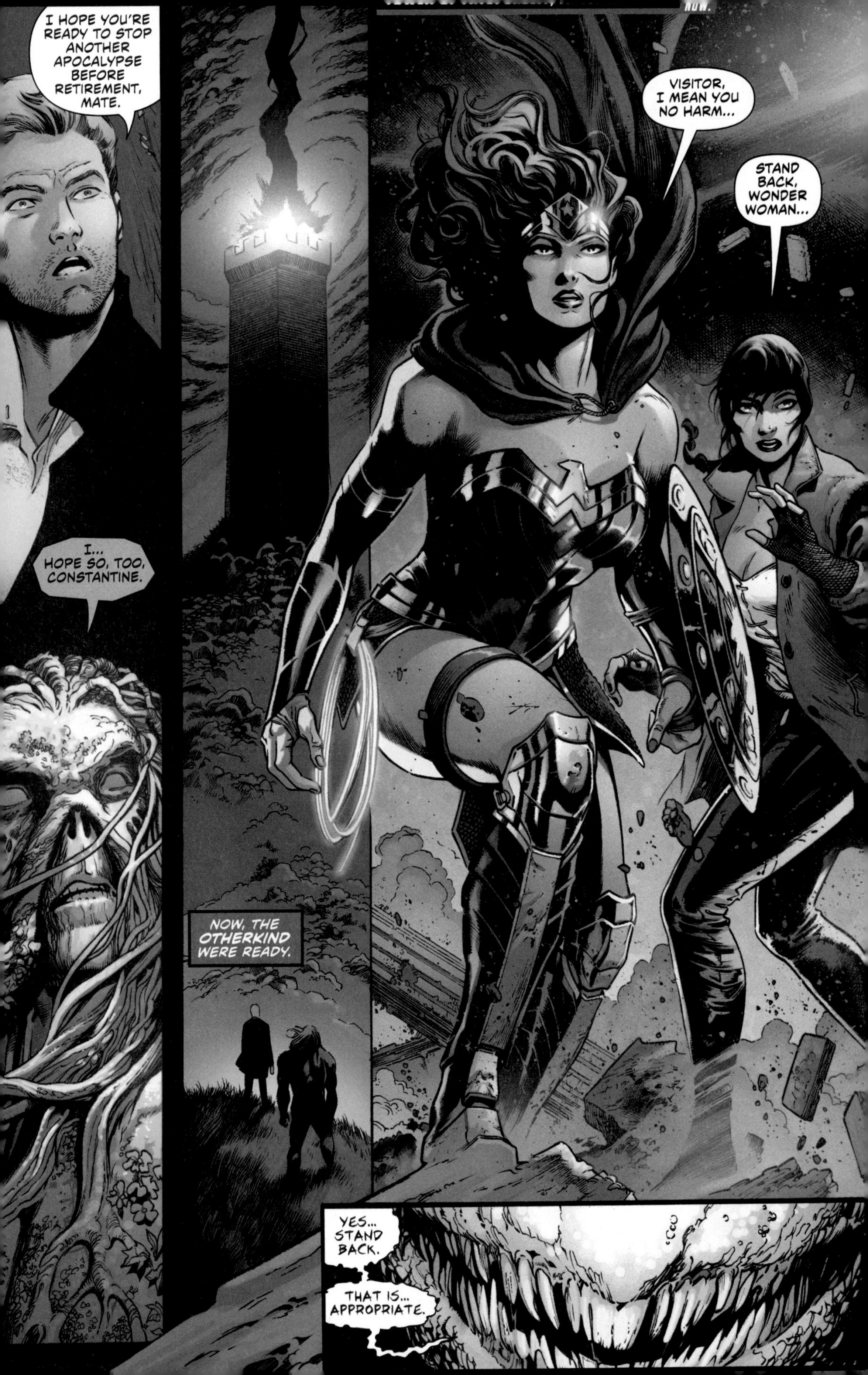

I HOPE YOU'RE READY TO STOP ANOTHER APOCALYPSE BEFORE RETIREMENT, MATE.
I... HOPE SO, TOO, CONSTANTINE.
NOW, THE OTHERKIND WERE READY.
NOW.
VISITOR, I MEAN YOU NO HARM...
STAND BACK, WONDER WOMAN...
YES... STAND BACK.
THAT IS... APPROPRIATE.

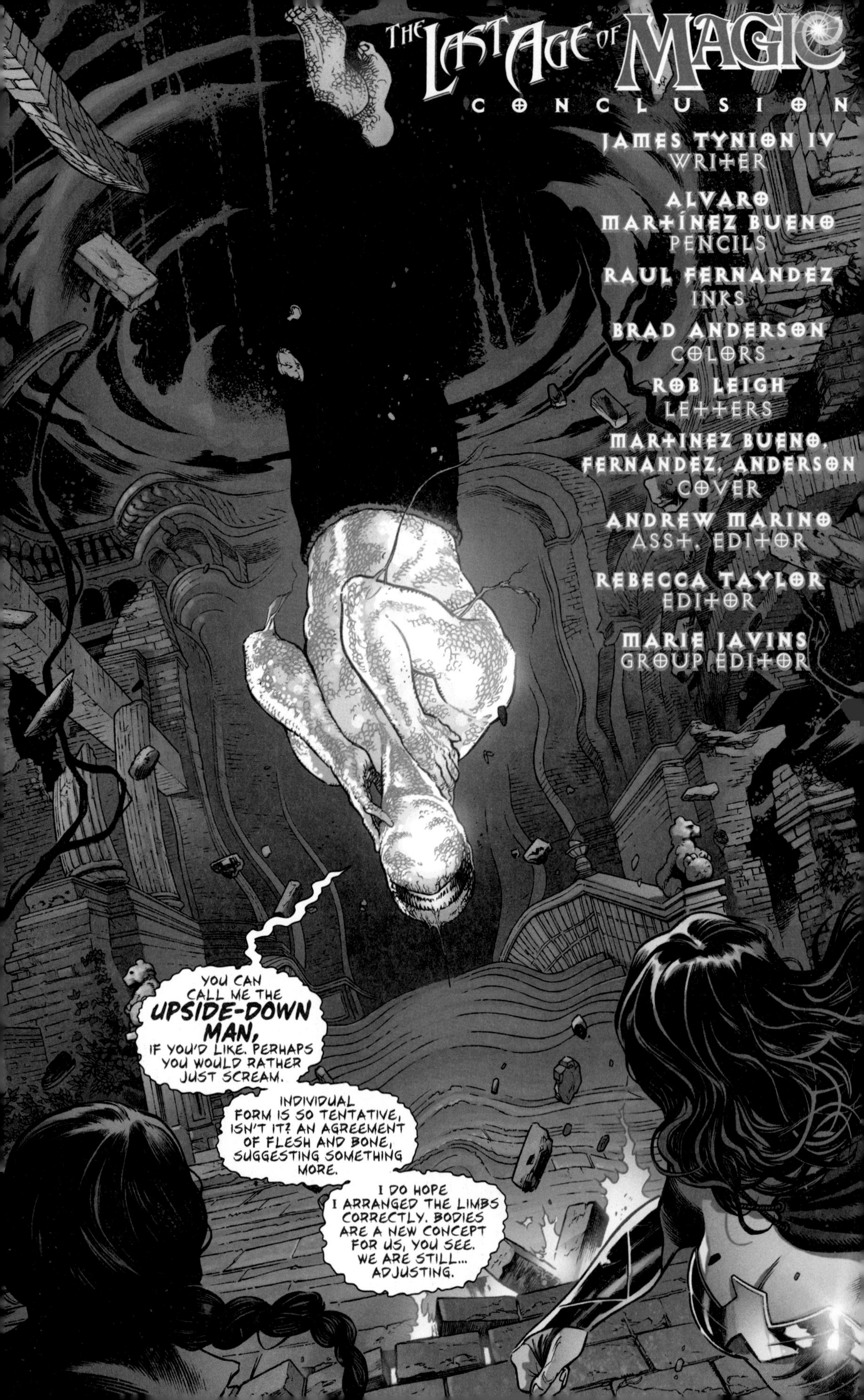
THE LAST AGE OF MAGIC
CONCLUSION
JAMES TYNION IV WRITER
ALVARO MARTÍNEZ BUENO PENCILS
RAUL FERNANDEZ INKS
BRAD ANDERSON COLORS
ROB LEIGH LETTERS
MARTINEZ BUENO, FERNANDEZ, ANDERSON COVER
ANDREW MARINO ASST. EDITOR
REBECCA TAYLOR EDITOR
MARIE JAVINS GROUP EDITOR
YOU CAN CALL ME THE UPSIDE-DOWN MAN, IF YOU'D LIKE. PERHAPS YOU WOULD RATHER JUST SCREAM.
INDIVIDUAL FORM IS SO TENTATIVE, ISN'T IT? AN AGREEMENT OF FLESH AND BONE, SUGGESTING SOMETHING MORE.
I DO HOPE I ARRANGED THE LIMBS CORRECTLY. BODIES ARE A NEW CONCEPT FOR US, YOU SEE. WE ARE STILL... ADJUSTING.

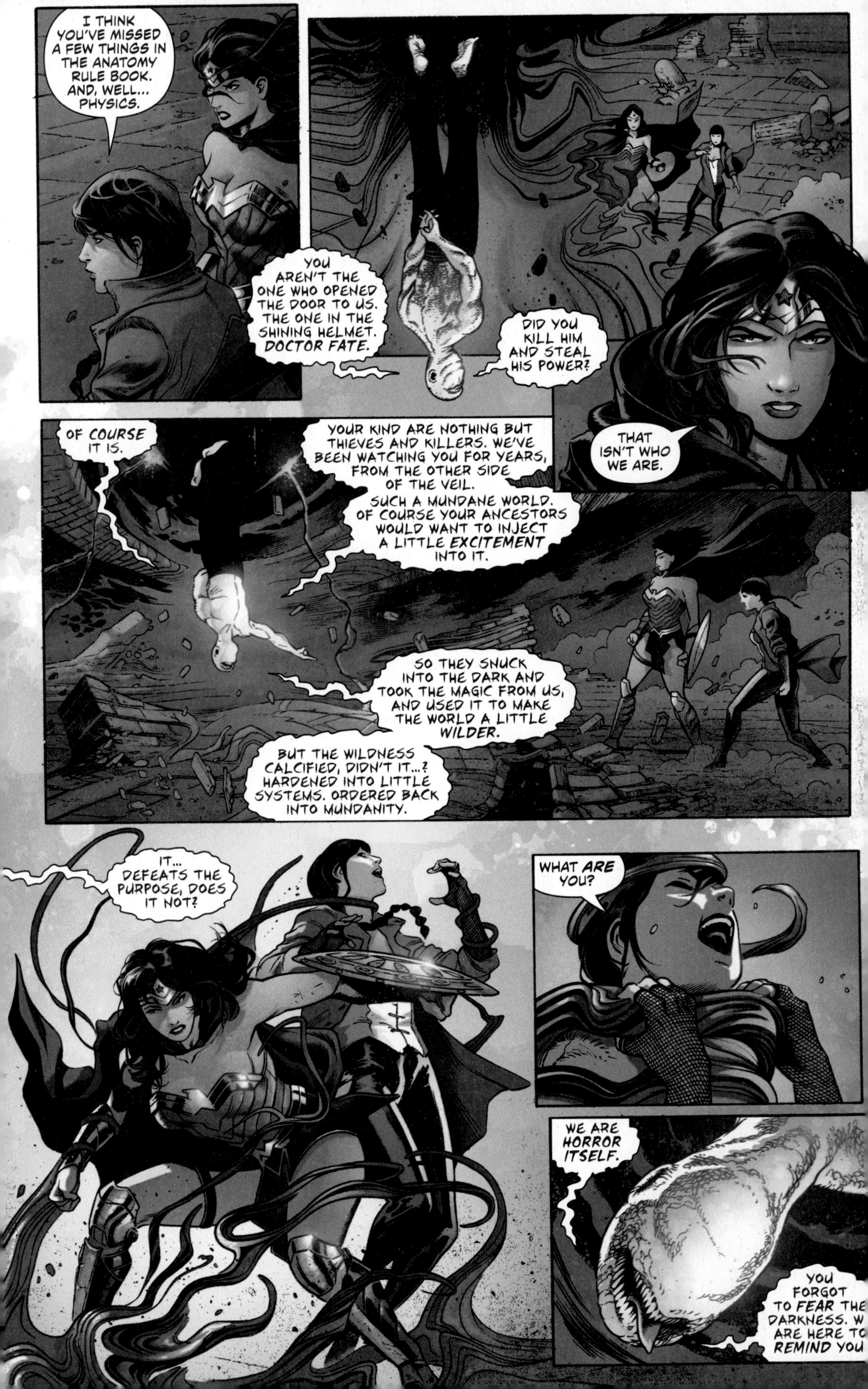
I THINK YOU'VE MISSED A FEW THINGS IN THE ANATOMY RULE BOOK. AND, WELL... PHYSICS.
YOU AREN'T THE ONE WHO OPENED THE DOOR TO US. THE ONE IN THE SHINING HELMET. DOCTOR FATE.
DID YOU KILL HIM AND STEAL HIS POWER?
THAT ISN'T WHO WE ARE.
OF COURSE IT IS.
YOUR KIND ARE NOTHING BUT THIEVES AND KILLERS. WE'VE BEEN WATCHING YOU FOR YEARS, FROM THE OTHER SIDE OF THE VEIL.
SUCH A MUNDANE WORLD. OF COURSE YOUR ANCESTORS WOULD WANT TO INJECT A LITTLE EXCITEMENT INTO IT.
SO THEY SNUCK INTO THE DARK AND TOOK THE MAGIC FROM US, AND USED IT TO MAKE THE WORLD A LITTLE WILDER.
BUT THE WILDNESS CALCIFIED, DIDN'T IT...? HARDENED INTO LITTLE SYSTEMS. ORDERED BACK INTO MUNDANITY.
IT... DEFEATS THE PURPOSE, DOES IT NOT?
WHAT ARE YOU?
WE ARE HORROR ITSELF.
YOU FORGOT TO FEAR THE DARKNESS. W ARE HERE TO REMIND YOU

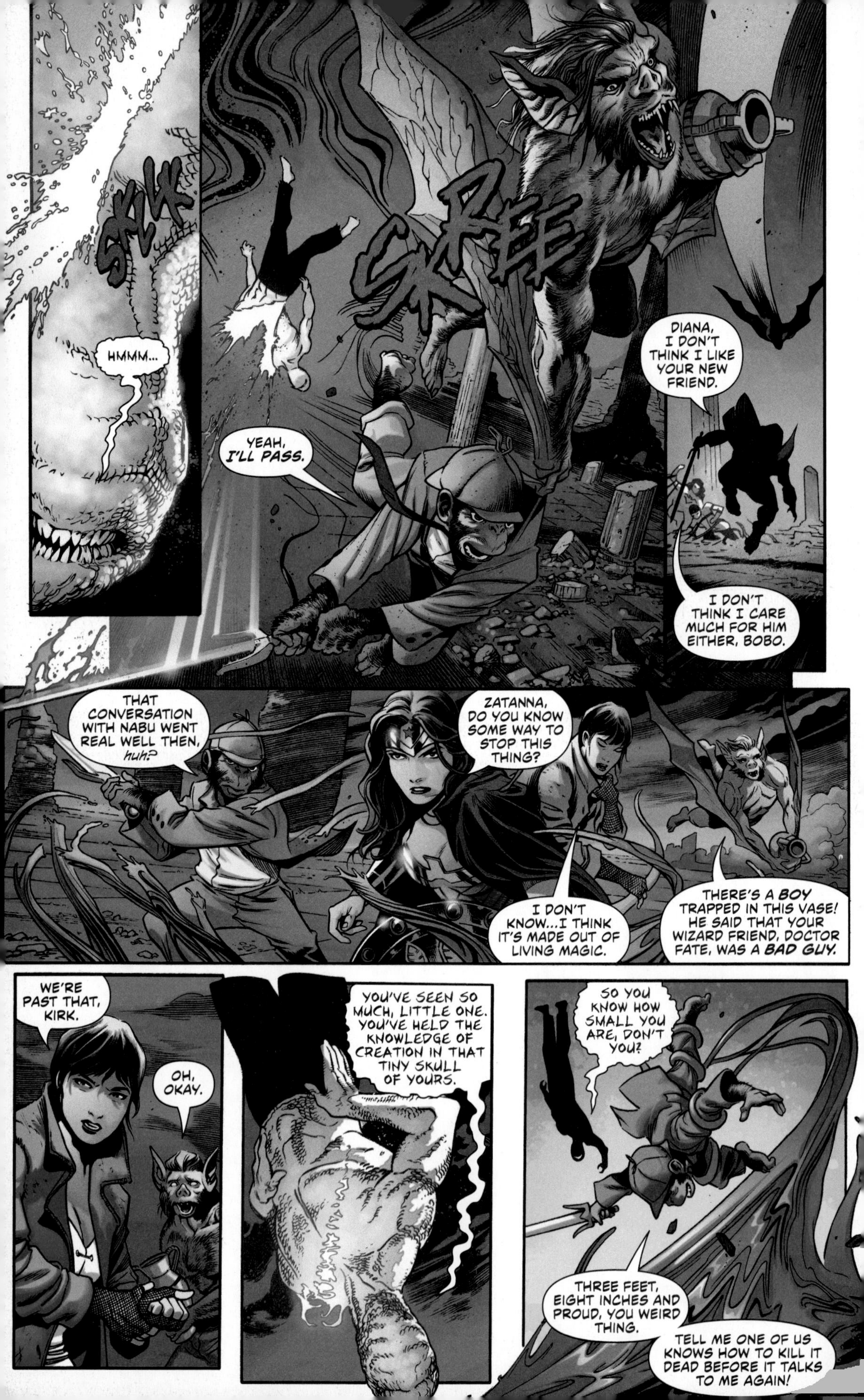
SKLK
HMMM...
SKREE
YEAH, I'LL PASS.
DIANA, I DON'T THINK I LIKE YOUR NEW FRIEND.
I DON'T THINK I CARE MUCH FOR HIM EITHER, BOBO.
THAT CONVERSATION WITH NABU WENT REAL WELL THEN, huh?
ZATANNA, DO YOU KNOW SOME WAY TO STOP THIS THING?
I DON'T KNOW...I THINK IT'S MADE OUT OF LIVING MAGIC.
THERE'S A BOY TRAPPED IN THIS VASE! HE SAID THAT YOUR WIZARD FRIEND, DOCTOR FATE, WAS A BAD GUY.
WE'RE PAST THAT, KIRK.
OH, OKAY.
YOU'VE SEEN SO MUCH, LITTLE ONE. YOU'VE HELD THE KNOWLEDGE OF CREATION IN THAT TINY SKULL OF YOURS.
SO YOU KNOW HOW SMALL YOU ARE, DON'T YOU?
THREE FEET, EIGHT INCHES AND PROUD, YOU WEIRD THING.
TELL ME ONE OF US KNOWS HOW TO KILL IT DEAD BEFORE IT TALKS TO ME AGAIN!

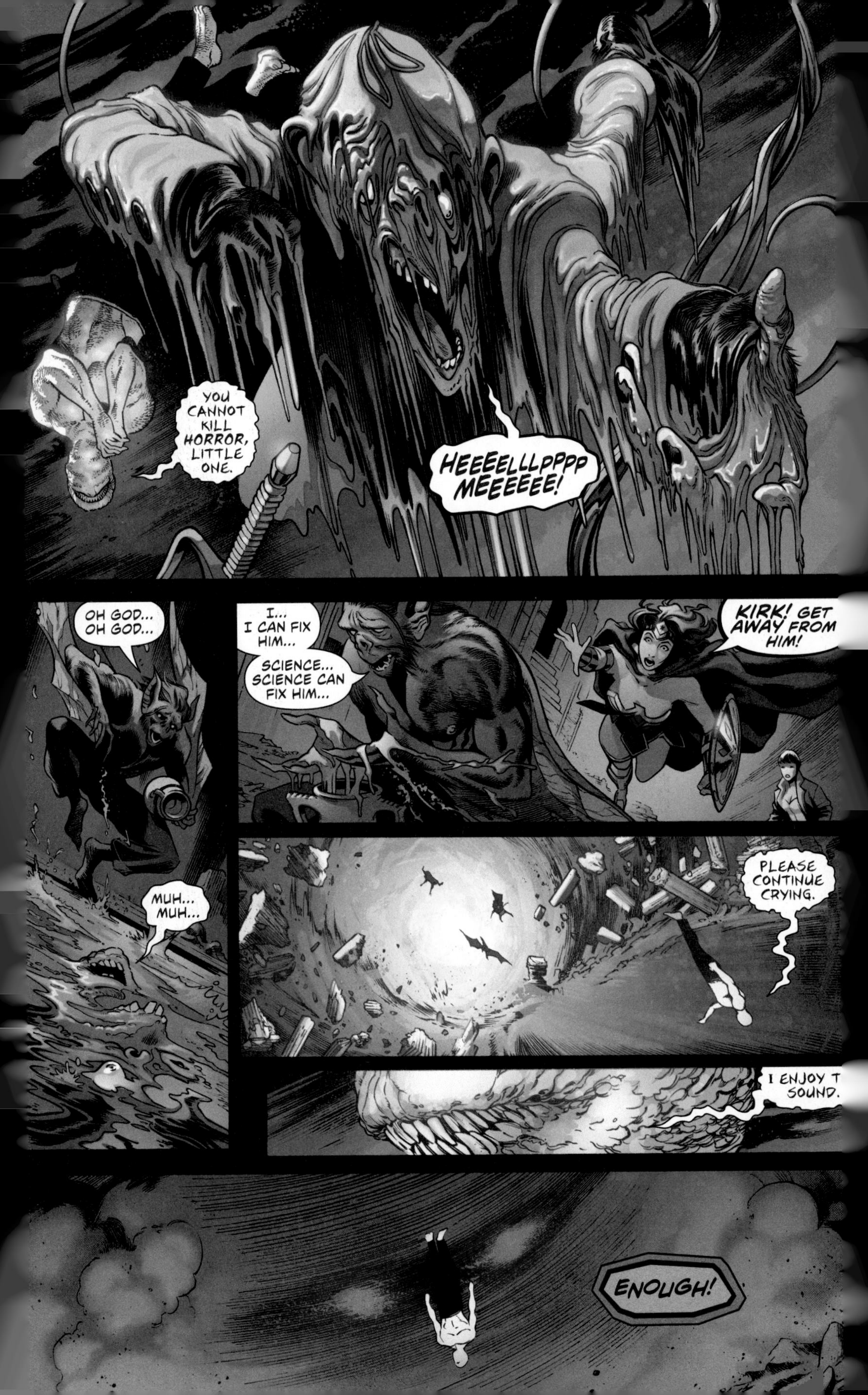

YOU CANNOT KILL HORROR, LITTLE ONE.
HEEEELLLPPPP MEEEEEE!
OH GOD... OH GOD...
I... I CAN FIX HIM...
SCIENCE... SCIENCE CAN FIX HIM...
KIRK! GET AWAY FROM HIM!
MUH... MUH...
PLEASE CONTINUE CRYING.
I ENJOY T
SOUND.
ENOUGH!

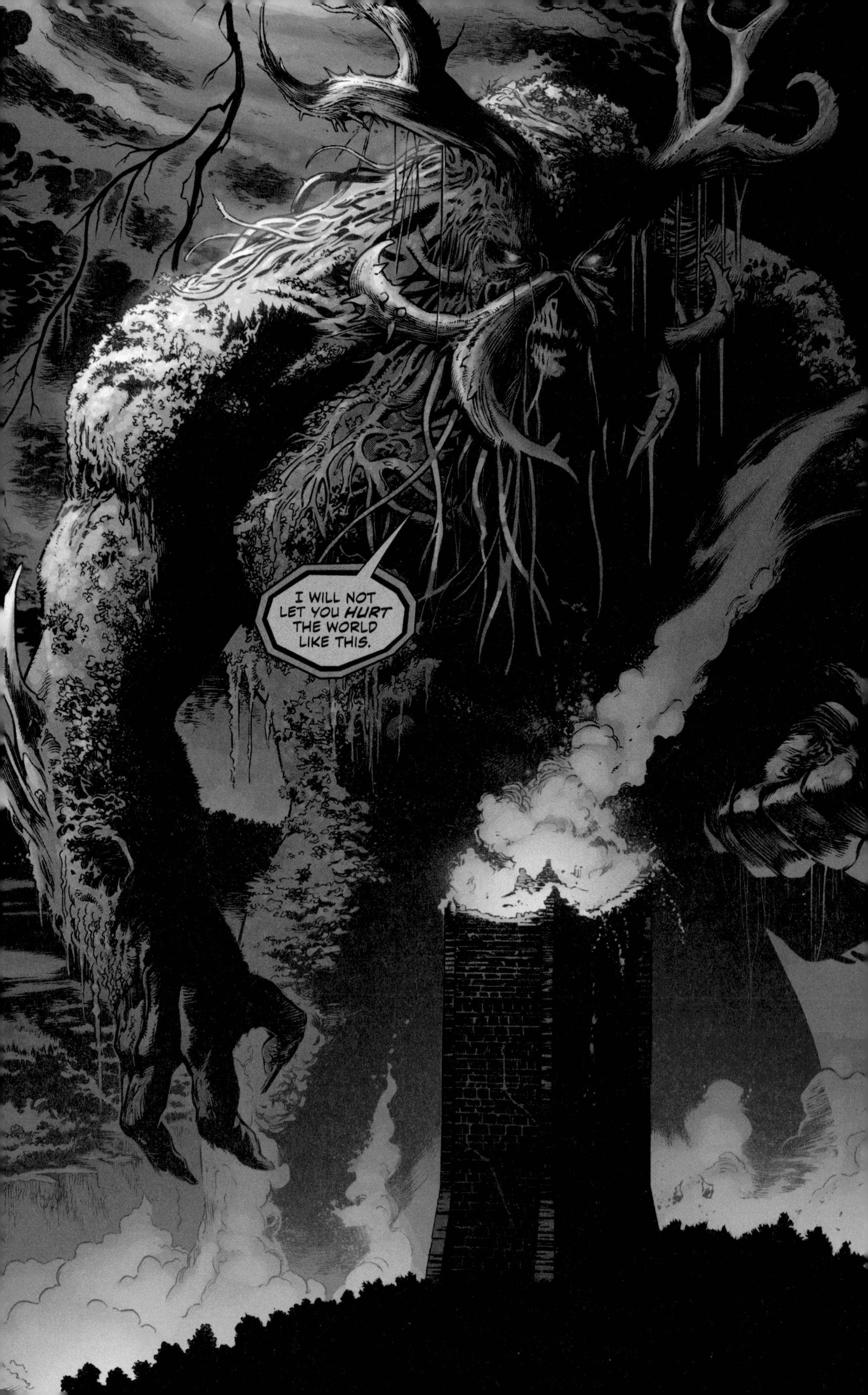
I WILL NOT LET YOU *HURT* THE WORLD LIKE THIS.

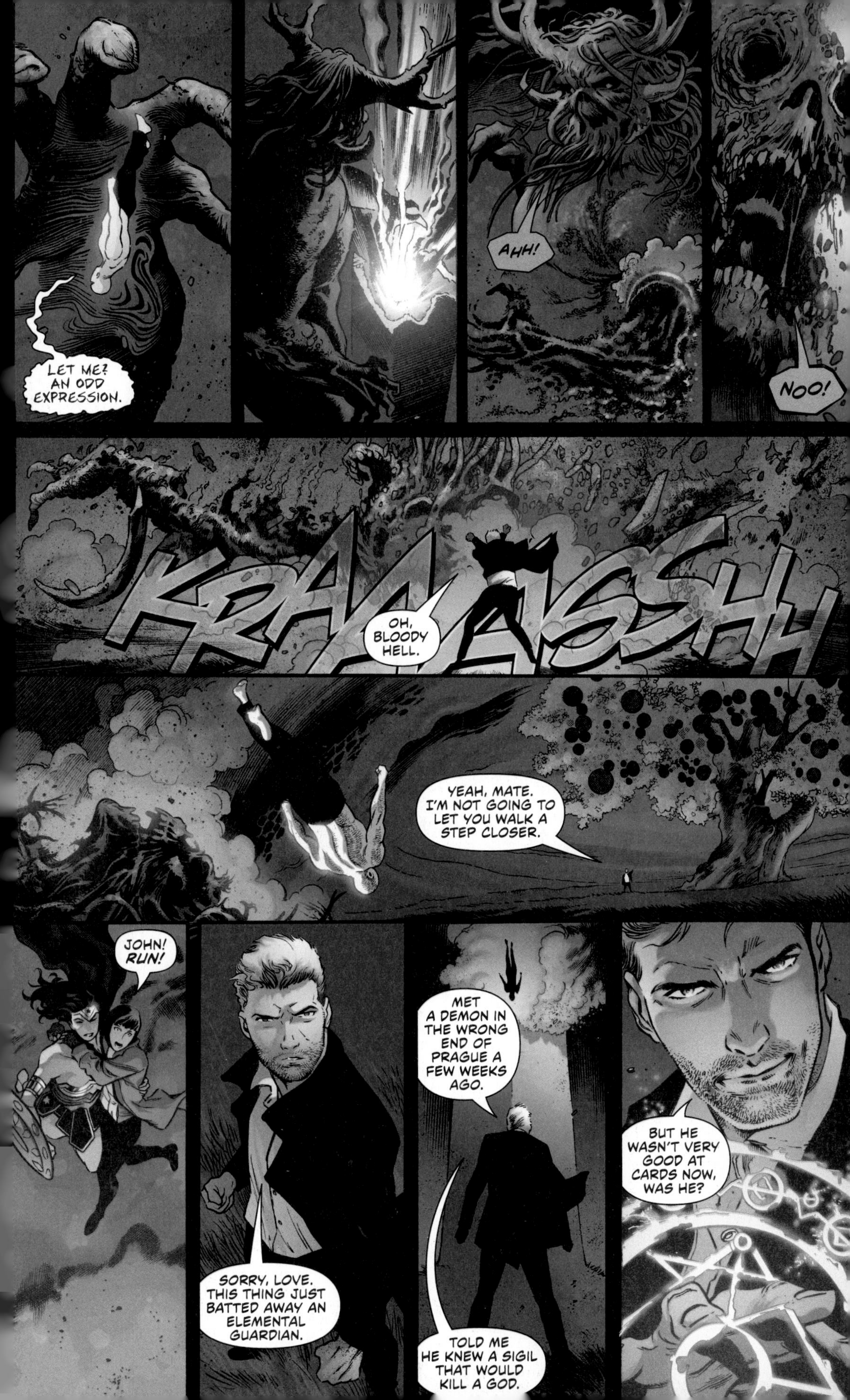
LET ME? AN ODD EXPRESSION.
AHH!
NOO!
KRAAASSHH
OH, BLOODY HELL.
YEAH, MATE. I'M NOT GOING TO LET YOU WALK A STEP CLOSER.
JOHN! RUN!
SORRY, LOVE. THIS THING JUST BATTED AWAY AN ELEMENTAL GUARDIAN.
MET A DEMON IN THE WRONG END OF PRAGUE A FEW WEEKS AGO.
TOLD ME HE KNEW A SIGIL THAT WOULD KILL A GOD.
BUT HE WASN'T VERY GOOD AT CARDS NOW, WAS HE?

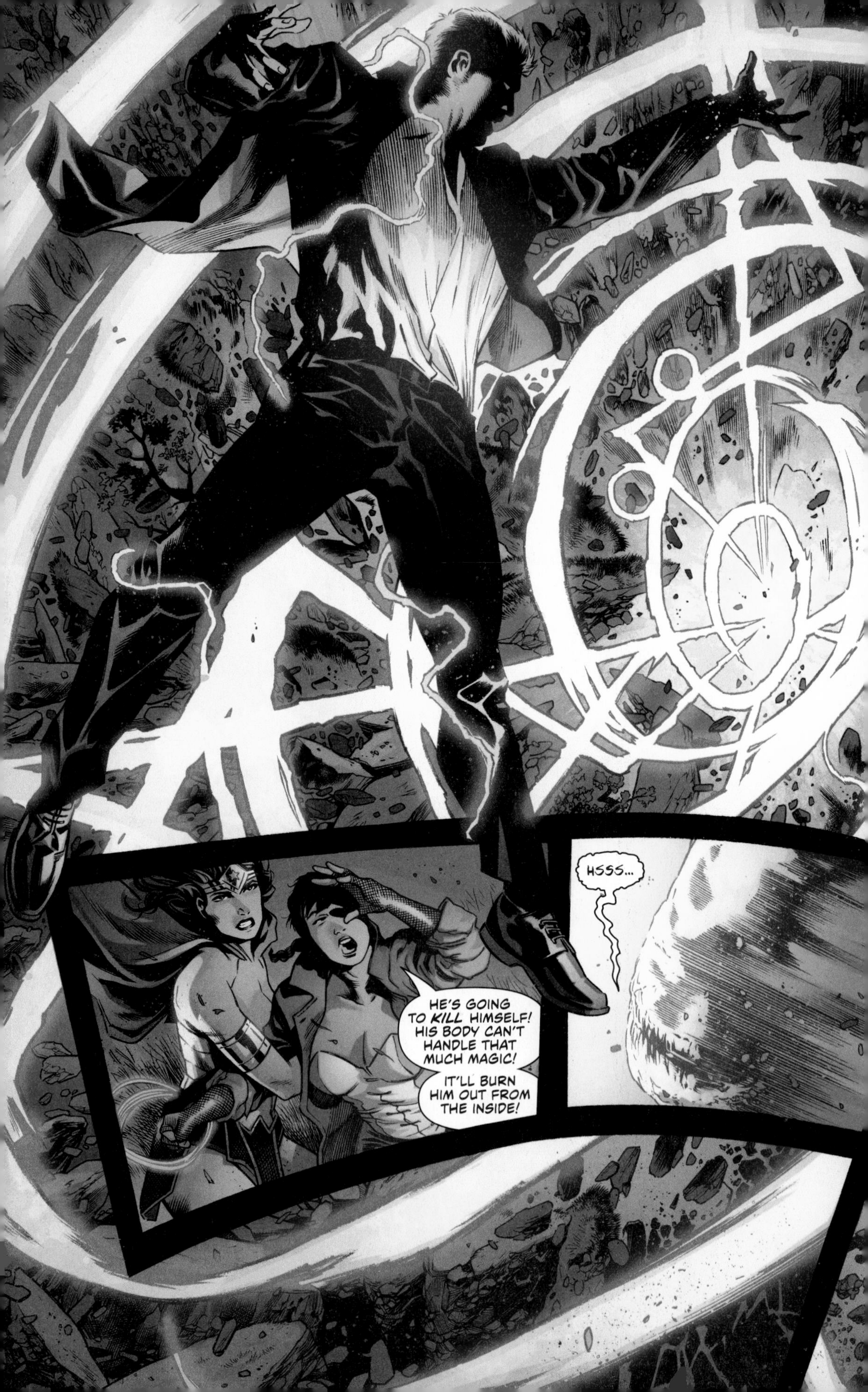
HE'S GOING TO KILL HIMSELF! HIS BODY CAN'T HANDLE THAT MUCH MAGIC!
IT'LL BURN HIM OUT FROM THE INSIDE!
HSSS...

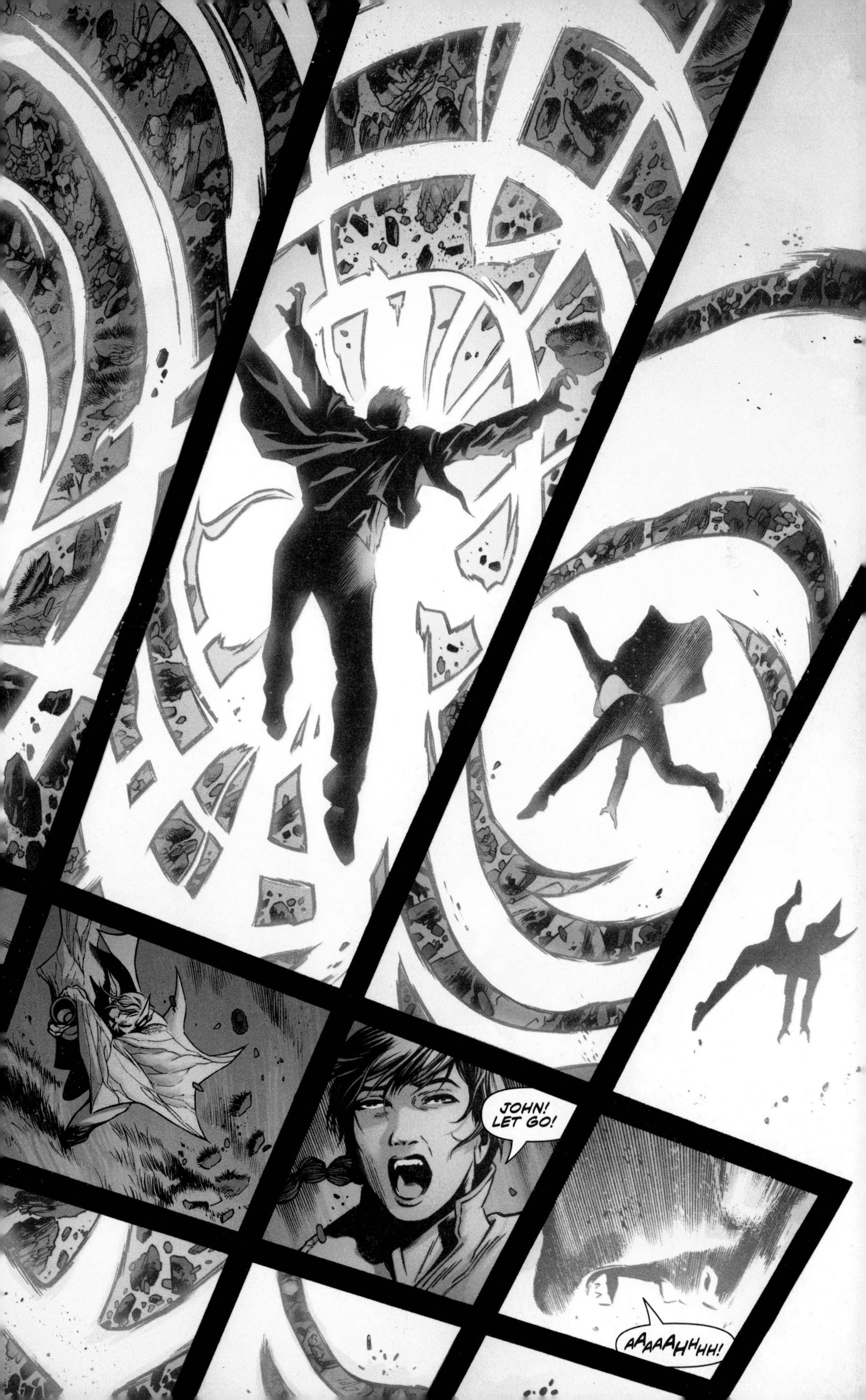
JOHN! LET GO!
AAAAAHHHH!

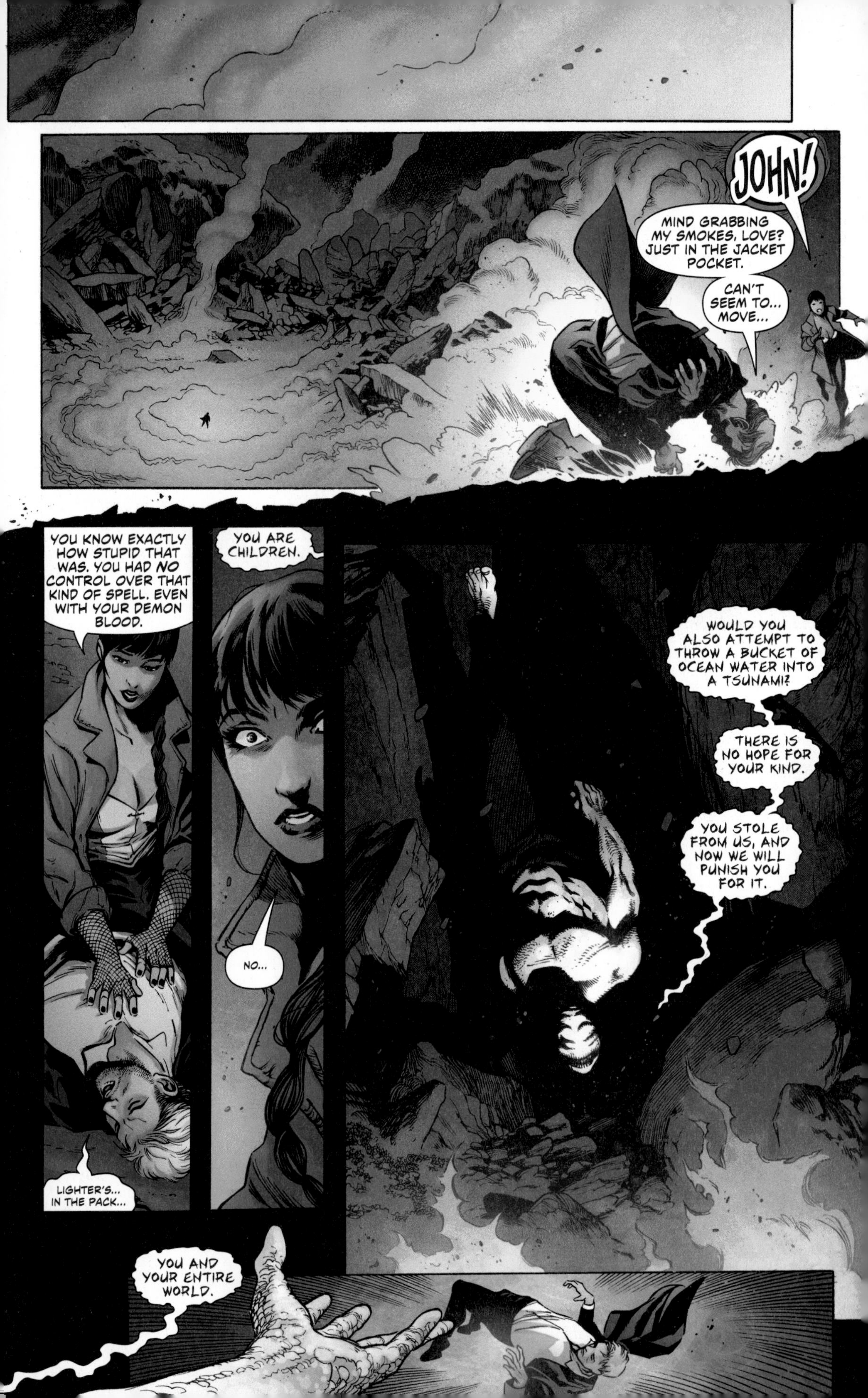
JOHN!
MIND GRABBING MY SMOKES, LOVE? JUST IN THE JACKET POCKET.
CAN'T SEEM TO... MOVE...
YOU KNOW EXACTLY HOW STUPID THAT WAS. YOU HAD NO CONTROL OVER THAT KIND OF SPELL. EVEN WITH YOUR DEMON BLOOD.
LIGHTER'S... IN THE PACK...
YOU ARE CHILDREN.
NO...
WOULD YOU ALSO ATTEMPT TO THROW A BUCKET OF OCEAN WATER INTO A TSUNAMI?
THERE IS NO HOPE FOR YOUR KIND.
YOU STOLE FROM US, AND NOW WE WILL PUNISH YOU FOR IT.
YOU AND YOUR ENTIRE WORLD.

YOU CHANNEL THE MAGIC THROUGH YOUR BLOOD, DON'T YOU?

DEMON'S BLOOD. CUTE.

LET US SEE HOW YOU FARE WITHOUT IT.

OG YAWA!

YOU ARE AS TEDIOUS AS YOUR FATHER, GIRL.

WE HAVE ENJOYED PLAYING WITH HIM, ALL THESE YEARS. TAKING HIM APART, AND PUTTING HIM BACK TOGETHER.

"ESAELER EM!" HE SHOUTS, OVER AND OVER.

"ESAELER EM! ESAELER EM!"

MY FATHER...

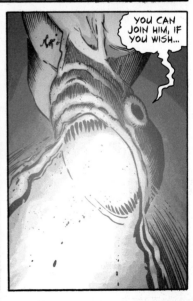

YOU CAN JOIN HIM, IF YOU WISH...

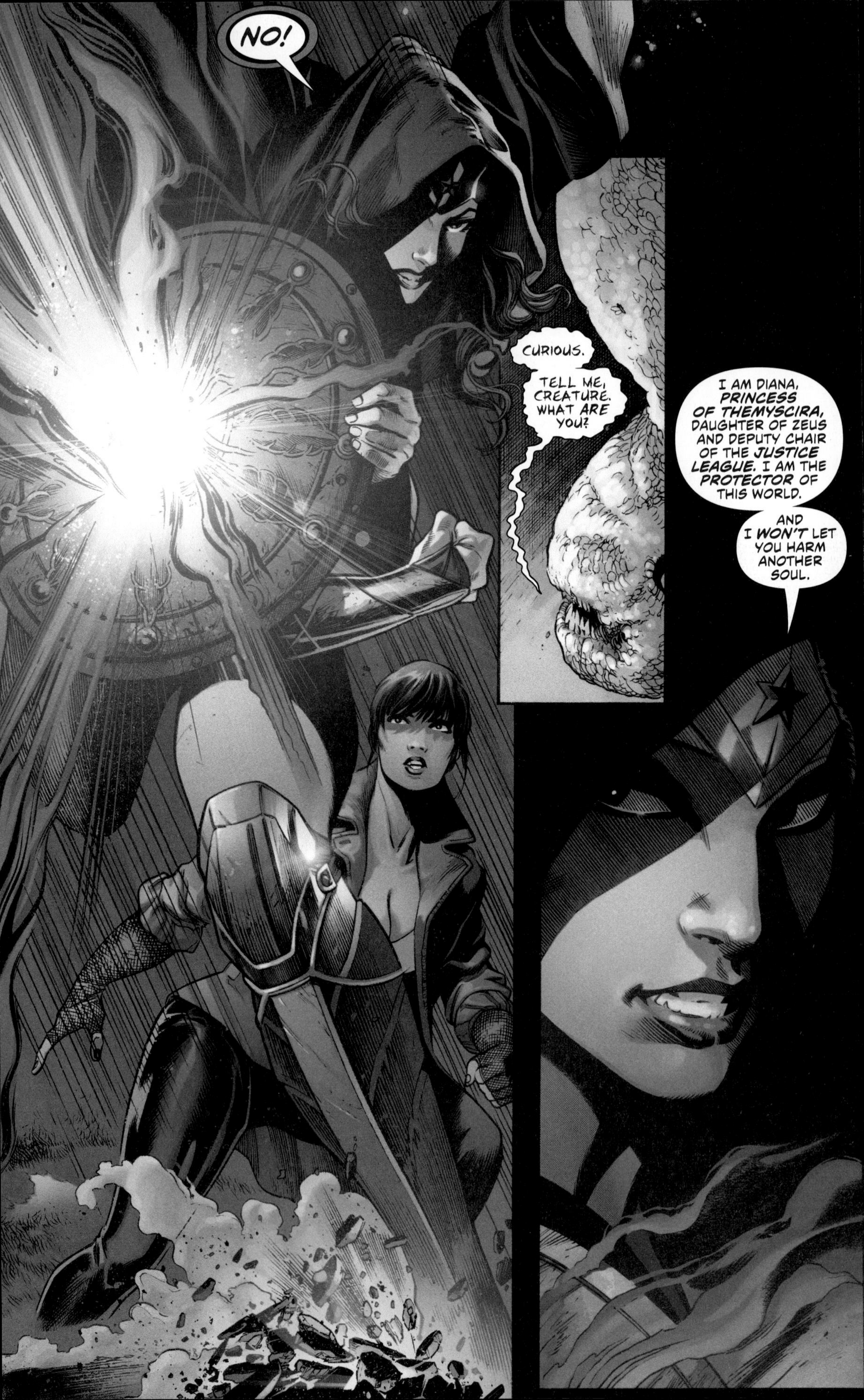
NO!
CURIOUS.
TELL ME, CREATURE. WHAT ARE YOU?
I AM DIANA, PRINCESS OF THEMYSCIRA, DAUGHTER OF ZEUS AND DEPUTY CHAIR OF THE JUSTICE LEAGUE. I AM THE PROTECTOR OF THIS WORLD.
AND I WON'T LET YOU HARM ANOTHER SOUL.

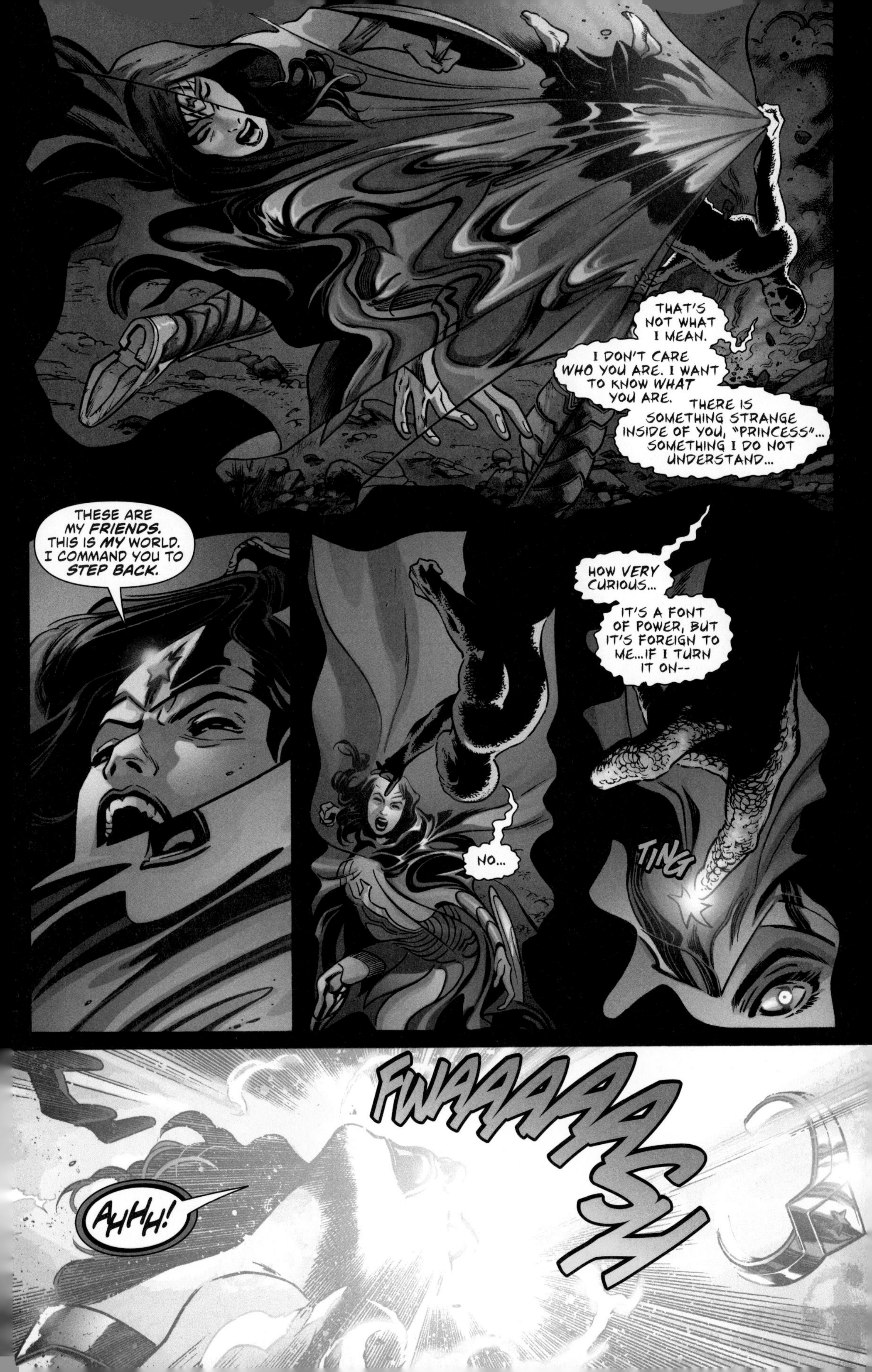
THAT'S NOT WHAT I MEAN.
I DON'T CARE WHO YOU ARE. I WANT TO KNOW WHAT YOU ARE.
THERE IS SOMETHING STRANGE INSIDE OF YOU, "PRINCESS"... SOMETHING I DO NOT UNDERSTAND...
THESE ARE MY FRIENDS. THIS IS MY WORLD. I COMMAND YOU TO STEP BACK.
HOW VERY CURIOUS...
IT'S A FONT OF POWER, BUT IT'S FOREIGN TO ME...IF I TURN IT ON--
NO...
TING
FWAAAAAASH
AHHH!

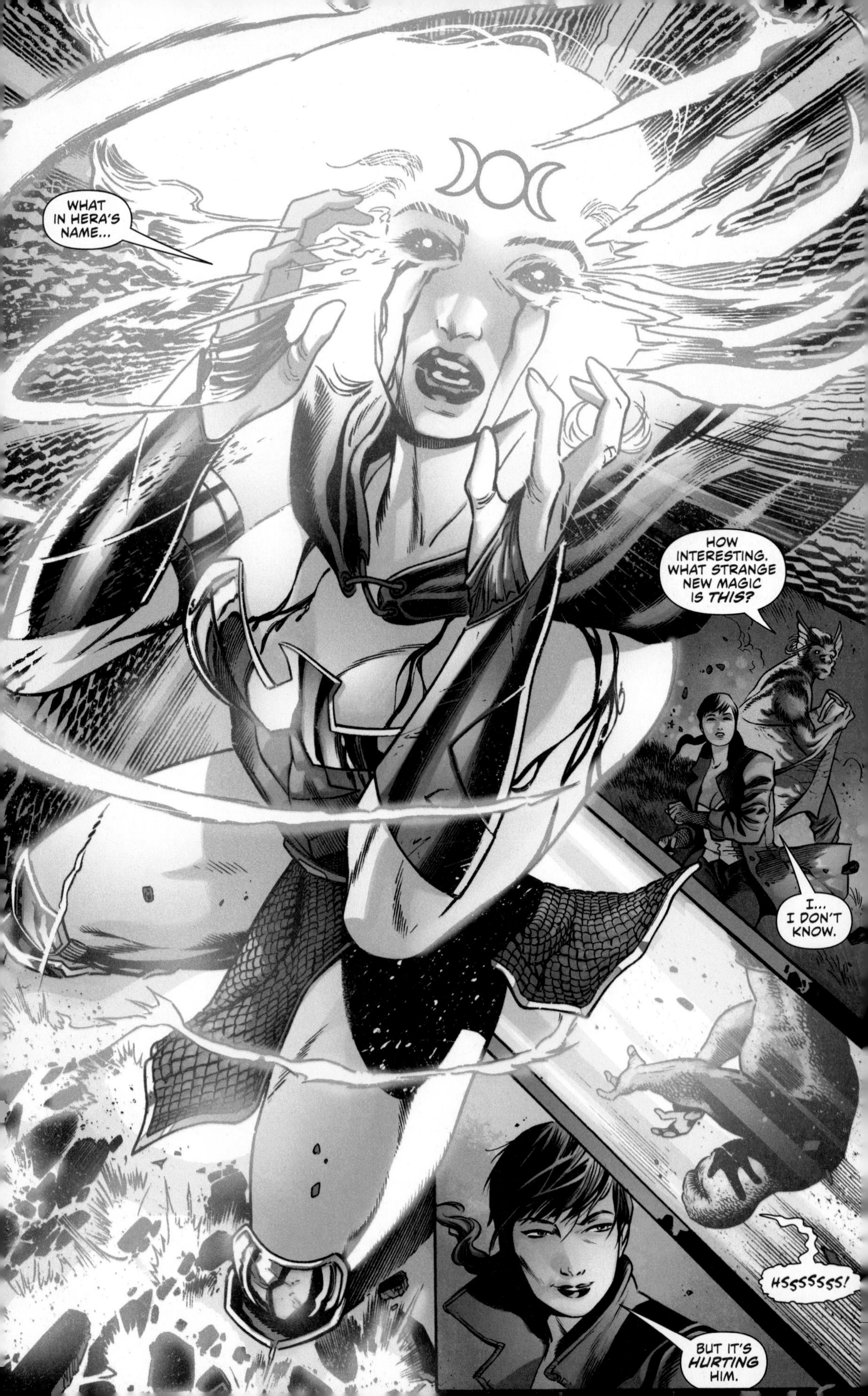
WHAT IN HERA'S NAME...
HOW INTERESTING. WHAT STRANGE NEW MAGIC IS THIS?
I... I DON'T KNOW.
HSSSSSSS!
BUT IT'S HURTING HIM.

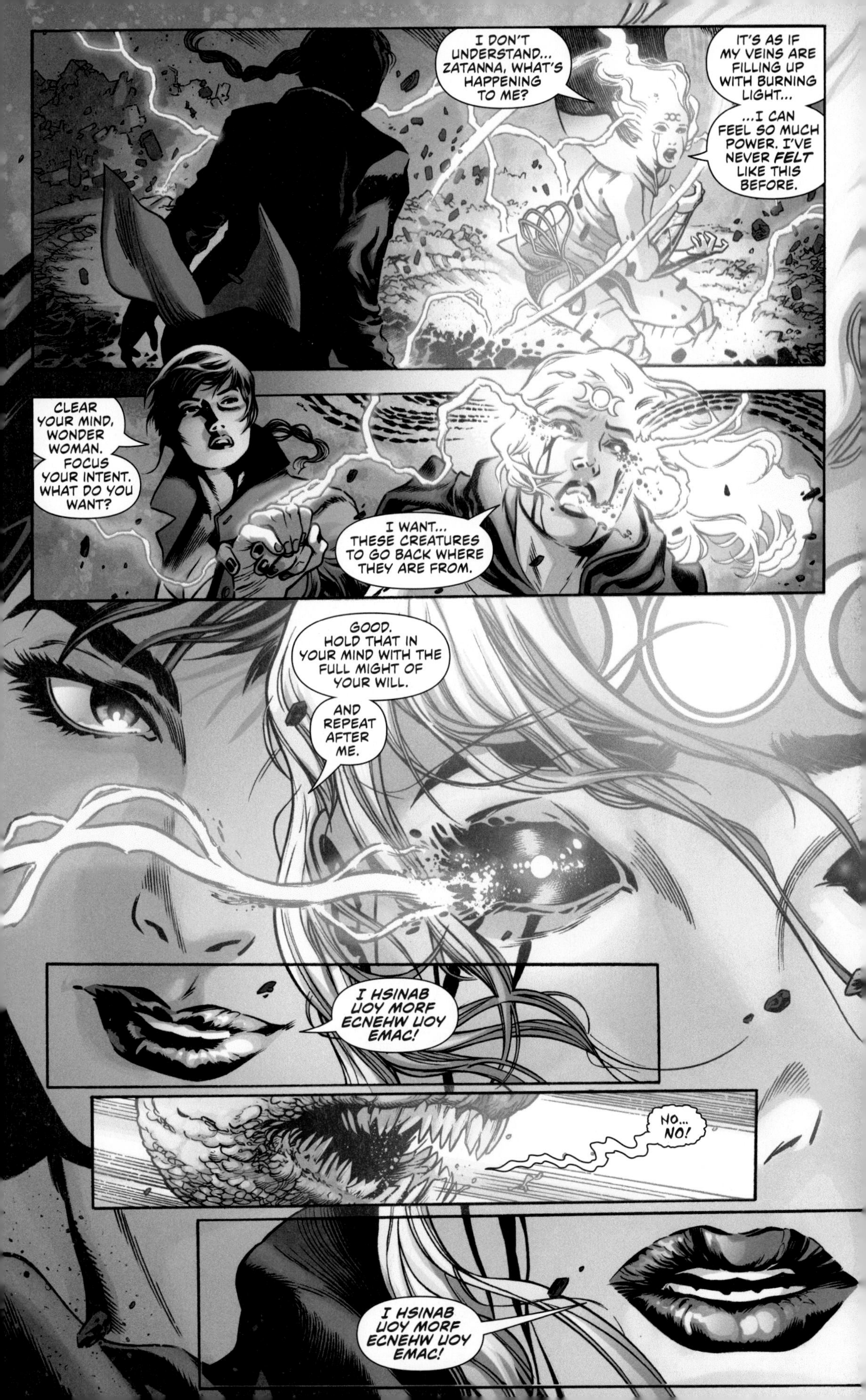
I DON'T UNDERSTAND... ZATANNA, WHAT'S HAPPENING TO ME?
IT'S AS IF MY VEINS ARE FILLING UP WITH BURNING LIGHT...
...I CAN FEEL SO MUCH POWER. I'VE NEVER FELT LIKE THIS BEFORE.
CLEAR YOUR MIND, WONDER WOMAN. FOCUS YOUR INTENT. WHAT DO YOU WANT?
I WANT... THESE CREATURES TO GO BACK WHERE THEY ARE FROM.
GOOD. HOLD THAT IN YOUR MIND WITH THE FULL MIGHT OF YOUR WILL.
AND REPEAT AFTER ME.
I HSINAB UOY MORF ECNEHW UOY EMAC!
NO... NO!
I HSINAB UOY MORF ECNEHW UOY EMAC!

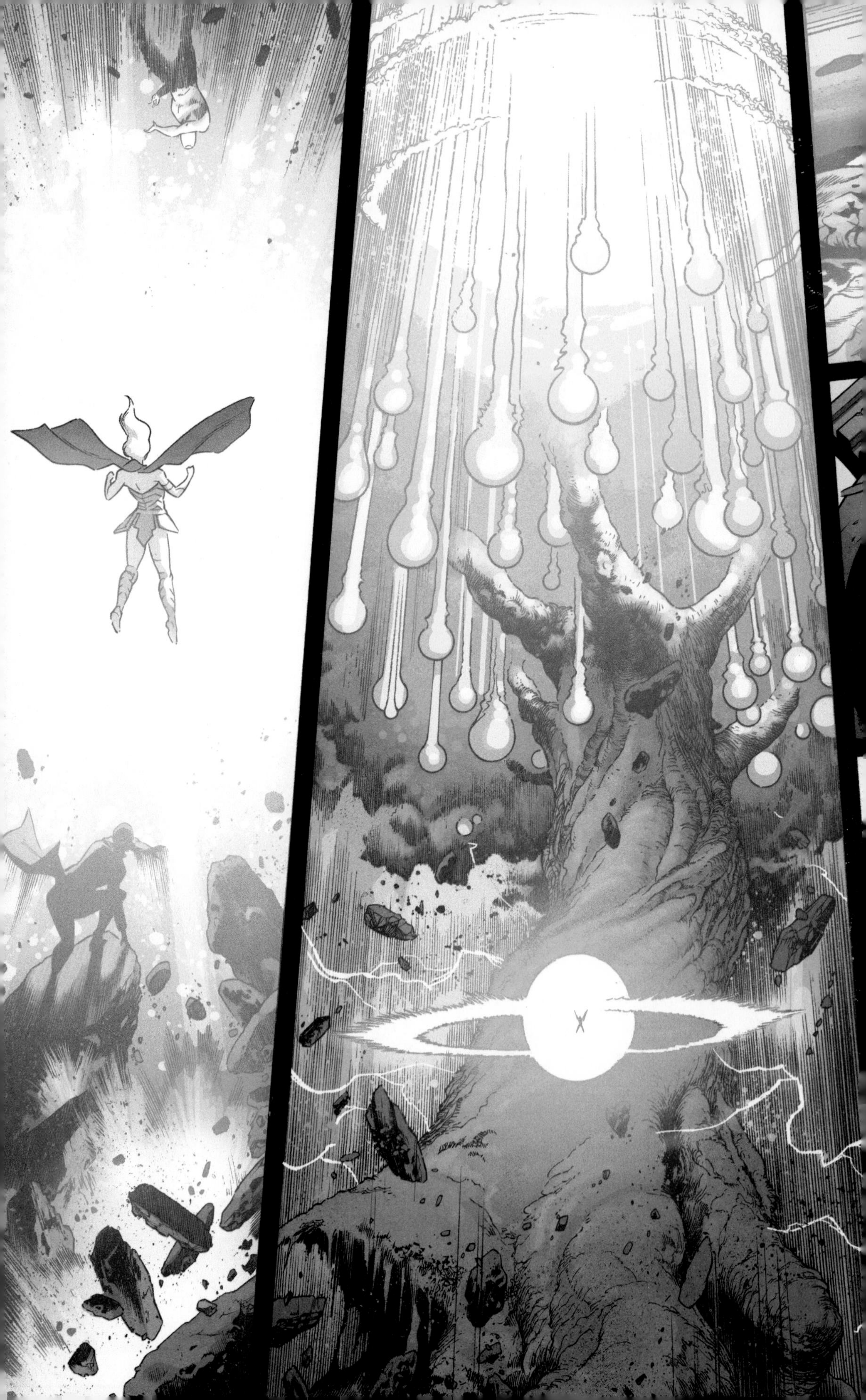

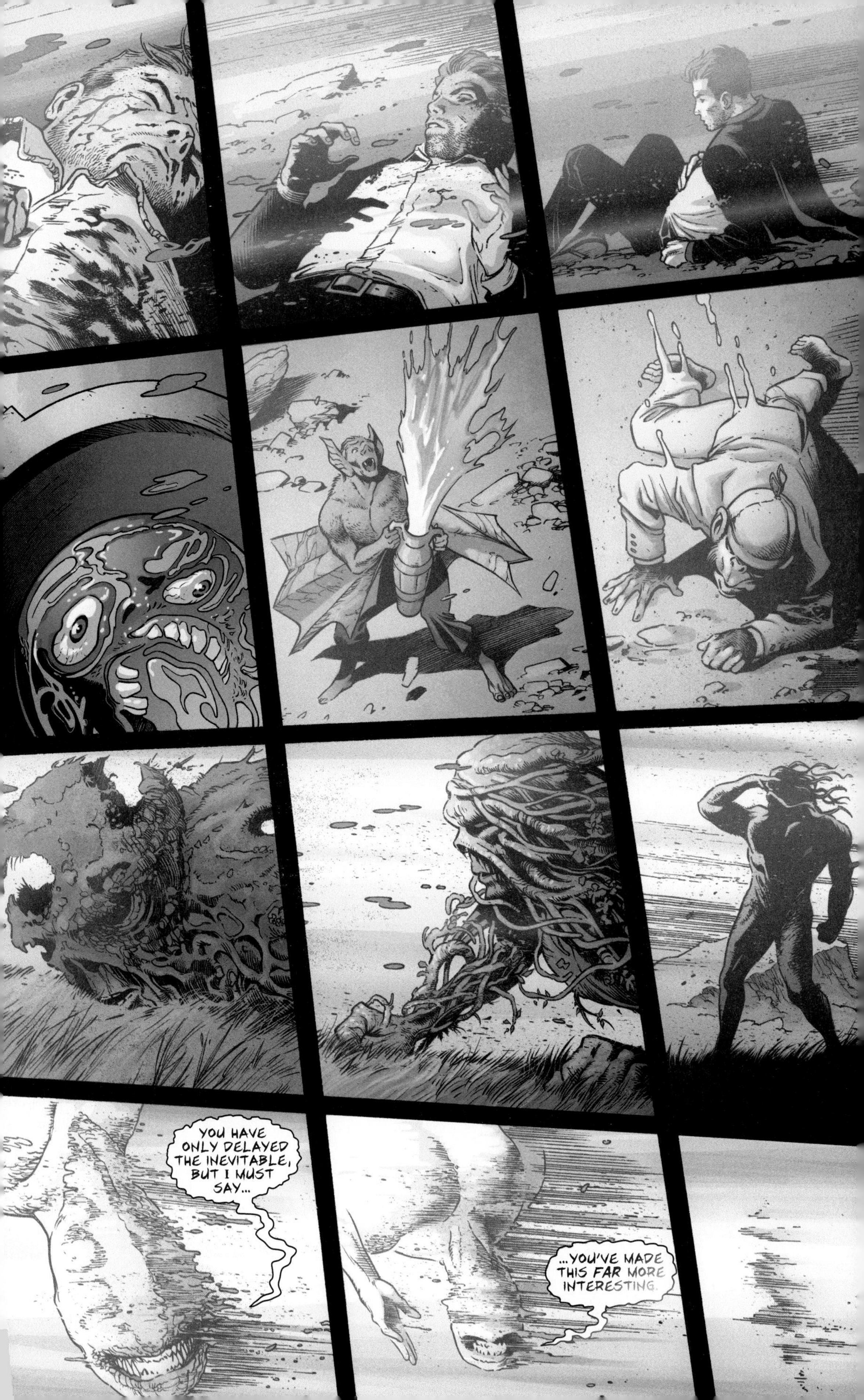
YOU HAVE ONLY DELAYED THE INEVITABLE, BUT I MUST SAY...
...YOU'VE MADE THIS FAR MORE INTERESTING.

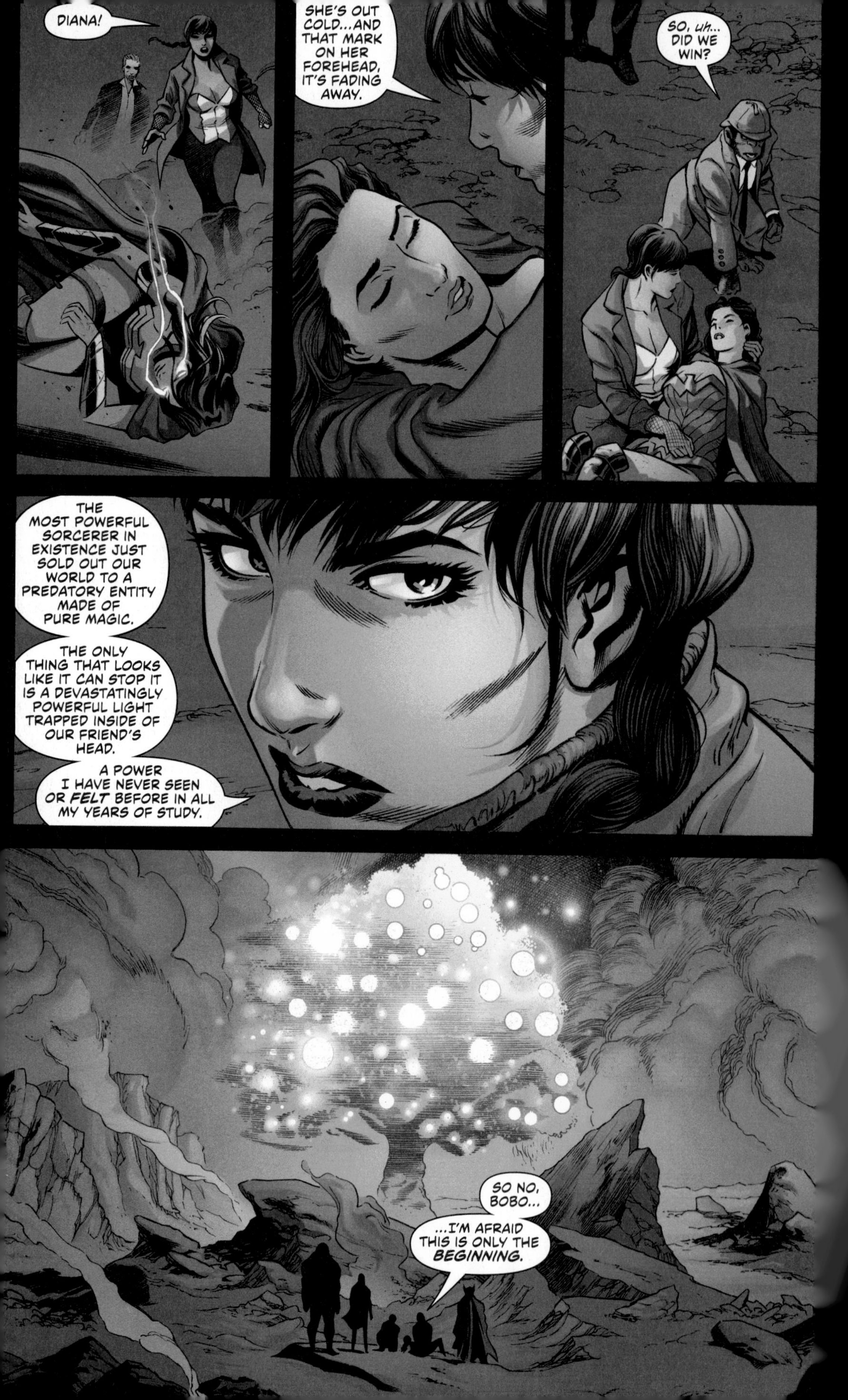

DIANA!
SHE'S OUT COLD...AND THAT MARK ON HER FOREHEAD, IT'S FADING AWAY.
SO, uh... DID WE WIN?
THE MOST POWERFUL SORCERER IN EXISTENCE JUST SOLD OUT OUR WORLD TO A PREDATORY ENTITY MADE OF PURE MAGIC.
THE ONLY THING THAT LOOKS LIKE IT CAN STOP IT IS A DEVASTATINGLY POWERFUL LIGHT TRAPPED INSIDE OF OUR FRIEND'S HEAD.
A POWER I HAVE NEVER SEEN OR FELT BEFORE IN ALL MY YEARS OF STUDY.
SO NO, BOBO...
...I'M AFRAID THIS IS ONLY THE BEGINNING.

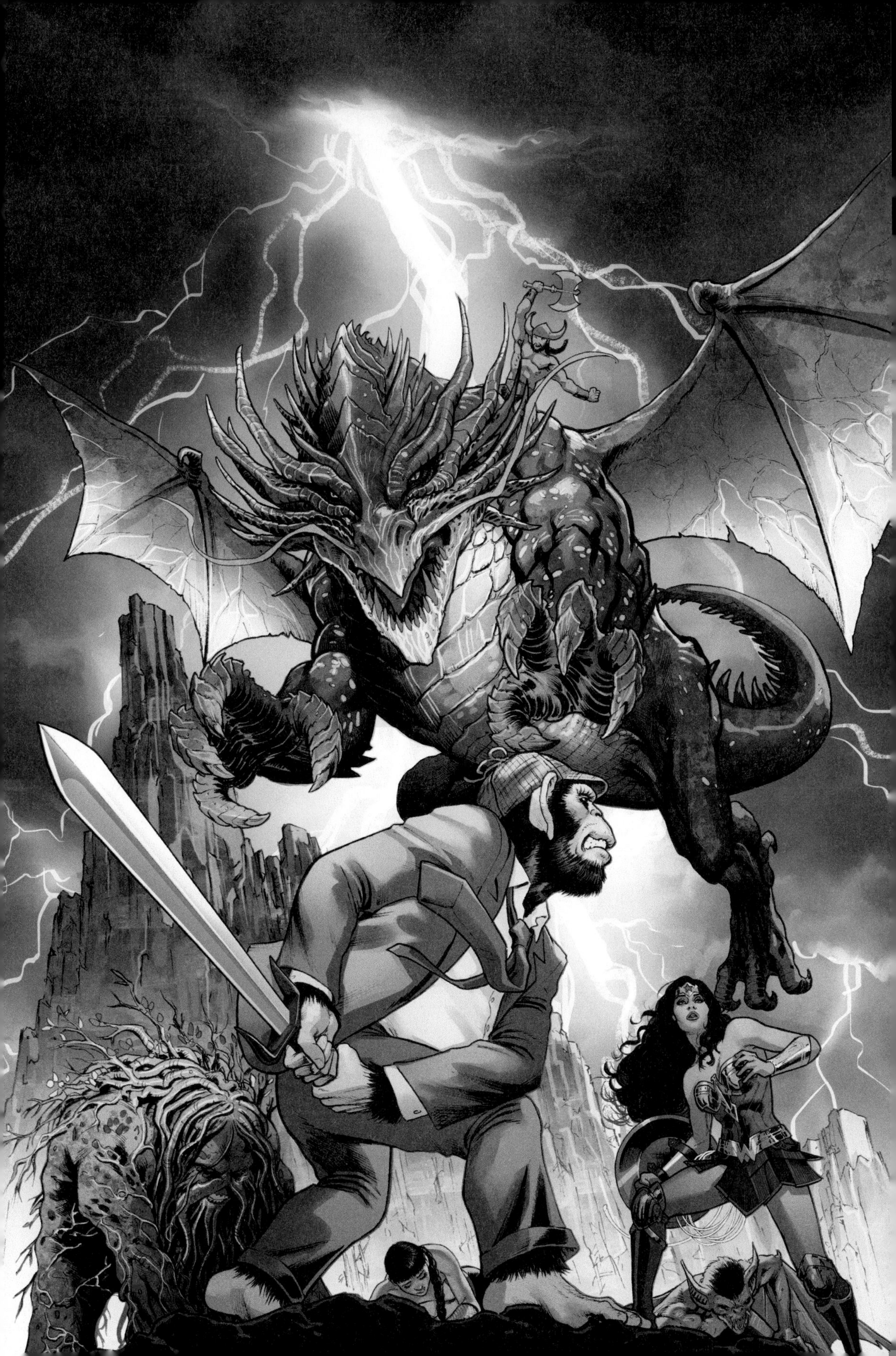

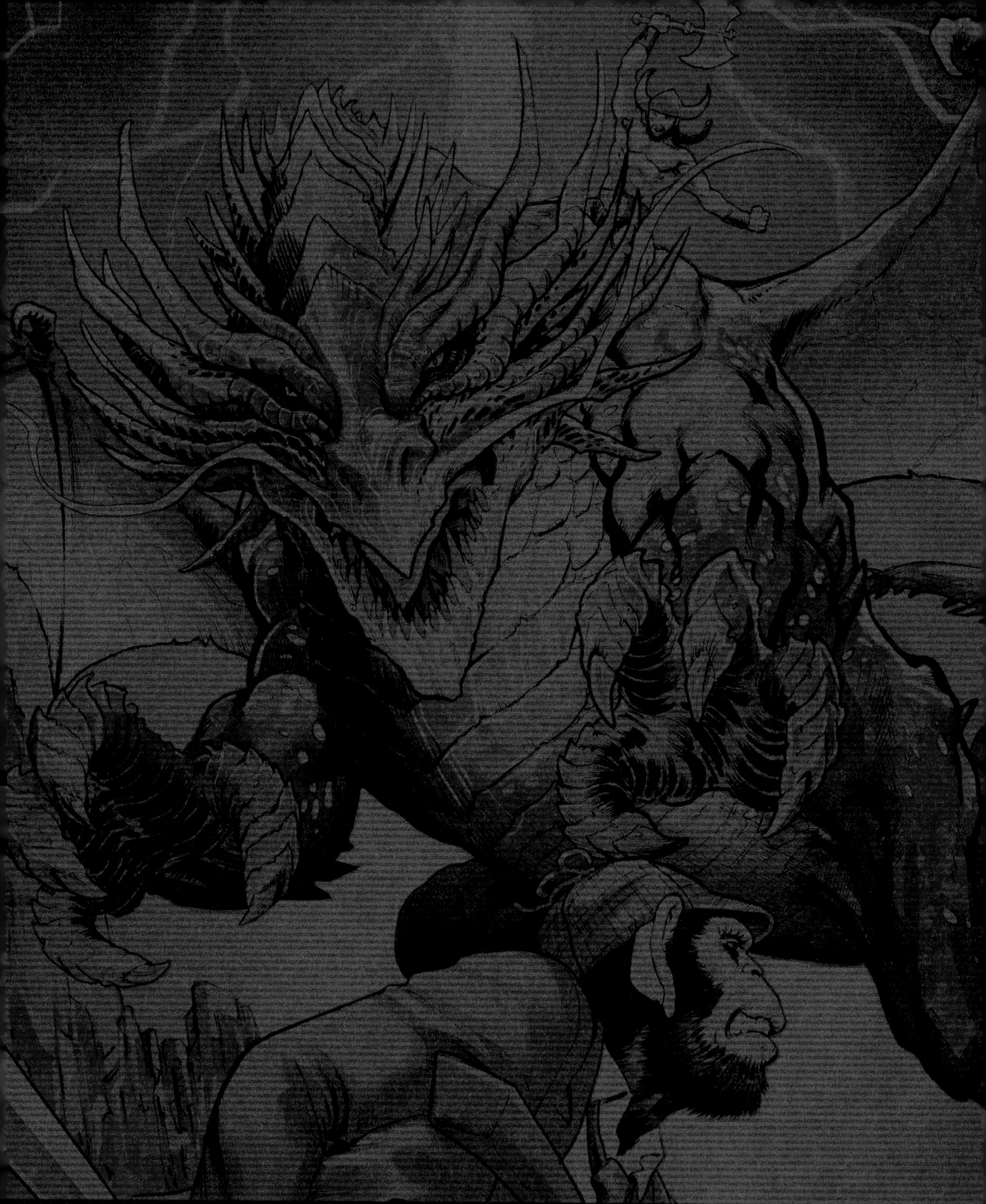

JUSTICE LEAGUE DARK

#5

Previously in WONDER WOMAN/JUSTICE LEAGUE DARK: THE WITCHING HOUR...

The Justice League Dark teamed with the rest of Earth's magical heroes to face Hecate, the Witch Goddess, in a battle for Wonder Woman's soul—and the very fate of magic! With no way to defeat Hecate on her own, Zatanna could only

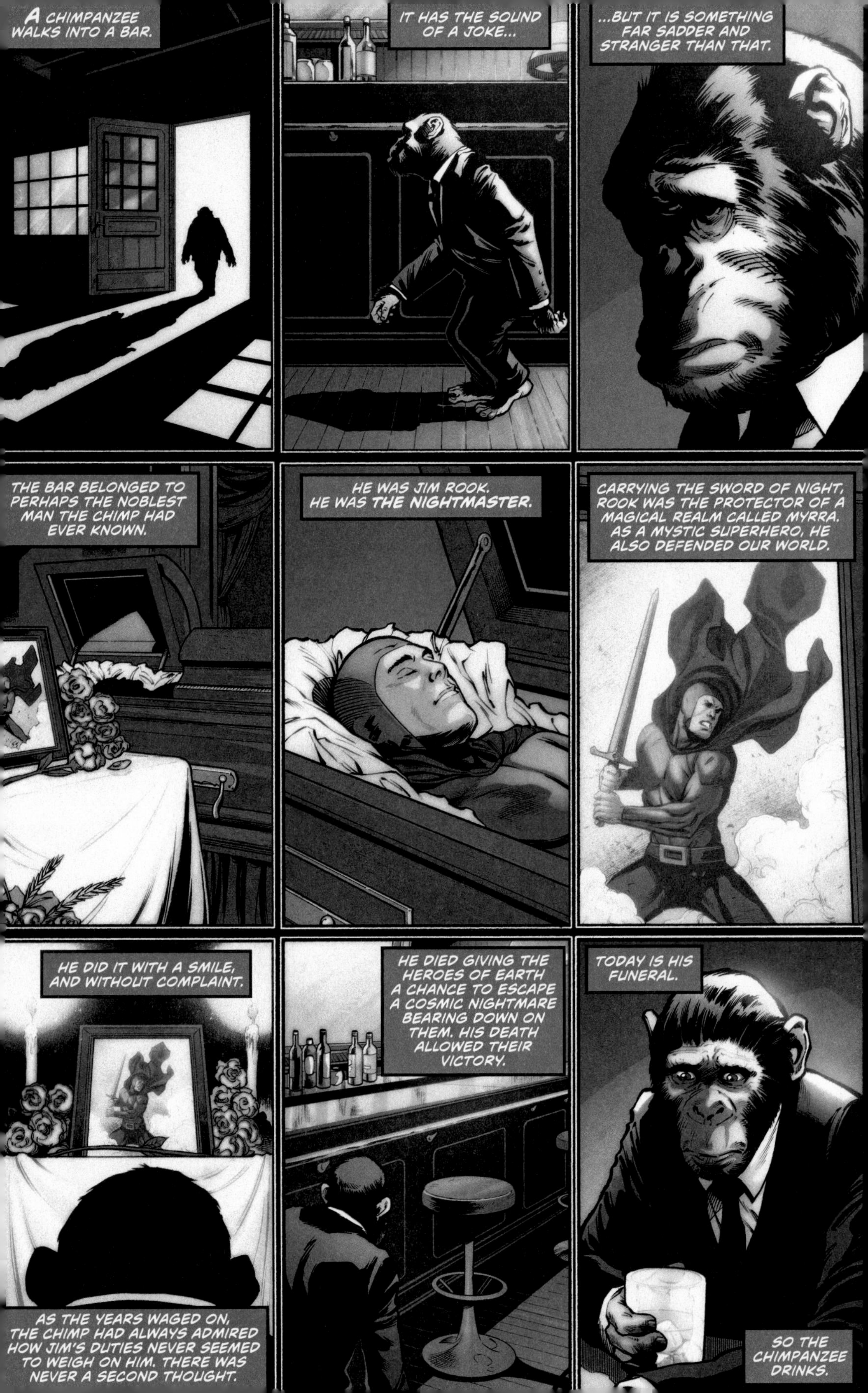
A CHIMPANZEE WALKS INTO A BAR.
IT HAS THE SOUND OF A JOKE...
...BUT IT IS SOMETHING FAR SADDER AND STRANGER THAN THAT.
THE BAR BELONGED TO PERHAPS THE NOBLEST MAN THE CHIMP HAD EVER KNOWN.
HE WAS JIM ROOK. HE WAS THE NIGHTMASTER.
CARRYING THE SWORD OF NIGHT, ROOK WAS THE PROTECTOR OF A MAGICAL REALM CALLED MYRRA. AS A MYSTIC SUPERHERO, HE ALSO DEFENDED OUR WORLD.
HE DID IT WITH A SMILE, AND WITHOUT COMPLAINT.
AS THE YEARS WAGED ON, THE CHIMP HAD ALWAYS ADMIRED HOW JIM'S DUTIES NEVER SEEMED TO WEIGH ON HIM. THERE WAS NEVER A SECOND THOUGHT.
HE DIED GIVING THE HEROES OF EARTH A CHANCE TO ESCAPE A COSMIC NIGHTMARE BEARING DOWN ON THEM. HIS DEATH ALLOWED THEIR VICTORY.
TODAY IS HIS FUNERAL.
SO THE CHIMPANZEE DRINKS.

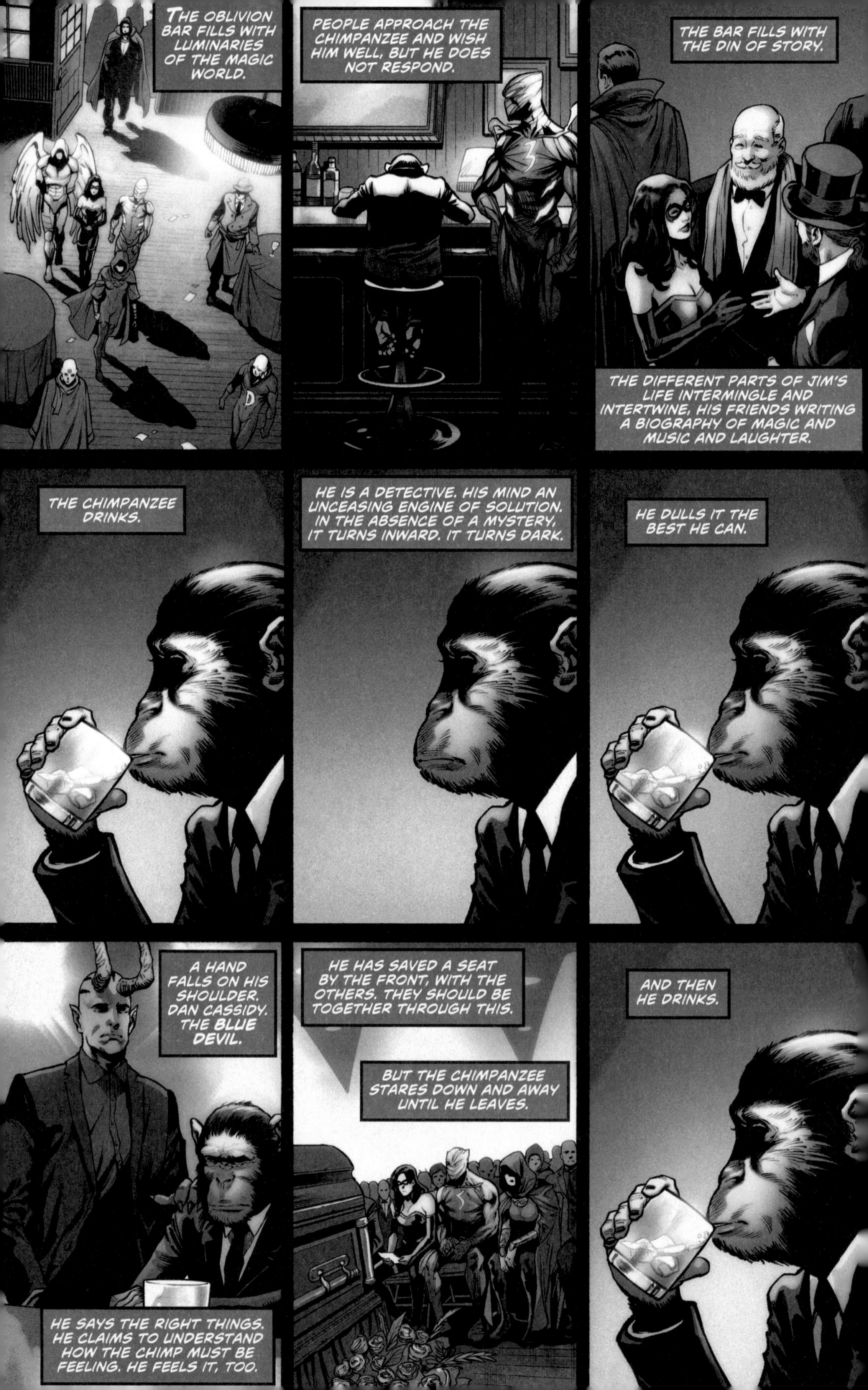
THE OBLIVION BAR FILLS WITH LUMINARIES OF THE MAGIC WORLD.
PEOPLE APPROACH THE CHIMPANZEE AND WISH HIM WELL, BUT HE DOES NOT RESPOND.
THE BAR FILLS WITH THE DIN OF STORY.
THE DIFFERENT PARTS OF JIM'S LIFE INTERMINGLE AND INTERTWINE, HIS FRIENDS WRITING A BIOGRAPHY OF MAGIC AND MUSIC AND LAUGHTER.
THE CHIMPANZEE DRINKS.
HE IS A DETECTIVE. HIS MIND AN UNCEASING ENGINE OF SOLUTION. IN THE ABSENCE OF A MYSTERY, IT TURNS INWARD. IT TURNS DARK.
HE DULLS IT THE BEST HE CAN.
A HAND FALLS ON HIS SHOULDER. DAN CASSIDY. THE BLUE DEVIL.
HE SAYS THE RIGHT THINGS. HE CLAIMS TO UNDERSTAND HOW THE CHIMP MUST BE FEELING. HE FEELS IT, TOO.
HE HAS SAVED A SEAT BY THE FRONT, WITH THE OTHERS. THEY SHOULD BE TOGETHER THROUGH THIS.
BUT THE CHIMPANZEE STARES DOWN AND AWAY UNTIL HE LEAVES.
AND THEN HE DRINKS.

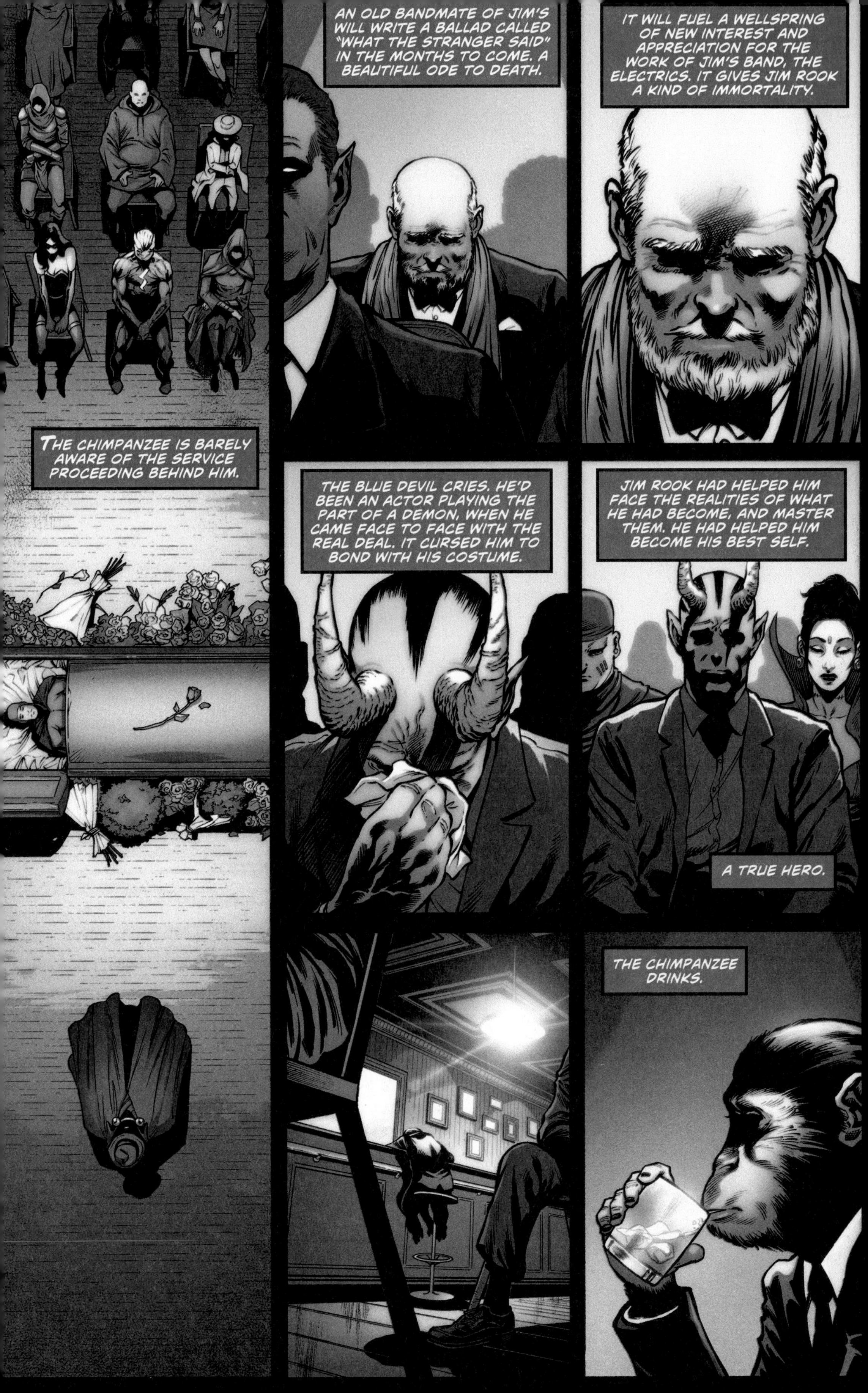
AN OLD BANDMATE OF JIM'S WILL WRITE A BALLAD CALLED "WHAT THE STRANGER SAID" IN THE MONTHS TO COME. A BEAUTIFUL ODE TO DEATH.
IT WILL FUEL A WELLSPRING OF NEW INTEREST AND APPRECIATION FOR THE WORK OF JIM'S BAND, THE ELECTRICS. IT GIVES JIM ROOK A KIND OF IMMORTALITY.
THE CHIMPANZEE IS BARELY AWARE OF THE SERVICE PROCEEDING BEHIND HIM.
THE BLUE DEVIL CRIES. HE'D BEEN AN ACTOR PLAYING THE PART OF A DEMON, WHEN HE CAME FACE TO FACE WITH THE REAL DEAL. IT CURSED HIM TO BOND WITH HIS COSTUME.
JIM ROOK HAD HELPED HIM FACE THE REALITIES OF WHAT HE HAD BECOME, AND MASTER THEM. HE HAD HELPED HIM BECOME HIS BEST SELF.
A TRUE HERO.
THE CHIMPANZEE DRINKS.

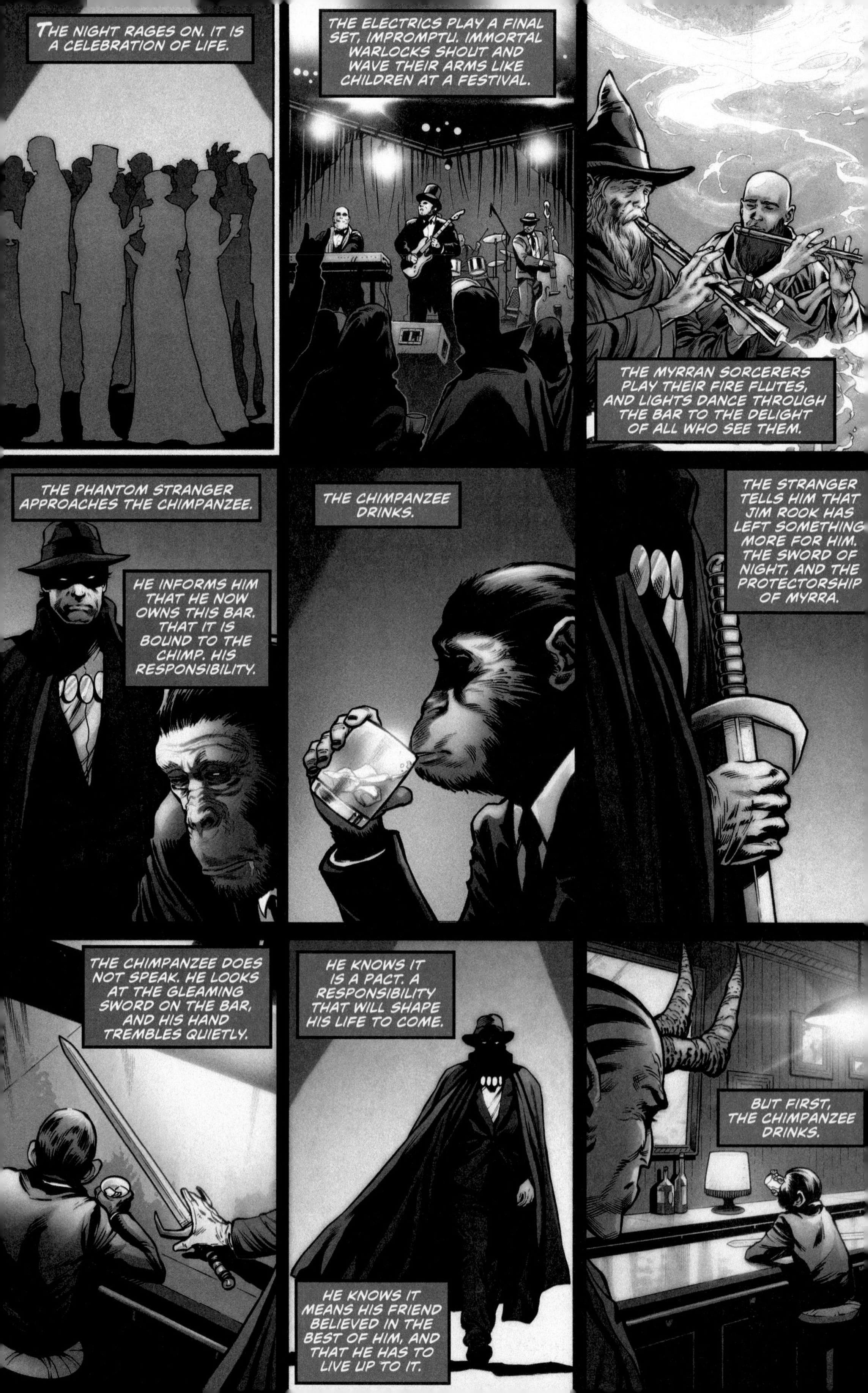
THE NIGHT RAGES ON. IT IS A CELEBRATION OF LIFE.
THE ELECTRICS PLAY A FINAL SET, IMPROMPTU. IMMORTAL WARLOCKS SHOUT AND WAVE THEIR ARMS LIKE CHILDREN AT A FESTIVAL.
THE MYRRAN SORCERERS PLAY THEIR FIRE FLUTES, AND LIGHTS DANCE THROUGH THE BAR TO THE DELIGHT OF ALL WHO SEE THEM.
THE PHANTOM STRANGER APPROACHES THE CHIMPANZEE.
HE INFORMS HIM THAT HE NOW OWNS THIS BAR. THAT IT IS BOUND TO THE CHIMP. HIS RESPONSIBILITY.
THE CHIMPANZEE DRINKS.
THE STRANGER TELLS HIM THAT JIM ROOK HAS LEFT SOMETHING MORE FOR HIM. THE SWORD OF NIGHT, AND THE PROTECTORSHIP OF MYRRA.
THE CHIMPANZEE DOES NOT SPEAK. HE LOOKS AT THE GLEAMING SWORD ON THE BAR, AND HIS HAND TREMBLES QUIETLY.
HE KNOWS IT IS A PACT. A RESPONSIBILITY THAT WILL SHAPE HIS LIFE TO COME.
HE KNOWS IT MEANS HIS FRIEND BELIEVED IN THE BEST OF HIM, AND THAT HE HAS TO LIVE UP TO IT.
BUT FIRST, THE CHIMPANZEE DRINKS.

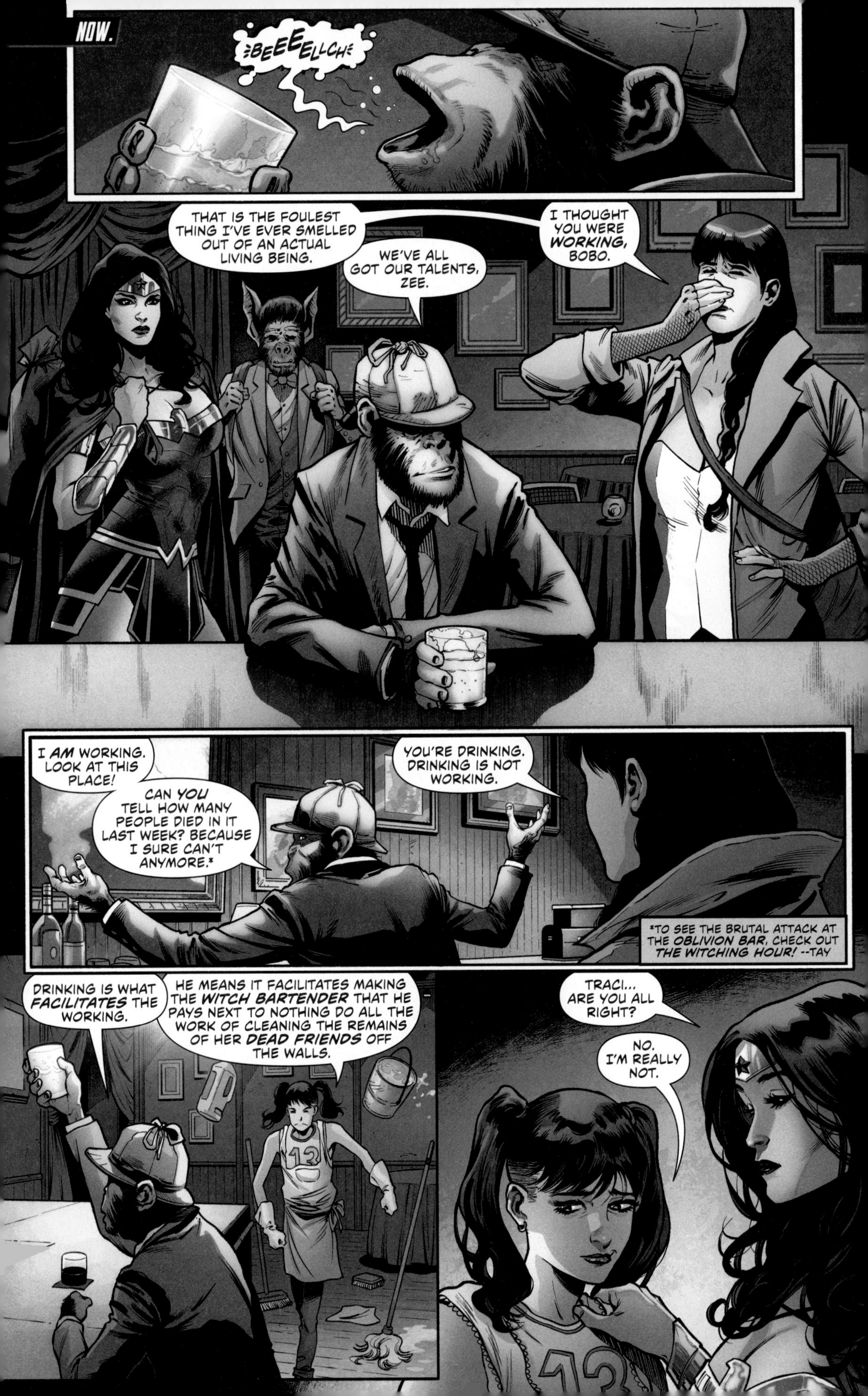
NOW.
BEEEELLCH
THAT IS THE FOULEST THING I'VE EVER SMELLED OUT OF AN ACTUAL LIVING BEING.
WE'VE ALL GOT OUR TALENTS, ZEE.
I THOUGHT YOU WERE WORKING, BOBO.
I AM WORKING. LOOK AT THIS PLACE!
CAN YOU TELL HOW MANY PEOPLE DIED IN IT LAST WEEK? BECAUSE I SURE CAN'T ANYMORE.*
YOU'RE DRINKING. DRINKING IS NOT WORKING.
*TO SEE THE BRUTAL ATTACK AT THE OBLIVION BAR, CHECK OUT THE WITCHING HOUR! --TAY
DRINKING IS WHAT FACILITATES THE WORKING.
HE MEANS IT FACILITATES MAKING THE WITCH BARTENDER THAT HE PAYS NEXT TO NOTHING DO ALL THE WORK OF CLEANING THE REMAINS OF HER DEAD FRIENDS OFF THE WALLS.
TRACI... ARE YOU ALL RIGHT?
NO. I'M REALLY NOT.

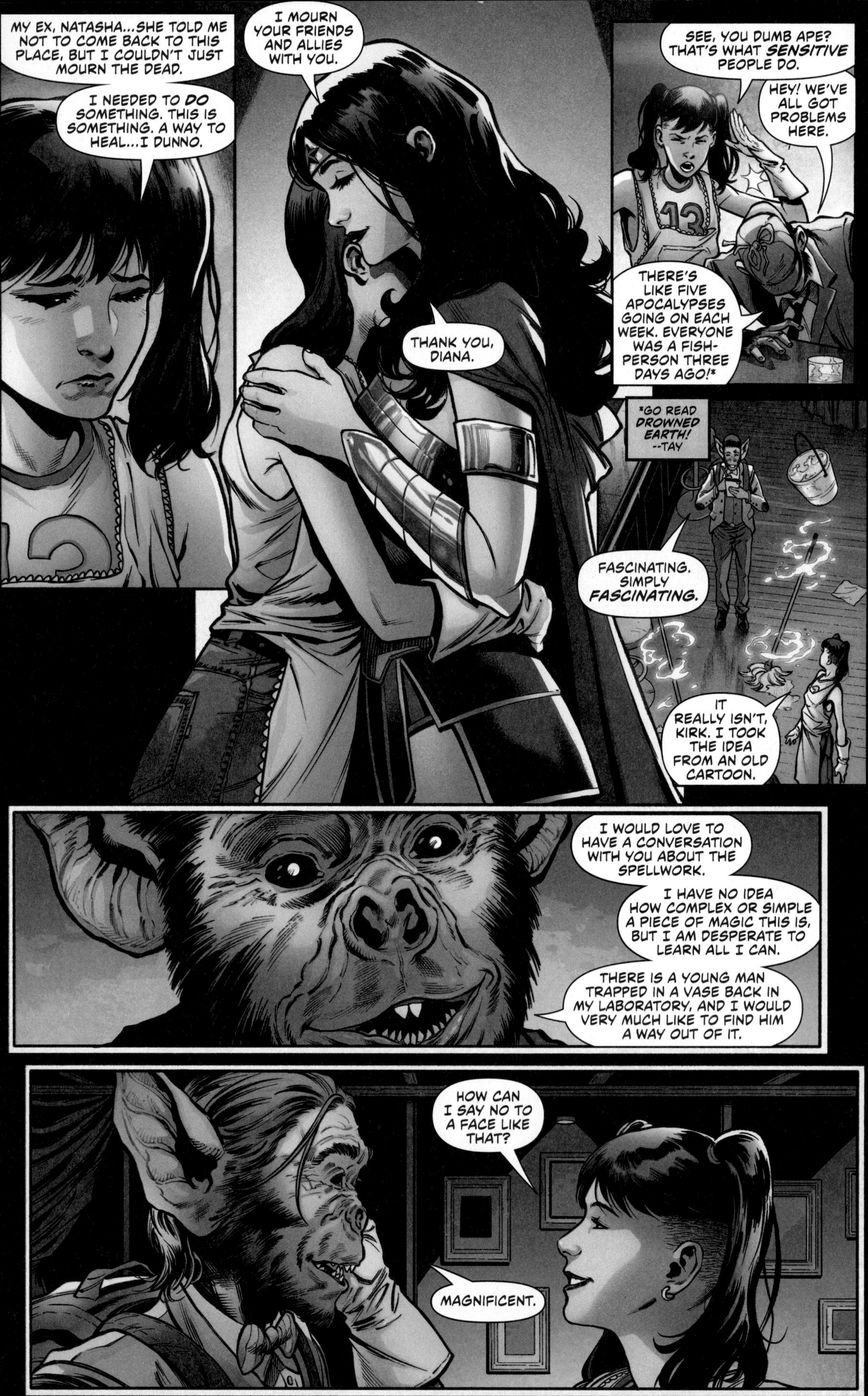
MY EX, NATASHA...SHE TOLD ME NOT TO COME BACK TO THIS PLACE, BUT I COULDN'T JUST MOURN THE DEAD.
I NEEDED TO DO SOMETHING. THIS IS SOMETHING. A WAY TO HEAL...I DUNNO.
I MOURN YOUR FRIENDS AND ALLIES WITH YOU.
THANK YOU, DIANA.
SEE, YOU DUMB APE? THAT'S WHAT SENSITIVE PEOPLE DO.
HEY! WE'VE ALL GOT PROBLEMS HERE.
THERE'S LIKE FIVE APOCALYPSES GOING ON EACH WEEK. EVERYONE WAS A FISH-PERSON THREE DAYS AGO!*
*GO READ DROWNED EARTH! --TAY
FASCINATING. SIMPLY FASCINATING.
IT REALLY ISN'T, KIRK. I TOOK THE IDEA FROM AN OLD CARTOON.
I WOULD LOVE TO HAVE A CONVERSATION WITH YOU ABOUT THE SPELLWORK.
I HAVE NO IDEA HOW COMPLEX OR SIMPLE A PIECE OF MAGIC THIS IS, BUT I AM DESPERATE TO LEARN ALL I CAN.
THERE IS A YOUNG MAN TRAPPED IN A VASE BACK IN MY LABORATORY, AND I WOULD VERY MUCH LIKE TO FIND HIM A WAY OUT OF IT.
HOW CAN I SAY NO TO A FACE LIKE THAT?
MAGNIFICENT.

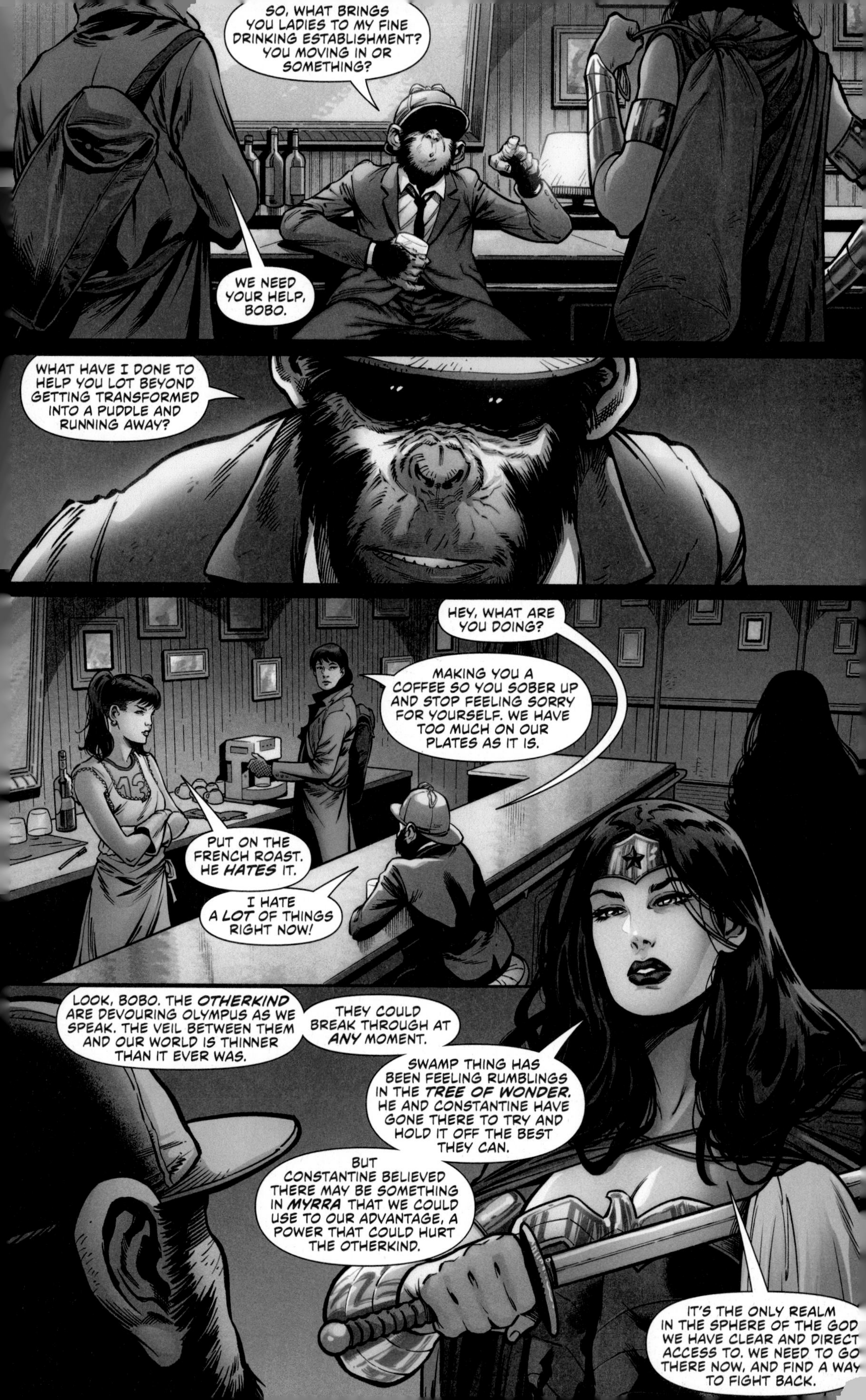
SO, WHAT BRINGS YOU LADIES TO MY FINE DRINKING ESTABLISHMENT? YOU MOVING IN OR SOMETHING?
WE NEED YOUR HELP, BOBO.
WHAT HAVE I DONE TO HELP YOU LOT BEYOND GETTING TRANSFORMED INTO A PUDDLE AND RUNNING AWAY?
HEY, WHAT ARE YOU DOING?
MAKING YOU A COFFEE SO YOU SOBER UP AND STOP FEELING SORRY FOR YOURSELF. WE HAVE TOO MUCH ON OUR PLATES AS IT IS.
PUT ON THE FRENCH ROAST. HE *HATES* IT.
I HATE A *LOT* OF THINGS RIGHT NOW!
LOOK, BOBO. THE *OTHERKIND* ARE DEVOURING OLYMPUS AS WE SPEAK. THE VEIL BETWEEN THEM AND OUR WORLD IS THINNER THAN IT EVER WAS.
THEY COULD BREAK THROUGH AT *ANY* MOMENT.
SWAMP THING HAS BEEN FEELING RUMBLINGS IN THE *TREE OF WONDER*. HE AND CONSTANTINE HAVE GONE THERE TO TRY AND HOLD IT OFF THE BEST THEY CAN.
BUT CONSTANTINE BELIEVED THERE MAY BE SOMETHING IN *MYRRA* THAT WE COULD USE TO OUR ADVANTAGE, A POWER THAT COULD HURT THE OTHERKIND.
IT'S THE ONLY REALM IN THE SPHERE OF THE GOD WE HAVE CLEAR AND DIRECT ACCESS TO. WE NEED TO GO THERE NOW, AND FIND A WAY TO FIGHT BACK.

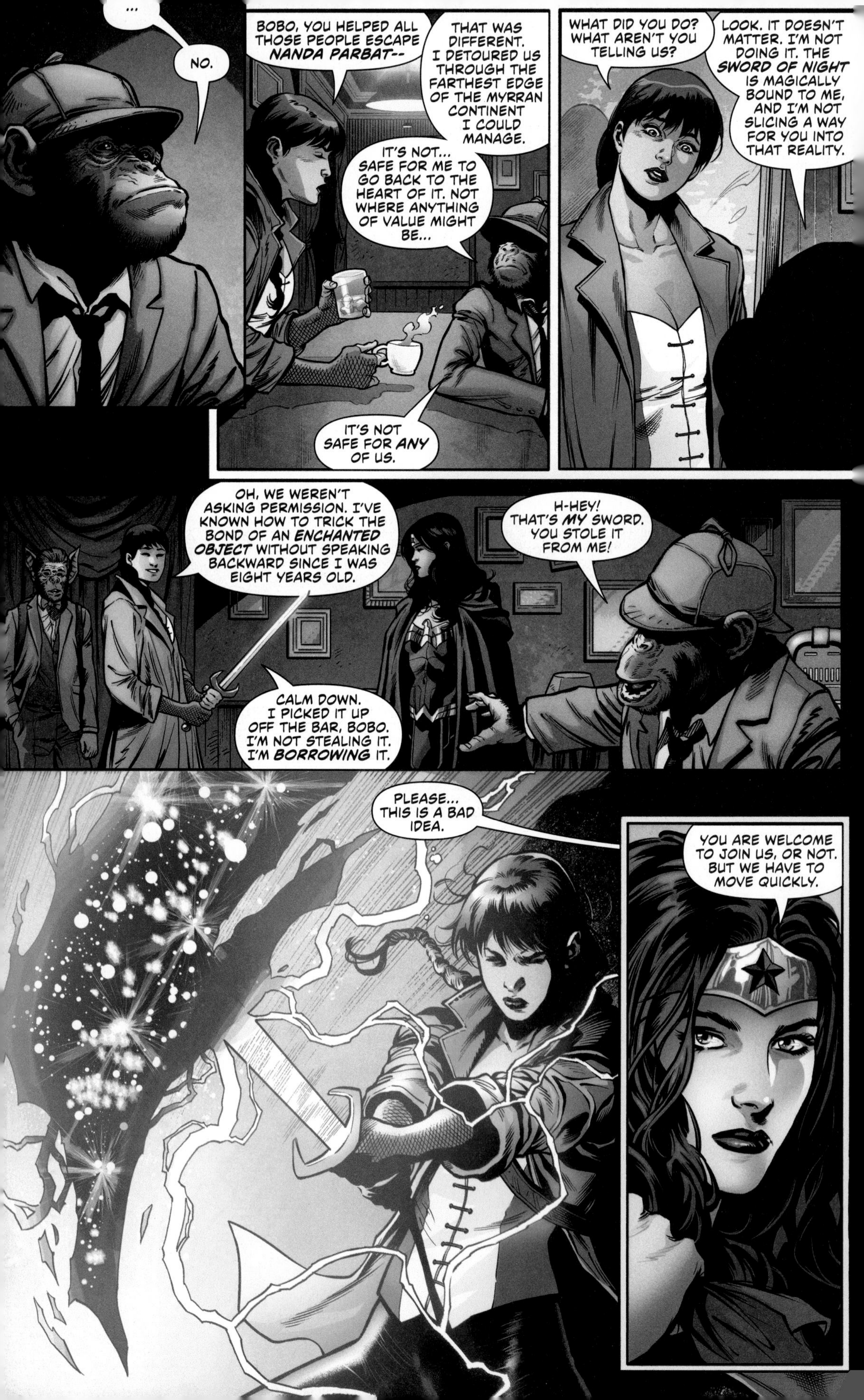
...
NO.
BOBO, YOU HELPED ALL THOSE PEOPLE ESCAPE NANDA PARBAT--
THAT WAS DIFFERENT. I DETOURED US THROUGH THE FARTHEST EDGE OF THE MYRRAN CONTINENT I COULD MANAGE.
IT'S NOT... SAFE FOR ME TO GO BACK TO THE HEART OF IT. NOT WHERE ANYTHING OF VALUE MIGHT BE...
IT'S NOT SAFE FOR ANY OF US.
WHAT DID YOU DO? WHAT AREN'T YOU TELLING US?
LOOK. IT DOESN'T MATTER. I'M NOT DOING IT. THE SWORD OF NIGHT IS MAGICALLY BOUND TO ME, AND I'M NOT SLICING A WAY FOR YOU INTO THAT REALITY.
OH, WE WEREN'T ASKING PERMISSION. I'VE KNOWN HOW TO TRICK THE BOND OF AN ENCHANTED OBJECT WITHOUT SPEAKING BACKWARD SINCE I WAS EIGHT YEARS OLD.
H-HEY! THAT'S MY SWORD. YOU STOLE IT FROM ME!
CALM DOWN. I PICKED IT UP OFF THE BAR, BOBO. I'M NOT STEALING IT. I'M BORROWING IT.
PLEASE... THIS IS A BAD IDEA.
YOU ARE WELCOME TO JOIN US, OR NOT. BUT WE HAVE TO MOVE QUICKLY.

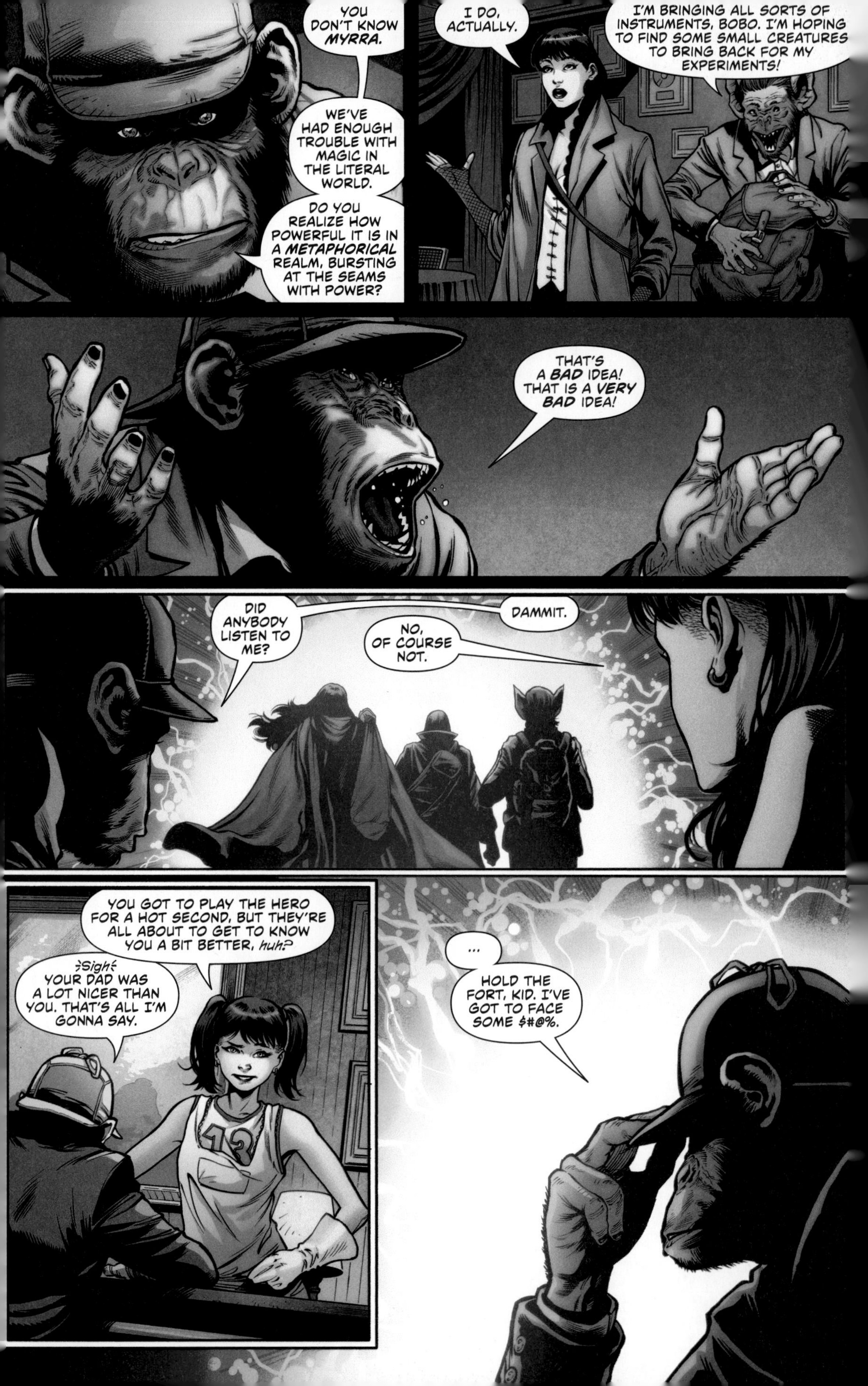
YOU DON'T KNOW *MYRRA.*
WE'VE HAD ENOUGH TROUBLE WITH MAGIC IN THE LITERAL WORLD.
DO YOU REALIZE HOW POWERFUL IT IS IN A *METAPHORICAL* REALM, BURSTING AT THE SEAMS WITH POWER?
I DO, ACTUALLY.
I'M BRINGING ALL SORTS OF INSTRUMENTS, BOBO. I'M HOPING TO FIND SOME SMALL CREATURES TO BRING BACK FOR MY EXPERIMENTS!
THAT'S A **BAD** IDEA! THAT IS A **VERY BAD** IDEA!
DID ANYBODY LISTEN TO ME?
DAMMIT.
NO, OF COURSE NOT.
YOU GOT TO PLAY THE HERO FOR A HOT SECOND, BUT THEY'RE ALL ABOUT TO GET TO KNOW YOU A BIT BETTER, *huh?*
Sigh YOUR DAD WAS A LOT NICER THAN YOU. THAT'S ALL I'M GONNA SAY.
...
HOLD THE FORT, KID. I'VE GOT TO FACE SOME $#@%.

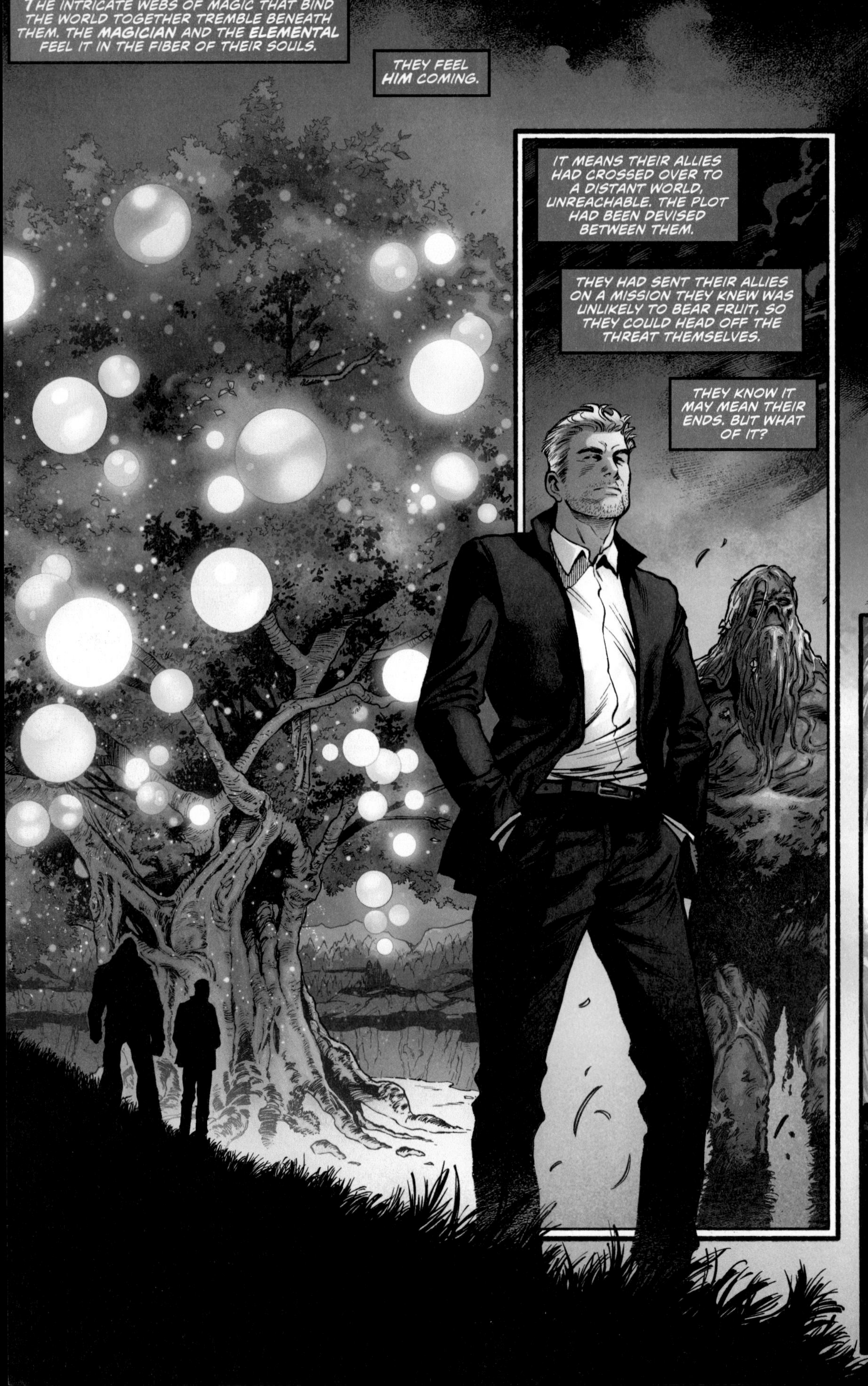
THE INTRICATE WEBS OF MAGIC THAT BIND THE WORLD TOGETHER TREMBLE BENEATH THEM. THE MAGICIAN AND THE ELEMENTAL FEEL IT IN THE FIBER OF THEIR SOULS.
THEY FEEL HIM COMING.
IT MEANS THEIR ALLIES HAD CROSSED OVER TO A DISTANT WORLD, UNREACHABLE. THE PLOT HAD BEEN DEVISED BETWEEN THEM.
THEY HAD SENT THEIR ALLIES ON A MISSION THEY KNEW WAS UNLIKELY TO BEAR FRUIT, SO THEY COULD HEAD OFF THE THREAT THEMSELVES.
THEY KNOW IT MAY MEAN THEIR ENDS. BUT WHAT OF IT?

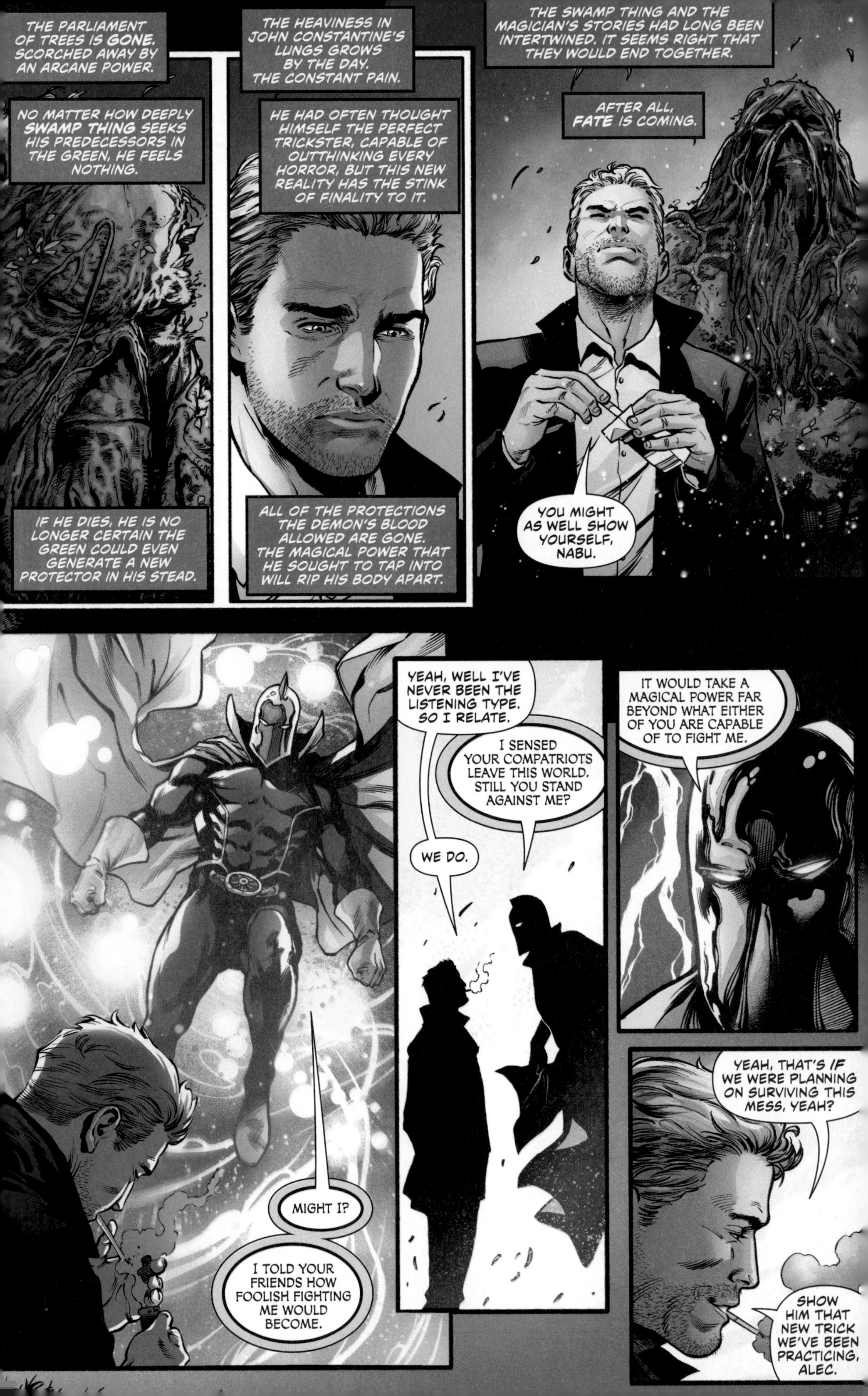
THE PARLIAMENT OF TREES IS **GONE**. SCORCHED AWAY BY AN ARCANE POWER.
NO MATTER HOW DEEPLY **SWAMP THING** SEEKS HIS PREDECESSORS IN THE GREEN, HE FEELS NOTHING.
IF HE DIES, HE IS NO LONGER CERTAIN THE GREEN COULD EVEN GENERATE A NEW PROTECTOR IN HIS STEAD.
THE HEAVINESS IN JOHN CONSTANTINE'S LUNGS GROWS BY THE DAY. THE CONSTANT PAIN.
HE HAD OFTEN THOUGHT HIMSELF THE PERFECT TRICKSTER, CAPABLE OF OUTTHINKING EVERY HORROR, BUT THIS NEW REALITY HAS THE STINK OF FINALITY TO IT.
ALL OF THE PROTECTIONS THE DEMON'S BLOOD ALLOWED ARE GONE. THE MAGICAL POWER THAT HE SOUGHT TO TAP INTO WILL RIP HIS BODY APART.
THE SWAMP THING AND THE MAGICIAN'S STORIES HAD LONG BEEN INTERTWINED. IT SEEMS RIGHT THAT THEY WOULD END TOGETHER.
AFTER ALL, **FATE** IS COMING.
YOU MIGHT AS WELL SHOW YOURSELF, NABU.
MIGHT I?
I TOLD YOUR FRIENDS HOW FOOLISH FIGHTING ME WOULD BECOME.
YEAH, WELL I'VE NEVER BEEN THE LISTENING TYPE. SO I RELATE.
I SENSED YOUR COMPATRIOTS LEAVE THIS WORLD. STILL YOU STAND AGAINST ME?
WE DO.
IT WOULD TAKE A MAGICAL POWER FAR BEYOND WHAT EITHER OF YOU ARE CAPABLE OF TO FIGHT ME.
YEAH, THAT'S *IF* WE WERE PLANNING ON SURVIVING THIS MESS, YEAH?
SHOW HIM THAT NEW TRICK WE'VE BEEN PRACTICING, ALEC.

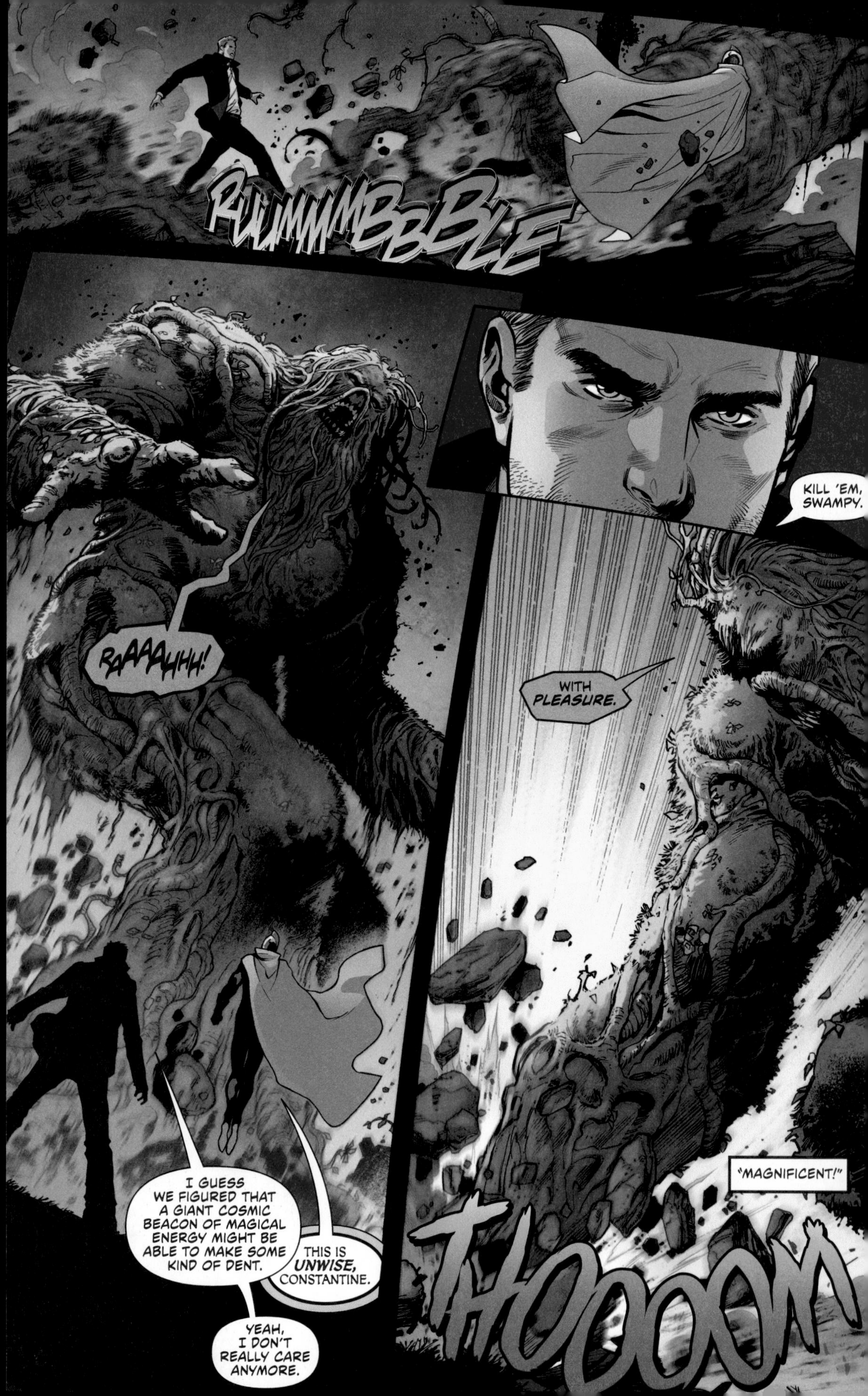
RUUMMMBBBLE
RAAAAHHH!
KILL 'EM, SWAMPY.
WITH PLEASURE.
I GUESS WE FIGURED THAT A GIANT COSMIC BEACON OF MAGICAL ENERGY MIGHT BE ABLE TO MAKE SOME KIND OF DENT.
THIS IS UNWISE, CONSTANTINE.
YEAH, I DON'T REALLY CARE ANYMORE.
"MAGNIFICENT!"
THOOOOM

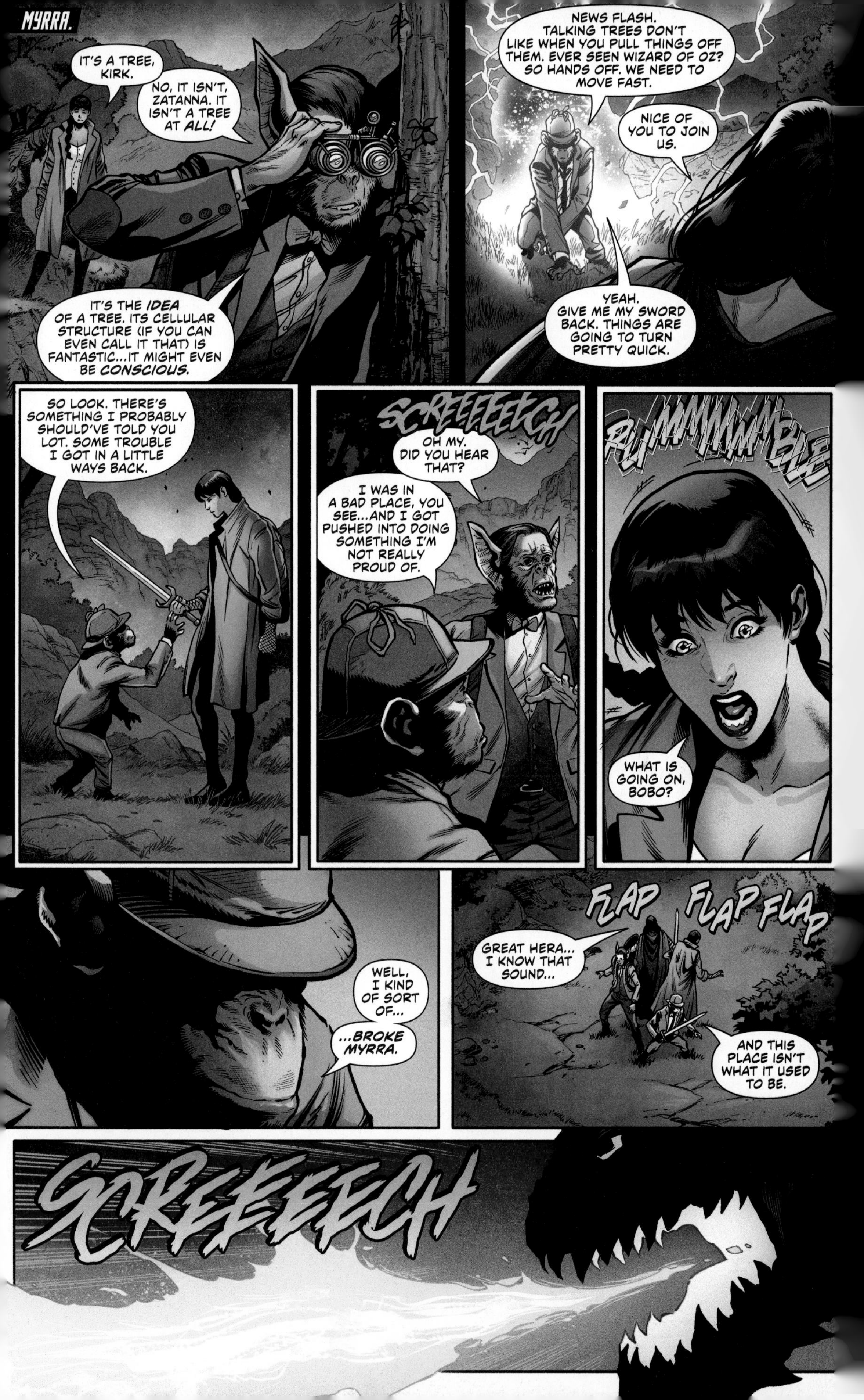
MYRRA.
IT'S A TREE, KIRK.
NO, IT ISN'T, ZATANNA. IT ISN'T A TREE AT ALL!
IT'S THE IDEA OF A TREE. ITS CELLULAR STRUCTURE (IF YOU CAN EVEN CALL IT THAT) IS FANTASTIC...IT MIGHT EVEN BE CONSCIOUS.
NEWS FLASH. TALKING TREES DON'T LIKE WHEN YOU PULL THINGS OFF THEM. EVER SEEN WIZARD OF OZ? SO HANDS OFF. WE NEED TO MOVE FAST.
NICE OF YOU TO JOIN US.
YEAH. GIVE ME MY SWORD BACK. THINGS ARE GOING TO TURN PRETTY QUICK.
SO LOOK. THERE'S SOMETHING I PROBABLY SHOULD'VE TOLD YOU LOT. SOME TROUBLE I GOT IN A LITTLE WAYS BACK.
SCREEEEECH
OH MY. DID YOU HEAR THAT?
I WAS IN A BAD PLACE, YOU SEE...AND I GOT PUSHED INTO DOING SOMETHING I'M NOT REALLY PROUD OF.
RUMMMMMBLE
WHAT IS GOING ON, BOBO?
WELL, I KIND OF SORT OF...
...BROKE MYRRA.
FLAP FLAP FLAP
GREAT HERA... I KNOW THAT SOUND...
AND THIS PLACE ISN'T WHAT IT USED TO BE.
SCREEEECH

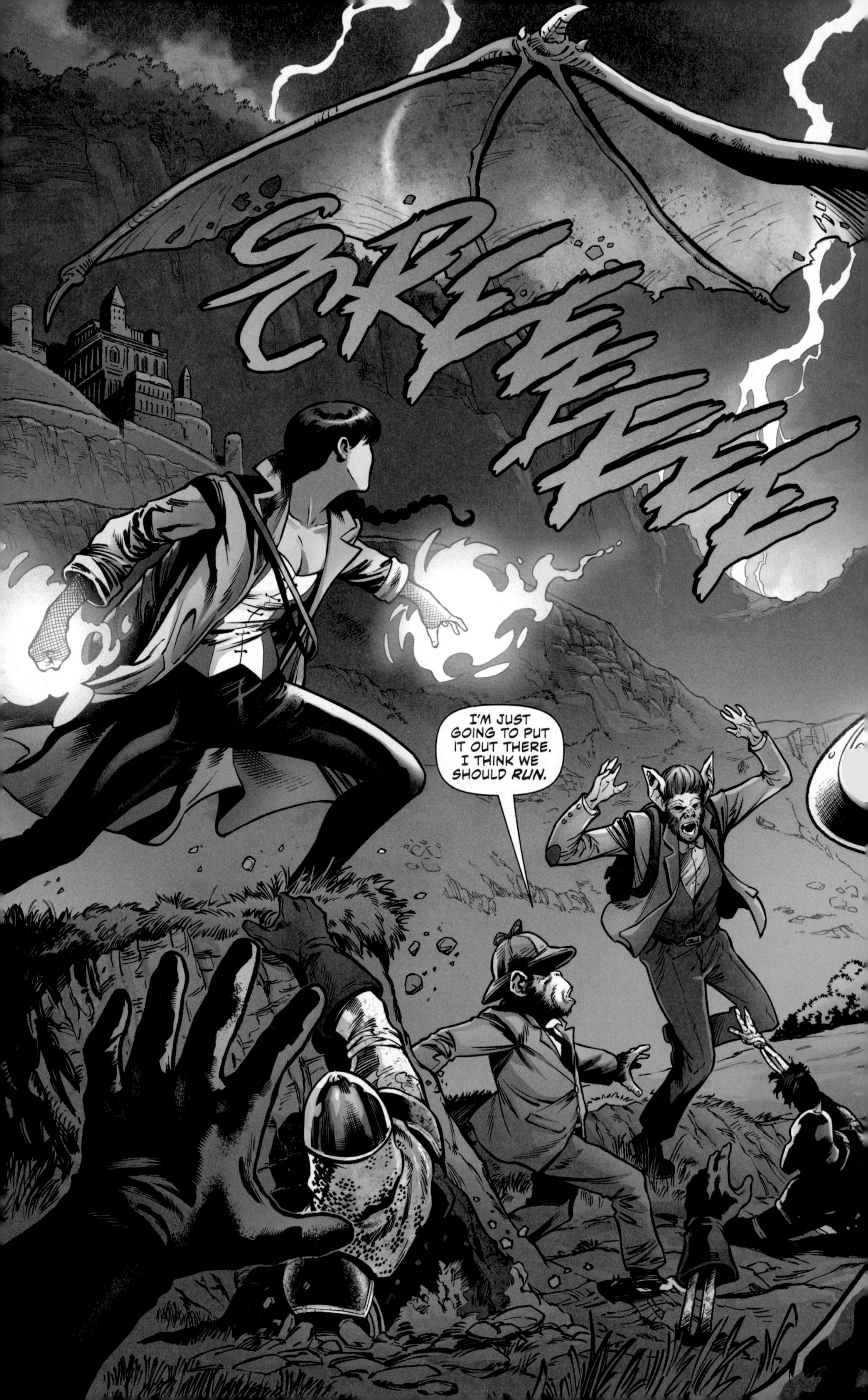
I'M JUST GOING TO PUT IT OUT THERE. I THINK WE SHOULD *RUN*.

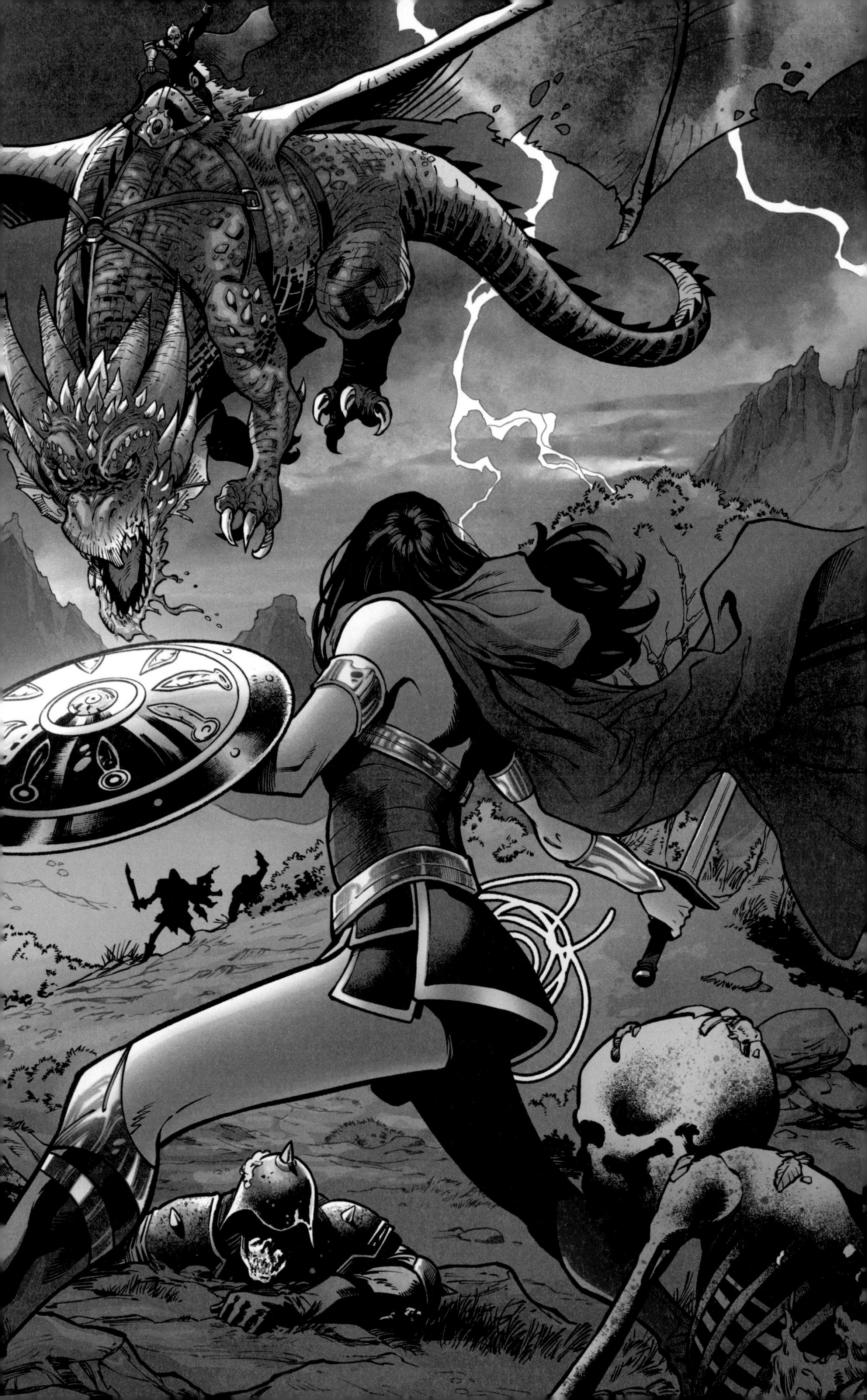

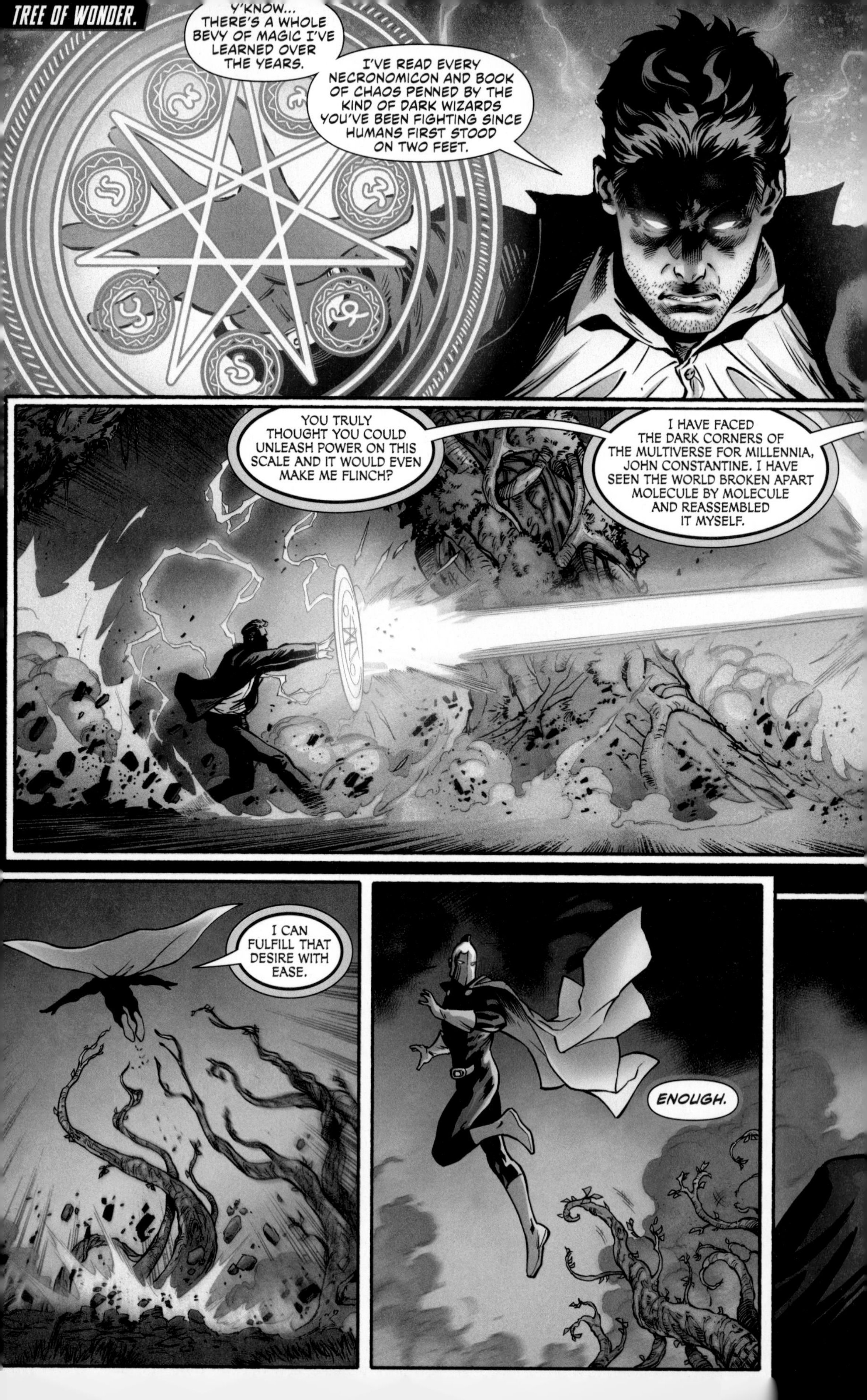
TREE OF WONDER.
Y'KNOW... THERE'S A WHOLE BEVY OF MAGIC I'VE LEARNED OVER THE YEARS.
I'VE READ EVERY NECRONOMICON AND BOOK OF CHAOS PENNED BY THE KIND OF DARK WIZARDS YOU'VE BEEN FIGHTING SINCE HUMANS FIRST STOOD ON TWO FEET.
YOU TRULY THOUGHT YOU COULD UNLEASH POWER ON THIS SCALE AND IT WOULD EVEN MAKE ME FLINCH?
I HAVE FACED THE DARK CORNERS OF THE MULTIVERSE FOR MILLENNIA, JOHN CONSTANTINE. I HAVE SEEN THE WORLD BROKEN APART MOLECULE BY MOLECULE AND REASSEMBLED IT MYSELF.
I CAN FULFILL THAT DESIRE WITH EASE.
ENOUGH.

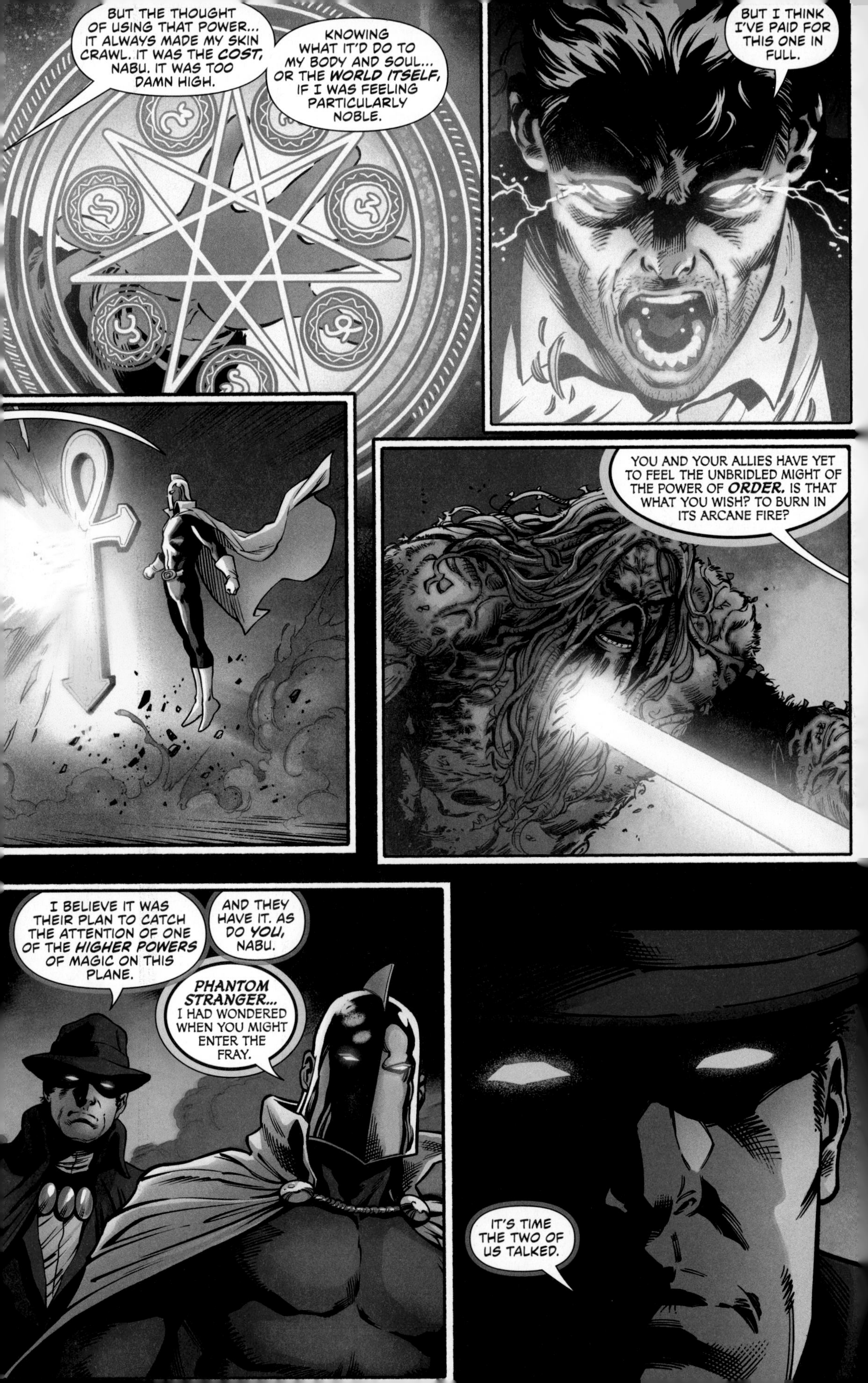
BUT THE THOUGHT OF USING THAT POWER... IT ALWAYS MADE MY SKIN CRAWL. IT WAS THE COST, NABU. IT WAS TOO DAMN HIGH.
KNOWING WHAT IT'D DO TO MY BODY AND SOUL... OR THE WORLD ITSELF, IF I WAS FEELING PARTICULARLY NOBLE.
BUT I THINK I'VE PAID FOR THIS ONE IN FULL.
YOU AND YOUR ALLIES HAVE YET TO FEEL THE UNBRIDLED MIGHT OF THE POWER OF ORDER. IS THAT WHAT YOU WISH? TO BURN IN ITS ARCANE FIRE?
I BELIEVE IT WAS THEIR PLAN TO CATCH THE ATTENTION OF ONE OF THE HIGHER POWERS OF MAGIC ON THIS PLANE.
AND THEY HAVE IT. AS DO YOU, NABU.
PHANTOM STRANGER... I HAD WONDERED WHEN YOU MIGHT ENTER THE FRAY.
IT'S TIME THE TWO OF US TALKED.

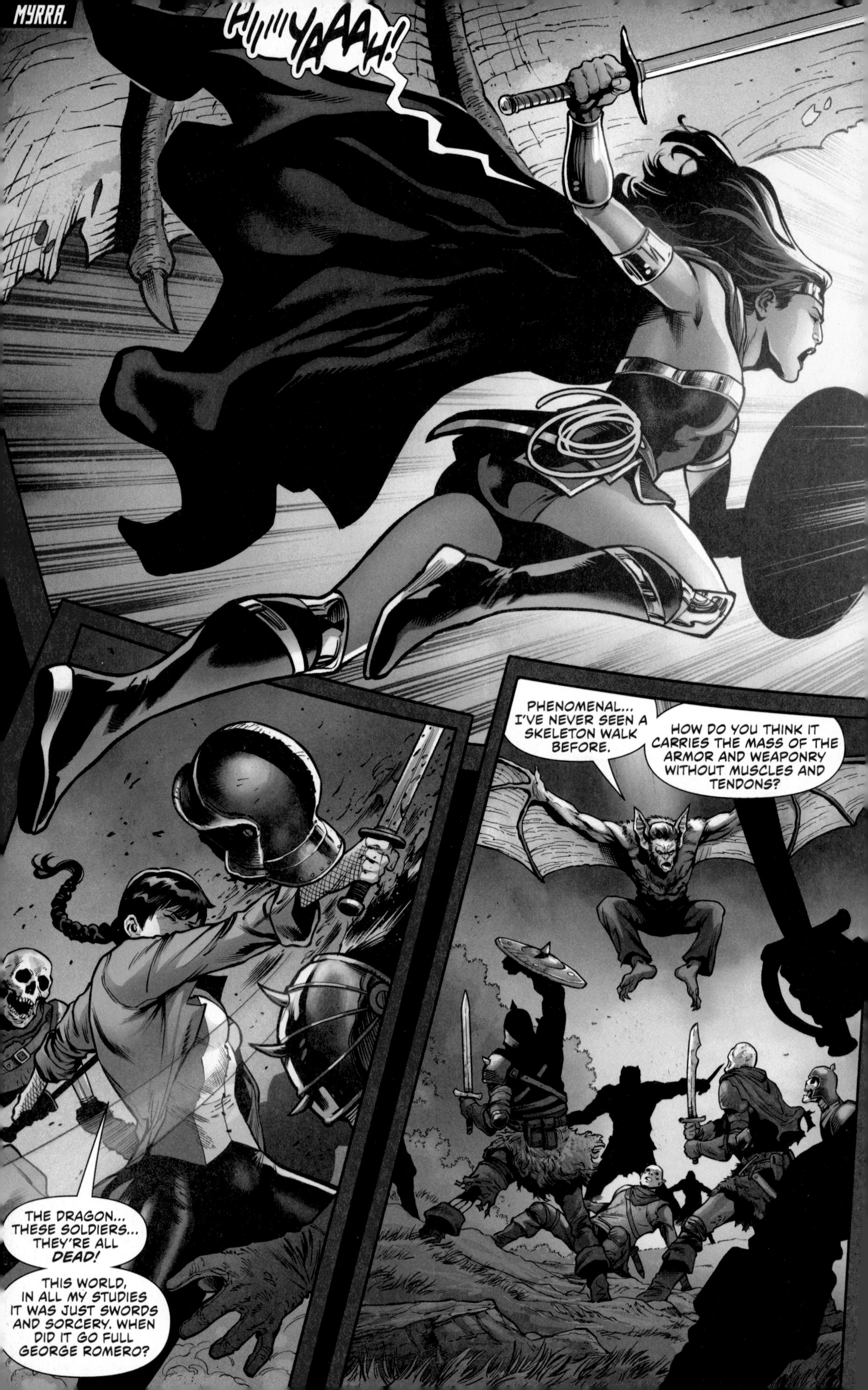
MYRRA.
HI'YAAAH!
THE DRAGON... THESE SOLDIERS... THEY'RE ALL DEAD!
THIS WORLD, IN ALL MY STUDIES IT WAS JUST SWORDS AND SORCERY. WHEN DID IT GO FULL GEORGE ROMERO?
PHENOMENAL... I'VE NEVER SEEN A SKELETON WALK BEFORE.
HOW DO YOU THINK IT CARRIES THE MASS OF THE ARMOR AND WEAPONRY WITHOUT MUSCLES AND TENDONS?

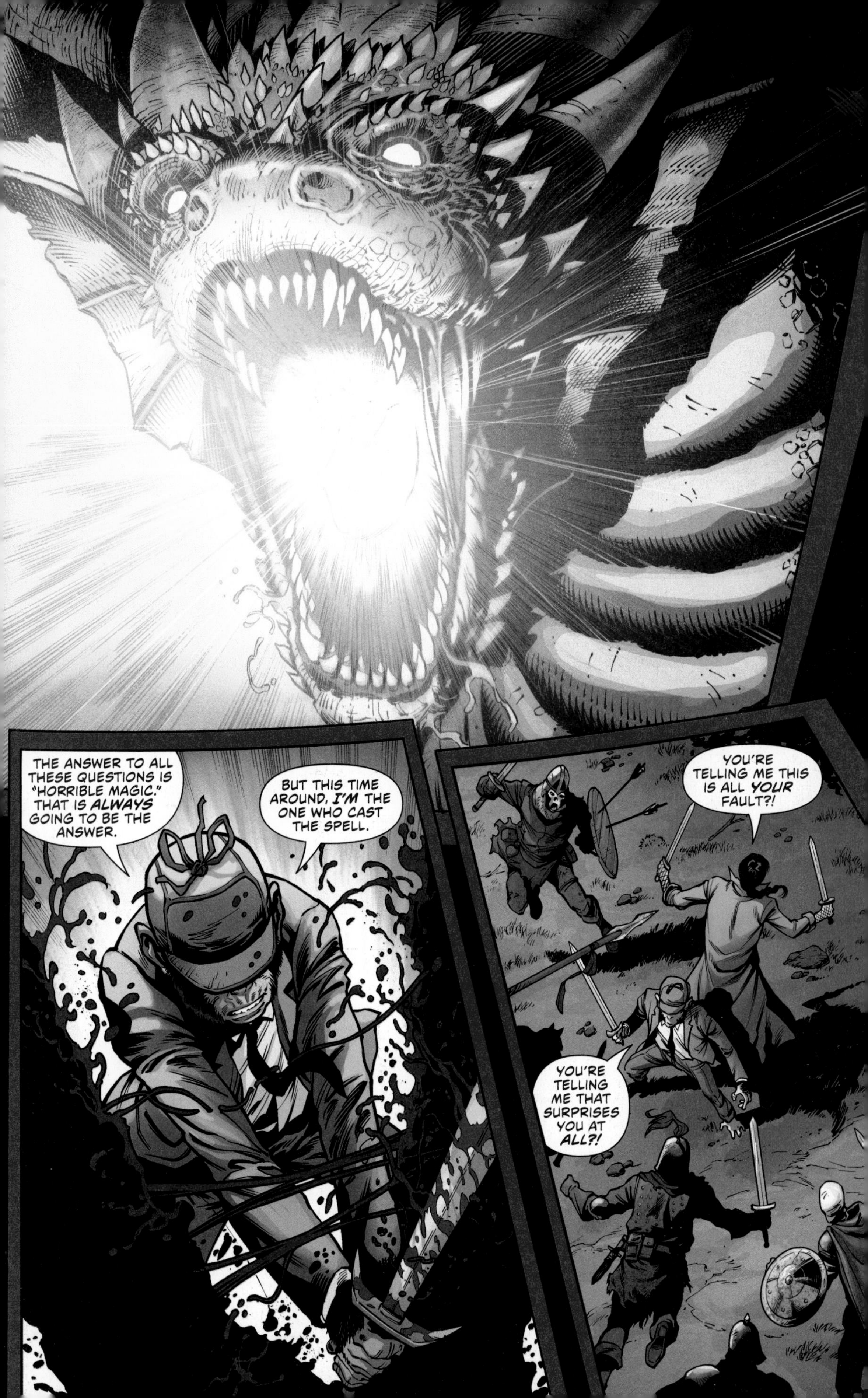
THE ANSWER TO ALL THESE QUESTIONS IS "HORRIBLE MAGIC." THAT IS ALWAYS GOING TO BE THE ANSWER.
BUT THIS TIME AROUND, I'M THE ONE WHO CAST THE SPELL.
YOU'RE TELLING ME THIS IS ALL YOUR FAULT?!
YOU'RE TELLING ME THAT SURPRISES YOU AT ALL?!

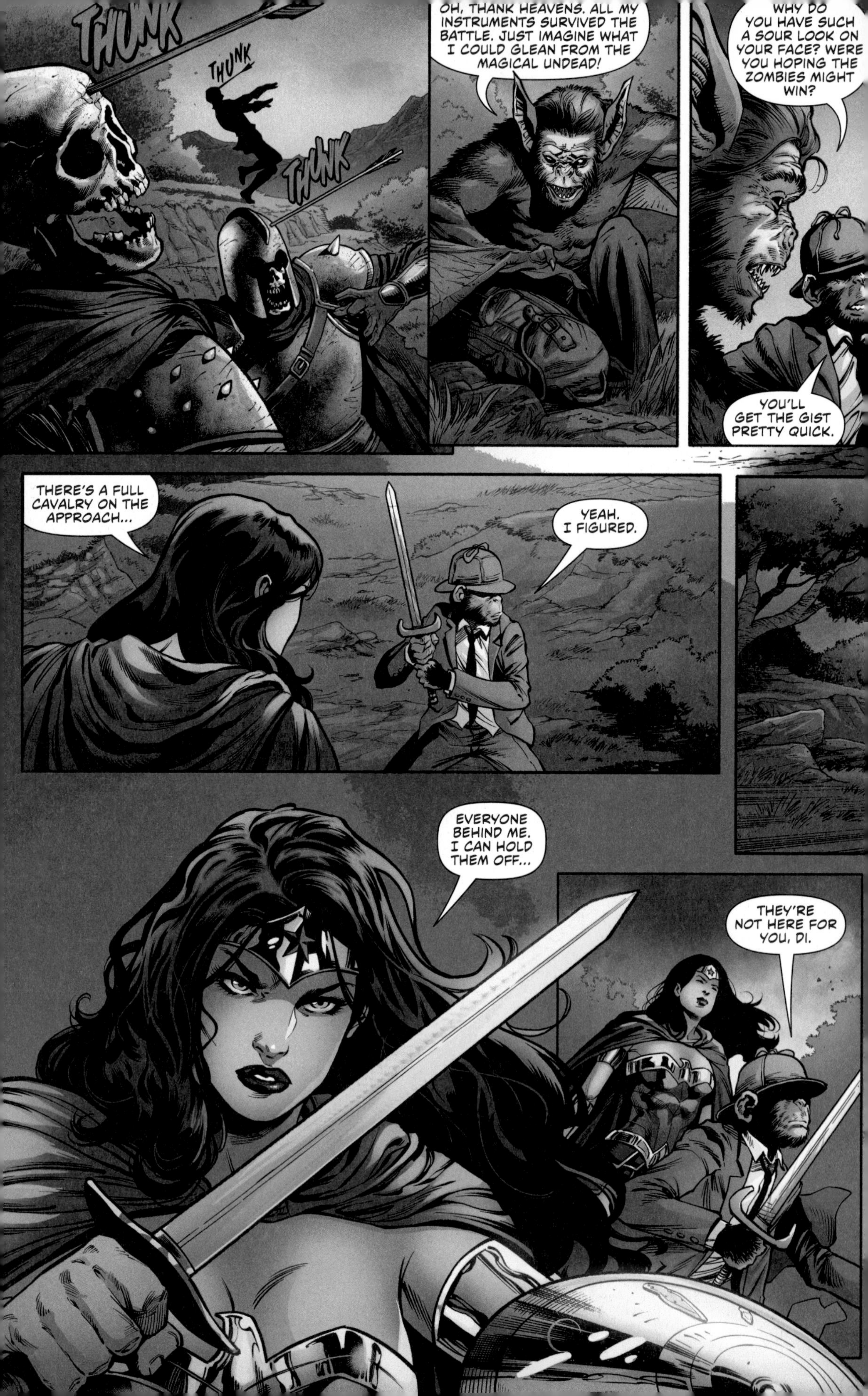
THUNK
THUNK
THUNK
OH, THANK HEAVENS. ALL MY INSTRUMENTS SURVIVED THE BATTLE. JUST IMAGINE WHAT I COULD GLEAN FROM THE MAGICAL UNDEAD!
WHY DO YOU HAVE SUCH A SOUR LOOK ON YOUR FACE? WERE YOU HOPING THE ZOMBIES MIGHT WIN?
YOU'LL GET THE GIST PRETTY QUICK.
THERE'S A FULL CAVALRY ON THE APPROACH...
YEAH. I FIGURED.
EVERYONE BEHIND ME. I CAN HOLD THEM OFF...
THEY'RE NOT HERE FOR YOU, DI.

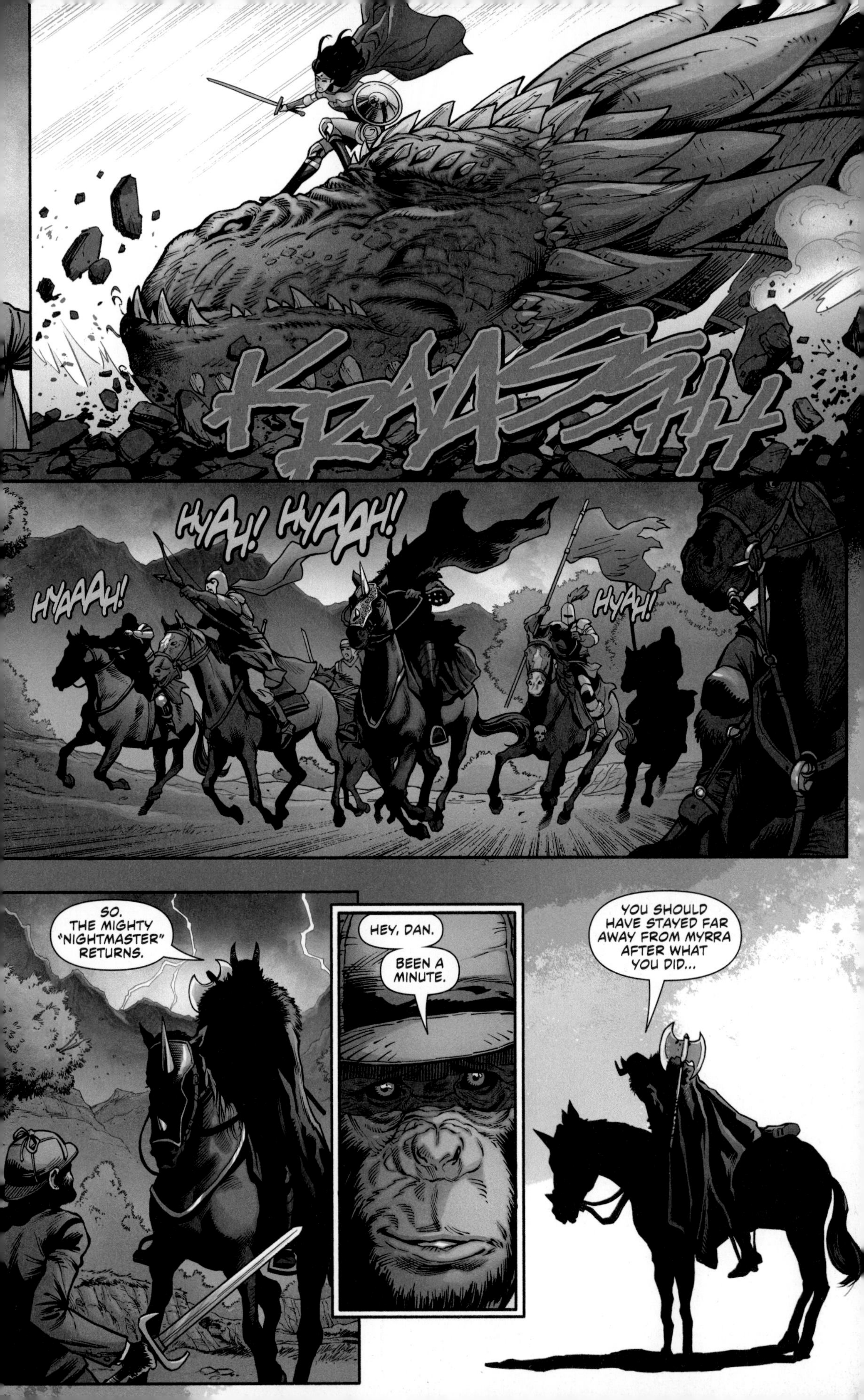
KRAASHH
HYAH! HYAAH!
HYAAAH!
HYAH!
SO. THE MIGHTY "NIGHTMASTER" RETURNS.
HEY, DAN.
BEEN A MINUTE.
YOU SHOULD HAVE STAYED FAR AWAY FROM MYRRA AFTER WHAT YOU DID...

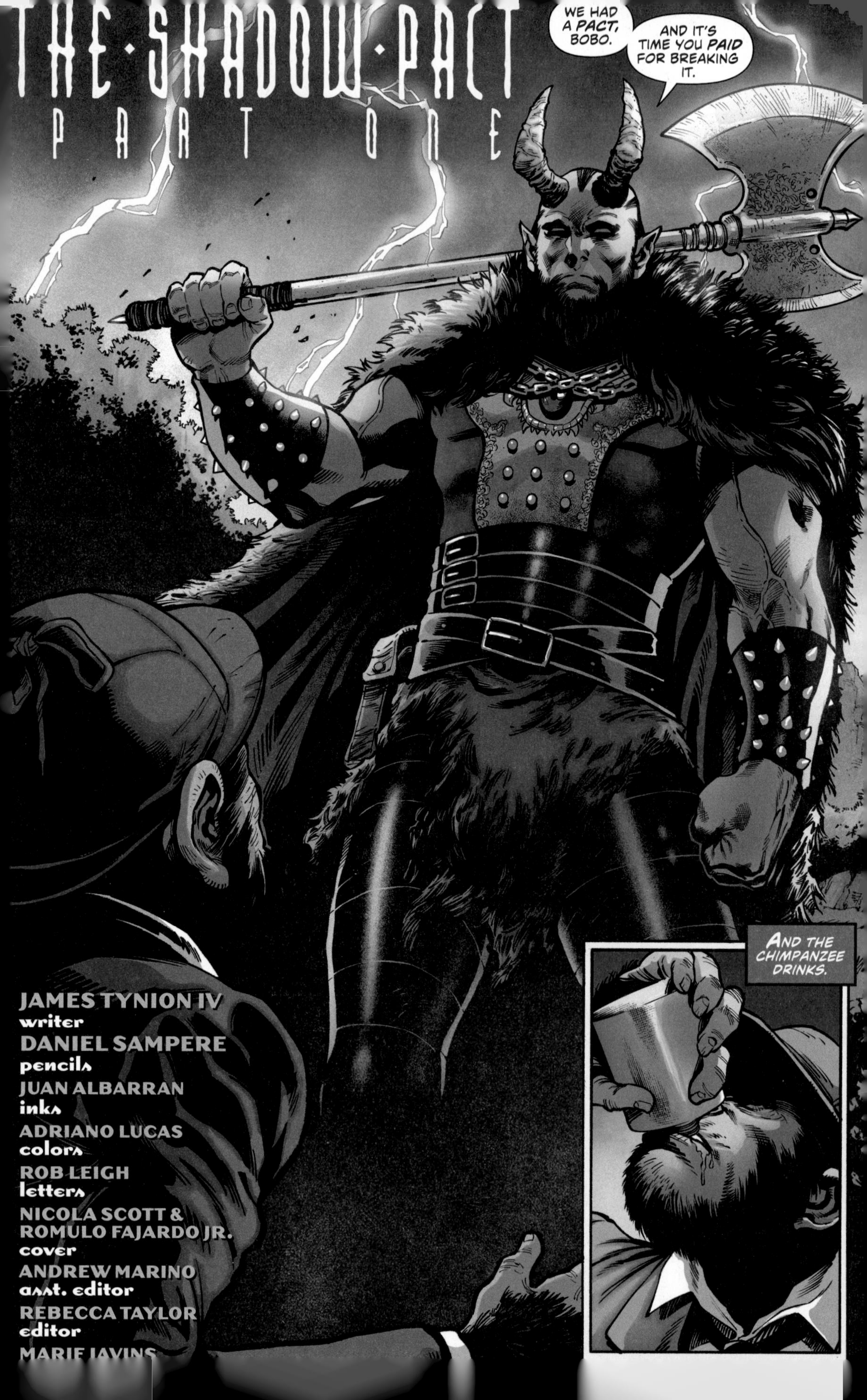
THE SHADOW PACT
PART ONE
WE HAD A PACT, BOBO.
AND IT'S TIME YOU PAID FOR BREAKING IT.
AND THE CHIMPANZEE DRINKS.
JAMES TYNION IV
writer
DANIEL SAMPERE
pencils
JUAN ALBARRAN
inks
ADRIANO LUCAS
colors
ROB LEIGH
letters
NICOLA SCOTT & ROMULO FAJARDO JR.
cover
ANDREW MARINO
asst. editor
REBECCA TAYLOR
editor
MARIE JAVINS

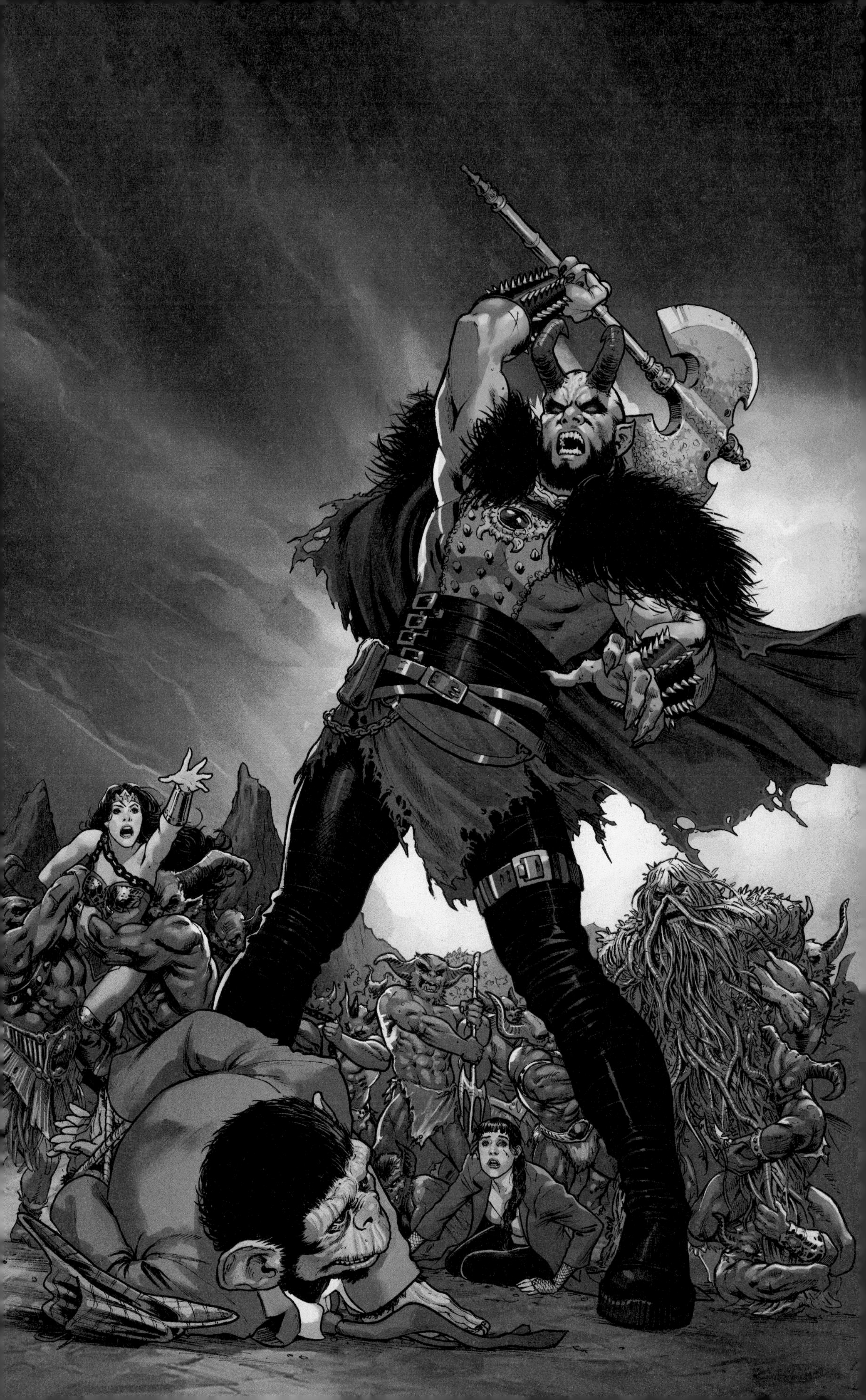

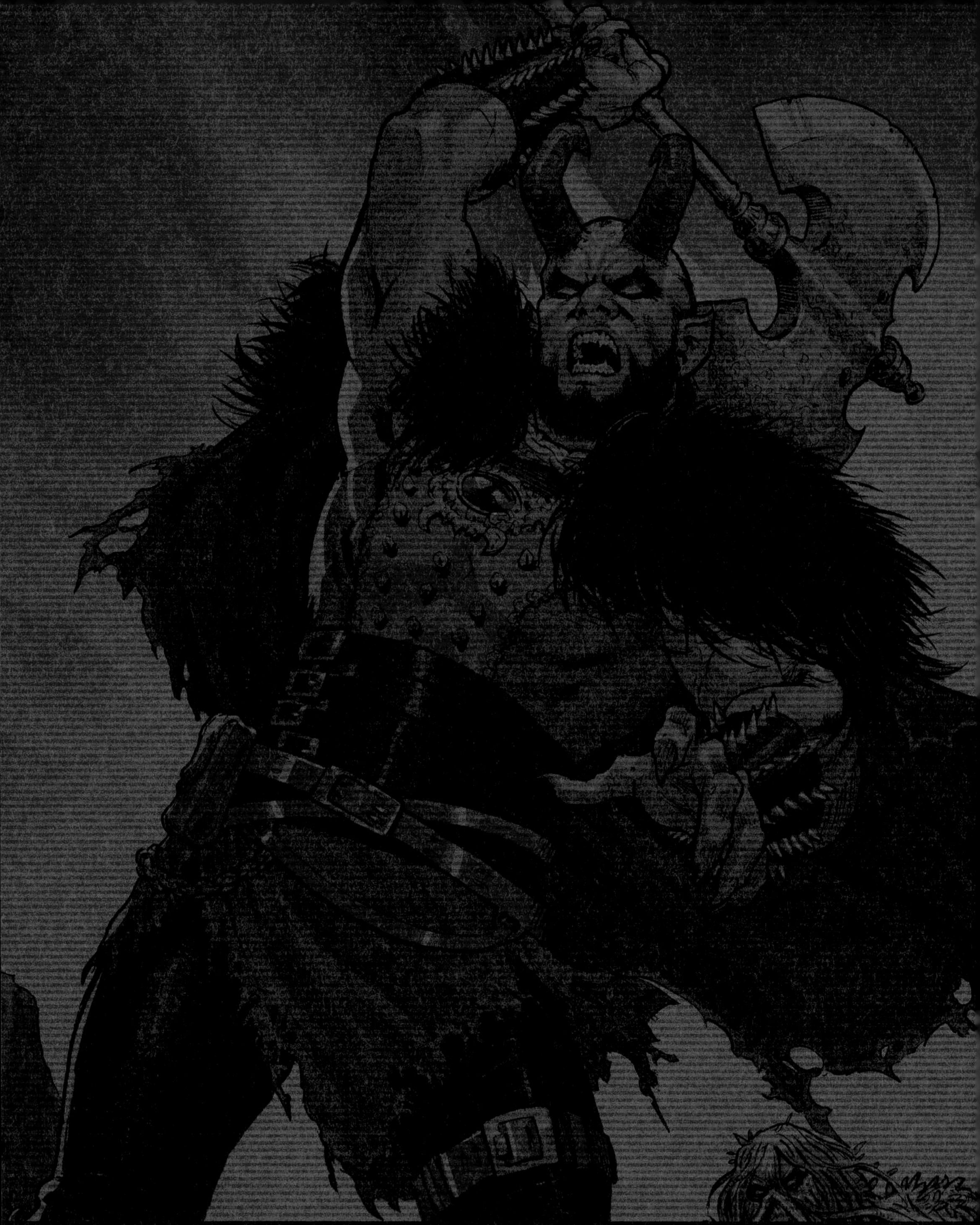

JUSTICE LEAGUE DARK
#6

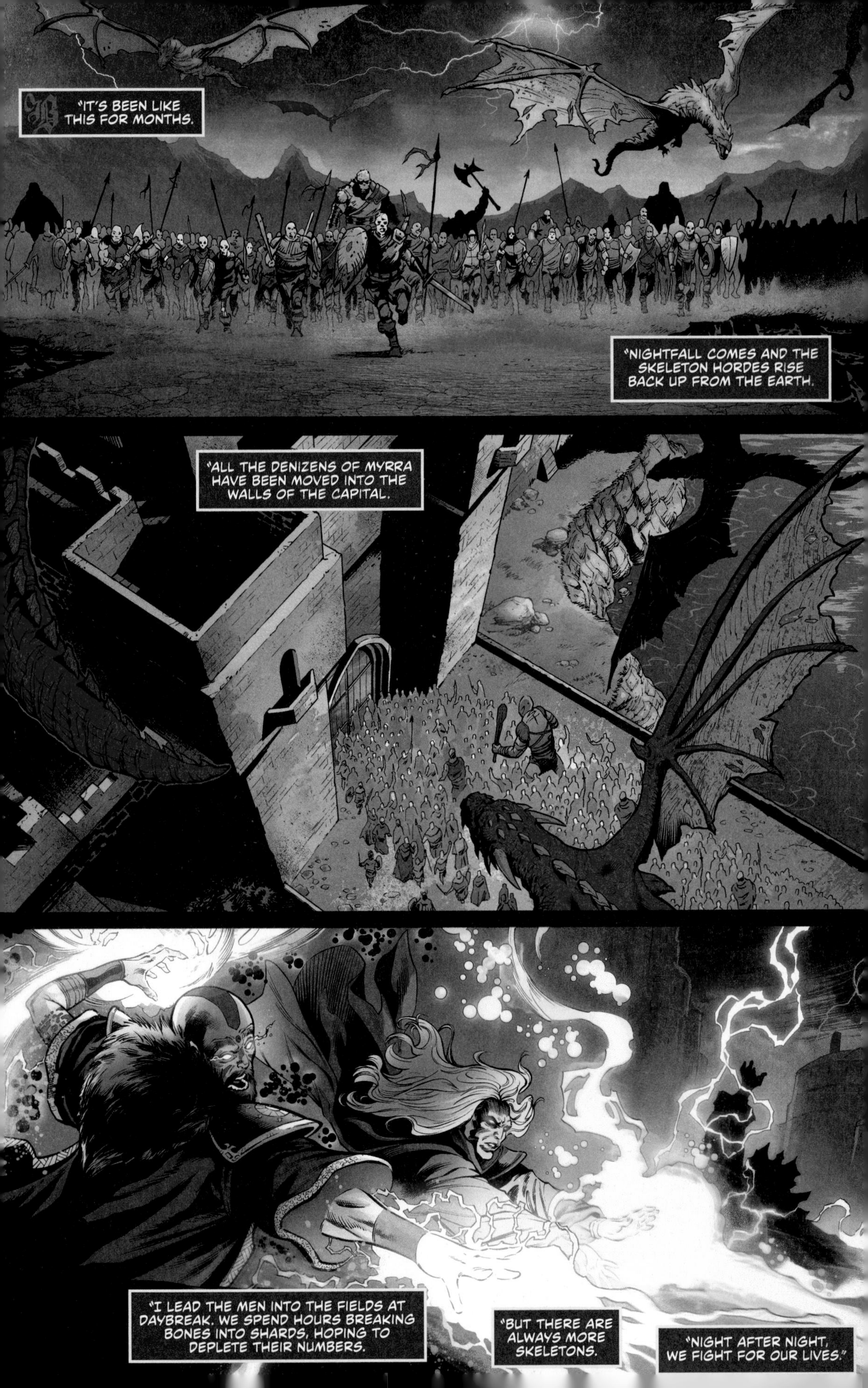
"IT'S BEEN LIKE THIS FOR MONTHS.
"NIGHTFALL COMES AND THE SKELETON HORDES RISE BACK UP FROM THE EARTH.
"ALL THE DENIZENS OF MYRRA HAVE BEEN MOVED INTO THE WALLS OF THE CAPITAL.
"I LEAD THE MEN INTO THE FIELDS AT DAYBREAK. WE SPEND HOURS BREAKING BONES INTO SHARDS, HOPING TO DEPLETE THEIR NUMBERS.
"BUT THERE ARE ALWAYS MORE SKELETONS.
"NIGHT AFTER NIGHT, WE FIGHT FOR OUR LIVES."

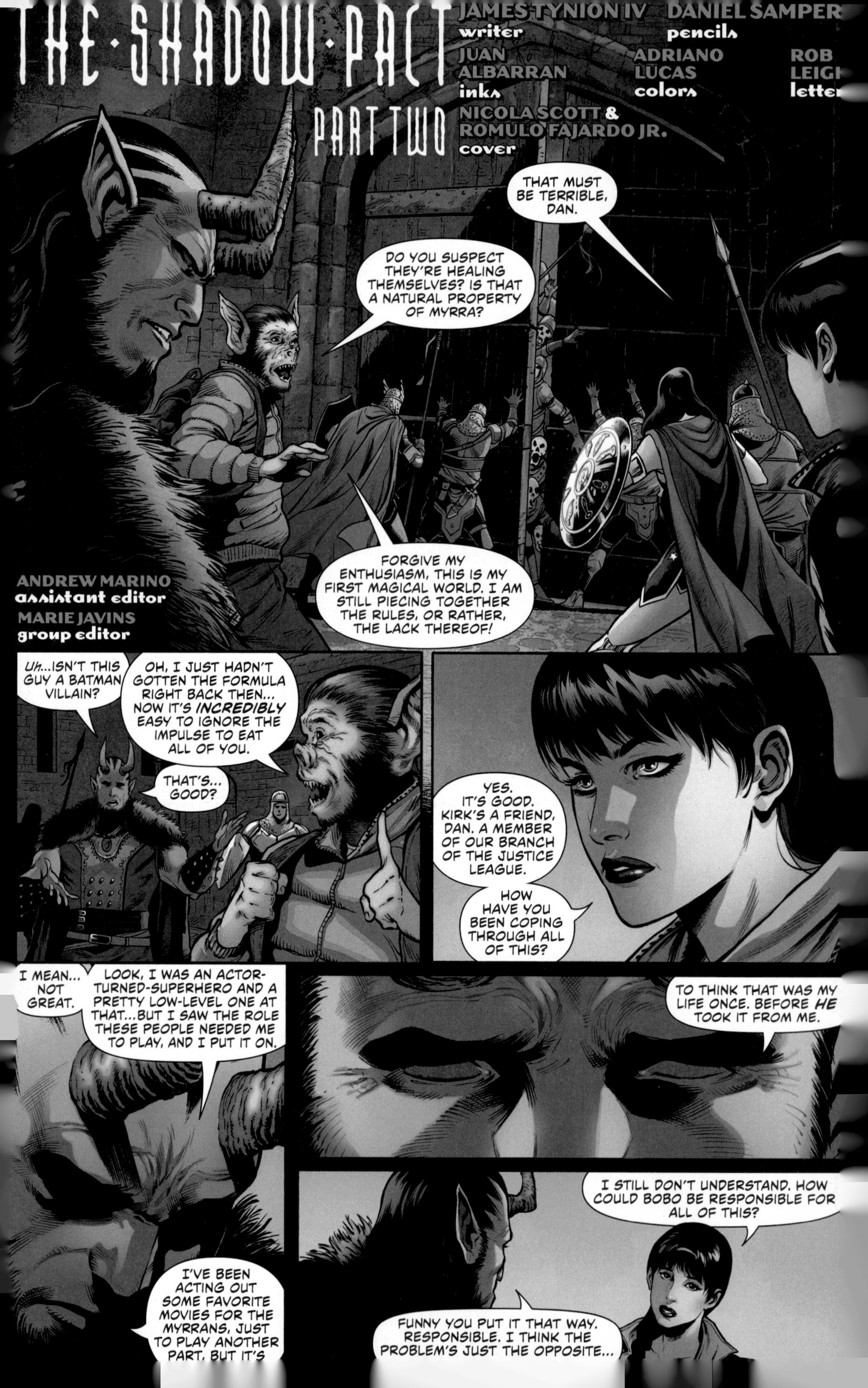
THE · SHADOW · PACT
PART TWO
JAMES TYNION IV writer
DANIEL SAMPER pencils
JUAN ALBARRAN inks
ADRIANO LUCAS colors
ROB LEIGH letters
NICOLA SCOTT & ROMULO FAJARDO JR. cover
THAT MUST BE TERRIBLE, DAN.
DO YOU SUSPECT THEY'RE HEALING THEMSELVES? IS THAT A NATURAL PROPERTY OF MYRRA?
FORGIVE MY ENTHUSIASM, THIS IS MY FIRST MAGICAL WORLD. I AM STILL PIECING TOGETHER THE RULES, OR RATHER, THE LACK THEREOF!
ANDREW MARINO assistant editor
MARIE JAVINS group editor
Uh...ISN'T THIS GUY A BATMAN VILLAIN?
OH, I JUST HADN'T GOTTEN THE FORMULA RIGHT BACK THEN... NOW IT'S INCREDIBLY EASY TO IGNORE THE IMPULSE TO EAT ALL OF YOU.
THAT'S... GOOD?
YES. IT'S GOOD. KIRK'S A FRIEND, DAN. A MEMBER OF OUR BRANCH OF THE JUSTICE LEAGUE.
HOW HAVE YOU BEEN COPING THROUGH ALL OF THIS?
I MEAN... NOT GREAT.
LOOK, I WAS AN ACTOR-TURNED-SUPERHERO AND A PRETTY LOW-LEVEL ONE AT THAT...BUT I SAW THE ROLE THESE PEOPLE NEEDED ME TO PLAY, AND I PUT IT ON.
TO THINK THAT WAS MY LIFE ONCE. BEFORE HE TOOK IT FROM ME.
I'VE BEEN ACTING OUT SOME FAVORITE MOVIES FOR THE MYRRANS, JUST TO PLAY ANOTHER PART. BUT IT'S
I STILL DON'T UNDERSTAND. HOW COULD BOBO BE RESPONSIBLE FOR ALL OF THIS?
FUNNY YOU PUT IT THAT WAY. RESPONSIBLE. I THINK THE PROBLEM'S JUST THE OPPOSITE...

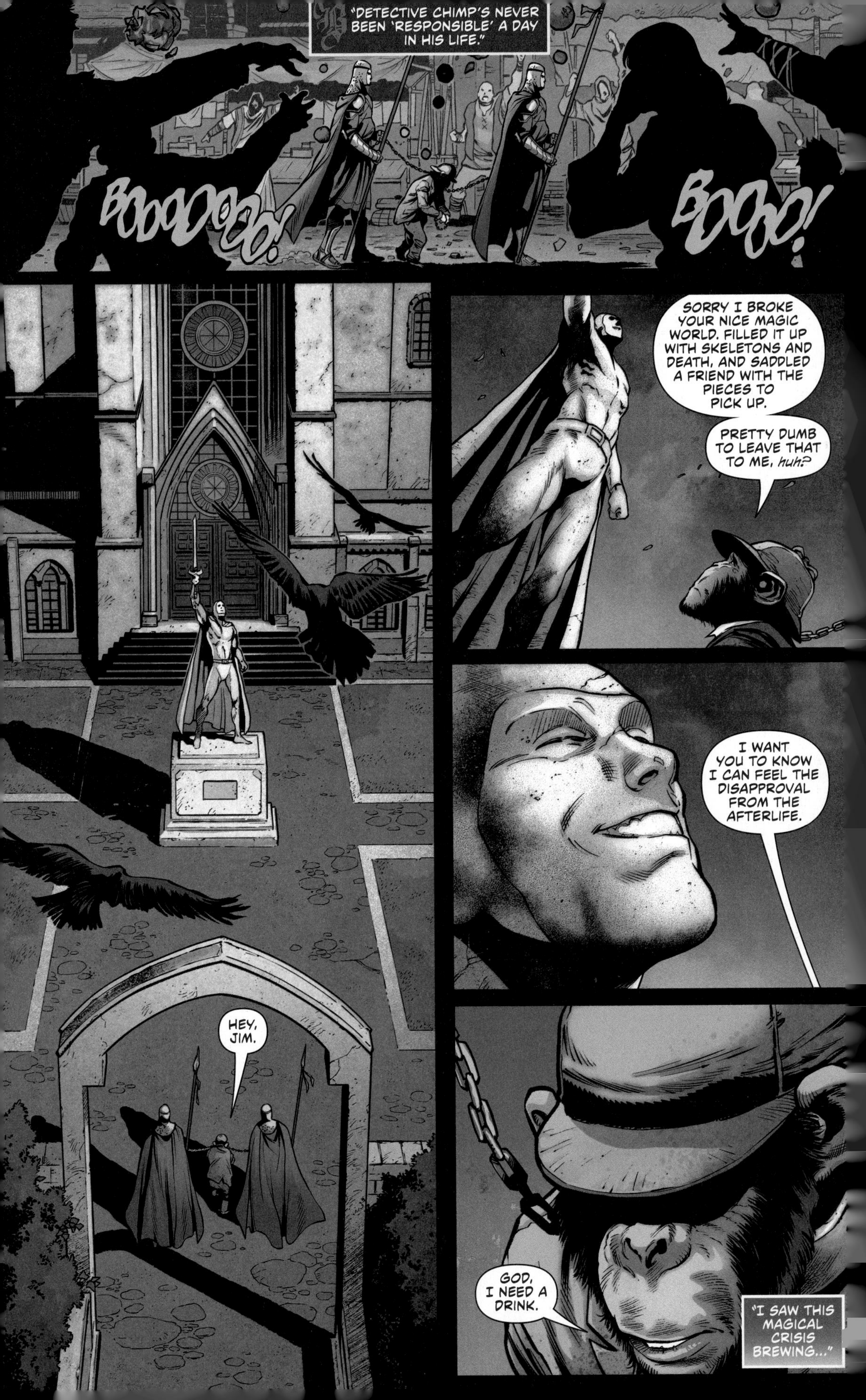
"DETECTIVE CHIMP'S NEVER BEEN 'RESPONSIBLE' A DAY IN HIS LIFE."
BOOOOOOOO!
BOOOO!
SORRY I BROKE YOUR NICE MAGIC WORLD. FILLED IT UP WITH SKELETONS AND DEATH, AND SADDLED A FRIEND WITH THE PIECES TO PICK UP.
PRETTY DUMB TO LEAVE THAT TO ME, huh?
HEY, JIM.
I WANT YOU TO KNOW I CAN FEEL THE DISAPPROVAL FROM THE AFTERLIFE.
GOD, I NEED A DRINK.
"I SAW THIS MAGICAL CRISIS BREWING..."

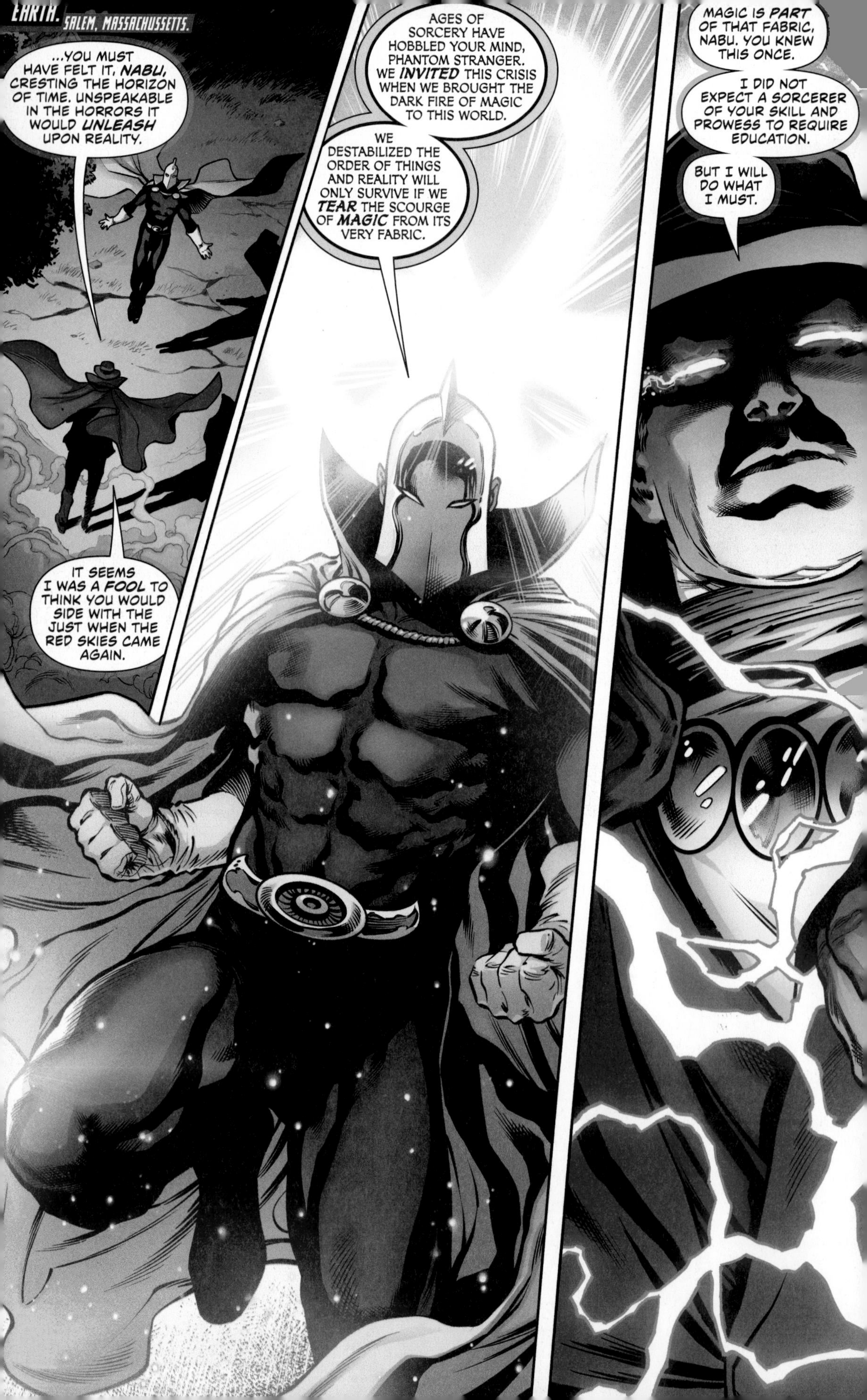
EARTH. SALEM, MASSACHUSSETTS.
...YOU MUST HAVE FELT IT, NABU, CRESTING THE HORIZON OF TIME. UNSPEAKABLE IN THE HORRORS IT WOULD UNLEASH UPON REALITY.
IT SEEMS I WAS A FOOL TO THINK YOU WOULD SIDE WITH THE JUST WHEN THE RED SKIES CAME AGAIN.
AGES OF SORCERY HAVE HOBBLED YOUR MIND, PHANTOM STRANGER. WE INVITED THIS CRISIS WHEN WE BROUGHT THE DARK FIRE OF MAGIC TO THIS WORLD.
WE DESTABILIZED THE ORDER OF THINGS AND REALITY WILL ONLY SURVIVE IF WE TEAR THE SCOURGE OF MAGIC FROM ITS VERY FABRIC.
MAGIC IS PART OF THAT FABRIC, NABU. YOU KNEW THIS ONCE.
I DID NOT EXPECT A SORCERER OF YOUR SKILL AND PROWESS TO REQUIRE EDUCATION.
BUT I WILL DO WHAT I MUST.

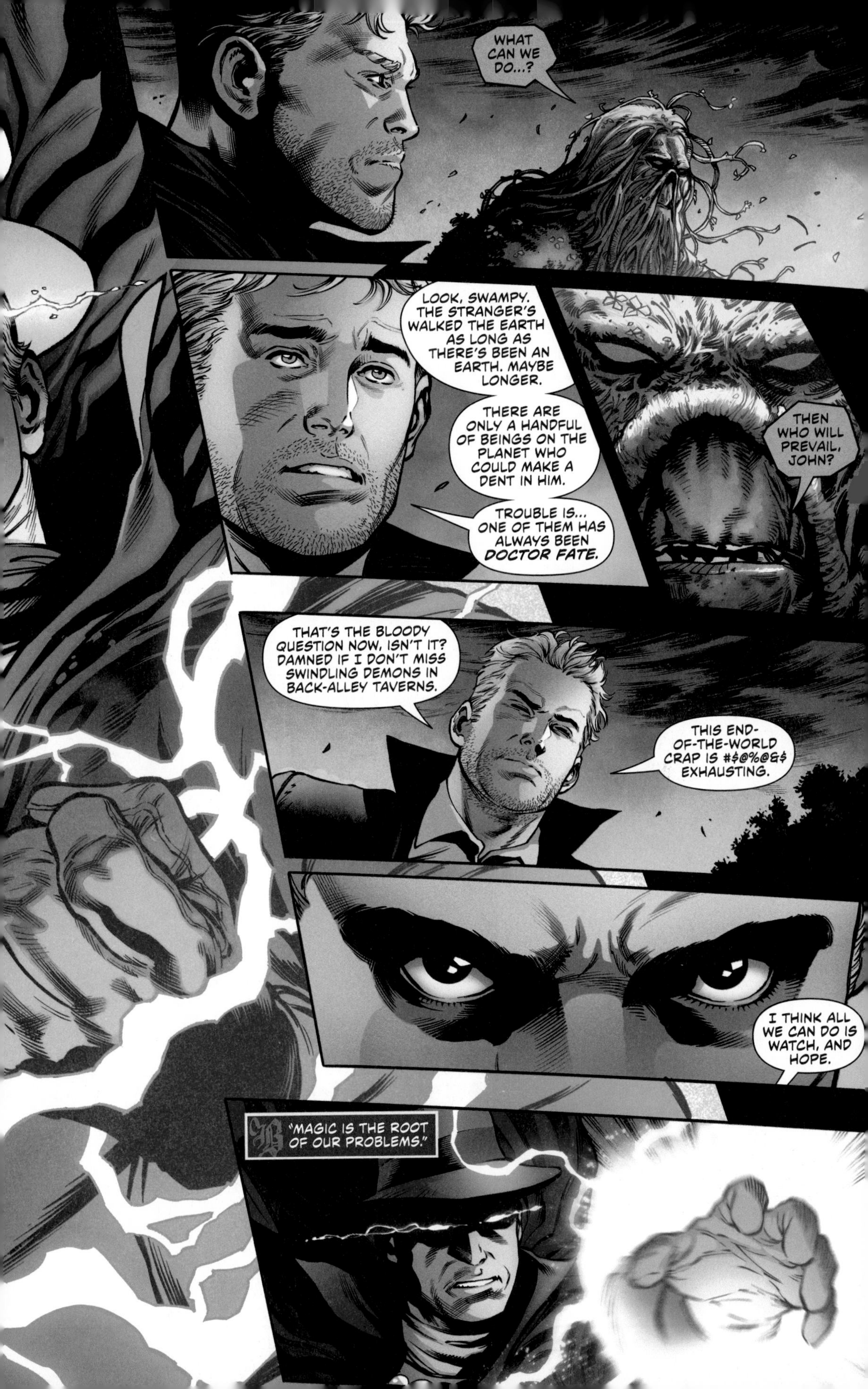
WHAT CAN WE DO...?
LOOK, SWAMPY. THE STRANGER'S WALKED THE EARTH AS LONG AS THERE'S BEEN AN EARTH. MAYBE LONGER.
THERE ARE ONLY A HANDFUL OF BEINGS ON THE PLANET WHO COULD MAKE A DENT IN HIM.
TROUBLE IS... ONE OF THEM HAS ALWAYS BEEN DOCTOR FATE.
THEN WHO WILL PREVAIL, JOHN?
THAT'S THE BLOODY QUESTION NOW, ISN'T IT? DAMNED IF I DON'T MISS SWINDLING DEMONS IN BACK-ALLEY TAVERNS.
THIS END-OF-THE-WORLD CRAP IS #$@%@&$ EXHAUSTING.
I THINK ALL WE CAN DO IS WATCH, AND HOPE.
"MAGIC IS THE ROOT OF OUR PROBLEMS."

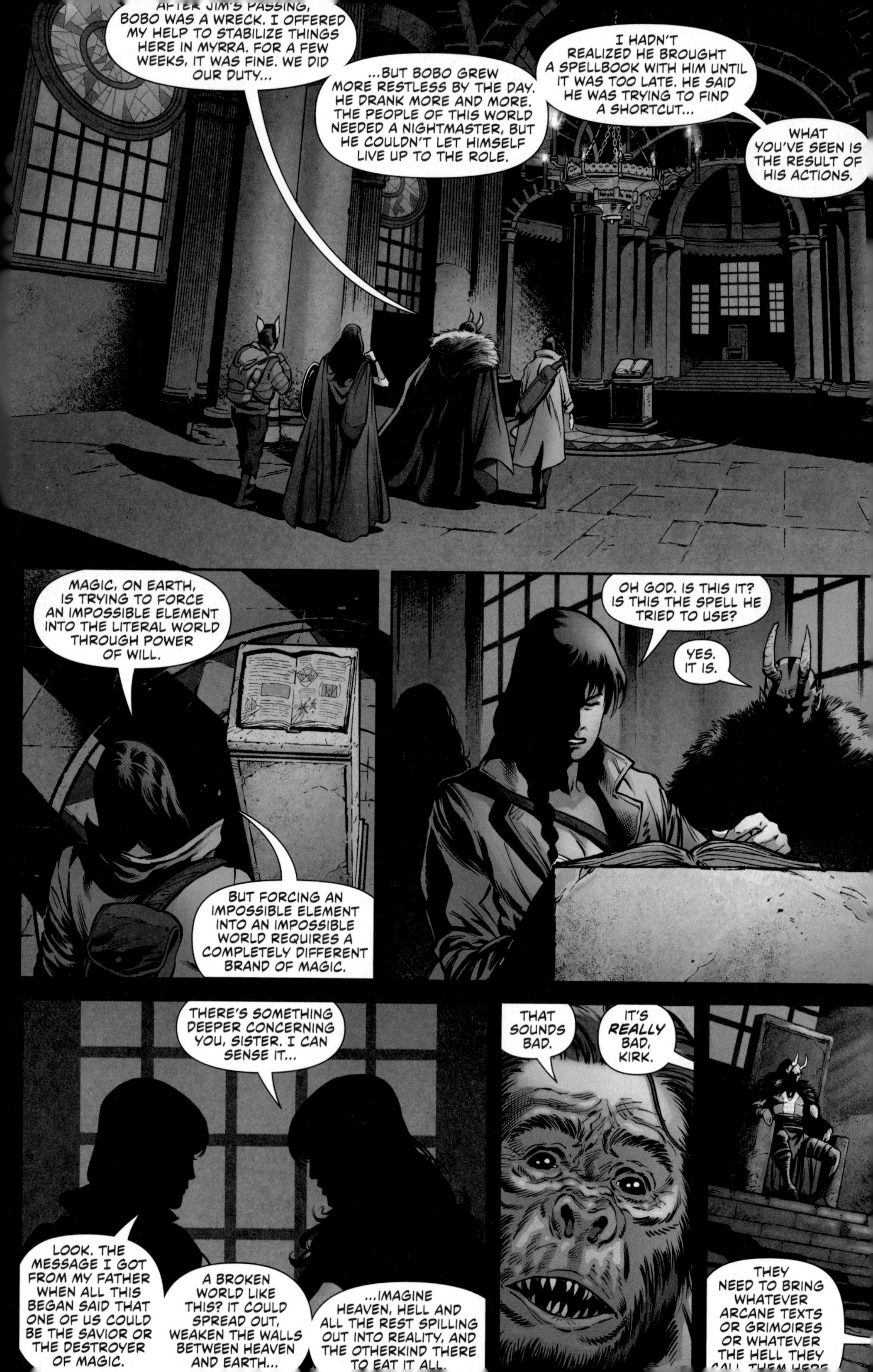
AFTER JIM'S PASSING, BOBO WAS A WRECK. I OFFERED MY HELP TO STABILIZE THINGS HERE IN MYRRA. FOR A FEW WEEKS, IT WAS FINE. WE DID OUR DUTY...
...BUT BOBO GREW MORE RESTLESS BY THE DAY. HE DRANK MORE AND MORE. THE PEOPLE OF THIS WORLD NEEDED A NIGHTMASTER, BUT HE COULDN'T LET HIMSELF LIVE UP TO THE ROLE.
I HADN'T REALIZED HE BROUGHT A SPELLBOOK WITH HIM UNTIL IT WAS TOO LATE. HE SAID HE WAS TRYING TO FIND A SHORTCUT...
WHAT YOU'VE SEEN IS THE RESULT OF HIS ACTIONS.
MAGIC, ON EARTH, IS TRYING TO FORCE AN IMPOSSIBLE ELEMENT INTO THE LITERAL WORLD THROUGH POWER OF WILL.
BUT FORCING AN IMPOSSIBLE ELEMENT INTO AN IMPOSSIBLE WORLD REQUIRES A COMPLETELY DIFFERENT BRAND OF MAGIC.
OH GOD. IS THIS IT? IS THIS THE SPELL HE TRIED TO USE?
YES. IT IS.
THERE'S SOMETHING DEEPER CONCERNING YOU, SISTER. I CAN SENSE IT...
LOOK. THE MESSAGE I GOT FROM MY FATHER WHEN ALL THIS BEGAN SAID THAT ONE OF US COULD BE THE SAVIOR OR THE DESTROYER OF MAGIC.
A BROKEN WORLD LIKE THIS? IT COULD SPREAD OUT, WEAKEN THE WALLS BETWEEN HEAVEN AND EARTH...
...IMAGINE HEAVEN, HELL AND ALL THE REST SPILLING OUT INTO REALITY, AND THE OTHERKIND THERE TO EAT IT ALL.
THAT SOUNDS BAD.
IT'S *REALLY* BAD, KIRK.
THEY NEED TO BRING WHATEVER ARCANE TEXTS OR GRIMOIRES OR WHATEVER THE HELL THEY

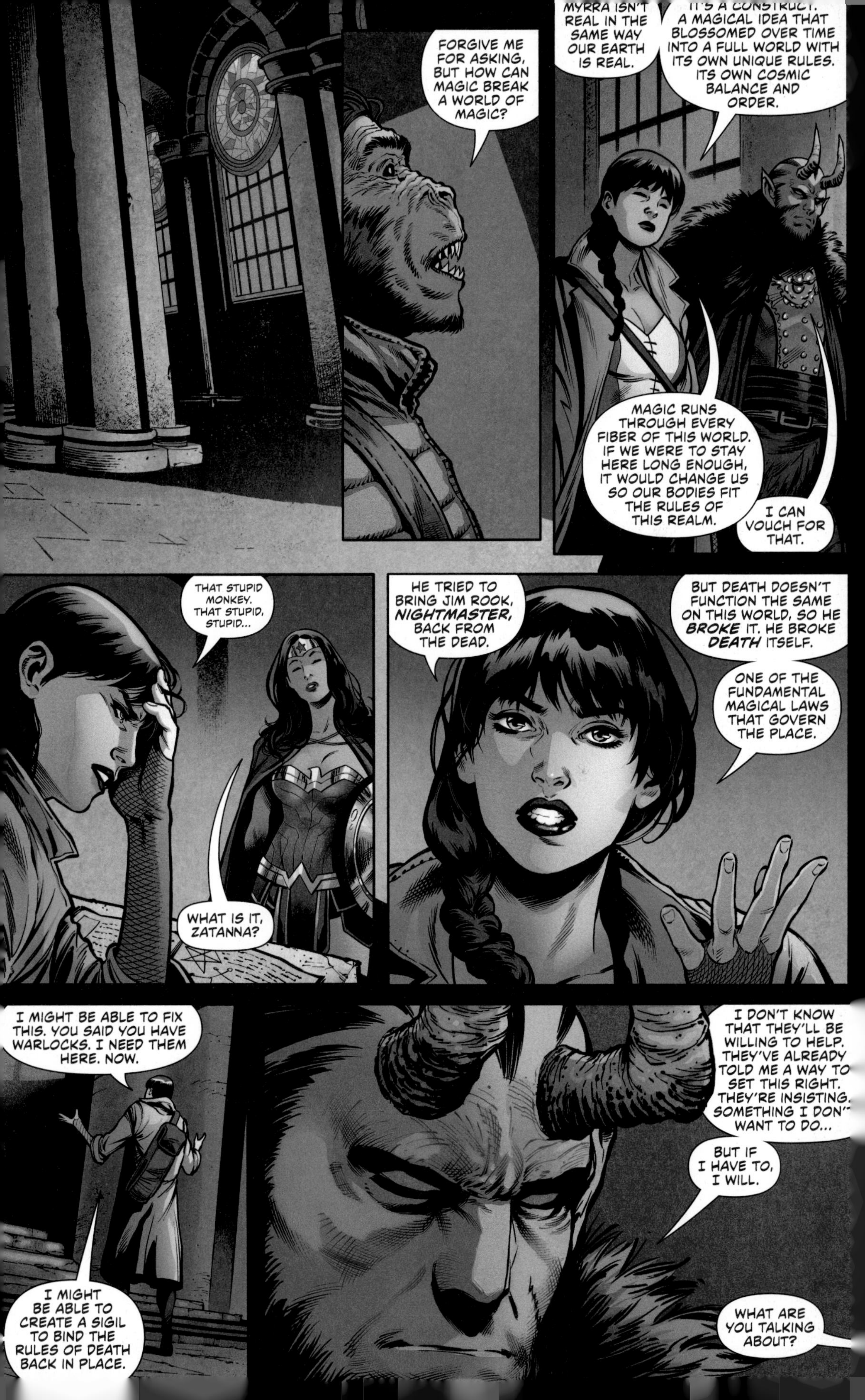
FORGIVE ME FOR ASKING, BUT HOW CAN MAGIC BREAK A WORLD OF MAGIC?
MYRRA ISN'T REAL IN THE SAME WAY OUR EARTH IS REAL.
IT'S A CONSTRUCT. A MAGICAL IDEA THAT BLOSSOMED OVER TIME INTO A FULL WORLD WITH ITS OWN UNIQUE RULES. ITS OWN COSMIC BALANCE AND ORDER.
MAGIC RUNS THROUGH EVERY FIBER OF THIS WORLD. IF WE WERE TO STAY HERE LONG ENOUGH, IT WOULD CHANGE US SO OUR BODIES FIT THE RULES OF THIS REALM.
I CAN VOUCH FOR THAT.
THAT STUPID MONKEY. THAT STUPID, STUPID...
WHAT IS IT, ZATANNA?
HE TRIED TO BRING JIM ROOK, NIGHTMASTER, BACK FROM THE DEAD.
BUT DEATH DOESN'T FUNCTION THE SAME ON THIS WORLD, SO HE BROKE IT. HE BROKE DEATH ITSELF.
ONE OF THE FUNDAMENTAL MAGICAL LAWS THAT GOVERN THE PLACE.
I MIGHT BE ABLE TO FIX THIS. YOU SAID YOU HAVE WARLOCKS. I NEED THEM HERE. NOW.
I MIGHT BE ABLE TO CREATE A SIGIL TO BIND THE RULES OF DEATH BACK IN PLACE.
I DON'T KNOW THAT THEY'LL BE WILLING TO HELP. THEY'VE ALREADY TOLD ME A WAY TO SET THIS RIGHT. THEY'RE INSISTING. SOMETHING I DON'T WANT TO DO...
BUT IF I HAVE TO, I WILL.
WHAT ARE YOU TALKING ABOUT?

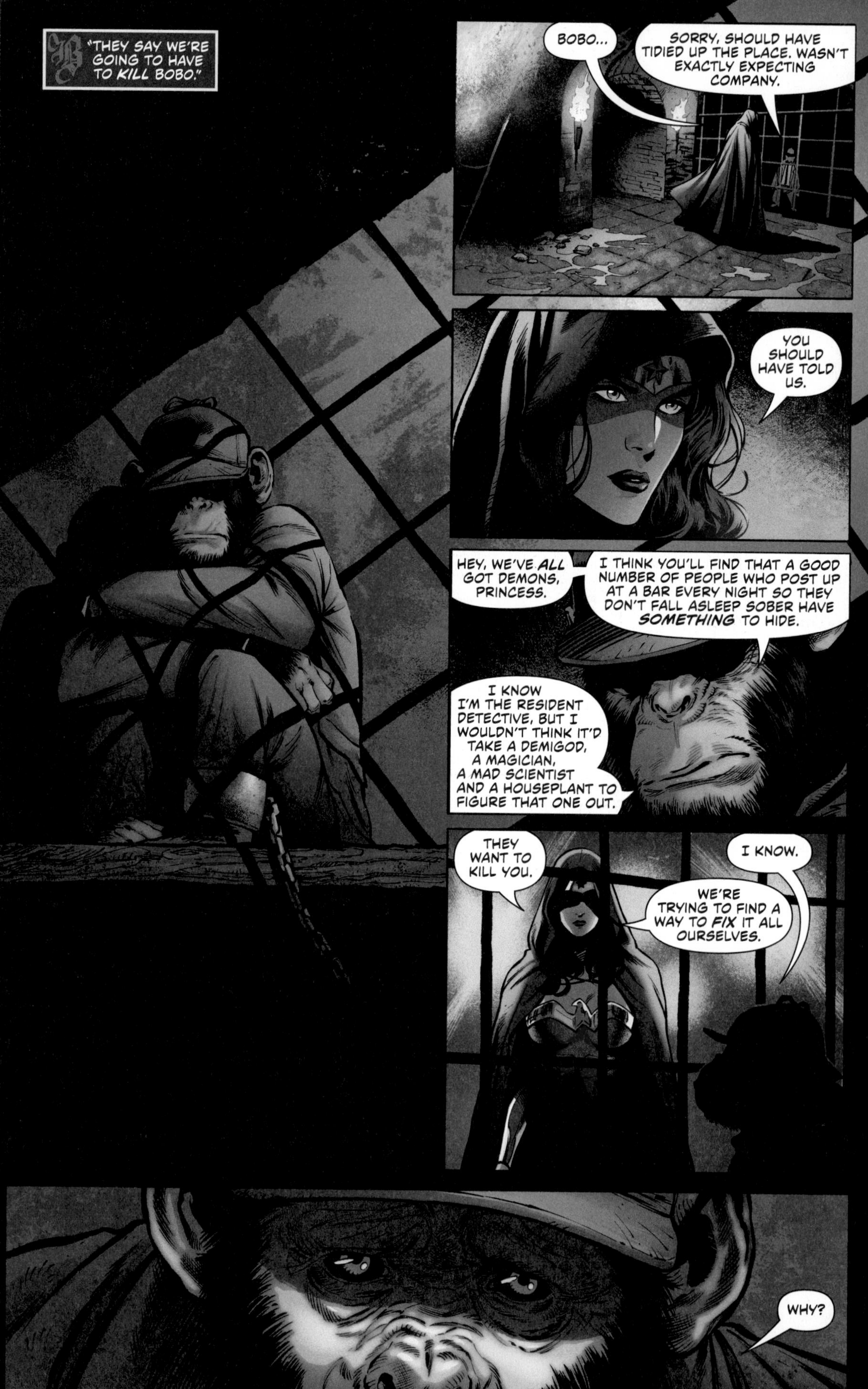
"THEY SAY WE'RE GOING TO HAVE TO KILL BOBO."
BOBO...
SORRY, SHOULD HAVE TIDIED UP THE PLACE. WASN'T EXACTLY EXPECTING COMPANY.
YOU SHOULD HAVE TOLD US.
HEY, WE'VE ALL GOT DEMONS, PRINCESS.
I THINK YOU'LL FIND THAT A GOOD NUMBER OF PEOPLE WHO POST UP AT A BAR EVERY NIGHT SO THEY DON'T FALL ASLEEP SOBER HAVE SOMETHING TO HIDE.
I KNOW I'M THE RESIDENT DETECTIVE, BUT I WOULDN'T THINK IT'D TAKE A DEMIGOD, A MAGICIAN, A MAD SCIENTIST AND A HOUSEPLANT TO FIGURE THAT ONE OUT.
THEY WANT TO KILL YOU.
I KNOW.
WE'RE TRYING TO FIND A WAY TO FIX IT ALL OURSELVES.
WHY?

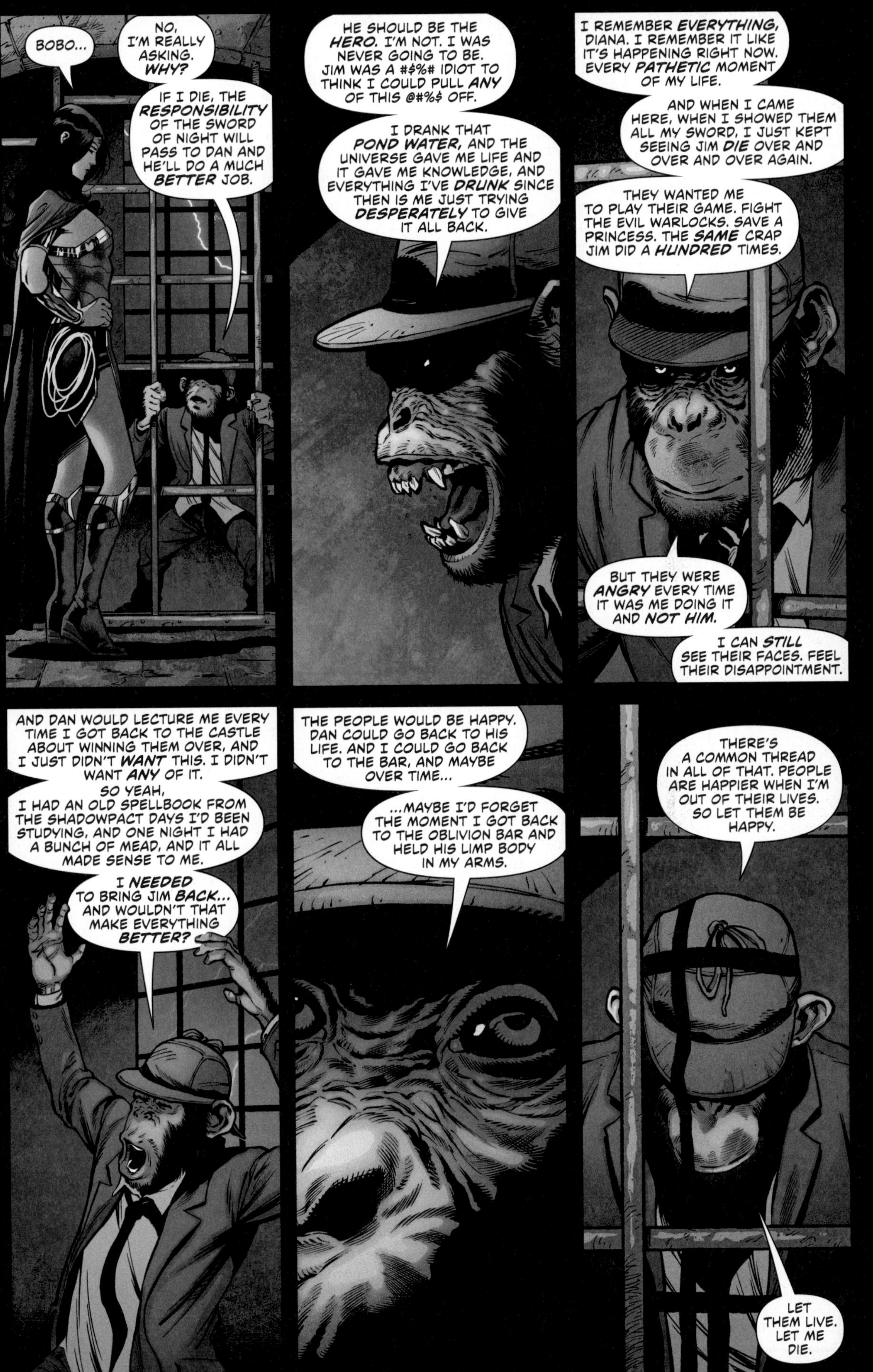
BOBO...
NO, I'M REALLY ASKING. WHY?
IF I DIE, THE RESPONSIBILITY OF THE SWORD OF NIGHT WILL PASS TO DAN AND HE'LL DO A MUCH BETTER JOB.
HE SHOULD BE THE HERO. I'M NOT. I WAS NEVER GOING TO BE. JIM WAS A #$%# IDIOT TO THINK I COULD PULL ANY OF THIS @#%$ OFF.
I DRANK THAT POND WATER, AND THE UNIVERSE GAVE ME LIFE AND IT GAVE ME KNOWLEDGE, AND EVERYTHING I'VE DRUNK SINCE THEN IS ME JUST TRYING DESPERATELY TO GIVE IT ALL BACK.
I REMEMBER EVERYTHING, DIANA. I REMEMBER IT LIKE IT'S HAPPENING RIGHT NOW. EVERY PATHETIC MOMENT OF MY LIFE.
AND WHEN I CAME HERE, WHEN I SHOWED THEM ALL MY SWORD, I JUST KEPT SEEING JIM DIE OVER AND OVER AND OVER AGAIN.
THEY WANTED ME TO PLAY THEIR GAME. FIGHT THE EVIL WARLOCKS. SAVE A PRINCESS. THE SAME CRAP JIM DID A HUNDRED TIMES.
BUT THEY WERE ANGRY EVERY TIME IT WAS ME DOING IT AND NOT HIM.
I CAN STILL SEE THEIR FACES. FEEL THEIR DISAPPOINTMENT.
AND DAN WOULD LECTURE ME EVERY TIME I GOT BACK TO THE CASTLE ABOUT WINNING THEM OVER, AND I JUST DIDN'T WANT THIS. I DIDN'T WANT ANY OF IT.
SO YEAH, I HAD AN OLD SPELLBOOK FROM THE SHADOWPACT DAYS I'D BEEN STUDYING, AND ONE NIGHT I HAD A BUNCH OF MEAD, AND IT ALL MADE SENSE TO ME.
I NEEDED TO BRING JIM BACK... AND WOULDN'T THAT MAKE EVERYTHING BETTER?
THE PEOPLE WOULD BE HAPPY. DAN COULD GO BACK TO HIS LIFE. AND I COULD GO BACK TO THE BAR, AND MAYBE OVER TIME...
...MAYBE I'D FORGET THE MOMENT I GOT BACK TO THE OBLIVION BAR AND HELD HIS LIMP BODY IN MY ARMS.
THERE'S A COMMON THREAD IN ALL OF THAT. PEOPLE ARE HAPPIER WHEN I'M OUT OF THEIR LIVES. SO LET THEM BE HAPPY.
LET THEM LIVE. LET ME DIE.

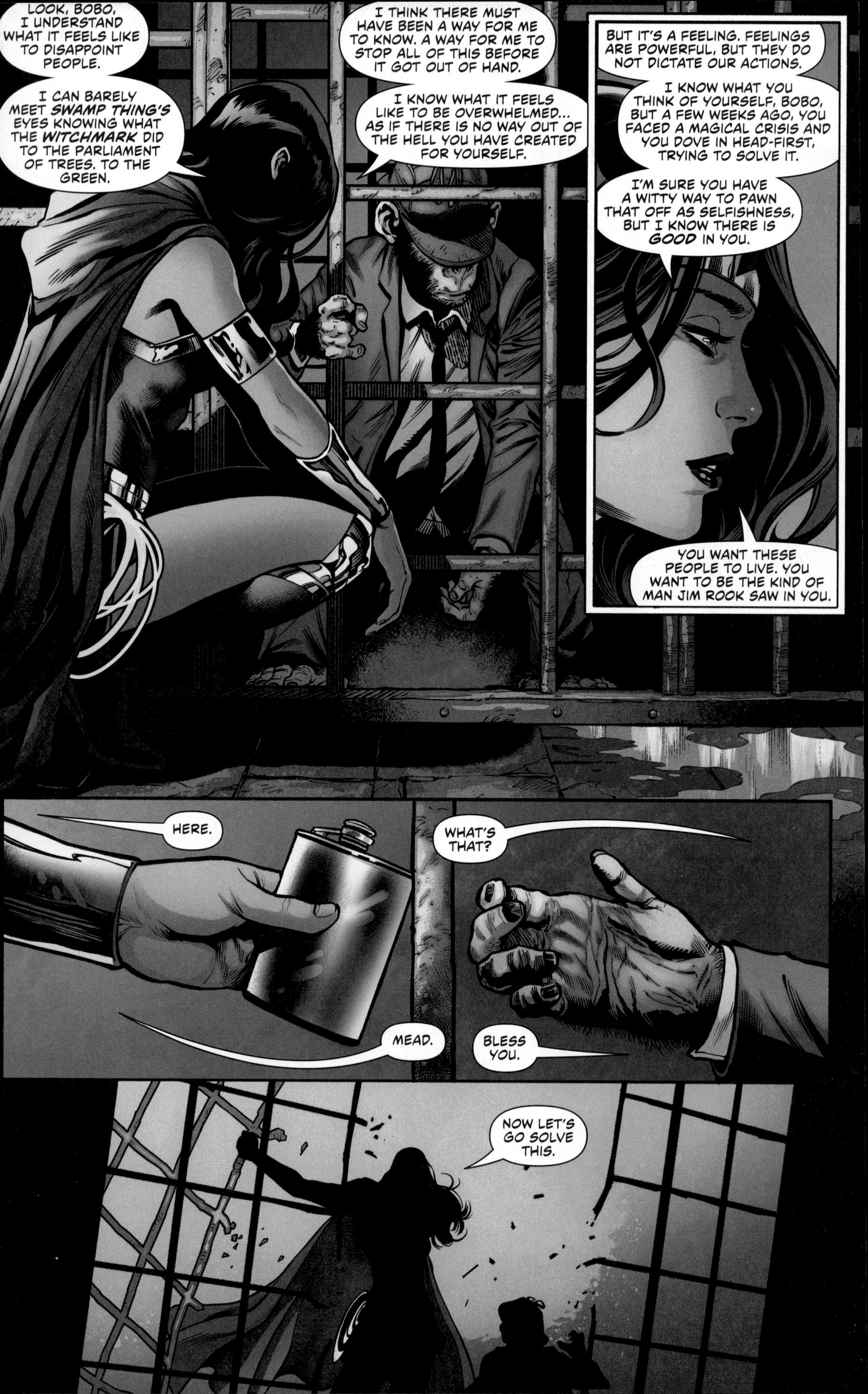
LOOK, BOBO, I UNDERSTAND WHAT IT FEELS LIKE TO DISAPPOINT PEOPLE.
I CAN BARELY MEET SWAMP THING'S EYES KNOWING WHAT THE WITCHMARK DID TO THE PARLIAMENT OF TREES. TO THE GREEN.
I THINK THERE MUST HAVE BEEN A WAY FOR ME TO KNOW. A WAY FOR ME TO STOP ALL OF THIS BEFORE IT GOT OUT OF HAND.
I KNOW WHAT IT FEELS LIKE TO BE OVERWHELMED... AS IF THERE IS NO WAY OUT OF THE HELL YOU HAVE CREATED FOR YOURSELF.
BUT IT'S A FEELING. FEELINGS ARE POWERFUL, BUT THEY DO NOT DICTATE OUR ACTIONS.
I KNOW WHAT YOU THINK OF YOURSELF, BOBO, BUT A FEW WEEKS AGO, YOU FACED A MAGICAL CRISIS AND YOU DOVE IN HEAD-FIRST, TRYING TO SOLVE IT.
I'M SURE YOU HAVE A WITTY WAY TO PAWN THAT OFF AS SELFISHNESS, BUT I KNOW THERE IS GOOD IN YOU.
YOU WANT THESE PEOPLE TO LIVE. YOU WANT TO BE THE KIND OF MAN JIM ROOK SAW IN YOU.
HERE.
MEAD.
WHAT'S THAT?
BLESS YOU.
NOW LET'S GO SOLVE THIS.

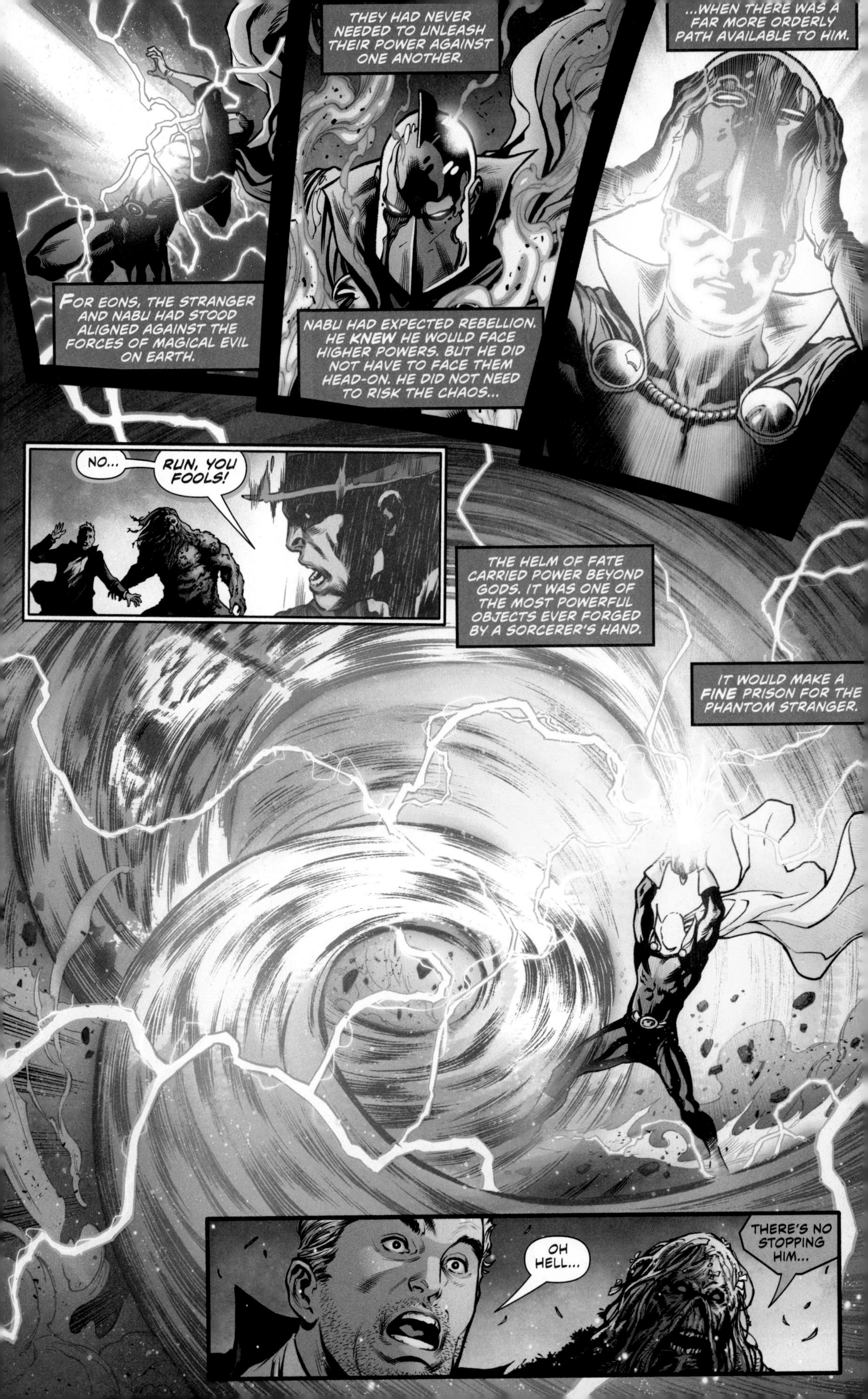
FOR EONS, THE STRANGER AND NABU HAD STOOD ALIGNED AGAINST THE FORCES OF MAGICAL EVIL ON EARTH.
THEY HAD NEVER NEEDED TO UNLEASH THEIR POWER AGAINST ONE ANOTHER.
NABU HAD EXPECTED REBELLION. HE KNEW HE WOULD FACE HIGHER POWERS. BUT HE DID NOT HAVE TO FACE THEM HEAD-ON. HE DID NOT NEED TO RISK THE CHAOS...
...WHEN THERE WAS A FAR MORE ORDERLY PATH AVAILABLE TO HIM.
NO...
RUN, YOU FOOLS!
THE HELM OF FATE CARRIED POWER BEYOND GODS. IT WAS ONE OF THE MOST POWERFUL OBJECTS EVER FORGED BY A SORCERER'S HAND.
IT WOULD MAKE A FINE PRISON FOR THE PHANTOM STRANGER.
OH HELL...
THERE'S NO STOPPING HIM...

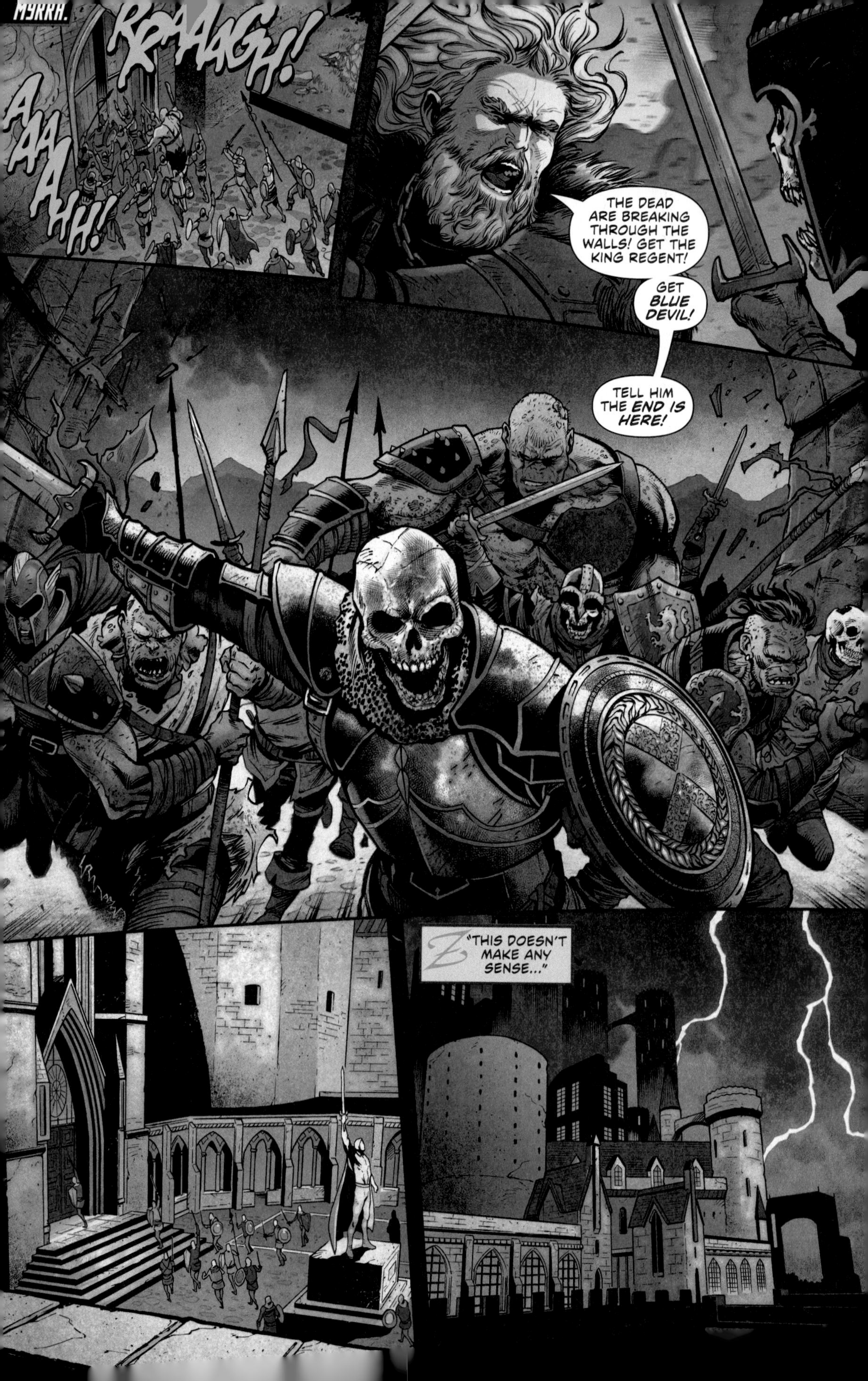
MYRRA.
RRAAAGH!
AAAAHH!
THE DEAD ARE BREAKING THROUGH THE WALLS! GET THE KING REGENT!
GET BLUE DEVIL!
TELL HIM THE END IS HERE!
"THIS DOESN'T MAKE ANY SENSE..."

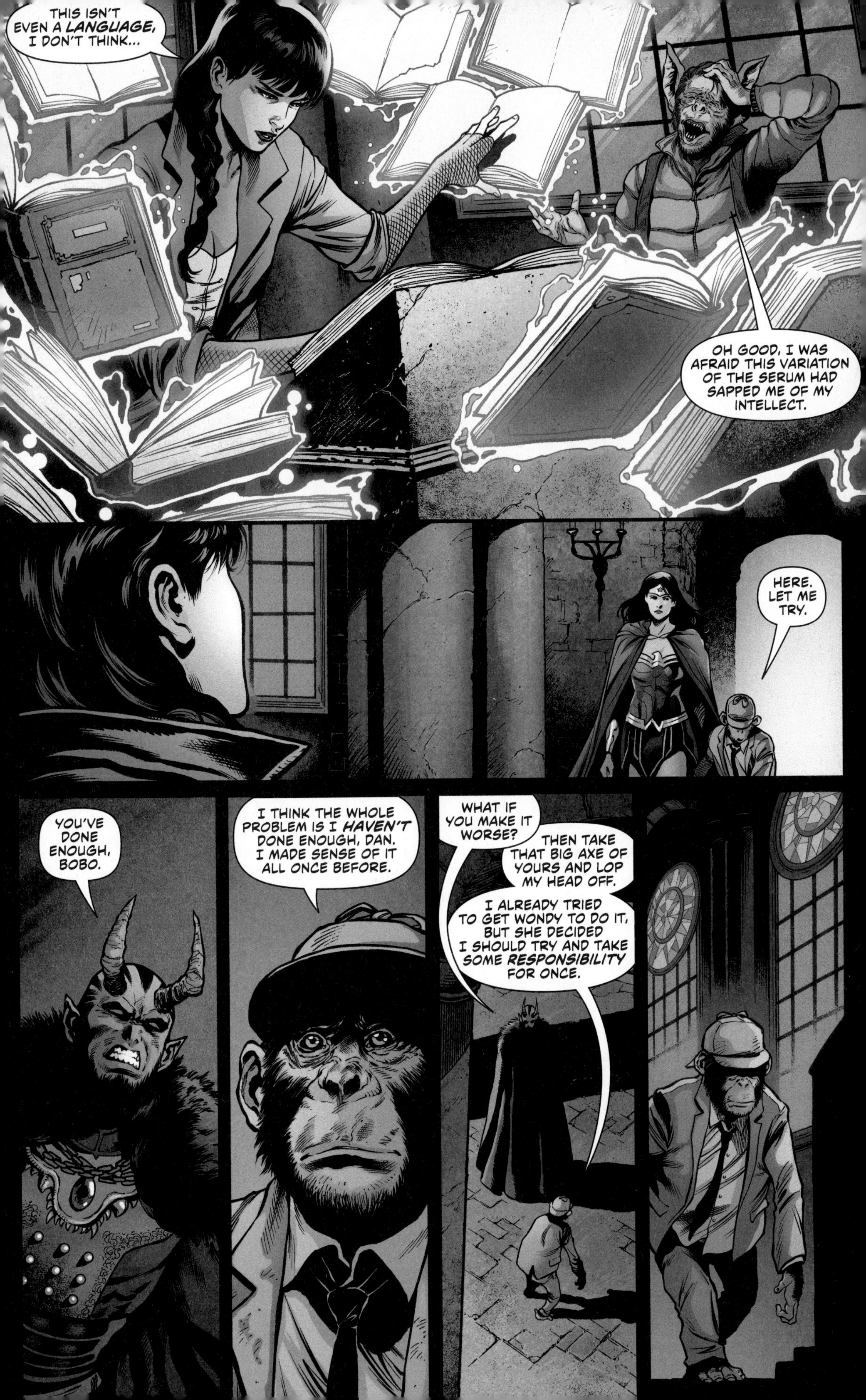
THIS ISN'T EVEN A LANGUAGE, I DON'T THINK...
OH GOOD, I WAS AFRAID THIS VARIATION OF THE SERUM HAD SAPPED ME OF MY INTELLECT.
HERE. LET ME TRY.
YOU'VE DONE ENOUGH, BOBO.
I THINK THE WHOLE PROBLEM IS I HAVEN'T DONE ENOUGH, DAN. I MADE SENSE OF IT ALL ONCE BEFORE.
WHAT IF YOU MAKE IT WORSE?
THEN TAKE THAT BIG AXE OF YOURS AND LOP MY HEAD OFF.
I ALREADY TRIED TO GET WONDY TO DO IT, BUT SHE DECIDED I SHOULD TRY AND TAKE SOME RESPONSIBILITY FOR ONCE.

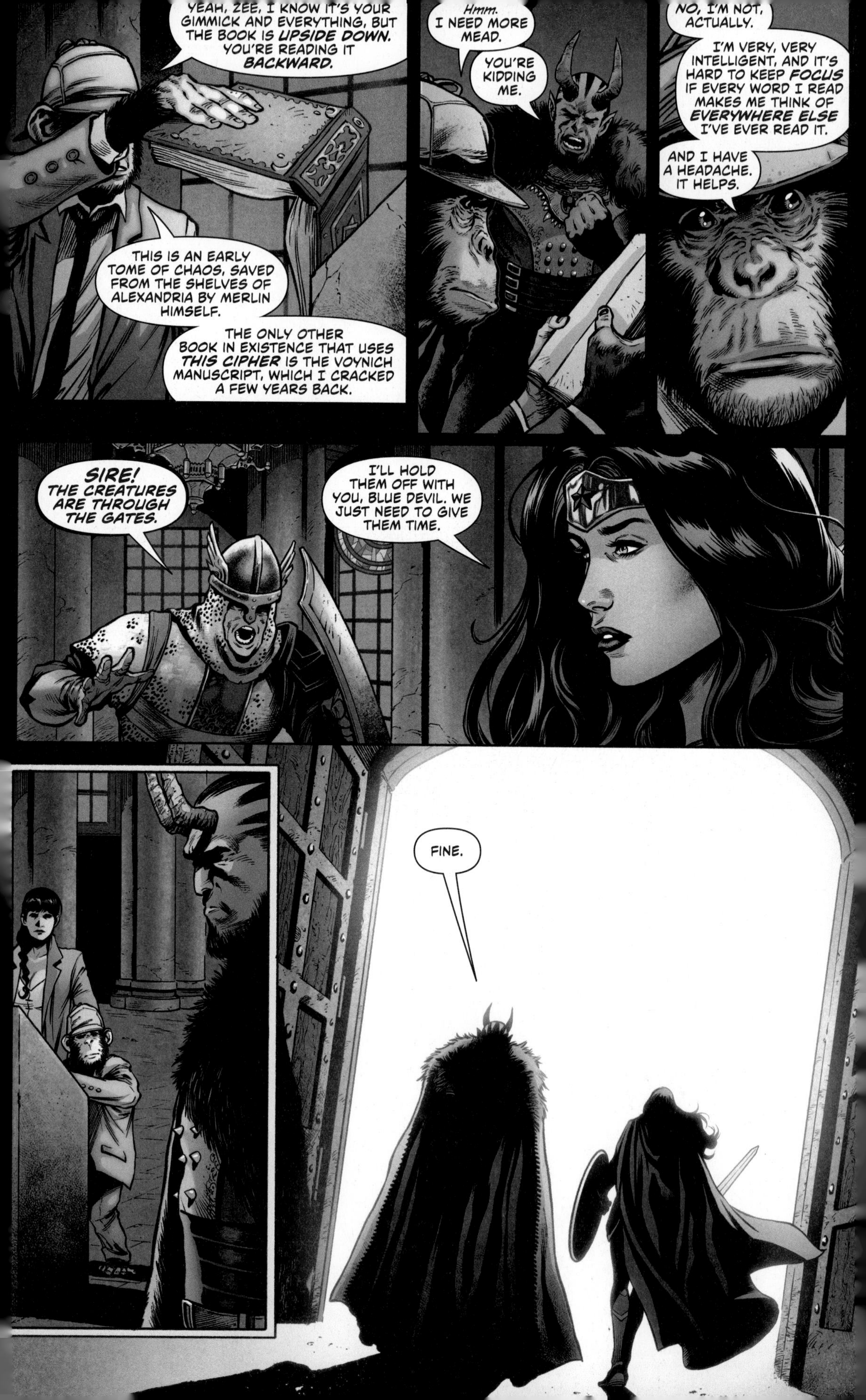
YEAH, ZEE, I KNOW IT'S YOUR GIMMICK AND EVERYTHING, BUT THE BOOK IS UPSIDE DOWN. YOU'RE READING IT BACKWARD.
THIS IS AN EARLY TOME OF CHAOS, SAVED FROM THE SHELVES OF ALEXANDRIA BY MERLIN HIMSELF.
THE ONLY OTHER BOOK IN EXISTENCE THAT USES THIS CIPHER IS THE VOYNICH MANUSCRIPT, WHICH I CRACKED A FEW YEARS BACK.
Hmm. I NEED MORE MEAD.
YOU'RE KIDDING ME.
NO, I'M NOT, ACTUALLY.
I'M VERY, VERY INTELLIGENT, AND IT'S HARD TO KEEP FOCUS IF EVERY WORD I READ MAKES ME THINK OF EVERYWHERE ELSE I'VE EVER READ IT.
AND I HAVE A HEADACHE. IT HELPS.
SIRE! THE CREATURES ARE THROUGH THE GATES.
I'LL HOLD THEM OFF WITH YOU, BLUE DEVIL. WE JUST NEED TO GIVE THEM TIME.
FINE.

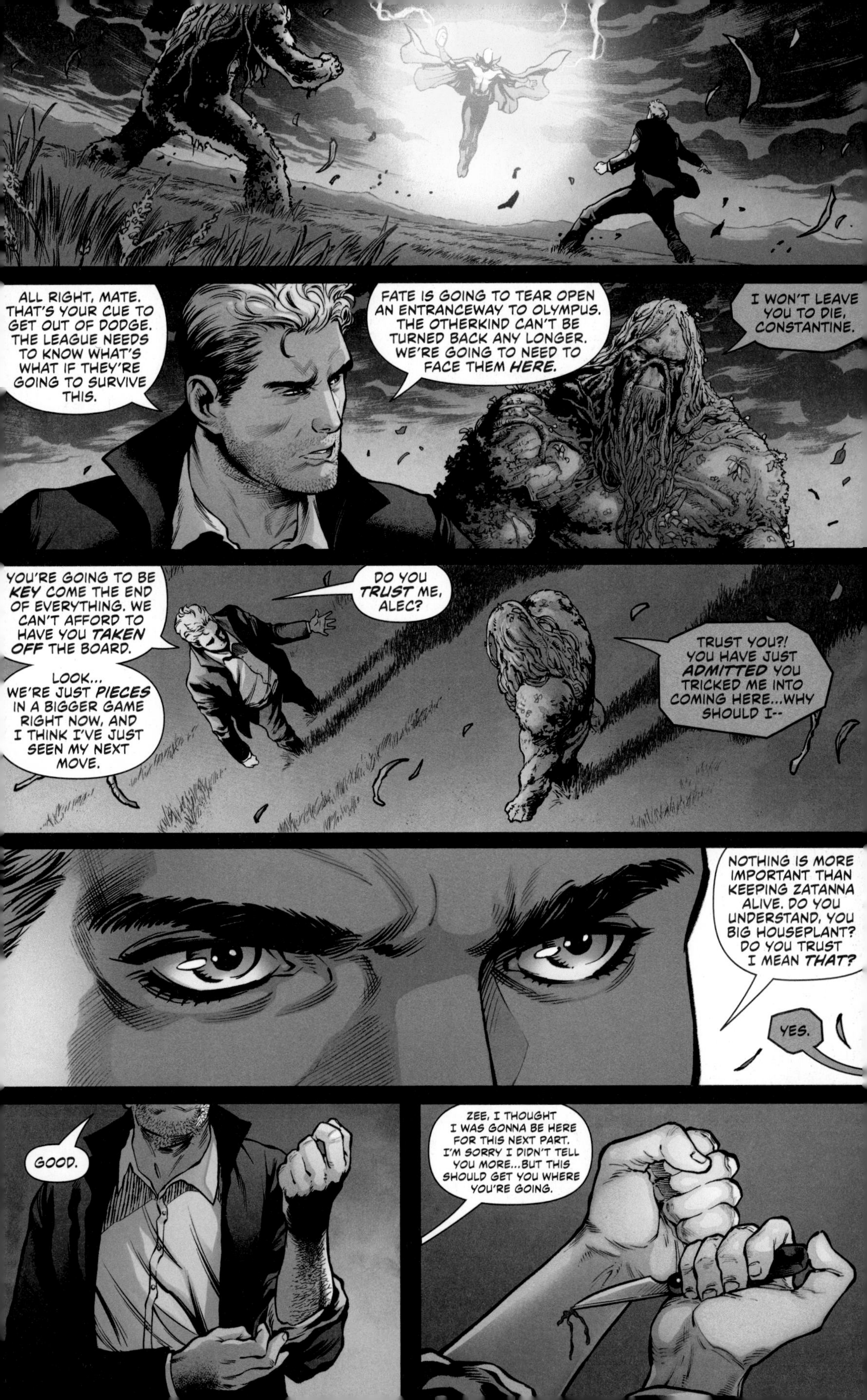
ALL RIGHT, MATE. THAT'S YOUR CUE TO GET OUT OF DODGE. THE LEAGUE NEEDS TO KNOW WHAT'S WHAT IF THEY'RE GOING TO SURVIVE THIS.
FATE IS GOING TO TEAR OPEN AN ENTRANCEWAY TO OLYMPUS. THE OTHERKIND CAN'T BE TURNED BACK ANY LONGER. WE'RE GOING TO NEED TO FACE THEM ***HERE.***
I WON'T LEAVE YOU TO DIE, CONSTANTINE.
YOU'RE GOING TO BE ***KEY*** COME THE END OF EVERYTHING. WE CAN'T AFFORD TO HAVE YOU ***TAKEN OFF*** THE BOARD.
LOOK... WE'RE JUST ***PIECES*** IN A BIGGER GAME RIGHT NOW, AND I THINK I'VE JUST SEEN MY NEXT MOVE.
DO YOU ***TRUST*** ME, ALEC?
TRUST YOU?! YOU HAVE JUST ***ADMITTED*** YOU TRICKED ME INTO COMING HERE...WHY SHOULD I--
NOTHING IS MORE IMPORTANT THAN KEEPING ZATANNA ALIVE. DO YOU UNDERSTAND, YOU BIG HOUSEPLANT? DO YOU TRUST I MEAN ***THAT?***
YES.
GOOD.
ZEE, I THOUGHT I WAS GONNA BE HERE FOR THIS NEXT PART. I'M SORRY I DIDN'T TELL YOU MORE...BUT THIS SHOULD GET YOU WHERE YOU'RE GOING.

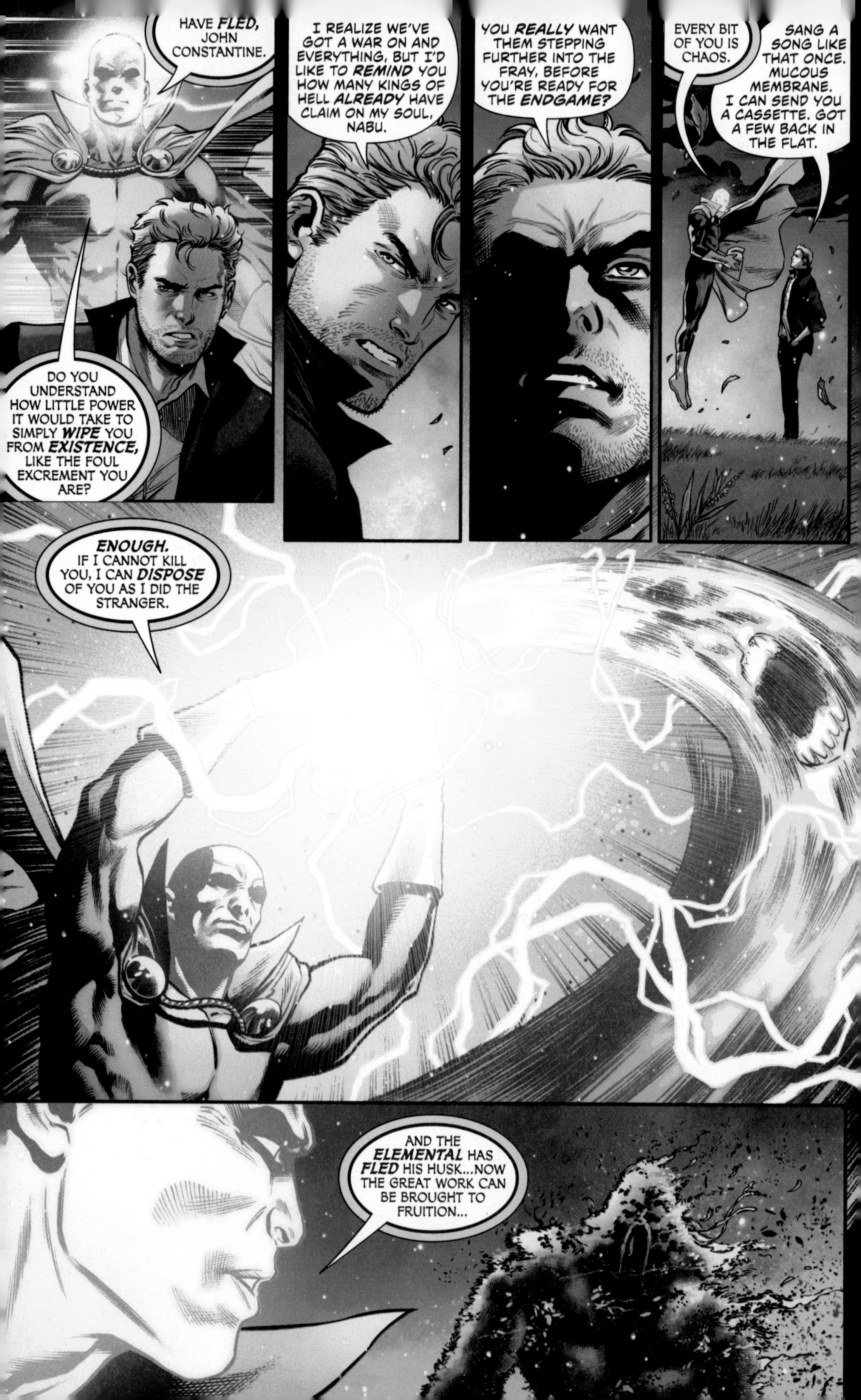
HAVE FLED, JOHN CONSTANTINE.
DO YOU UNDERSTAND HOW LITTLE POWER IT WOULD TAKE TO SIMPLY WIPE YOU FROM EXISTENCE, LIKE THE FOUL EXCREMENT YOU ARE?
I REALIZE WE'VE GOT A WAR ON AND EVERYTHING, BUT I'D LIKE TO REMIND YOU HOW MANY KINGS OF HELL ALREADY HAVE CLAIM ON MY SOUL, NABU.
YOU REALLY WANT THEM STEPPING FURTHER INTO THE FRAY, BEFORE YOU'RE READY FOR THE ENDGAME?
EVERY BIT OF YOU IS CHAOS.
SANG A SONG LIKE THAT ONCE. MUCOUS MEMBRANE. I CAN SEND YOU A CASSETTE. GOT A FEW BACK IN THE FLAT.
ENOUGH. IF I CANNOT KILL YOU, I CAN DISPOSE OF YOU AS I DID THE STRANGER.
AND THE ELEMENTAL HAS FLED HIS HUSK...NOW THE GREAT WORK CAN BE BROUGHT TO FRUITION...

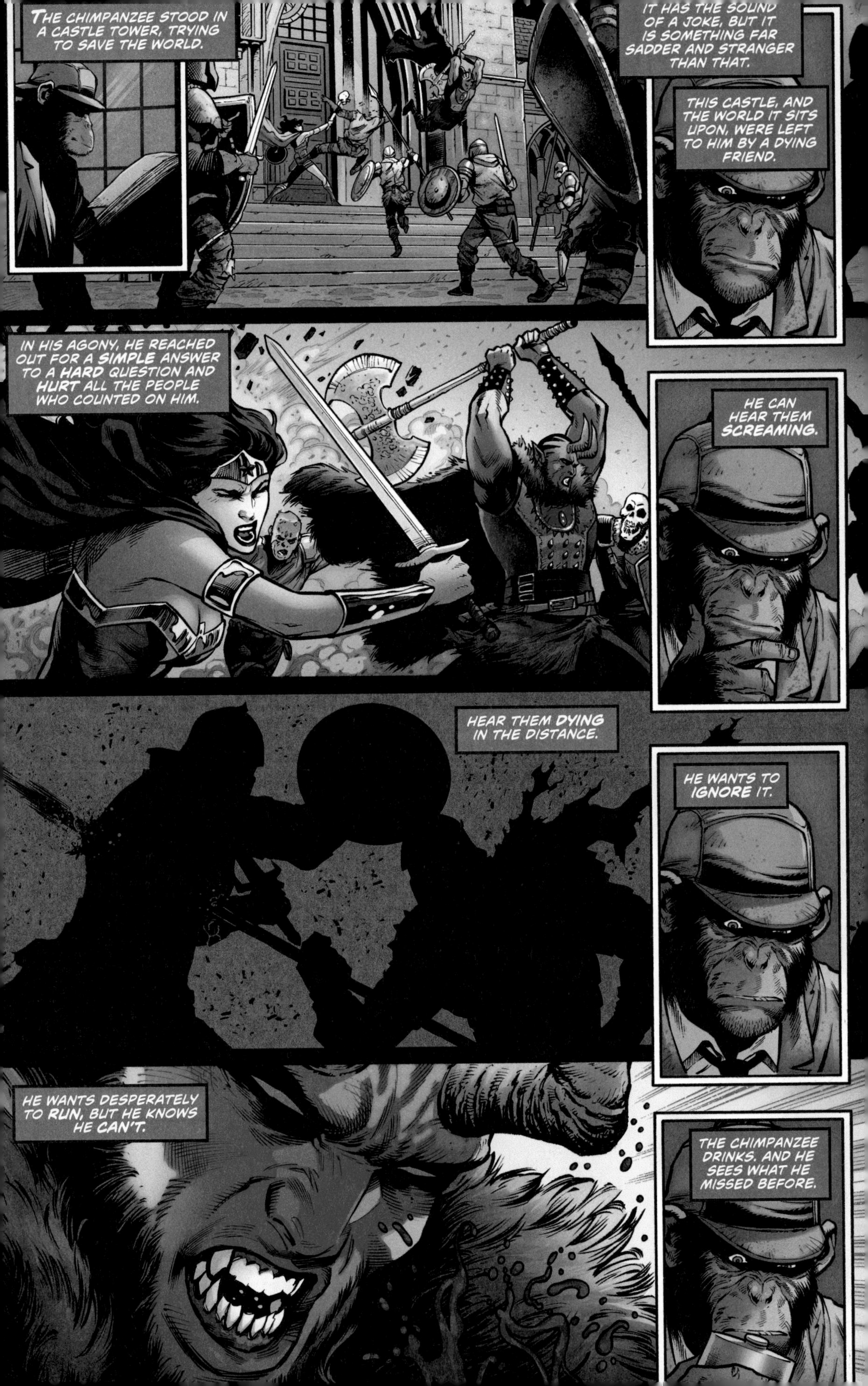
THE CHIMPANZEE STOOD IN A CASTLE TOWER, TRYING TO SAVE THE WORLD.
IT HAS THE SOUND OF A JOKE, BUT IT IS SOMETHING FAR SADDER AND STRANGER THAN THAT.
THIS CASTLE, AND THE WORLD IT SITS UPON, WERE LEFT TO HIM BY A DYING FRIEND.
IN HIS AGONY, HE REACHED OUT FOR A SIMPLE ANSWER TO A HARD QUESTION AND HURT ALL THE PEOPLE WHO COUNTED ON HIM.
HE CAN HEAR THEM SCREAMING.
HEAR THEM DYING IN THE DISTANCE.
HE WANTS TO IGNORE IT.
HE WANTS DESPERATELY TO RUN, BUT HE KNOWS HE CAN'T.
THE CHIMPANZEE DRINKS. AND HE SEES WHAT HE MISSED BEFORE.

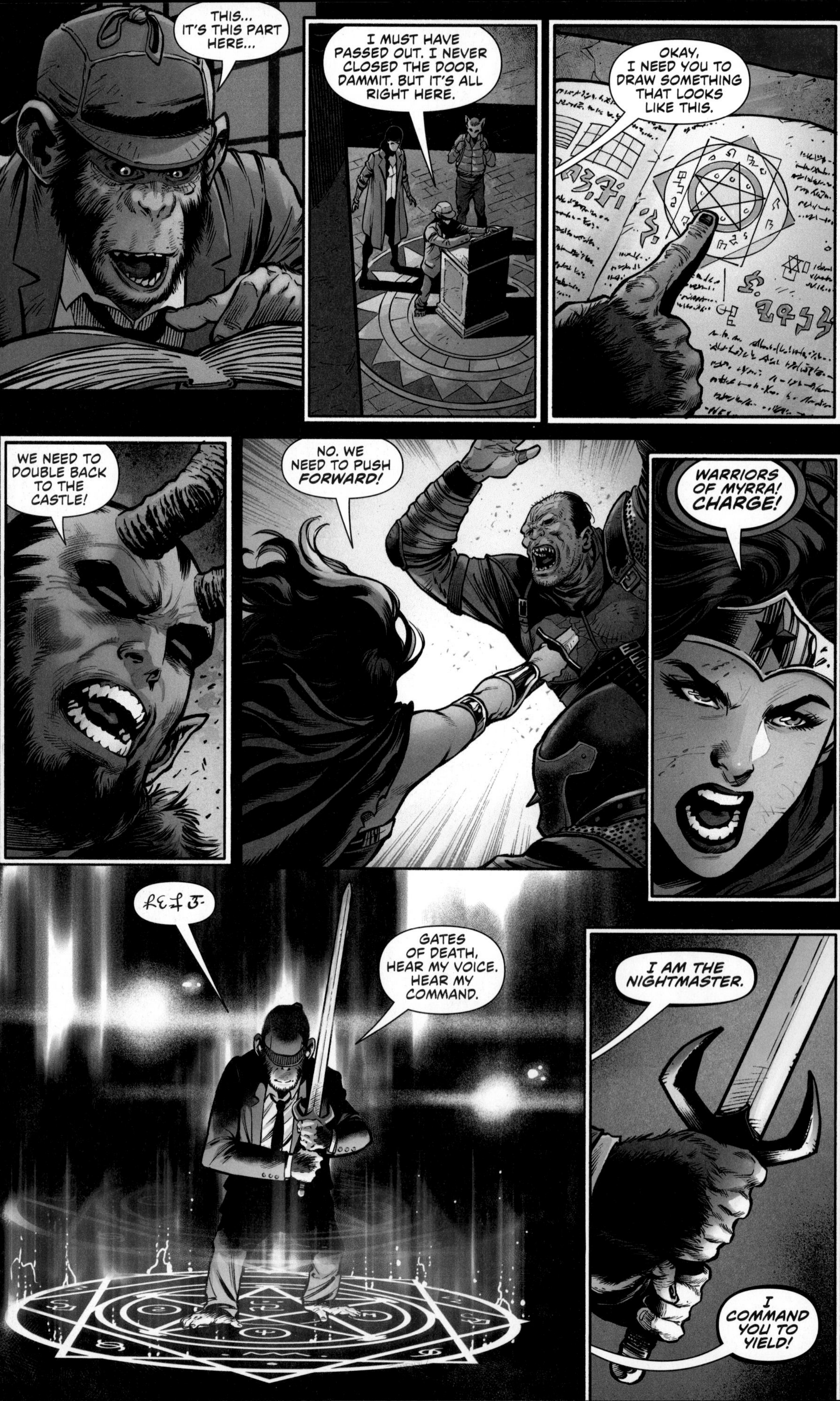
THIS... IT'S THIS PART HERE...
I MUST HAVE PASSED OUT. I NEVER CLOSED THE DOOR, DAMMIT. BUT IT'S ALL RIGHT HERE.
OKAY, I NEED YOU TO DRAW SOMETHING THAT LOOKS LIKE THIS.
WE NEED TO DOUBLE BACK TO THE CASTLE!
NO. WE NEED TO PUSH FORWARD!
WARRIORS OF MYRRA! CHARGE!
GATES OF DEATH, HEAR MY VOICE. HEAR MY COMMAND.
I AM THE NIGHTMASTER.
I COMMAND YOU TO YIELD!

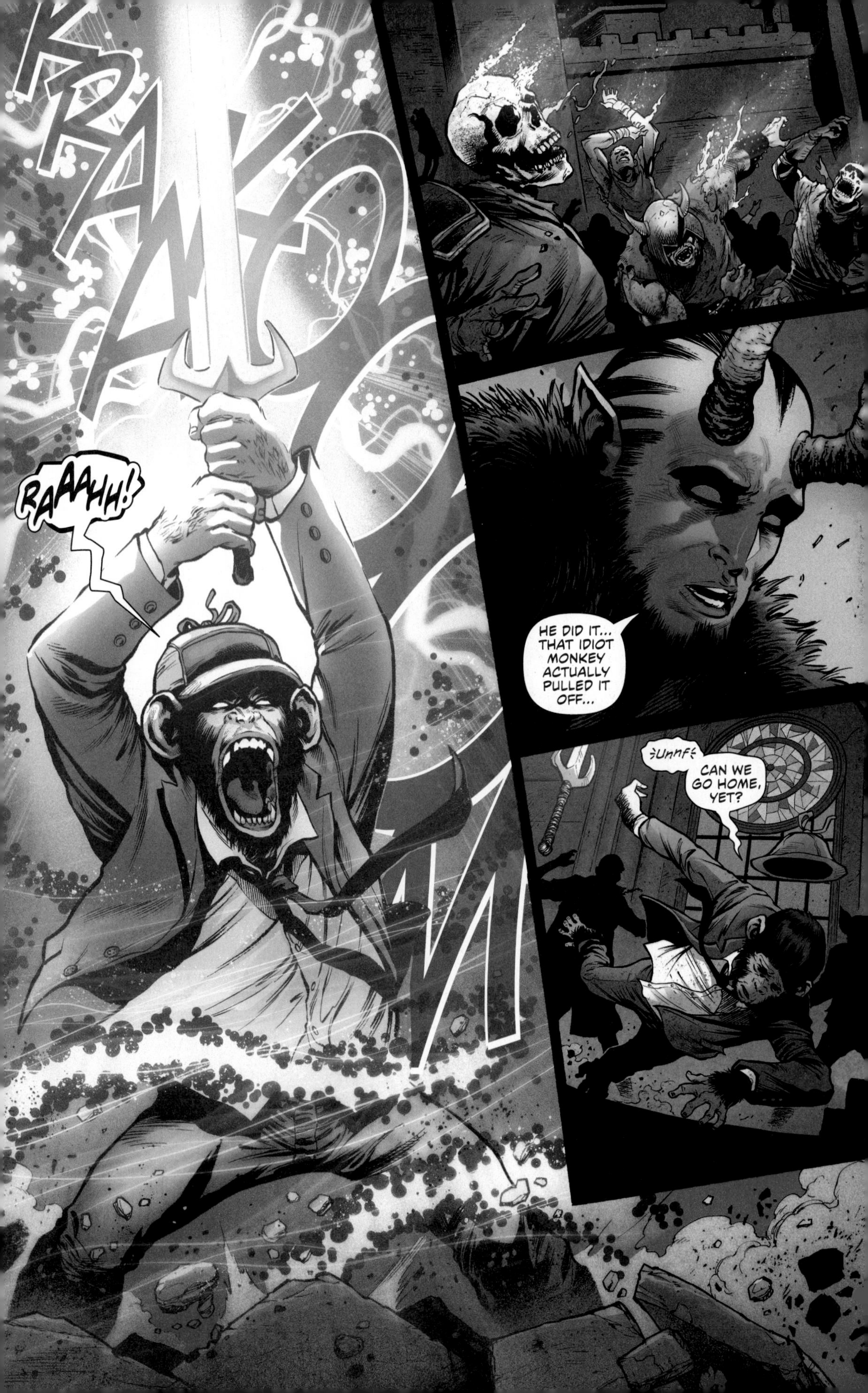
KRAKOOM
RAAAHH!
HE DID IT... THAT IDIOT MONKEY ACTUALLY PULLED IT OFF...
UNNF
CAN WE GO HOME, YET?

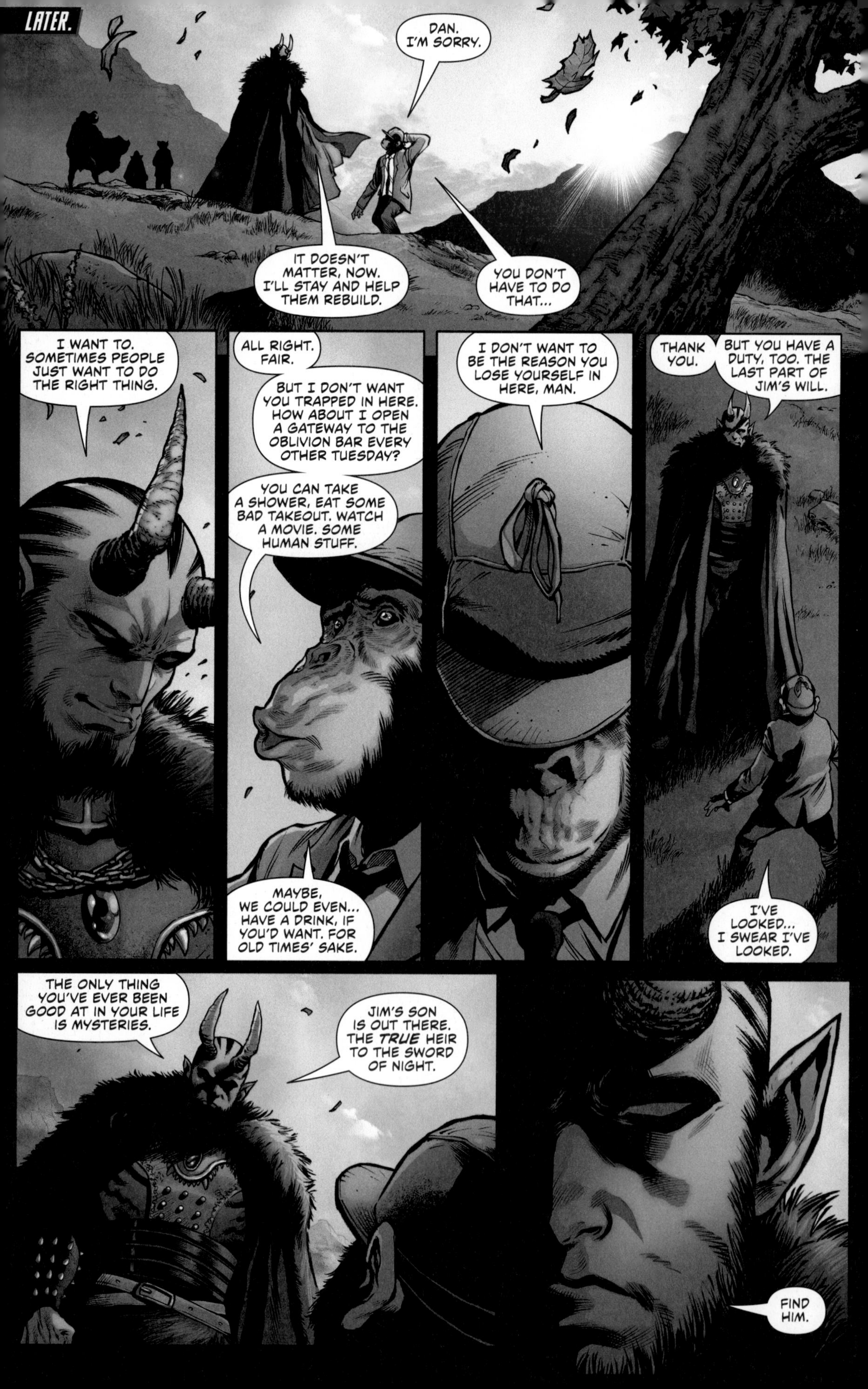
LATER.
DAN. I'M SORRY.
IT DOESN'T MATTER, NOW. I'LL STAY AND HELP THEM REBUILD.
YOU DON'T HAVE TO DO THAT...
I WANT TO. SOMETIMES PEOPLE JUST WANT TO DO THE RIGHT THING.
ALL RIGHT. FAIR.
BUT I DON'T WANT YOU TRAPPED IN HERE. HOW ABOUT I OPEN A GATEWAY TO THE OBLIVION BAR EVERY OTHER TUESDAY?
YOU CAN TAKE A SHOWER, EAT SOME BAD TAKEOUT. WATCH A MOVIE. SOME HUMAN STUFF.
MAYBE, WE COULD EVEN... HAVE A DRINK, IF YOU'D WANT. FOR OLD TIMES' SAKE.
I DON'T WANT TO BE THE REASON YOU LOSE YOURSELF IN HERE, MAN.
THANK YOU.
BUT YOU HAVE A DUTY, TOO. THE LAST PART OF JIM'S WILL.
I'VE LOOKED... I SWEAR I'VE LOOKED.
THE ONLY THING YOU'VE EVER BEEN GOOD AT IN YOUR LIFE IS MYSTERIES.
JIM'S SON IS OUT THERE. THE TRUE HEIR TO THE SWORD OF NIGHT.
FIND HIM.

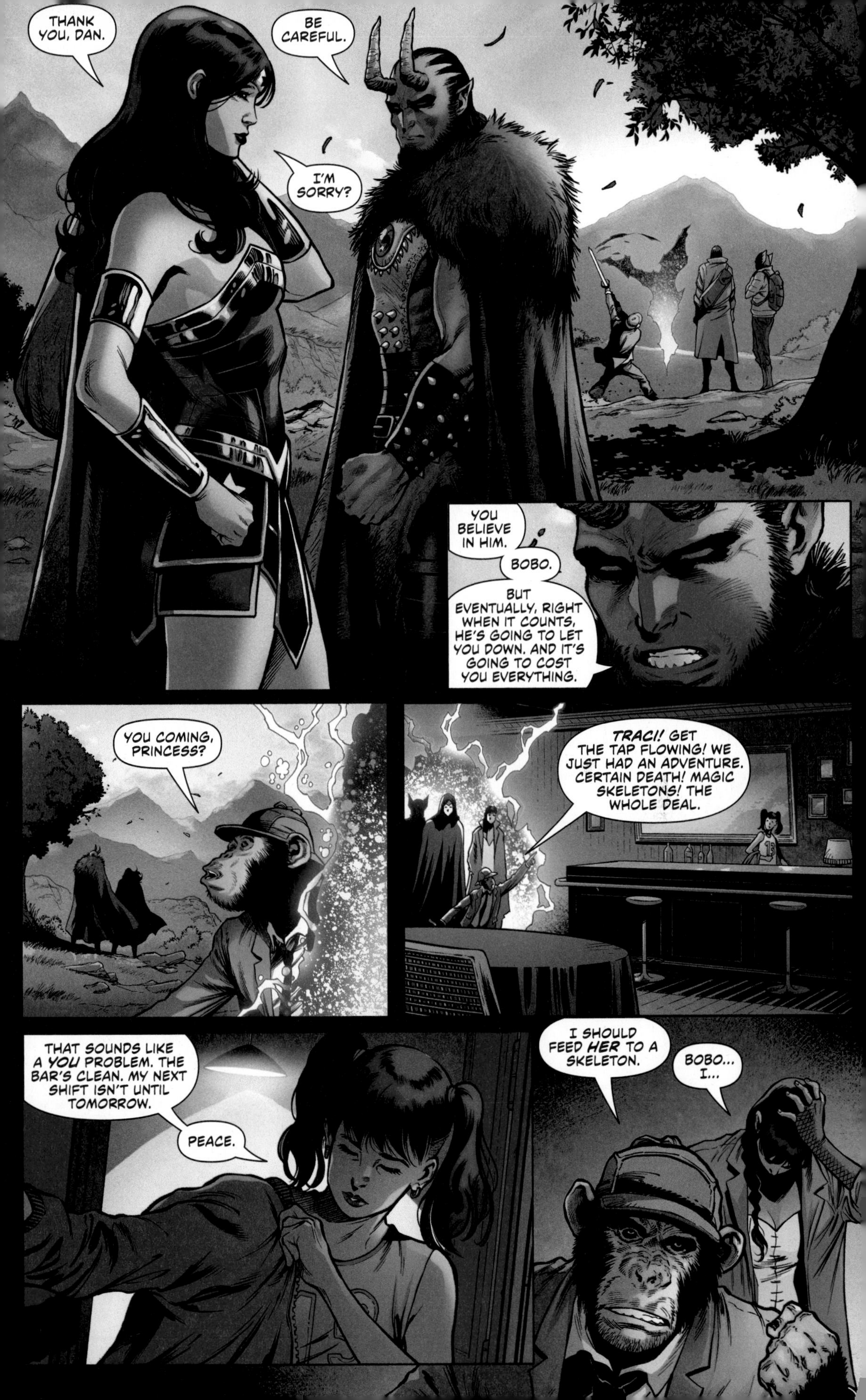
THANK YOU, DAN.
BE CAREFUL.
I'M SORRY?
YOU BELIEVE IN HIM.
BOBO.
BUT EVENTUALLY, RIGHT WHEN IT COUNTS, HE'S GOING TO LET YOU DOWN. AND IT'S GOING TO COST YOU EVERYTHING.
YOU COMING, PRINCESS?
TRACI! GET THE TAP FLOWING! WE JUST HAD AN ADVENTURE. CERTAIN DEATH! MAGIC SKELETONS! THE WHOLE DEAL.
THAT SOUNDS LIKE A YOU PROBLEM. THE BAR'S CLEAN. MY NEXT SHIFT ISN'T UNTIL TOMORROW.
PEACE.
I SHOULD FEED HER TO A SKELETON.
BOBO... I...

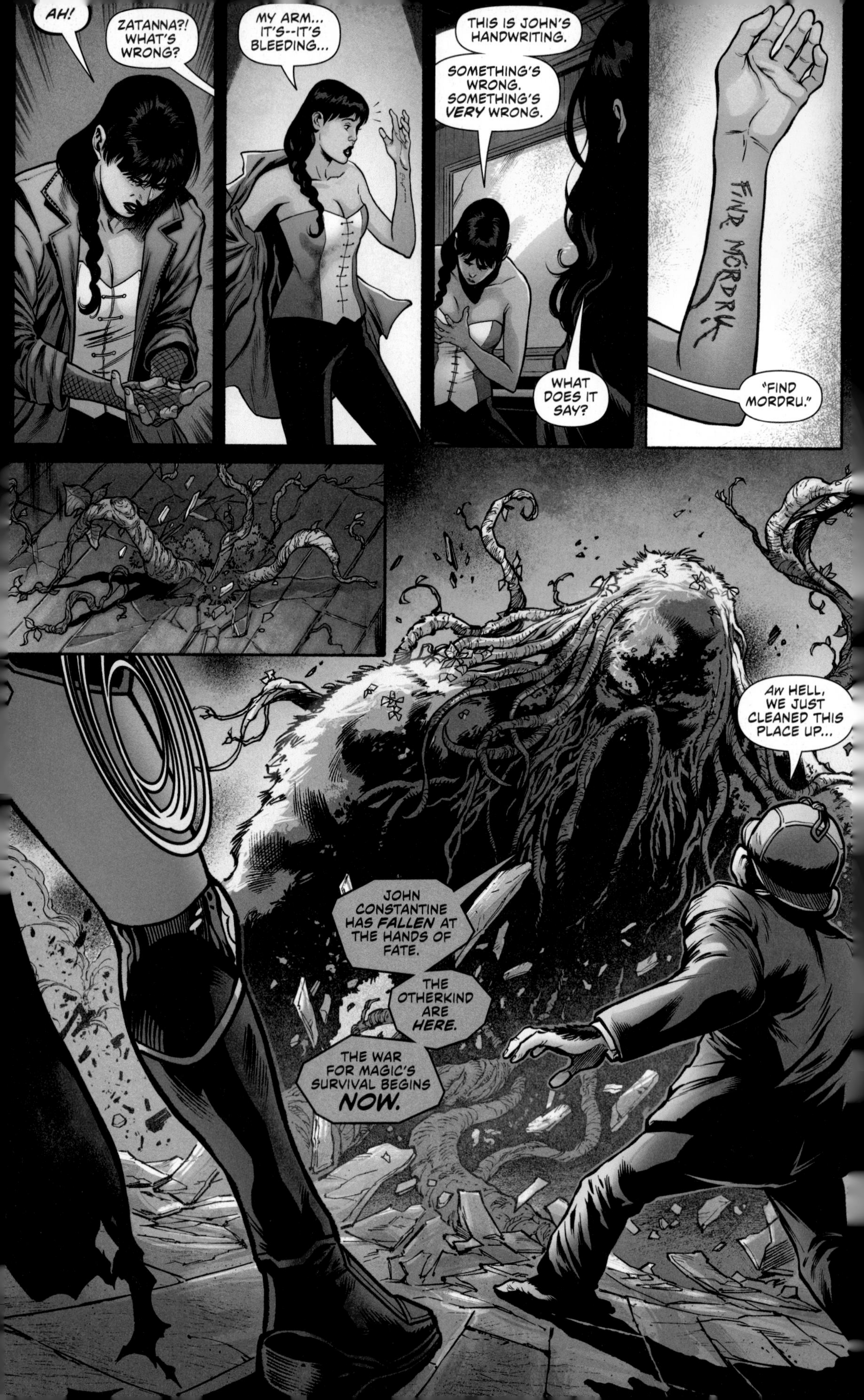
AH!
ZATANNA?! WHAT'S WRONG?
MY ARM... IT'S--IT'S BLEEDING...
THIS IS JOHN'S HANDWRITING.
SOMETHING'S WRONG. SOMETHING'S VERY WRONG.
WHAT DOES IT SAY?
FIND MORDRU
"FIND MORDRU."
AW HELL, WE JUST CLEANED THIS PLACE UP...
JOHN CONSTANTINE HAS FALLEN AT THE HANDS OF FATE.
THE OTHERKIND ARE HERE.
THE WAR FOR MAGIC'S SURVIVAL BEGINS NOW.

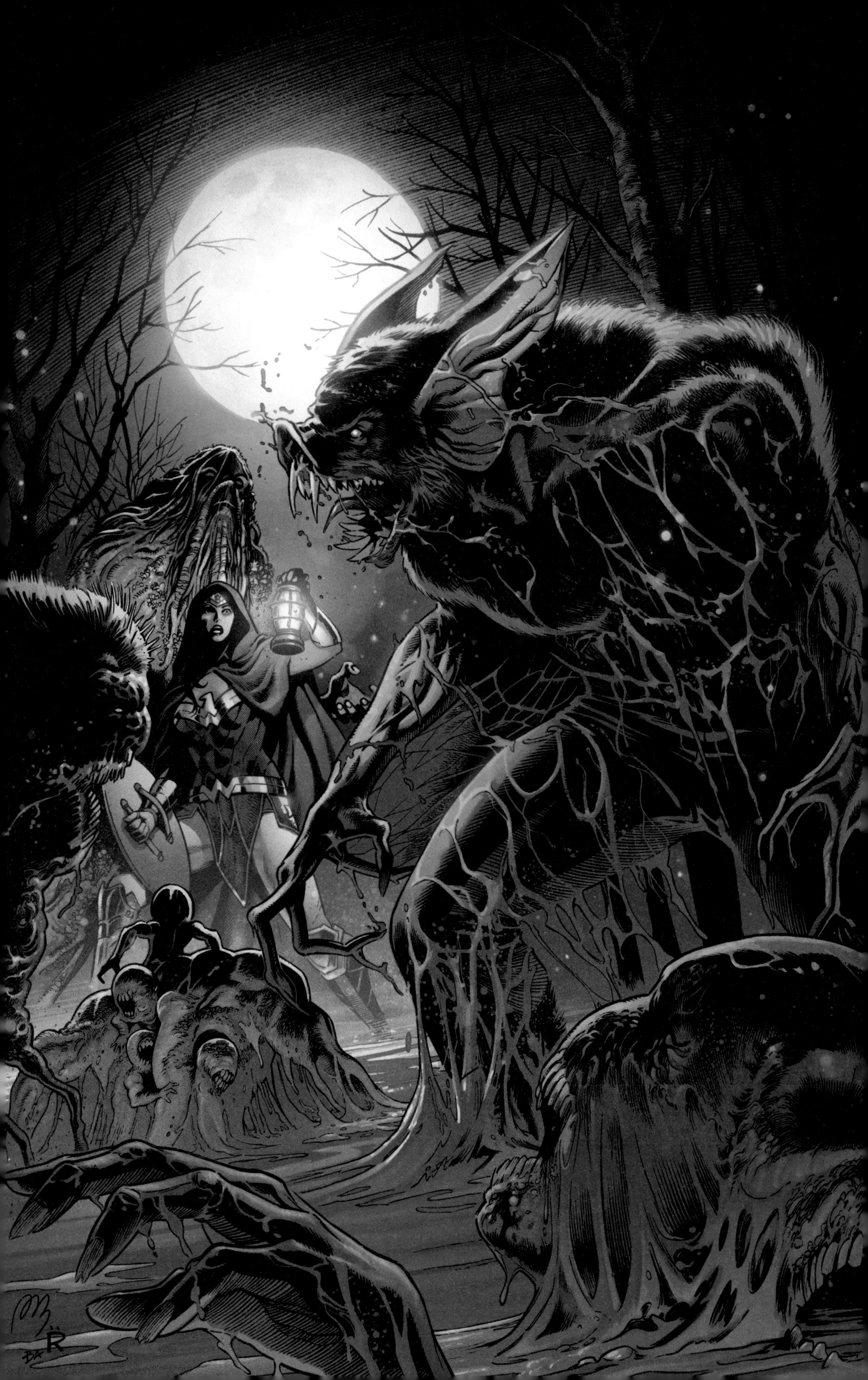

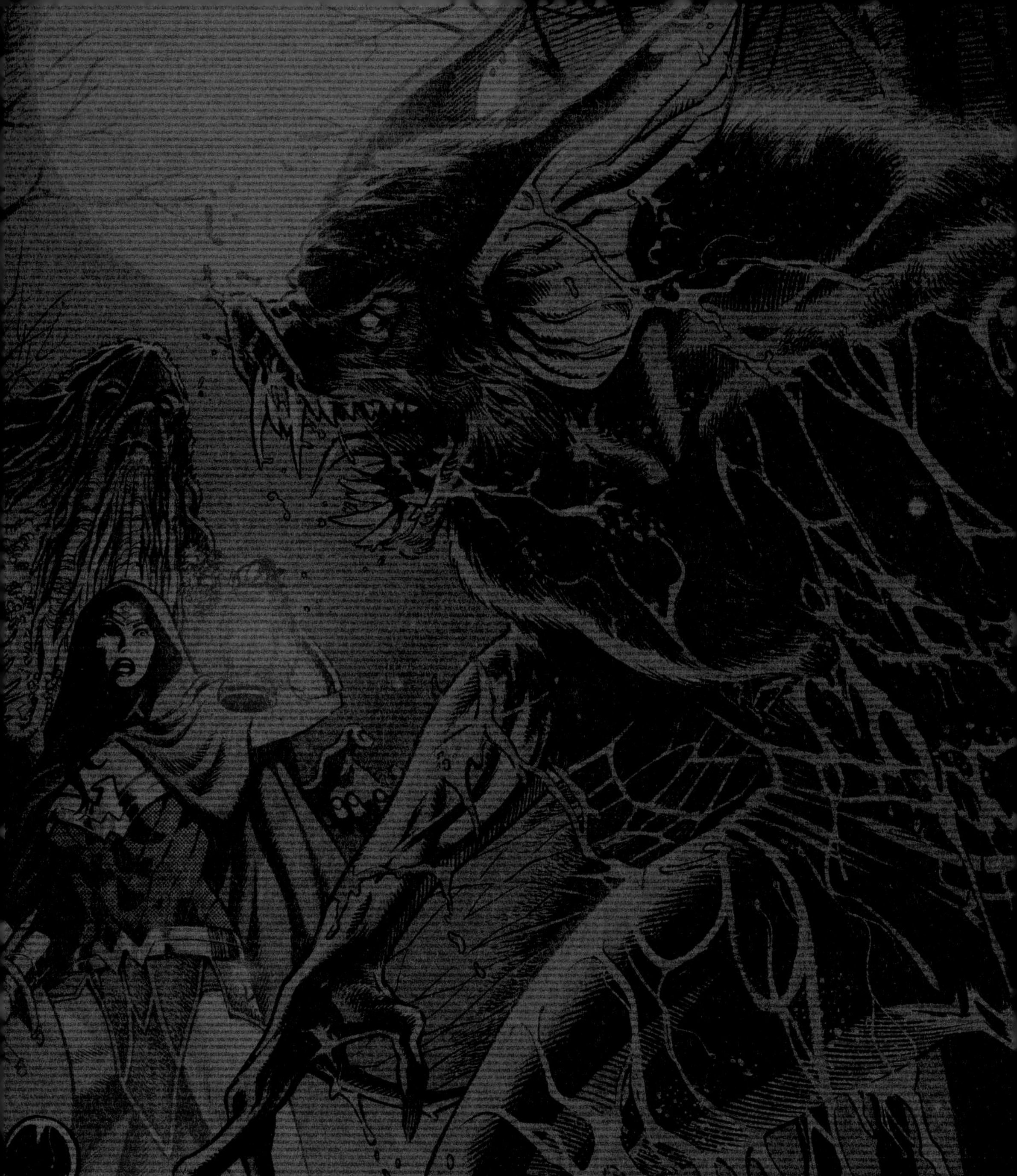

JUSTICE LEAGUE DARK

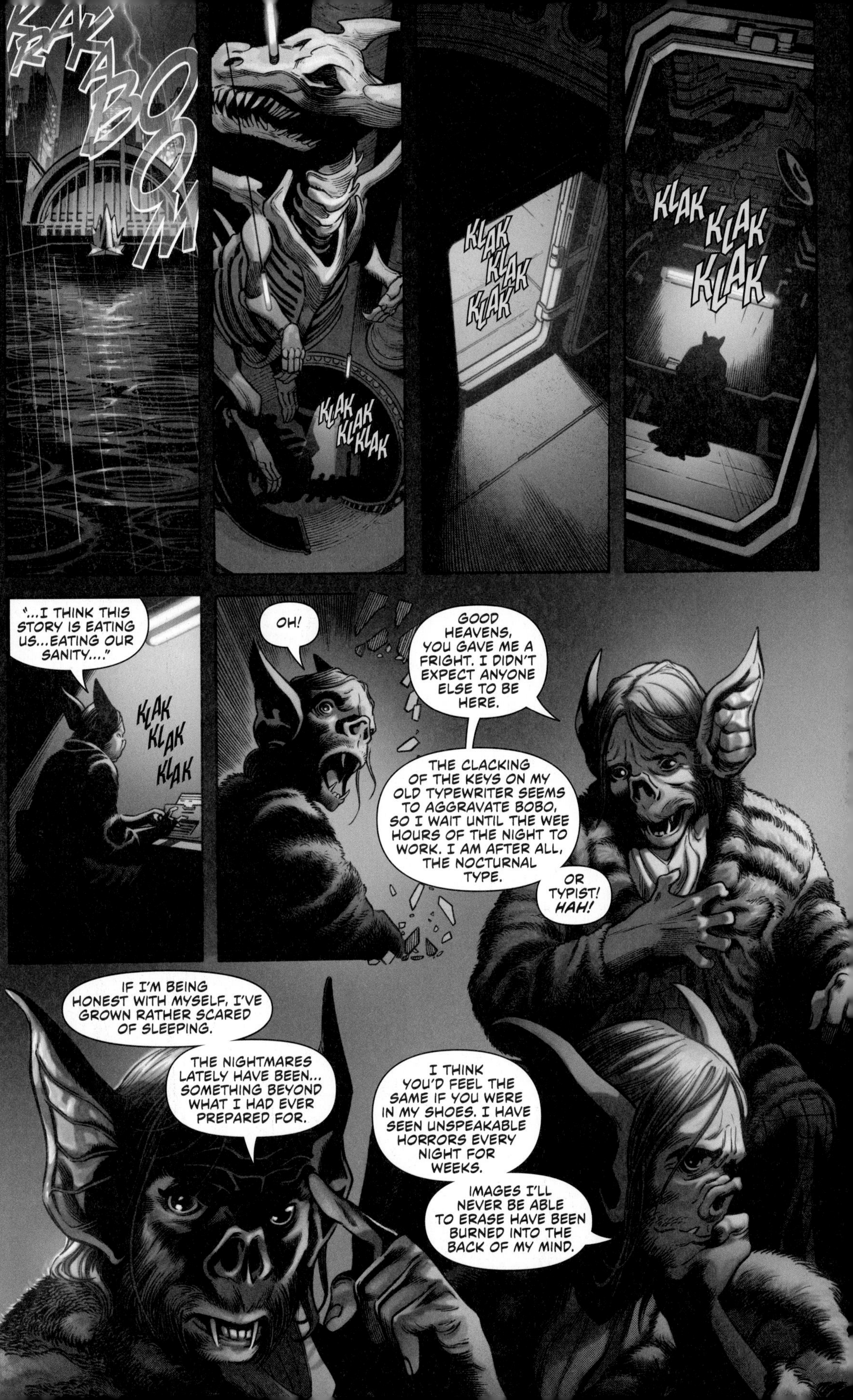
KRAKATHABOOM
KLAK KLAK KLAK
KLAK KLAK KLAK
KLAK KLAK KLAK
"...I THINK THIS STORY IS EATING US...EATING OUR SANITY...."
KLAK KLAK KLAK
OH!
GOOD HEAVENS, YOU GAVE ME A FRIGHT. I DIDN'T EXPECT ANYONE ELSE TO BE HERE.
THE CLACKING OF THE KEYS ON MY OLD TYPEWRITER SEEMS TO AGGRAVATE BOBO, SO I WAIT UNTIL THE WEE HOURS OF THE NIGHT TO WORK. I AM AFTER ALL, THE NOCTURNAL TYPE.
OR TYPIST! HAH!
IF I'M BEING HONEST WITH MYSELF, I'VE GROWN RATHER SCARED OF SLEEPING.
THE NIGHTMARES LATELY HAVE BEEN... SOMETHING BEYOND WHAT I HAD EVER PREPARED FOR.
I THINK YOU'D FEEL THE SAME IF YOU WERE IN MY SHOES. I HAVE SEEN UNSPEAKABLE HORRORS EVERY NIGHT FOR WEEKS.
IMAGES I'LL NEVER BE ABLE TO ERASE HAVE BEEN BURNED INTO THE BACK OF MY MIND.

TALES from the OTHERKIND

JAMES TYNION IV WRITER · ALVARO MARTÍNEZ BUENO PENCILLER · RAUL FERNANDEZ INKER · BRAD ANDERSON COLORIST · ROB LEIGH LETTERER
MARTÍNEZ BUENO, FERNANDEZ, ANDERSON COVER · ANDREW MARINO ASSISTANT EDITOR · MARIE JAVINS GROUP EDITOR

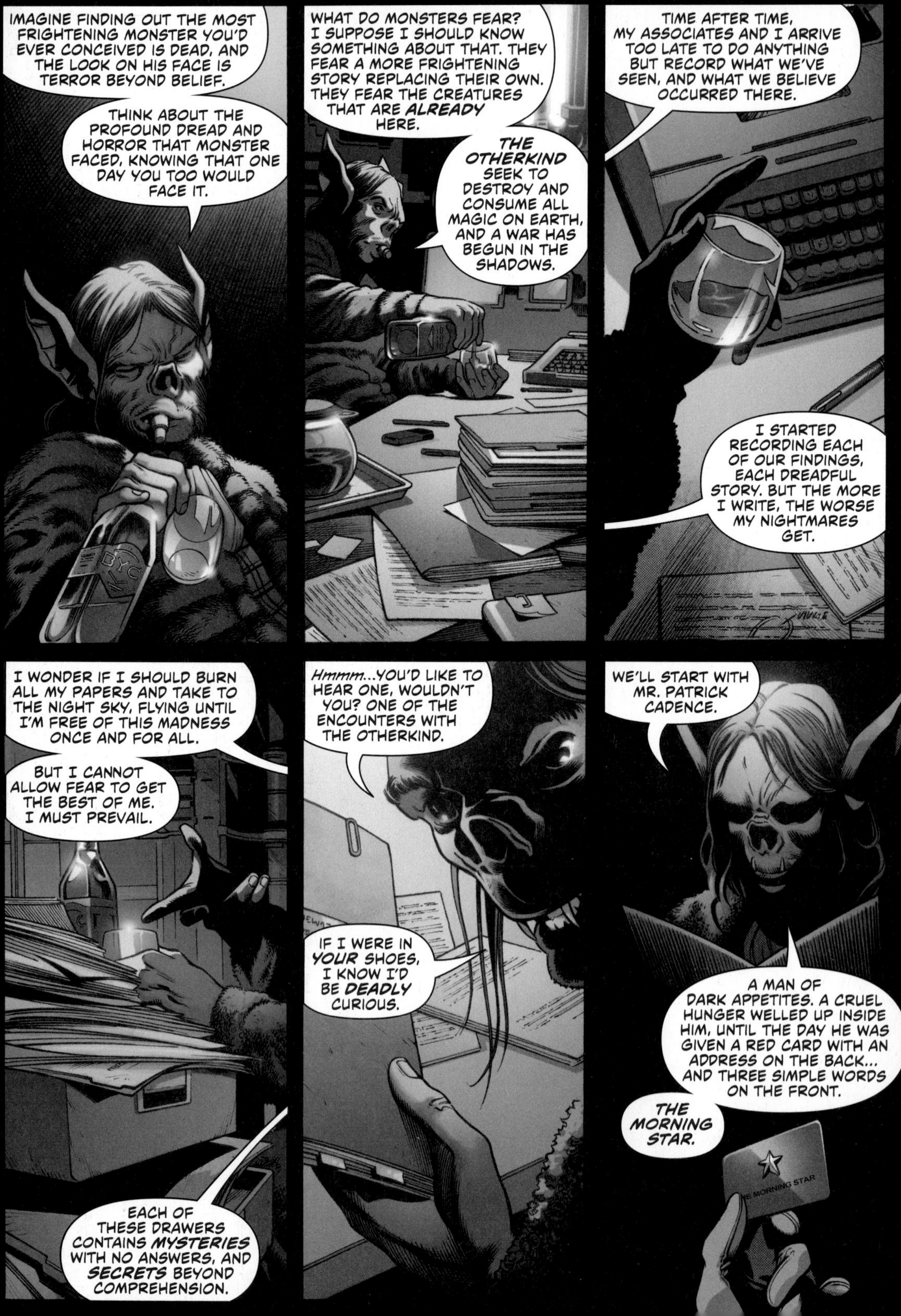

IMAGINE FINDING OUT THE MOST FRIGHTENING MONSTER YOU'D EVER CONCEIVED IS DEAD, AND THE LOOK ON HIS FACE IS TERROR BEYOND BELIEF.
THINK ABOUT THE PROFOUND DREAD AND HORROR THAT MONSTER FACED, KNOWING THAT ONE DAY YOU TOO WOULD FACE IT.
WHAT DO MONSTERS FEAR? I SUPPOSE I SHOULD KNOW SOMETHING ABOUT THAT. THEY FEAR A MORE FRIGHTENING STORY REPLACING THEIR OWN. THEY FEAR THE CREATURES THAT ARE *ALREADY* HERE.
THE OTHERKIND SEEK TO DESTROY AND CONSUME ALL MAGIC ON EARTH, AND A WAR HAS BEGUN IN THE SHADOWS.
TIME AFTER TIME, MY ASSOCIATES AND I ARRIVE TOO LATE TO DO ANYTHING BUT RECORD WHAT WE'VE SEEN, AND WHAT WE BELIEVE OCCURRED THERE.
I STARTED RECORDING EACH OF OUR FINDINGS, EACH DREADFUL STORY. BUT THE MORE I WRITE, THE WORSE MY NIGHTMARES GET.
I WONDER IF I SHOULD BURN ALL MY PAPERS AND TAKE TO THE NIGHT SKY, FLYING UNTIL I'M FREE OF THIS MADNESS ONCE AND FOR ALL.
BUT I CANNOT ALLOW FEAR TO GET THE BEST OF ME. I MUST PREVAIL.
EACH OF THESE DRAWERS CONTAINS *MYSTERIES* WITH NO ANSWERS, AND *SECRETS* BEYOND COMPREHENSION.
Hmmm...YOU'D LIKE TO HEAR ONE, WOULDN'T YOU? ONE OF THE ENCOUNTERS WITH THE OTHERKIND.
IF I WERE IN *YOUR* SHOES, I KNOW I'D BE *DEADLY* CURIOUS.
WE'LL START WITH MR. PATRICK CADENCE.
A MAN OF DARK APPETITES. A CRUEL HUNGER WELLED UP INSIDE HIM, UNTIL THE DAY HE WAS GIVEN A RED CARD WITH AN ADDRESS ON THE BACK... AND THREE SIMPLE WORDS ON THE FRONT.
THE MORNING STAR.

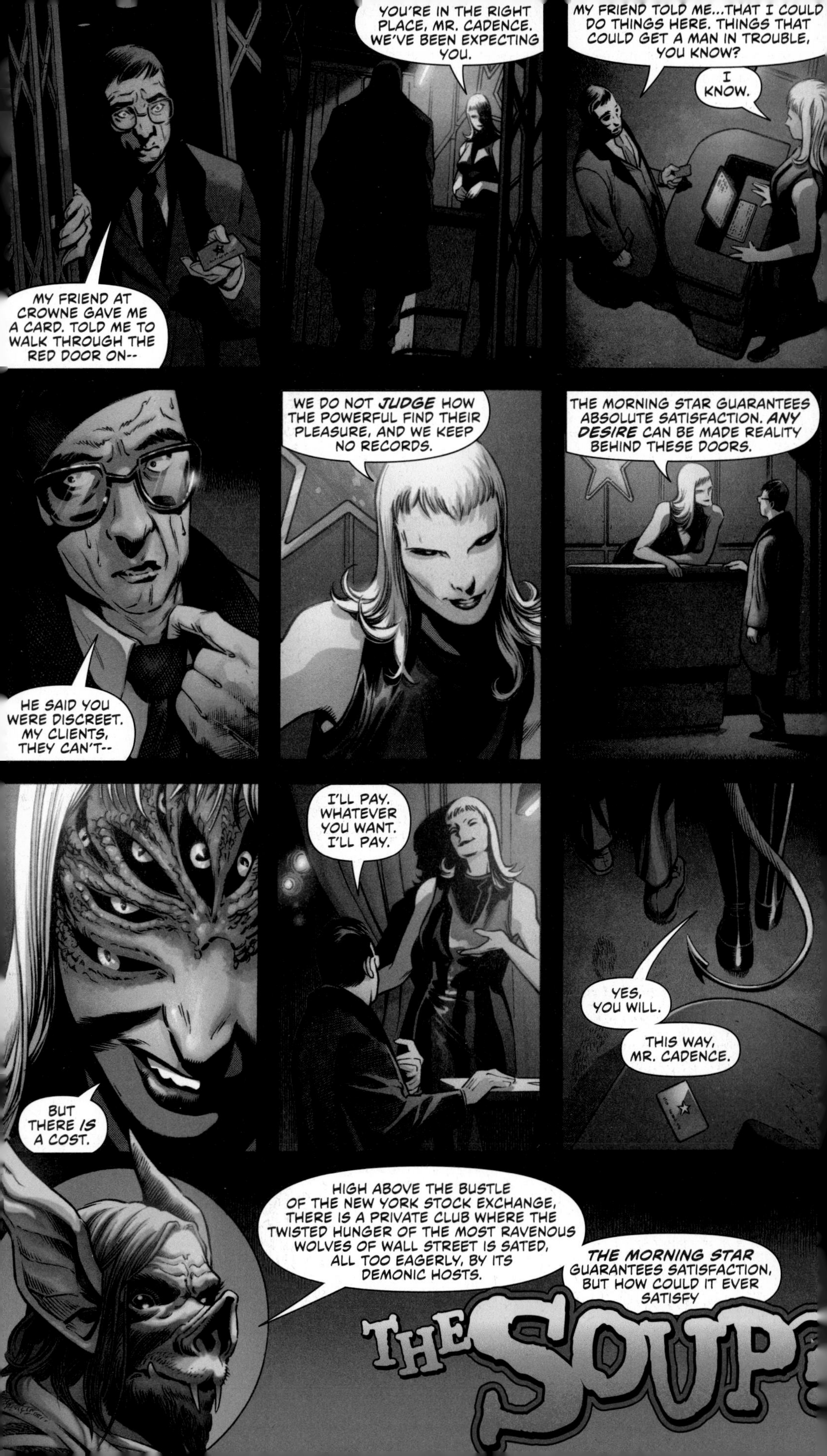
MY FRIEND AT CROWNE GAVE ME A CARD. TOLD ME TO WALK THROUGH THE RED DOOR ON--
YOU'RE IN THE RIGHT PLACE, MR. CADENCE. WE'VE BEEN EXPECTING YOU.
MY FRIEND TOLD ME...THAT I COULD DO THINGS HERE. THINGS THAT COULD GET A MAN IN TROUBLE, YOU KNOW?
I KNOW.
HE SAID YOU WERE DISCREET. MY CLIENTS, THEY CAN'T--
WE DO NOT JUDGE HOW THE POWERFUL FIND THEIR PLEASURE, AND WE KEEP NO RECORDS.
THE MORNING STAR GUARANTEES ABSOLUTE SATISFACTION. ANY DESIRE CAN BE MADE REALITY BEHIND THESE DOORS.
BUT THERE IS A COST.
I'LL PAY. WHATEVER YOU WANT. I'LL PAY.
YES, YOU WILL.
THIS WAY, MR. CADENCE.
HIGH ABOVE THE BUSTLE OF THE NEW YORK STOCK EXCHANGE, THERE IS A PRIVATE CLUB WHERE THE TWISTED HUNGER OF THE MOST RAVENOUS WOLVES OF WALL STREET IS SATED, ALL TOO EAGERLY, BY ITS DEMONIC HOSTS.
THE MORNING STAR GUARANTEES SATISFACTION, BUT HOW COULD IT EVER SATISFY
THE SOUP

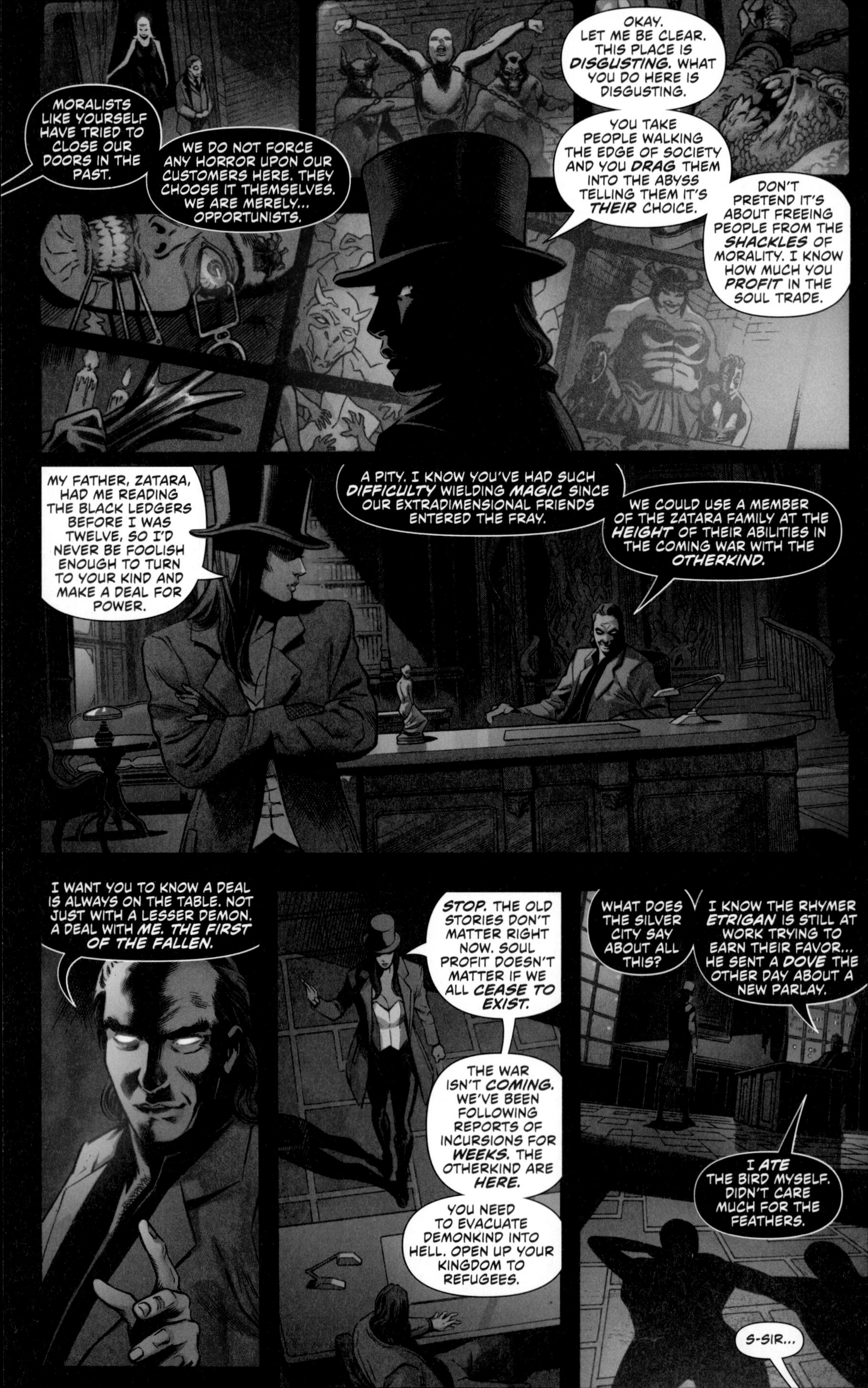
MORALISTS LIKE YOURSELF HAVE TRIED TO CLOSE OUR DOORS IN THE PAST.
WE DO NOT FORCE ANY HORROR UPON OUR CUSTOMERS HERE. THEY CHOOSE IT THEMSELVES. WE ARE MERELY... OPPORTUNISTS.
OKAY. LET ME BE CLEAR. THIS PLACE IS DISGUSTING. WHAT YOU DO HERE IS DISGUSTING.
YOU TAKE PEOPLE WALKING THE EDGE OF SOCIETY AND YOU DRAG THEM INTO THE ABYSS TELLING THEM IT'S THEIR CHOICE.
DON'T PRETEND IT'S ABOUT FREEING PEOPLE FROM THE SHACKLES OF MORALITY. I KNOW HOW MUCH YOU PROFIT IN THE SOUL TRADE.
MY FATHER, ZATARA, HAD ME READING THE BLACK LEDGERS BEFORE I WAS TWELVE, SO I'D NEVER BE FOOLISH ENOUGH TO TURN TO YOUR KIND AND MAKE A DEAL FOR POWER.
A PITY. I KNOW YOU'VE HAD SUCH DIFFICULTY WIELDING MAGIC SINCE OUR EXTRADIMENSIONAL FRIENDS ENTERED THE FRAY.
WE COULD USE A MEMBER OF THE ZATARA FAMILY AT THE HEIGHT OF THEIR ABILITIES IN THE COMING WAR WITH THE OTHERKIND.
I WANT YOU TO KNOW A DEAL IS ALWAYS ON THE TABLE. NOT JUST WITH A LESSER DEMON. A DEAL WITH ME. THE FIRST OF THE FALLEN.
STOP. THE OLD STORIES DON'T MATTER RIGHT NOW. SOUL PROFIT DOESN'T MATTER IF WE ALL CEASE TO EXIST.
THE WAR ISN'T COMING. WE'VE BEEN FOLLOWING REPORTS OF INCURSIONS FOR WEEKS. THE OTHERKIND ARE HERE.
YOU NEED TO EVACUATE DEMONKIND INTO HELL. OPEN UP YOUR KINGDOM TO REFUGEES.
WHAT DOES THE SILVER CITY SAY ABOUT ALL THIS?
I KNOW THE RHYMER ETRIGAN IS STILL AT WORK TRYING TO EARN THEIR FAVOR... HE SENT A DOVE THE OTHER DAY ABOUT A NEW PARLAY.
I ATE THE BIRD MYSELF. DIDN'T CARE MUCH FOR THE FEATHERS.
S-SIR...

IT...IT JUST KEPT WALKING. I TRIED TO STOP IT...TRIED TO FIND OUT WHAT IT WANTED. BUT IT WOULDN'T TELL ME...

IT WENT ROOM TO ROOM...IT MADE ME WATCH. PLEASE...IS THIS WHAT FEAR IS LIKE...?

I DON'T LIKE IT... I DON'T WANT THIS...

SPLASH

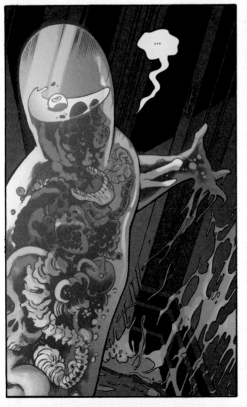

YOU ARE OF THE OTHERKIND. I HAVE HEARD MUCH ABOUT YOU.

I'LL CALL THE OTHERS, NOW...GET US BACKUP--

RUN ALONG, DEAR. THE GROWN-UPS ARE TALKING.

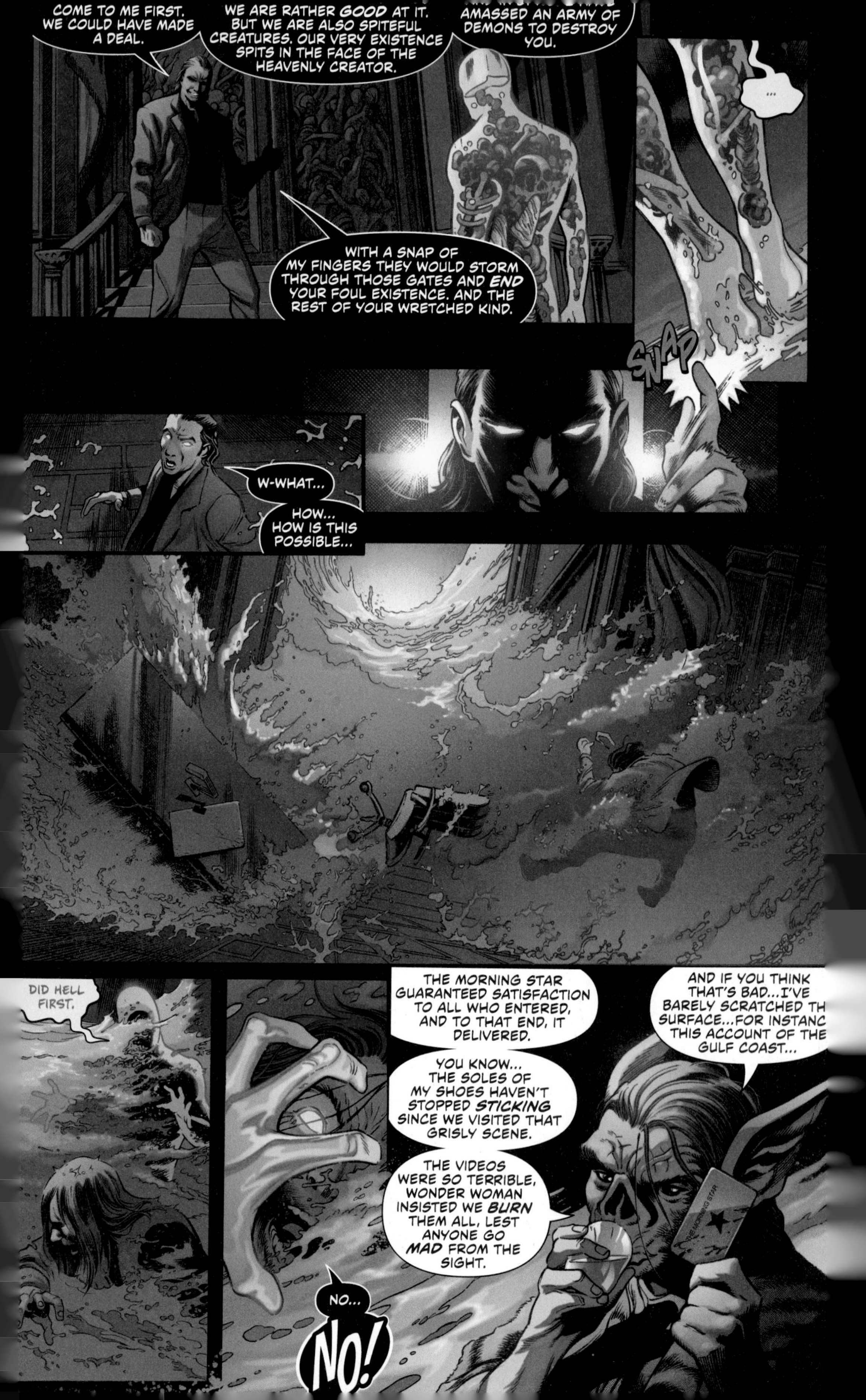
COME TO ME FIRST. WE COULD HAVE MADE A DEAL.
WE ARE RATHER GOOD AT IT. BUT WE ARE ALSO SPITEFUL CREATURES. OUR VERY EXISTENCE SPITS IN THE FACE OF THE HEAVENLY CREATOR.
AMASSED AN ARMY OF DEMONS TO DESTROY YOU.
WITH A SNAP OF MY FINGERS THEY WOULD STORM THROUGH THOSE GATES AND END YOUR FOUL EXISTENCE. AND THE REST OF YOUR WRETCHED KIND.
...
SNAP
W-WHAT...
HOW... HOW IS THIS POSSIBLE...
DID HELL FIRST.
THE MORNING STAR GUARANTEED SATISFACTION TO ALL WHO ENTERED, AND TO THAT END, IT DELIVERED.
YOU KNOW... THE SOLES OF MY SHOES HAVEN'T STOPPED STICKING SINCE WE VISITED THAT GRISLY SCENE.
THE VIDEOS WERE SO TERRIBLE, WONDER WOMAN INSISTED WE BURN THEM ALL, LEST ANYONE GO MAD FROM THE SIGHT.
NO...
NO!
AND IF YOU THINK THAT'S BAD...I'VE BARELY SCRATCHED TH SURFACE...FOR INSTANC THIS ACCOUNT OF THE GULF COAST...

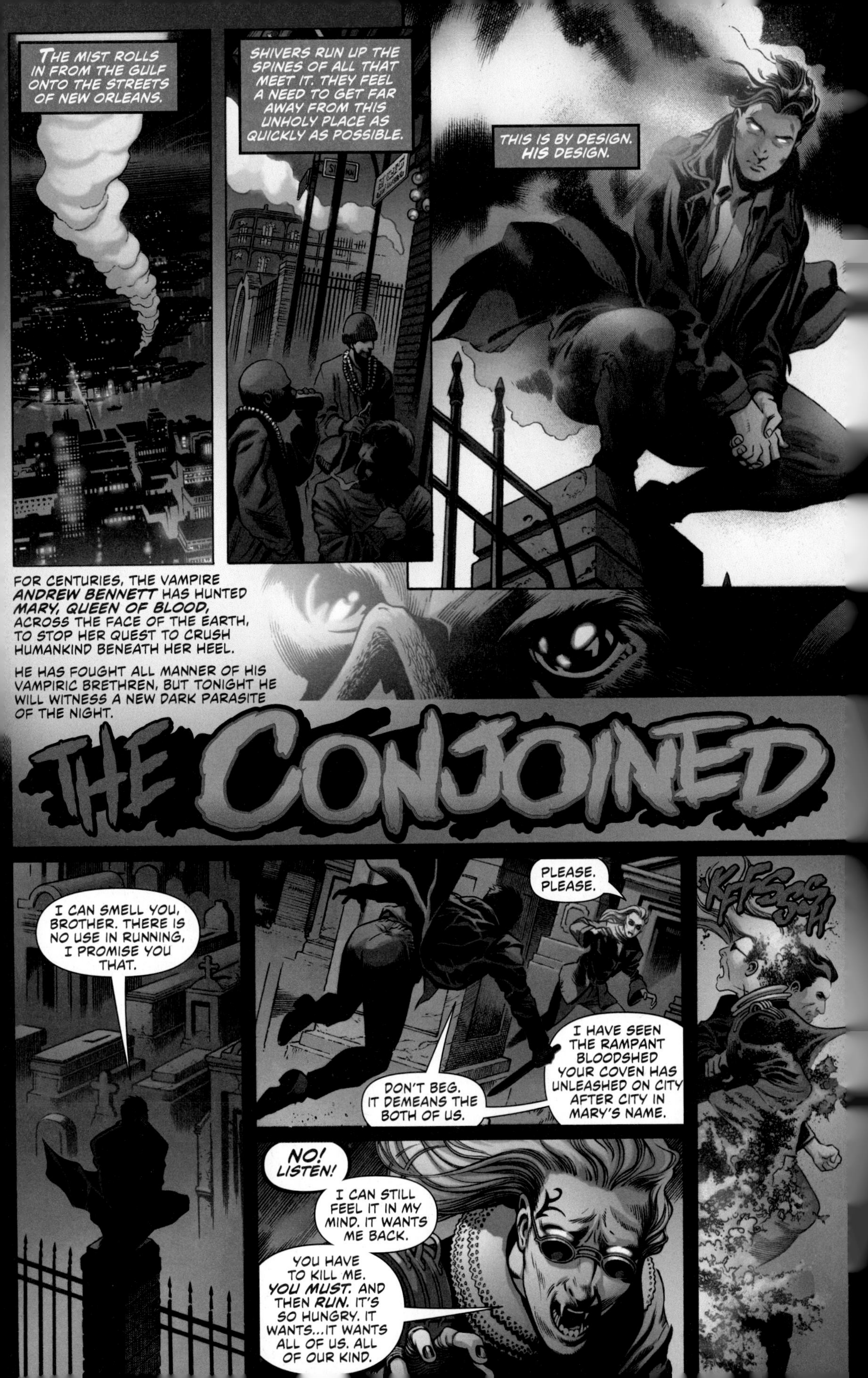
THE MIST ROLLS IN FROM THE GULF ONTO THE STREETS OF NEW ORLEANS.
SHIVERS RUN UP THE SPINES OF ALL THAT MEET IT. THEY FEEL A NEED TO GET FAR AWAY FROM THIS UNHOLY PLACE AS QUICKLY AS POSSIBLE.
THIS IS BY DESIGN. HIS DESIGN.
FOR CENTURIES, THE VAMPIRE ANDREW BENNETT HAS HUNTED MARY, QUEEN OF BLOOD, ACROSS THE FACE OF THE EARTH, TO STOP HER QUEST TO CRUSH HUMANKIND BENEATH HER HEEL.
HE HAS FOUGHT ALL MANNER OF HIS VAMPIRIC BRETHREN, BUT TONIGHT HE WILL WITNESS A NEW DARK PARASITE OF THE NIGHT.
THE CONJOINED
I CAN SMELL YOU, BROTHER. THERE IS NO USE IN RUNNING, I PROMISE YOU THAT.
PLEASE. PLEASE.
DON'T BEG. IT DEMEANS THE BOTH OF US.
I HAVE SEEN THE RAMPANT BLOODSHED YOUR COVEN HAS UNLEASHED ON CITY AFTER CITY IN MARY'S NAME.
NO! LISTEN!
I CAN STILL FEEL IT IN MY MIND. IT WANTS ME BACK.
YOU HAVE TO KILL ME. YOU MUST. AND THEN RUN. IT'S SO HUNGRY. IT WANTS...IT WANTS ALL OF US. ALL OF OUR KIND.

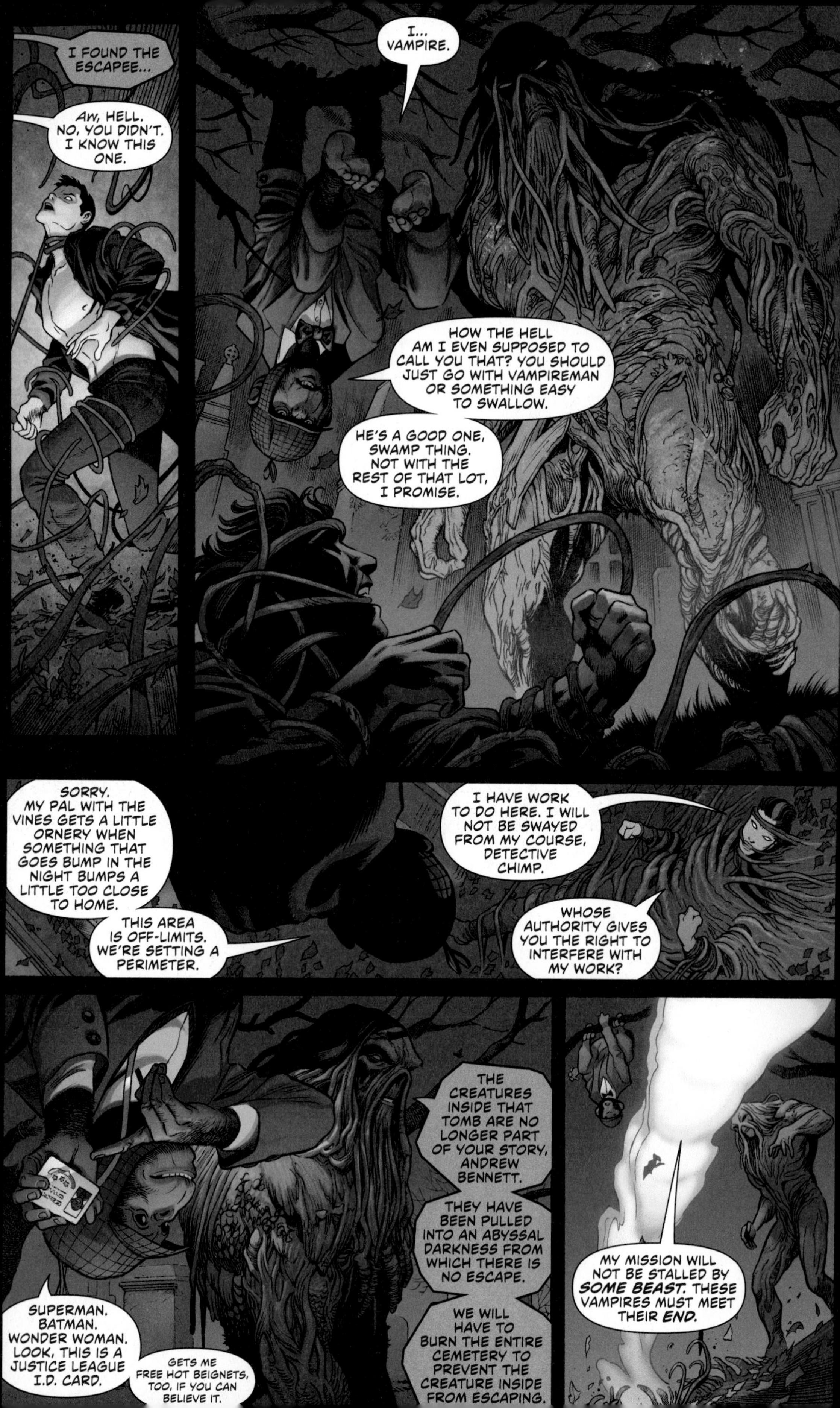

I FOUND THE ESCAPEE...
AW, HELL. NO, YOU DIDN'T. I KNOW THIS ONE.
I... VAMPIRE.
HOW THE HELL AM I EVEN SUPPOSED TO CALL YOU THAT? YOU SHOULD JUST GO WITH VAMPIREMAN OR SOMETHING EASY TO SWALLOW.
HE'S A GOOD ONE, SWAMP THING. NOT WITH THE REST OF THAT LOT, I PROMISE.
SORRY. MY PAL WITH THE VINES GETS A LITTLE ORNERY WHEN SOMETHING THAT GOES BUMP IN THE NIGHT BUMPS A LITTLE TOO CLOSE TO HOME.
THIS AREA IS OFF-LIMITS. WE'RE SETTING A PERIMETER.
I HAVE WORK TO DO HERE. I WILL NOT BE SWAYED FROM MY COURSE, DETECTIVE CHIMP.
WHOSE AUTHORITY GIVES YOU THE RIGHT TO INTERFERE WITH MY WORK?
SUPERMAN. BATMAN. WONDER WOMAN. LOOK, THIS IS A JUSTICE LEAGUE I.D. CARD.
GETS ME FREE HOT BEIGNETS, TOO, IF YOU CAN BELIEVE IT.
THE CREATURES INSIDE THAT TOMB ARE NO LONGER PART OF YOUR STORY, ANDREW BENNETT.
THEY HAVE BEEN PULLED INTO AN ABYSSAL DARKNESS FROM WHICH THERE IS NO ESCAPE.
WE WILL HAVE TO BURN THE ENTIRE CEMETERY TO PREVENT THE CREATURE INSIDE FROM ESCAPING.
MY MISSION WILL NOT BE STALLED BY ***SOME BEAST.*** THESE VAMPIRES MUST MEET THEIR ***END.***

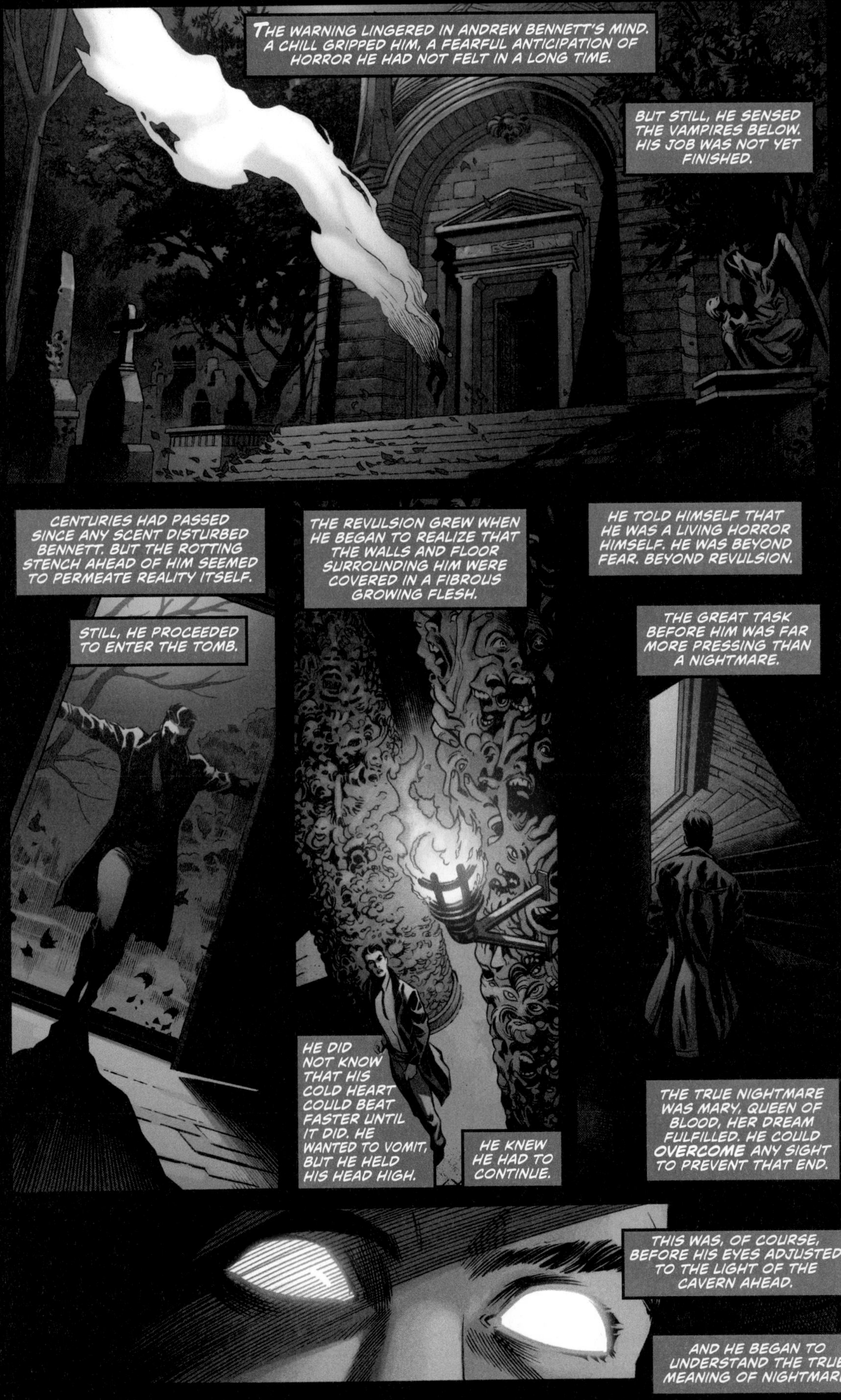
THE WARNING LINGERED IN ANDREW BENNETT'S MIND. A CHILL GRIPPED HIM, A FEARFUL ANTICIPATION OF HORROR HE HAD NOT FELT IN A LONG TIME.
BUT STILL, HE SENSED THE VAMPIRES BELOW. HIS JOB WAS NOT YET FINISHED.
CENTURIES HAD PASSED SINCE ANY SCENT DISTURBED BENNETT. BUT THE ROTTING STENCH AHEAD OF HIM SEEMED TO PERMEATE REALITY ITSELF.
STILL, HE PROCEEDED TO ENTER THE TOMB.
THE REVULSION GREW WHEN HE BEGAN TO REALIZE THAT THE WALLS AND FLOOR SURROUNDING HIM WERE COVERED IN A FIBROUS GROWING FLESH.
HE DID NOT KNOW THAT HIS COLD HEART COULD BEAT FASTER UNTIL IT DID. HE WANTED TO VOMIT, BUT HE HELD HIS HEAD HIGH.
HE KNEW HE HAD TO CONTINUE.
HE TOLD HIMSELF THAT HE WAS A LIVING HORROR HIMSELF. HE WAS BEYOND FEAR. BEYOND REVULSION.
THE GREAT TASK BEFORE HIM WAS FAR MORE PRESSING THAN A NIGHTMARE.
THE TRUE NIGHTMARE WAS MARY, QUEEN OF BLOOD, HER DREAM FULFILLED. HE COULD OVERCOME ANY SIGHT TO PREVENT THAT END.
THIS WAS, OF COURSE, BEFORE HIS EYES ADJUSTED TO THE LIGHT OF THE CAVERN AHEAD.
AND HE BEGAN TO UNDERSTAND THE TRUE MEANING OF NIGHTMARE.

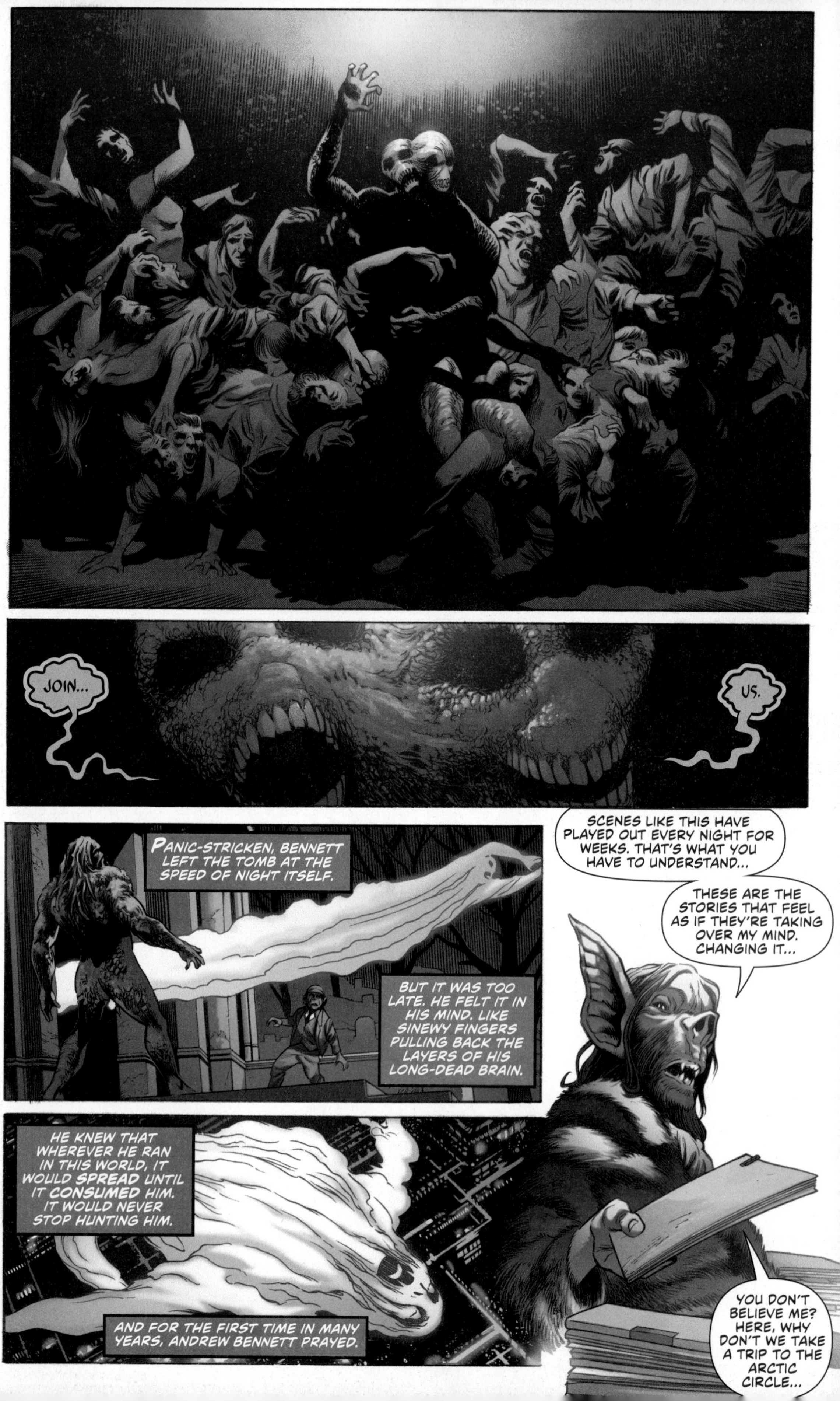
JOIN...
US.
PANIC-STRICKEN, BENNETT LEFT THE TOMB AT THE SPEED OF NIGHT ITSELF.
SCENES LIKE THIS HAVE PLAYED OUT EVERY NIGHT FOR WEEKS. THAT'S WHAT YOU HAVE TO UNDERSTAND...
THESE ARE THE STORIES THAT FEEL AS IF THEY'RE TAKING OVER MY MIND. CHANGING IT...
BUT IT WAS TOO LATE. HE FELT IT IN HIS MIND. LIKE SINEWY FINGERS PULLING BACK THE LAYERS OF HIS LONG-DEAD BRAIN.
HE KNEW THAT WHEREVER HE RAN IN THIS WORLD, IT WOULD SPREAD UNTIL IT CONSUMED HIM. IT WOULD NEVER STOP HUNTING HIM.
AND FOR THE FIRST TIME IN MANY YEARS, ANDREW BENNETT PRAYED.
YOU DON'T BELIEVE ME? HERE, WHY DON'T WE TAKE A TRIP TO THE ARCTIC CIRCLE...

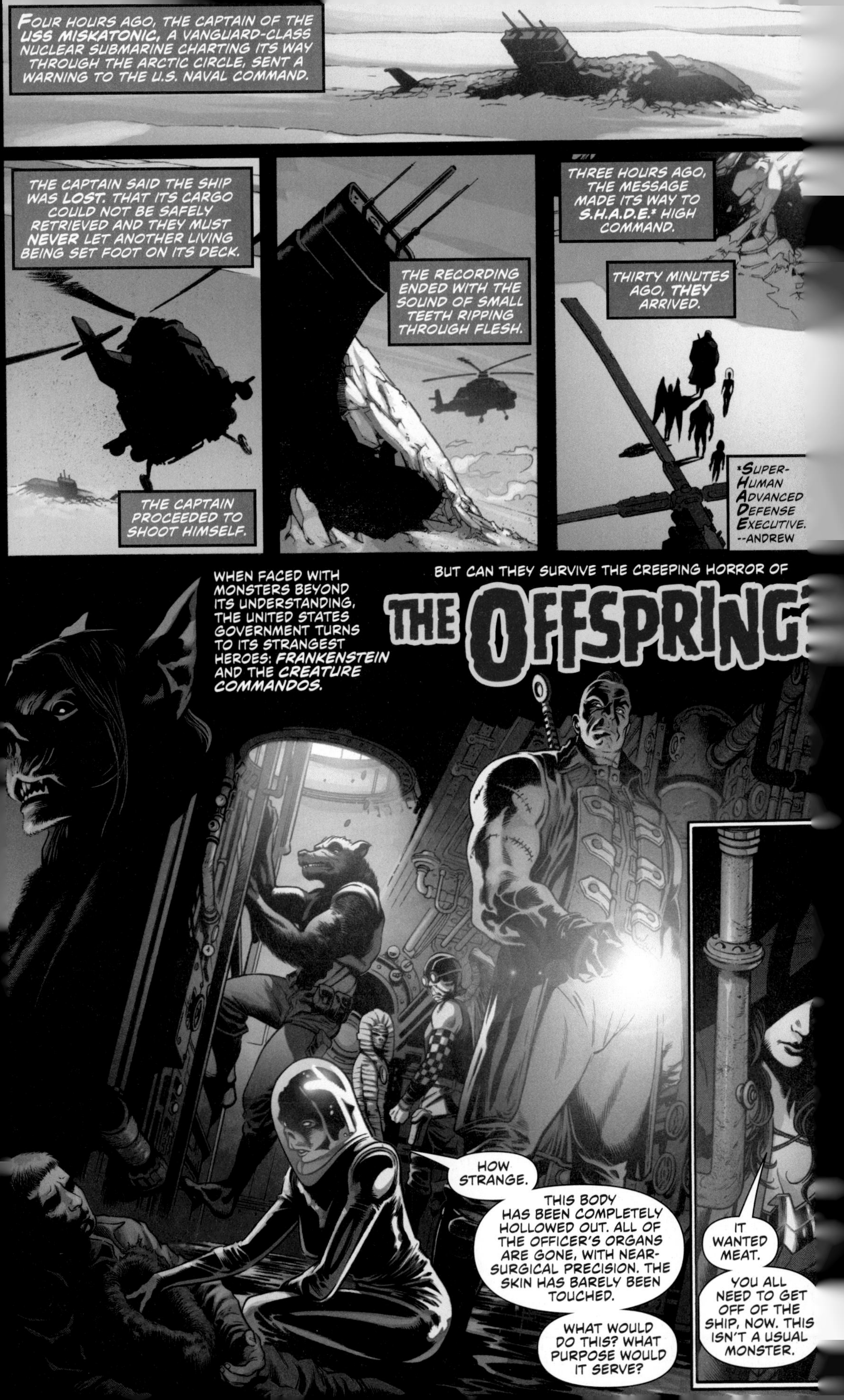
FOUR HOURS AGO, THE CAPTAIN OF THE USS MISKATONIC, A VANGUARD-CLASS NUCLEAR SUBMARINE CHARTING ITS WAY THROUGH THE ARCTIC CIRCLE, SENT A WARNING TO THE U.S. NAVAL COMMAND.
THE CAPTAIN SAID THE SHIP WAS LOST. THAT ITS CARGO COULD NOT BE SAFELY RETRIEVED AND THEY MUST NEVER LET ANOTHER LIVING BEING SET FOOT ON ITS DECK.
THE CAPTAIN PROCEEDED TO SHOOT HIMSELF.
THE RECORDING ENDED WITH THE SOUND OF SMALL TEETH RIPPING THROUGH FLESH.
THREE HOURS AGO, THE MESSAGE MADE ITS WAY TO S.H.A.D.E.* HIGH COMMAND.
THIRTY MINUTES AGO, THEY ARRIVED.
*SUPER-HUMAN ADVANCED DEFENSE EXECUTIVE. --ANDREW
WHEN FACED WITH MONSTERS BEYOND ITS UNDERSTANDING, THE UNITED STATES GOVERNMENT TURNS TO ITS STRANGEST HEROES: FRANKENSTEIN AND THE CREATURE COMMANDOS.
BUT CAN THEY SURVIVE THE CREEPING HORROR OF
THE OFFSPRING?
HOW STRANGE.
THIS BODY HAS BEEN COMPLETELY HOLLOWED OUT. ALL OF THE OFFICER'S ORGANS ARE GONE, WITH NEAR-SURGICAL PRECISION. THE SKIN HAS BARELY BEEN TOUCHED.
WHAT WOULD DO THIS? WHAT PURPOSE WOULD IT SERVE?
IT WANTED MEAT.
YOU ALL NEED TO GET OFF OF THE SHIP, NOW. THIS ISN'T A USUAL MONSTER.

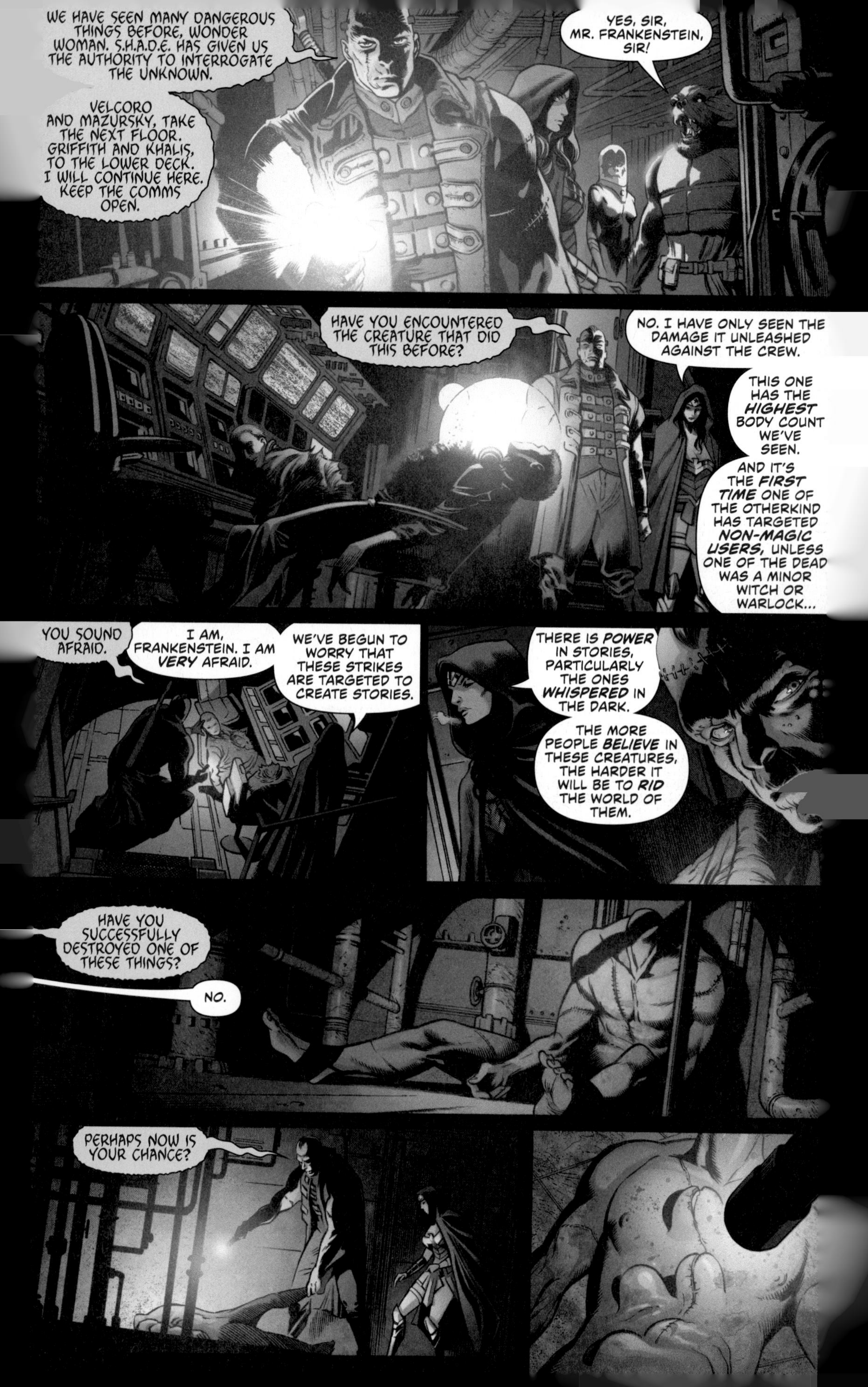
WE HAVE SEEN MANY DANGEROUS THINGS BEFORE, WONDER WOMAN. S.H.A.D.E. HAS GIVEN US THE AUTHORITY TO INTERROGATE THE UNKNOWN.
VELCORO AND MAZURSKY, TAKE THE NEXT FLOOR. GRIFFITH AND KHALIS, TO THE LOWER DECK. I WILL CONTINUE HERE. KEEP THE COMMS OPEN.
YES, SIR, MR. FRANKENSTEIN, SIR!
HAVE YOU ENCOUNTERED THE CREATURE THAT DID THIS BEFORE?
NO. I HAVE ONLY SEEN THE DAMAGE IT UNLEASHED AGAINST THE CREW.
THIS ONE HAS THE HIGHEST BODY COUNT WE'VE SEEN.
AND IT'S THE FIRST TIME ONE OF THE OTHERKIND HAS TARGETED NON-MAGIC USERS, UNLESS ONE OF THE DEAD WAS A MINOR WITCH OR WARLOCK...
YOU SOUND AFRAID.
I AM, FRANKENSTEIN. I AM VERY AFRAID.
WE'VE BEGUN TO WORRY THAT THESE STRIKES ARE TARGETED TO CREATE STORIES.
THERE IS POWER IN STORIES, PARTICULARLY THE ONES WHISPERED IN THE DARK.
THE MORE PEOPLE BELIEVE IN THESE CREATURES, THE HARDER IT WILL BE TO RID THE WORLD OF THEM.
HAVE YOU SUCCESSFULLY DESTROYED ONE OF THESE THINGS?
NO.
PERHAPS NOW IS YOUR CHANCE?

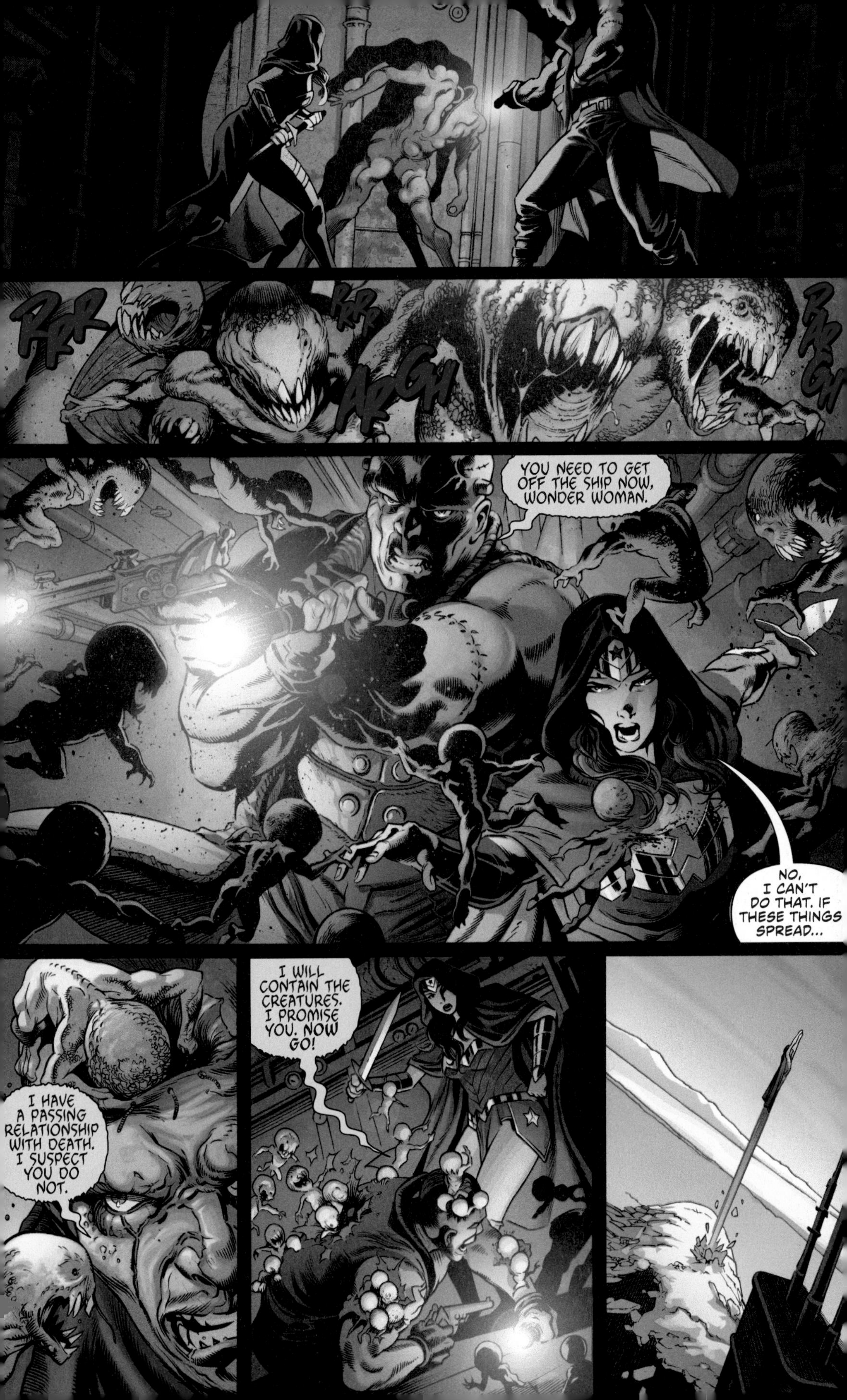
RRR
RRRR
ARGH
RARGH
YOU NEED TO GET OFF THE SHIP NOW, WONDER WOMAN.
NO, I CAN'T DO THAT. IF THESE THINGS SPREAD...
I HAVE A PASSING RELATIONSHIP WITH DEATH. I SUSPECT YOU DO NOT.
I WILL CONTAIN THE CREATURES. I PROMISE YOU. NOW GO!

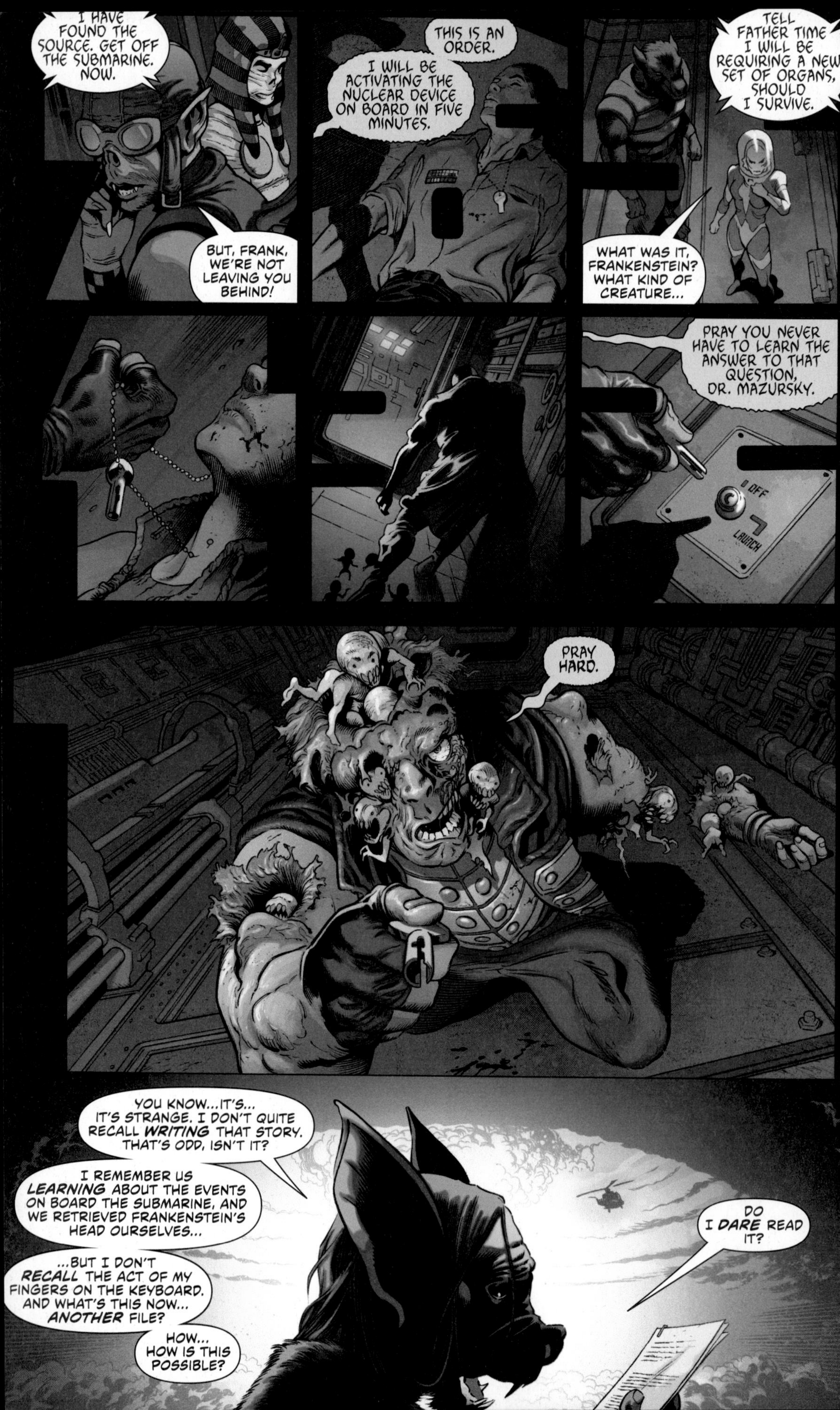
I HAVE FOUND THE SOURCE. GET OFF THE SUBMARINE. NOW.
BUT, FRANK, WE'RE NOT LEAVING YOU BEHIND!
THIS IS AN ORDER.
I WILL BE ACTIVATING THE NUCLEAR DEVICE ON BOARD IN FIVE MINUTES.
TELL FATHER TIME I WILL BE REQUIRING A NEW SET OF ORGANS, SHOULD I SURVIVE.
WHAT WAS IT, FRANKENSTEIN? WHAT KIND OF CREATURE...
PRAY YOU NEVER HAVE TO LEARN THE ANSWER TO THAT QUESTION, DR. MAZURSKY.
OFF
LAUNCH
PRAY HARD.
YOU KNOW...IT'S... IT'S STRANGE. I DON'T QUITE RECALL *WRITING* THAT STORY. THAT'S ODD, ISN'T IT?
I REMEMBER US *LEARNING* ABOUT THE EVENTS ON BOARD THE SUBMARINE, AND WE RETRIEVED FRANKENSTEIN'S HEAD OURSELVES...
...BUT I DON'T *RECALL* THE ACT OF MY FINGERS ON THE KEYBOARD. AND WHAT'S THIS NOW... *ANOTHER* FILE?
HOW... HOW IS THIS POSSIBLE?
DO I *DARE* READ IT?

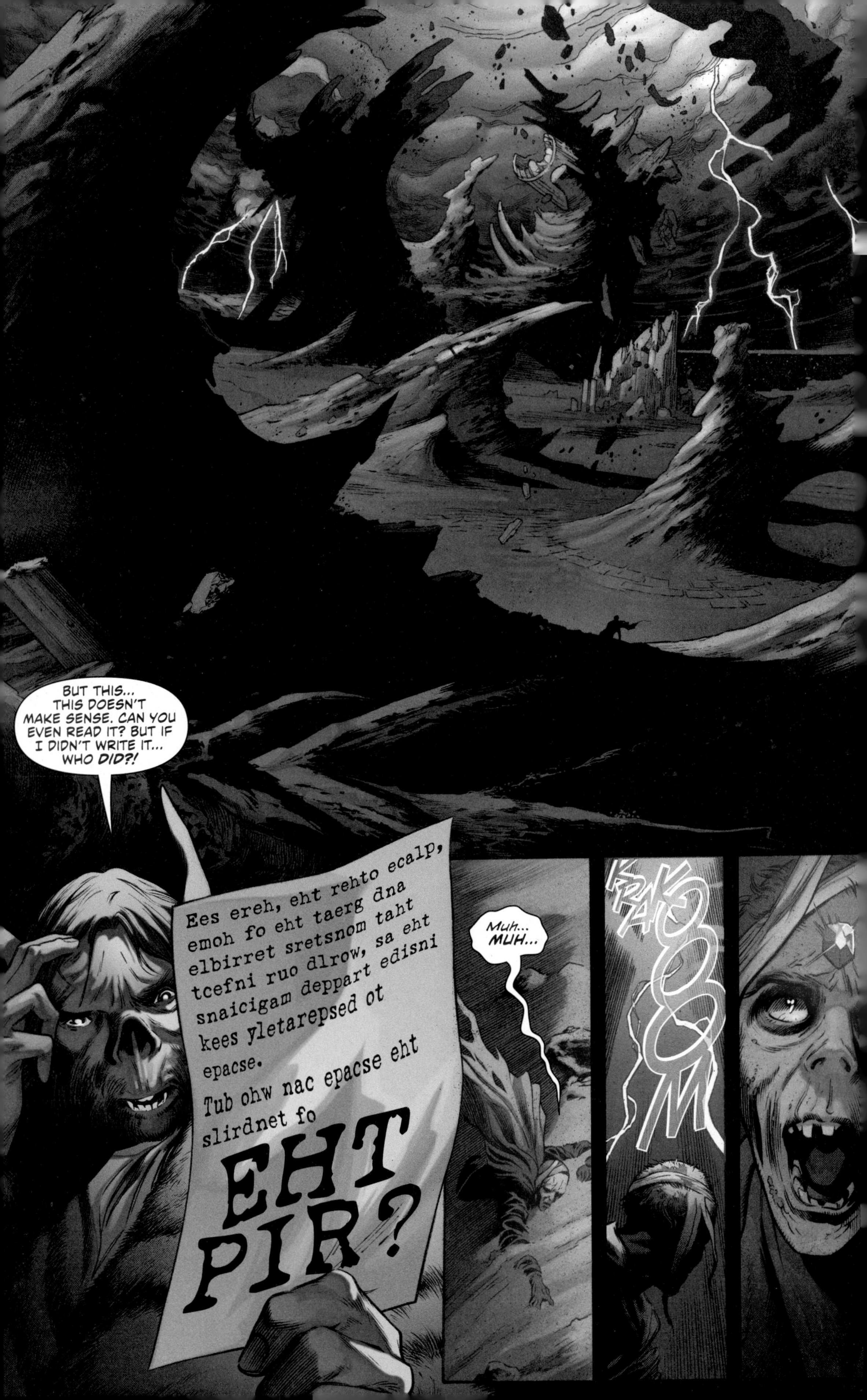
BUT THIS... THIS DOESN'T MAKE SENSE. CAN YOU EVEN READ IT? BUT IF I DIDN'T WRITE IT... WHO *DID?!*
Ees ereh, eht rehto ecalp, emoh fo eht taerg dna elbirret sretsnom taht tcefni ruo dlrow, sa eht snaicigam deppart edisni kees yletarepsed ot epacse.
Tub ohw nac epacse eht slirdnet fo
EHT PIR?
Muh... **MUH...**
KRAKOOOM

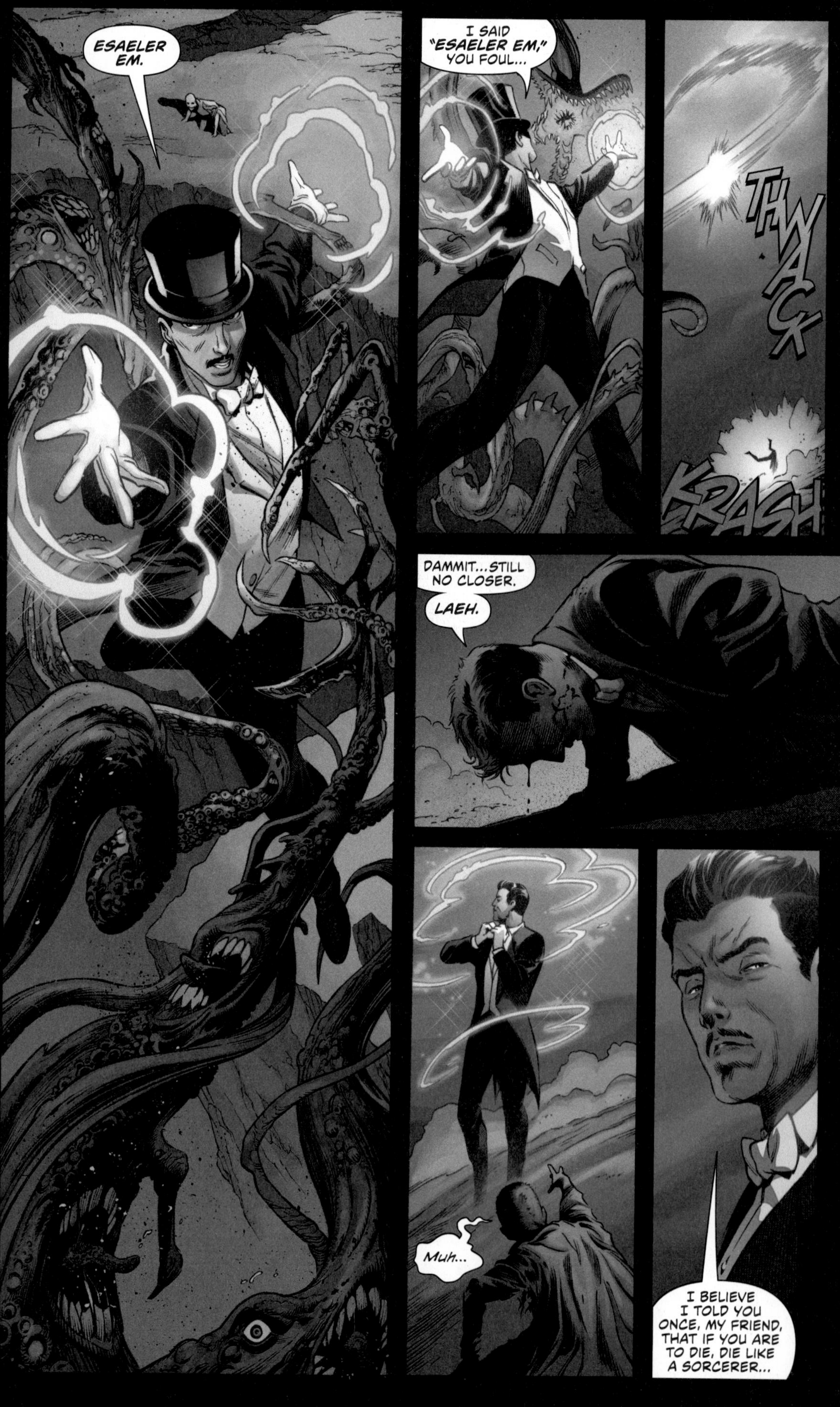
ESAELER EM.
I SAID "ESAELER EM," YOU FOUL...
THWACK
KRASH
DAMMIT...STILL NO CLOSER.
LAEH.
Muh...
I BELIEVE I TOLD YOU ONCE, MY FRIEND, THAT IF YOU ARE TO DIE, DIE LIKE A SORCERER...

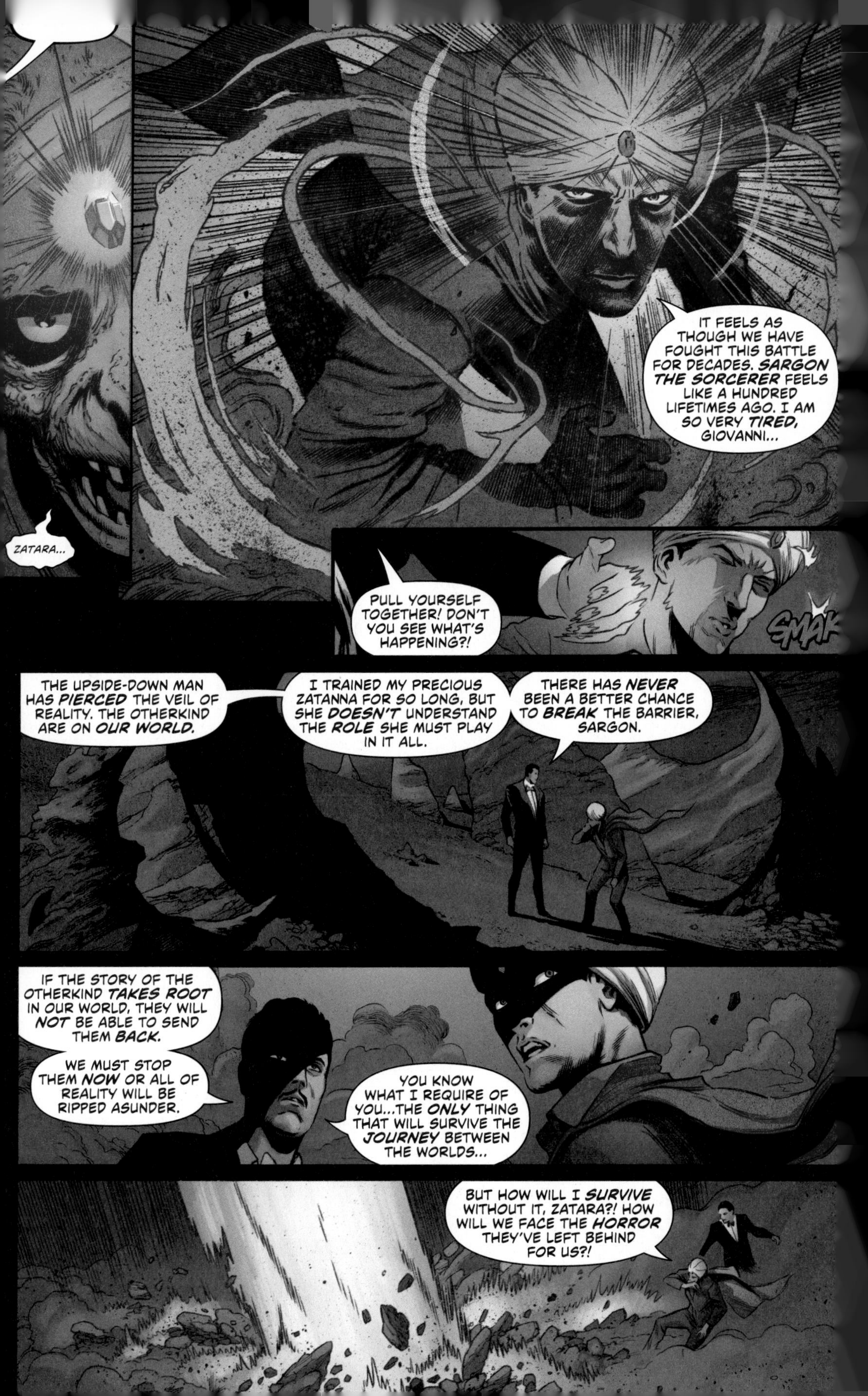
IT FEELS AS THOUGH WE HAVE FOUGHT THIS BATTLE FOR DECADES. SARGON THE SORCERER FEELS LIKE A HUNDRED LIFETIMES AGO. I AM SO VERY TIRED, GIOVANNI...
ZATARA...
PULL YOURSELF TOGETHER! DON'T YOU SEE WHAT'S HAPPENING?!
SMAK
THE UPSIDE-DOWN MAN HAS PIERCED THE VEIL OF REALITY. THE OTHERKIND ARE ON OUR WORLD.
I TRAINED MY PRECIOUS ZATANNA FOR SO LONG, BUT SHE DOESN'T UNDERSTAND THE ROLE SHE MUST PLAY IN IT ALL.
THERE HAS NEVER BEEN A BETTER CHANCE TO BREAK THE BARRIER, SARGON.
IF THE STORY OF THE OTHERKIND TAKES ROOT IN OUR WORLD, THEY WILL NOT BE ABLE TO SEND THEM BACK.
WE MUST STOP THEM NOW OR ALL OF REALITY WILL BE RIPPED ASUNDER.
YOU KNOW WHAT I REQUIRE OF YOU...THE ONLY THING THAT WILL SURVIVE THE JOURNEY BETWEEN THE WORLDS...
BUT HOW WILL I SURVIVE WITHOUT IT, ZATARA?! HOW WILL WE FACE THE HORROR THEY'VE LEFT BEHIND FOR US?!

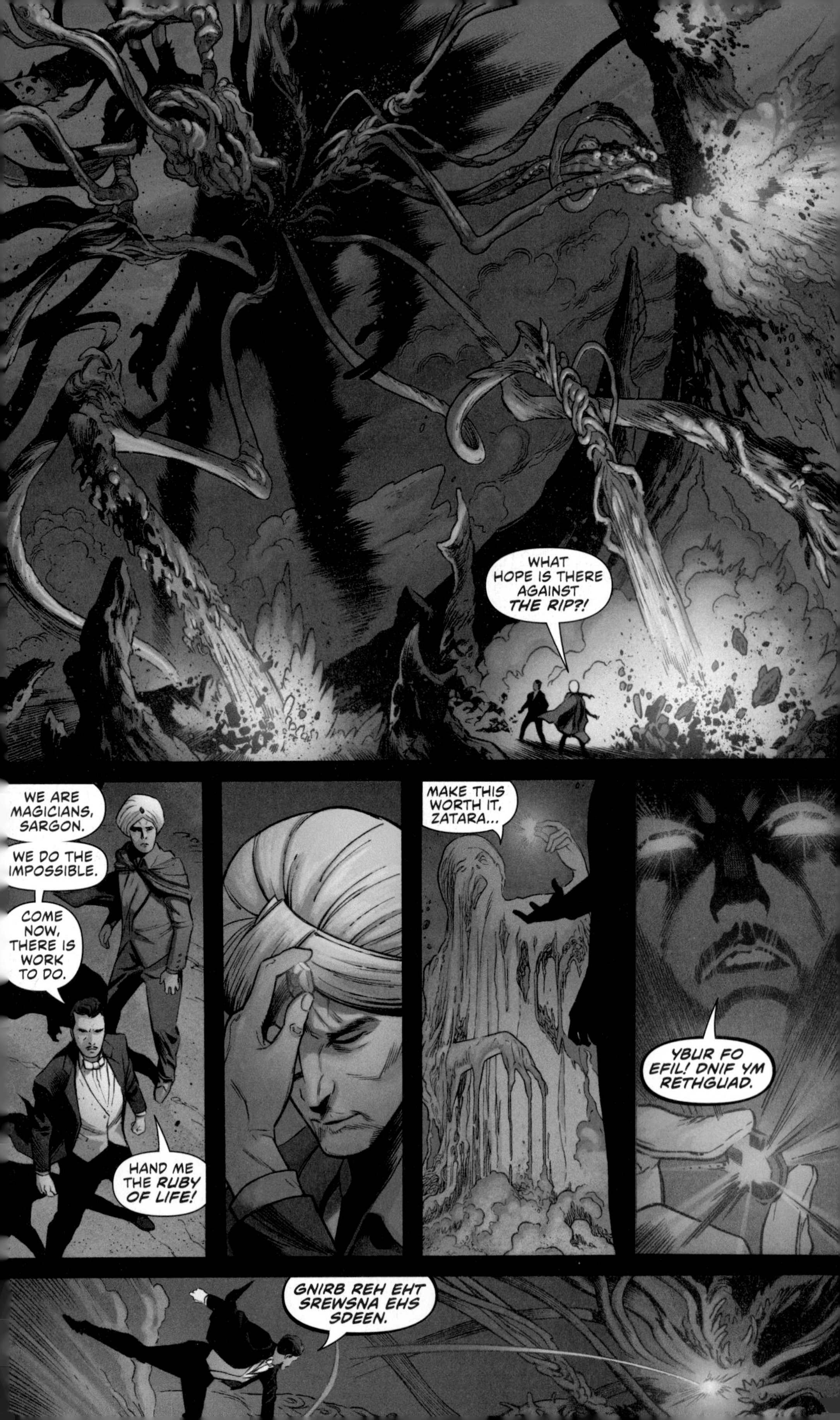
WHAT HOPE IS THERE AGAINST THE RIP?!
WE ARE MAGICIANS, SARGON.
WE DO THE IMPOSSIBLE.
COME NOW, THERE IS WORK TO DO.
HAND ME THE RUBY OF LIFE!
MAKE THIS WORTH IT, ZATARA...
YBUR FO EFIL! DNIF YM RETHGUAD.
GNIRB REH EHT SREWSNA EHS SDEEN.

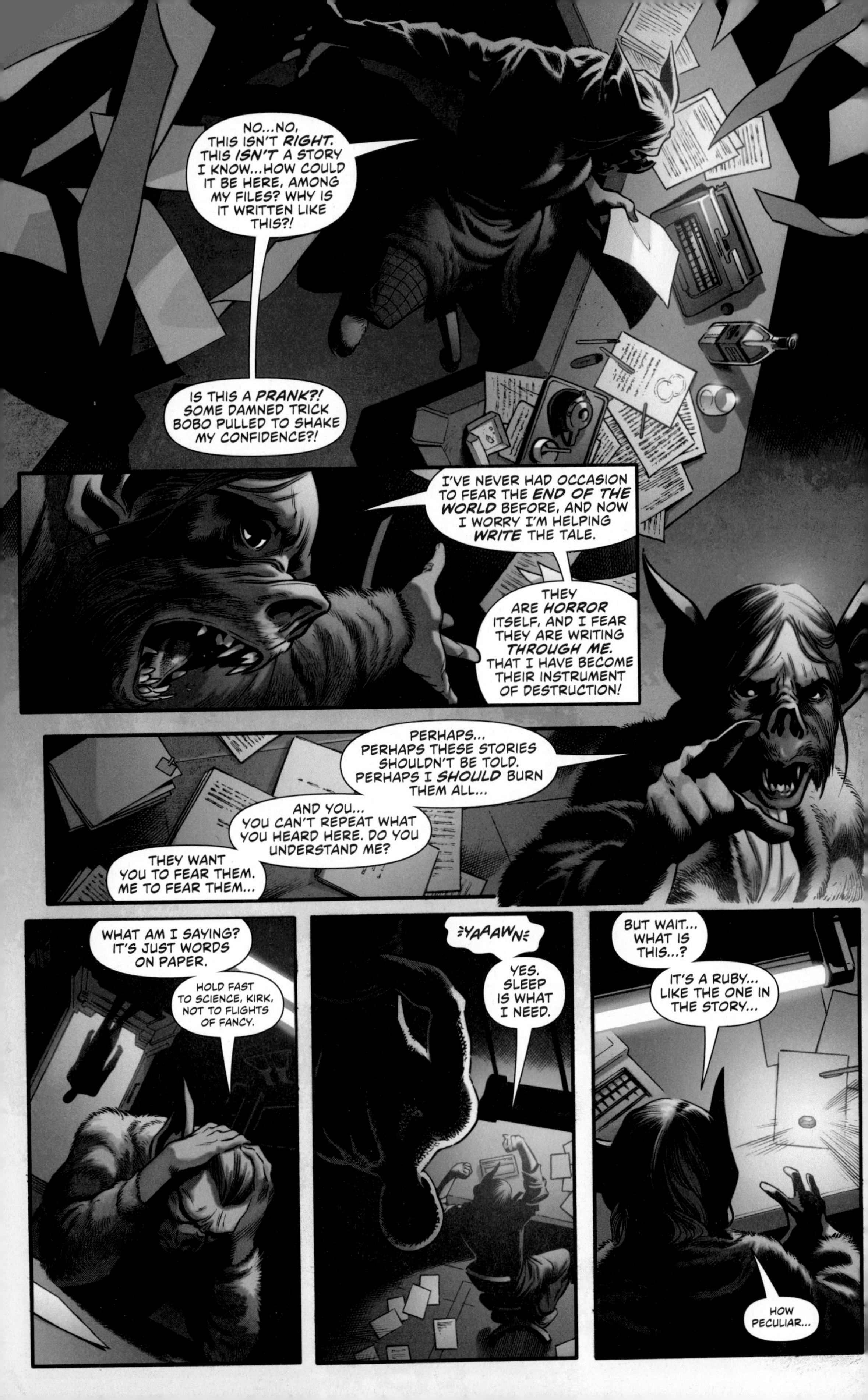
NO...NO, THIS ISN'T *RIGHT.* THIS *ISN'T* A STORY I KNOW...HOW COULD IT BE HERE, AMONG MY FILES? WHY IS IT WRITTEN LIKE THIS?!
IS THIS A *PRANK?!* SOME DAMNED TRICK BOBO PULLED TO SHAKE MY CONFIDENCE?!
I'VE NEVER HAD OCCASION TO FEAR THE *END OF THE WORLD* BEFORE, AND NOW I WORRY I'M HELPING *WRITE* THE TALE.
THEY ARE *HORROR* ITSELF, AND I FEAR THEY ARE WRITING *THROUGH ME.* THAT I HAVE BECOME THEIR INSTRUMENT OF DESTRUCTION!
PERHAPS... PERHAPS THESE STORIES SHOULDN'T BE TOLD. PERHAPS I *SHOULD* BURN THEM ALL...
AND YOU... YOU CAN'T REPEAT WHAT YOU HEARD HERE. DO YOU UNDERSTAND ME?
THEY WANT YOU TO FEAR THEM. ME TO FEAR THEM...
WHAT AM I SAYING? IT'S JUST WORDS ON PAPER.
HOLD FAST TO SCIENCE, KIRK, NOT TO FLIGHTS OF FANCY.
YAAAWN
YES. SLEEP IS WHAT I NEED.
BUT WAIT... WHAT IS THIS...?
IT'S A RUBY... LIKE THE ONE IN THE STORY...
HOW PECULIAR...

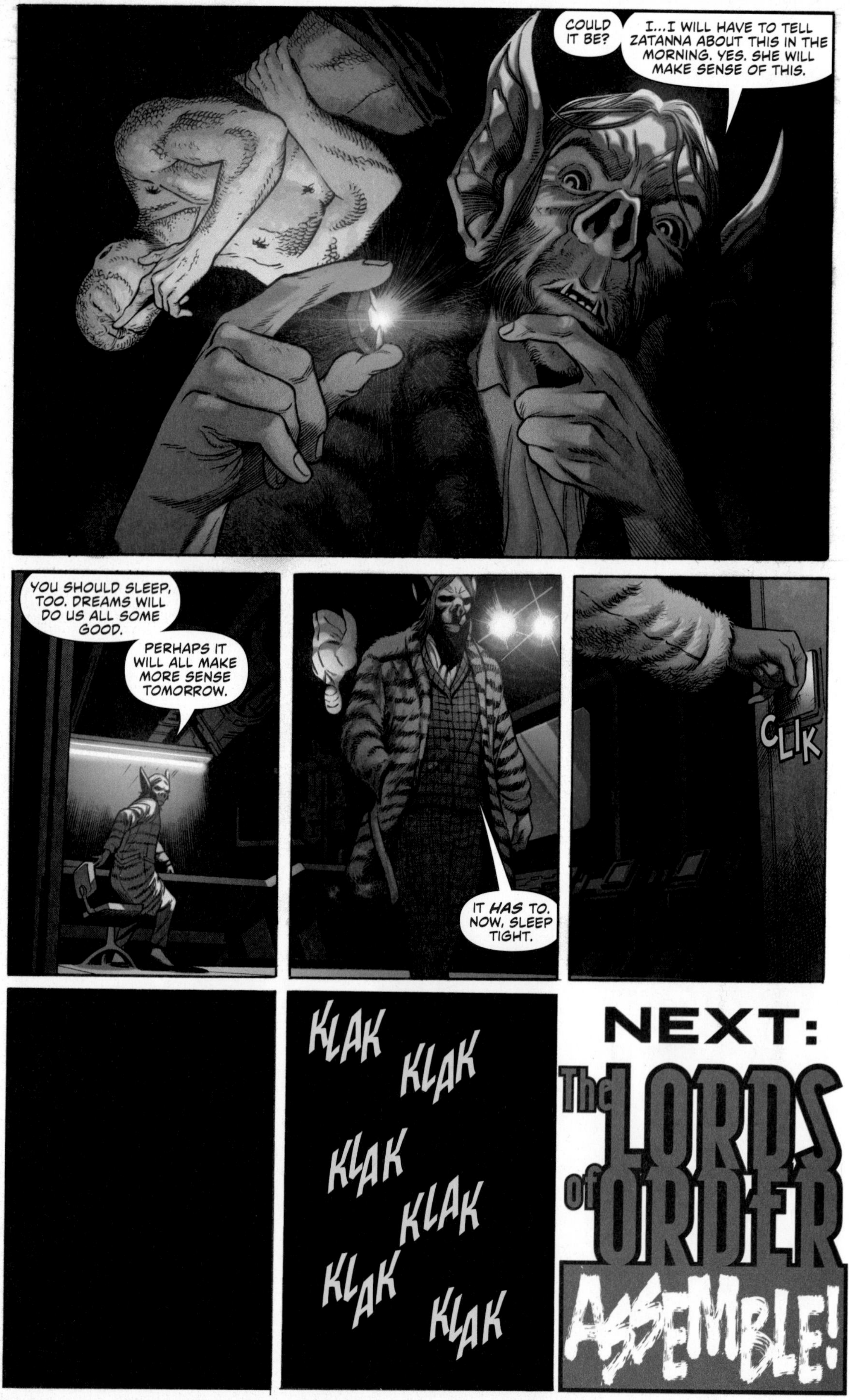
COULD IT BE?
I...I WILL HAVE TO TELL ZATANNA ABOUT THIS IN THE MORNING. YES. SHE WILL MAKE SENSE OF THIS.
YOU SHOULD SLEEP, TOO. DREAMS WILL DO US ALL SOME GOOD.
PERHAPS IT WILL ALL MAKE MORE SENSE TOMORROW.
IT HAS TO. NOW, SLEEP TIGHT.
CLIK
KLAK KLAK KLAK KLAK KLAK KLAK
NEXT:
The LORDS of ORDER ASSEMBLE!

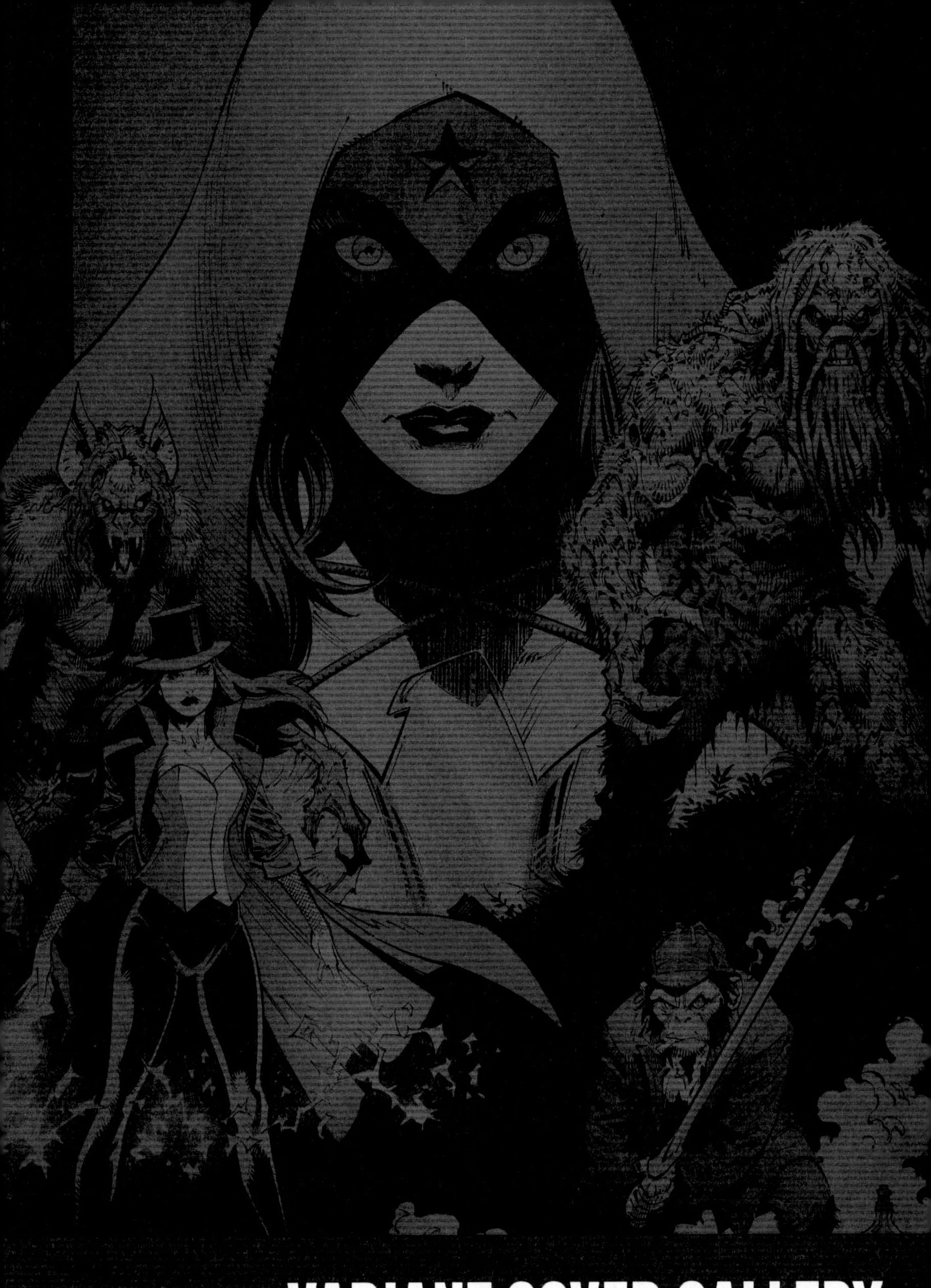

VARIANT COVER GALLERY

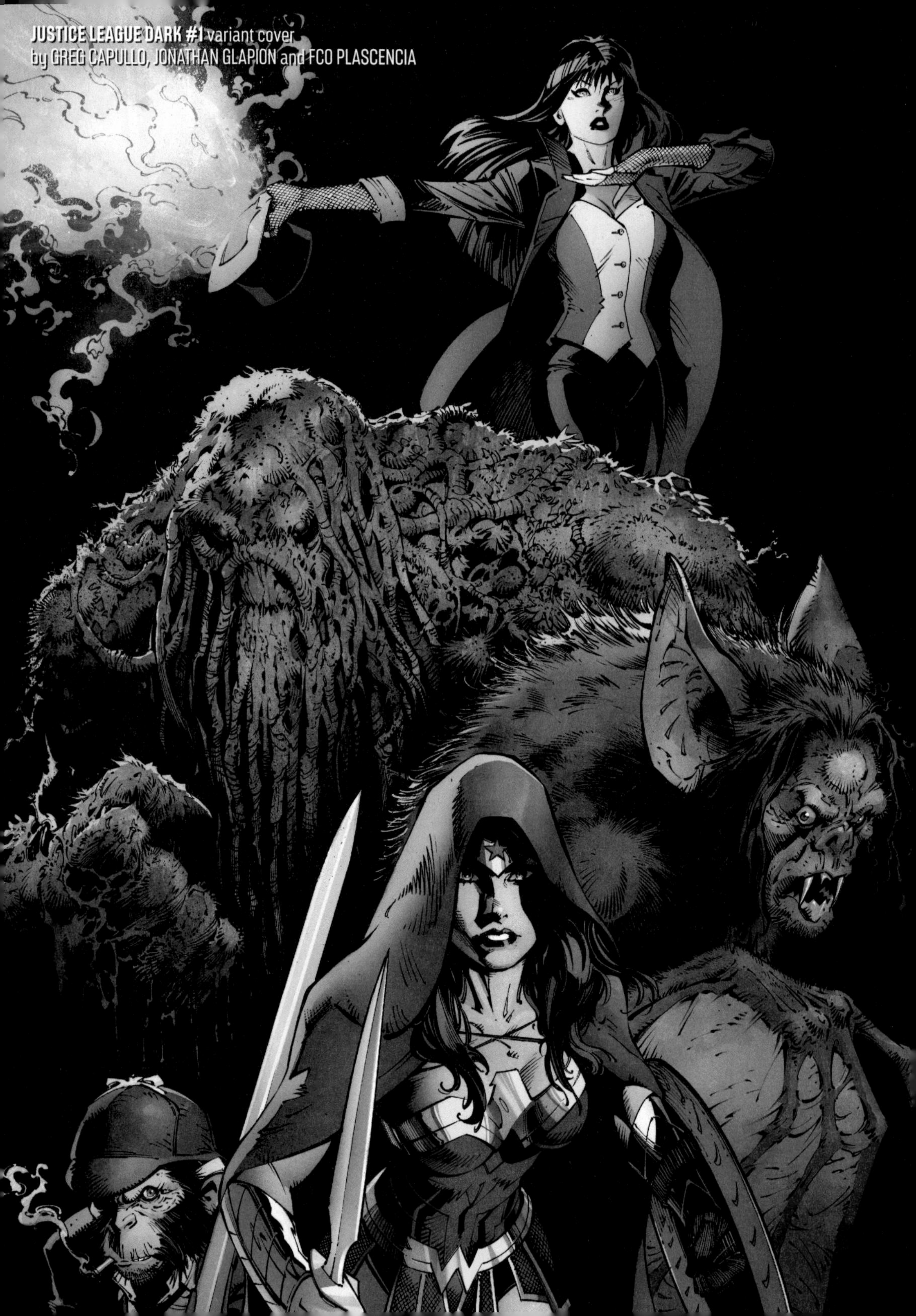

JUSTICE LEAGUE DARK #1 variant cover
by GREG CAPULLO, JONATHAN GLAPION and FCO PLASCENCIA

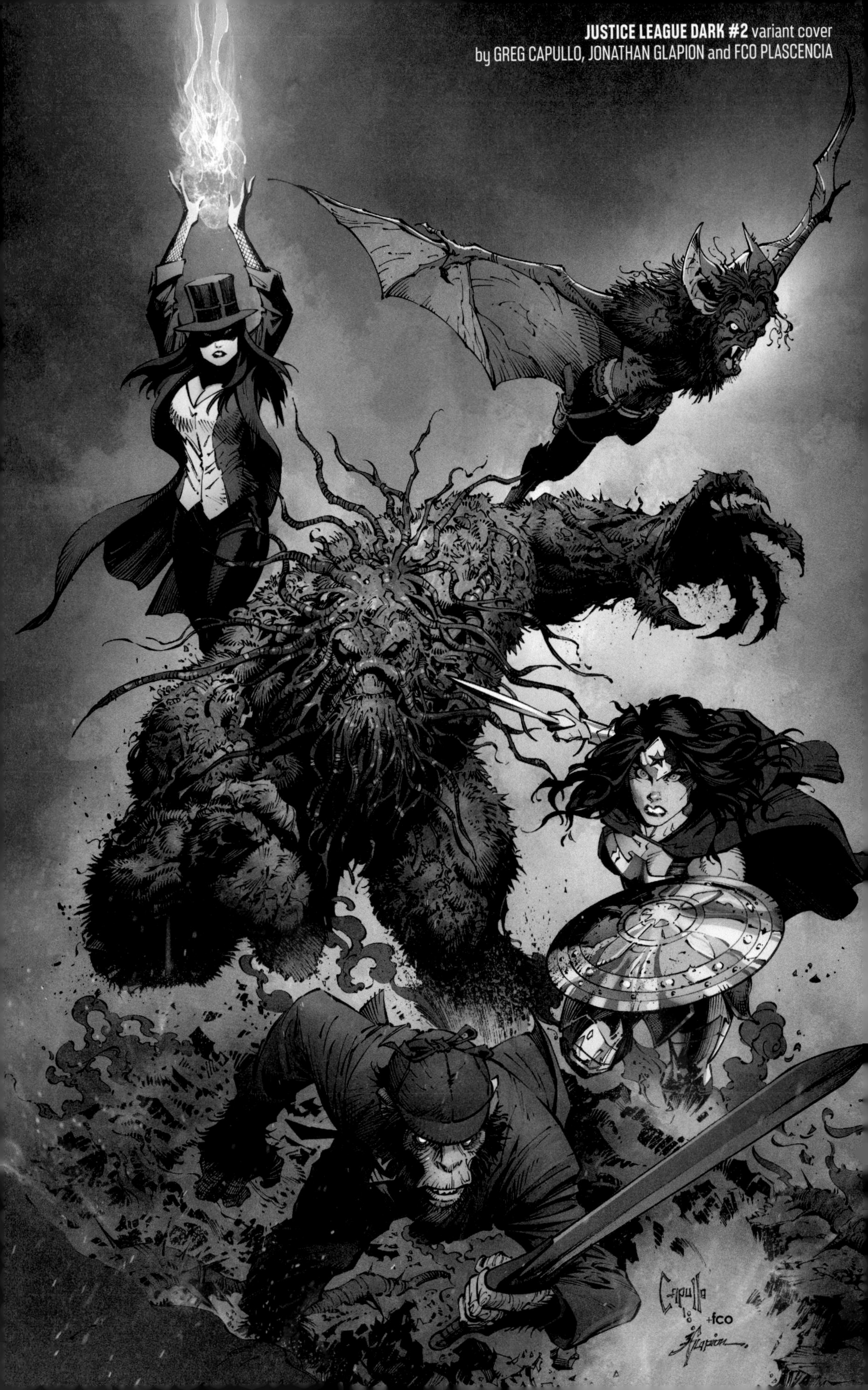

JUSTICE LEAGUE DARK #2 variant cover
by GREG CAPULLO, JONATHAN GLAPION and FCO PLASCENCIA

JUSTICE LEAGUE DARK #3 variant cover
by GREG CAPULLO, JONATHAN GLAPION and FCO PLASCENCIA

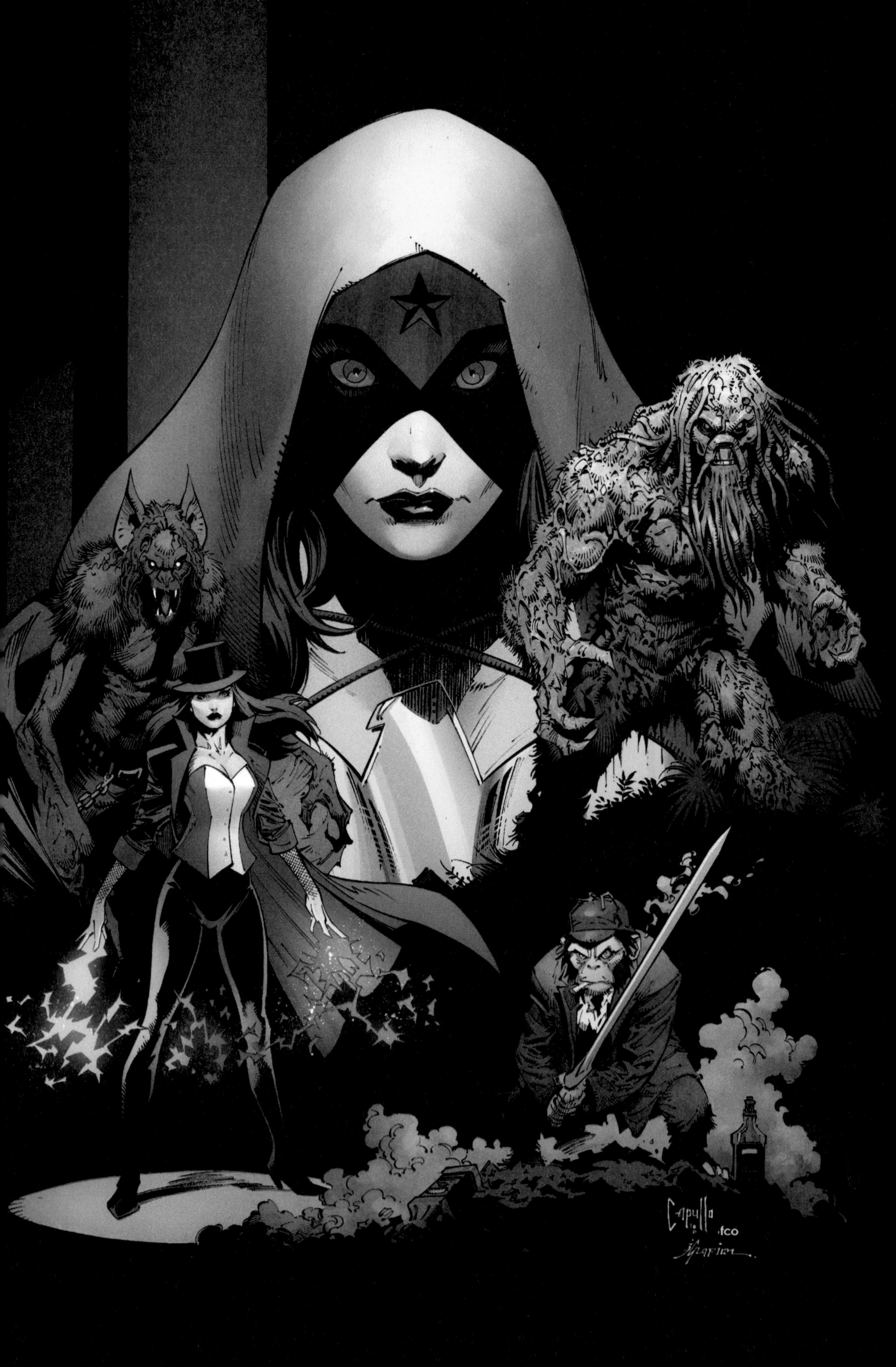
Capullo
fco
Glapion

JUSTICE LEAGUE DARK #5 variant cover
by CLAYTON CRAIN

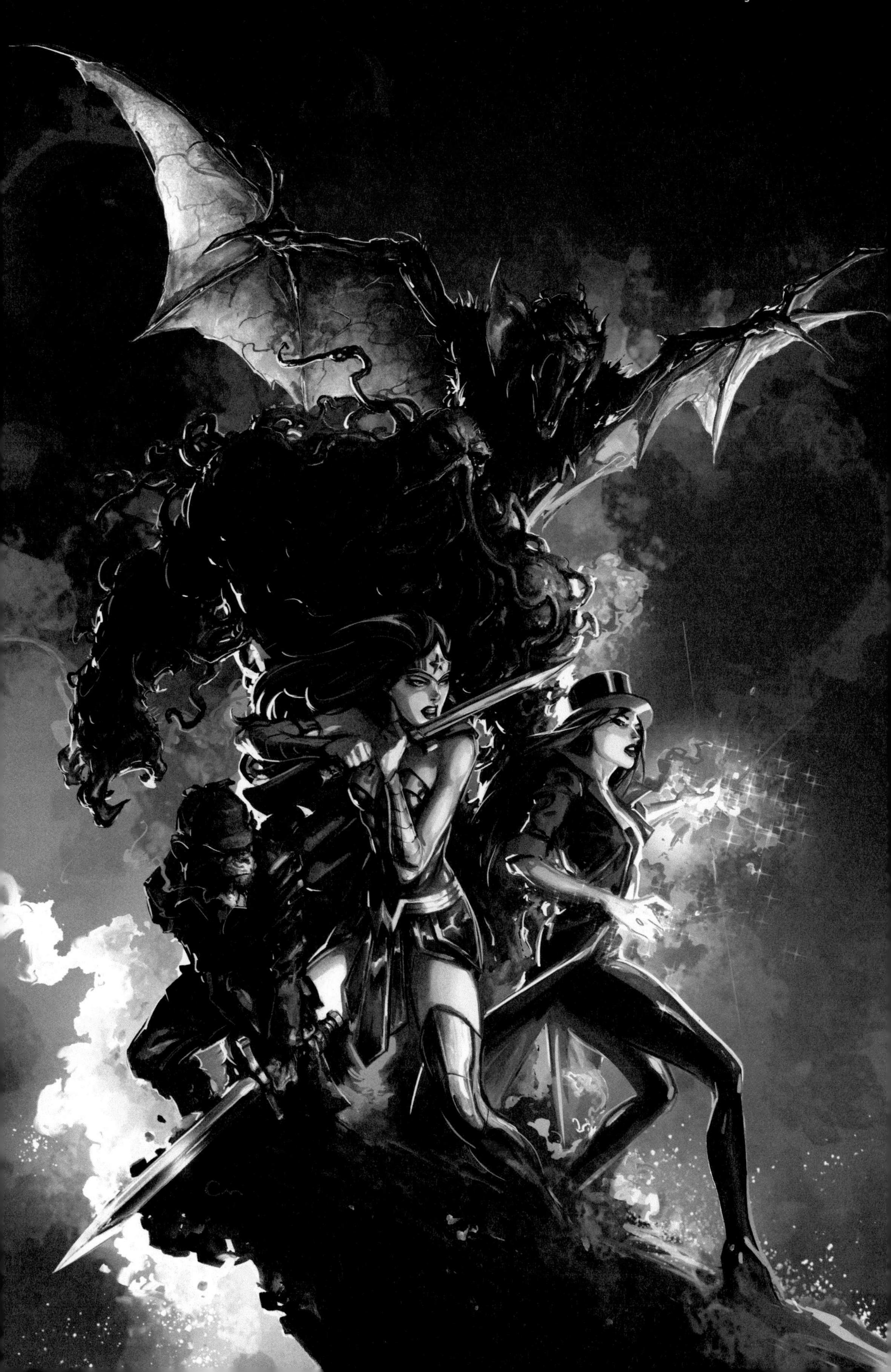

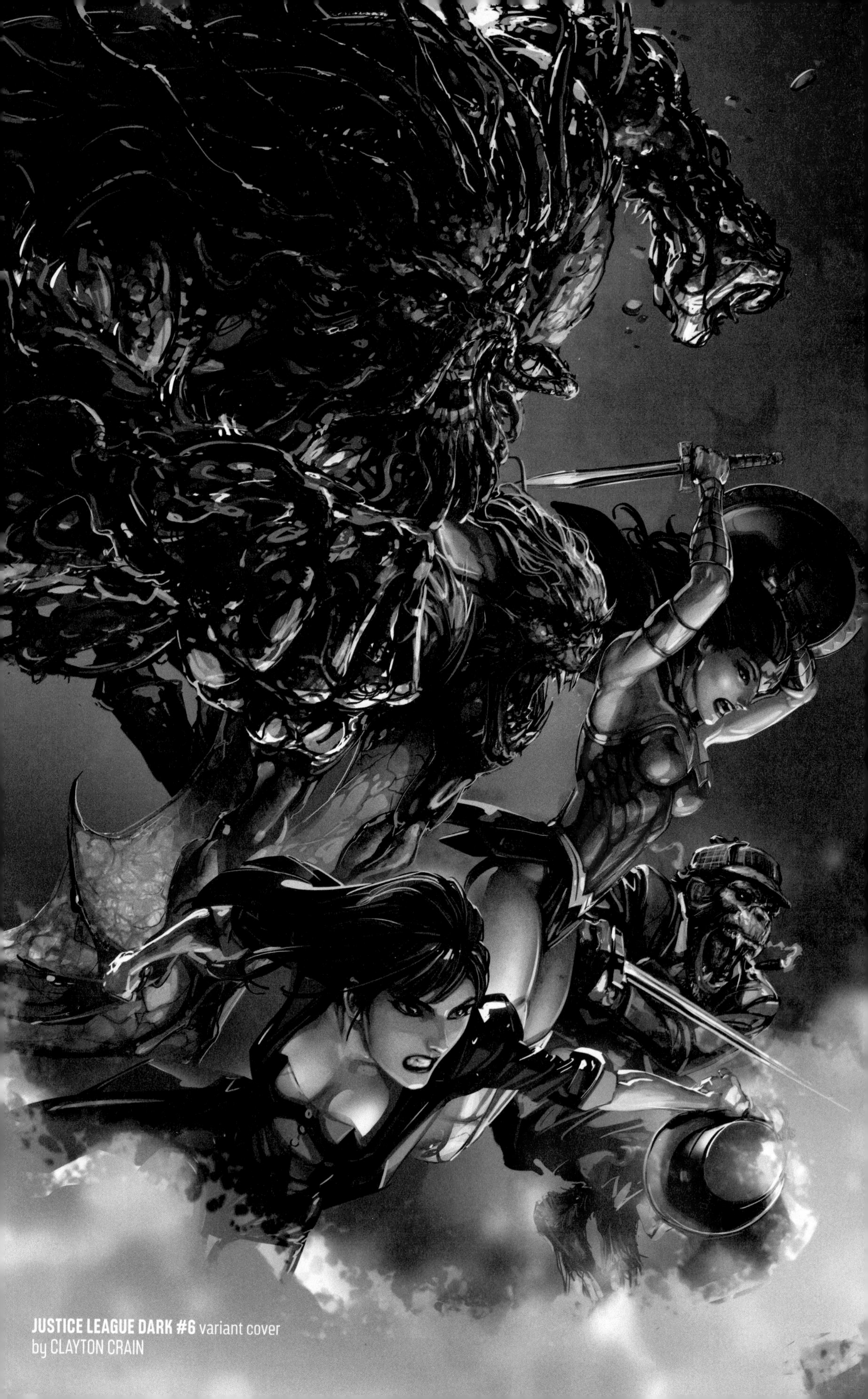

JUSTICE LEAGUE DARK #6 variant cover
by CLAYTON CRAIN

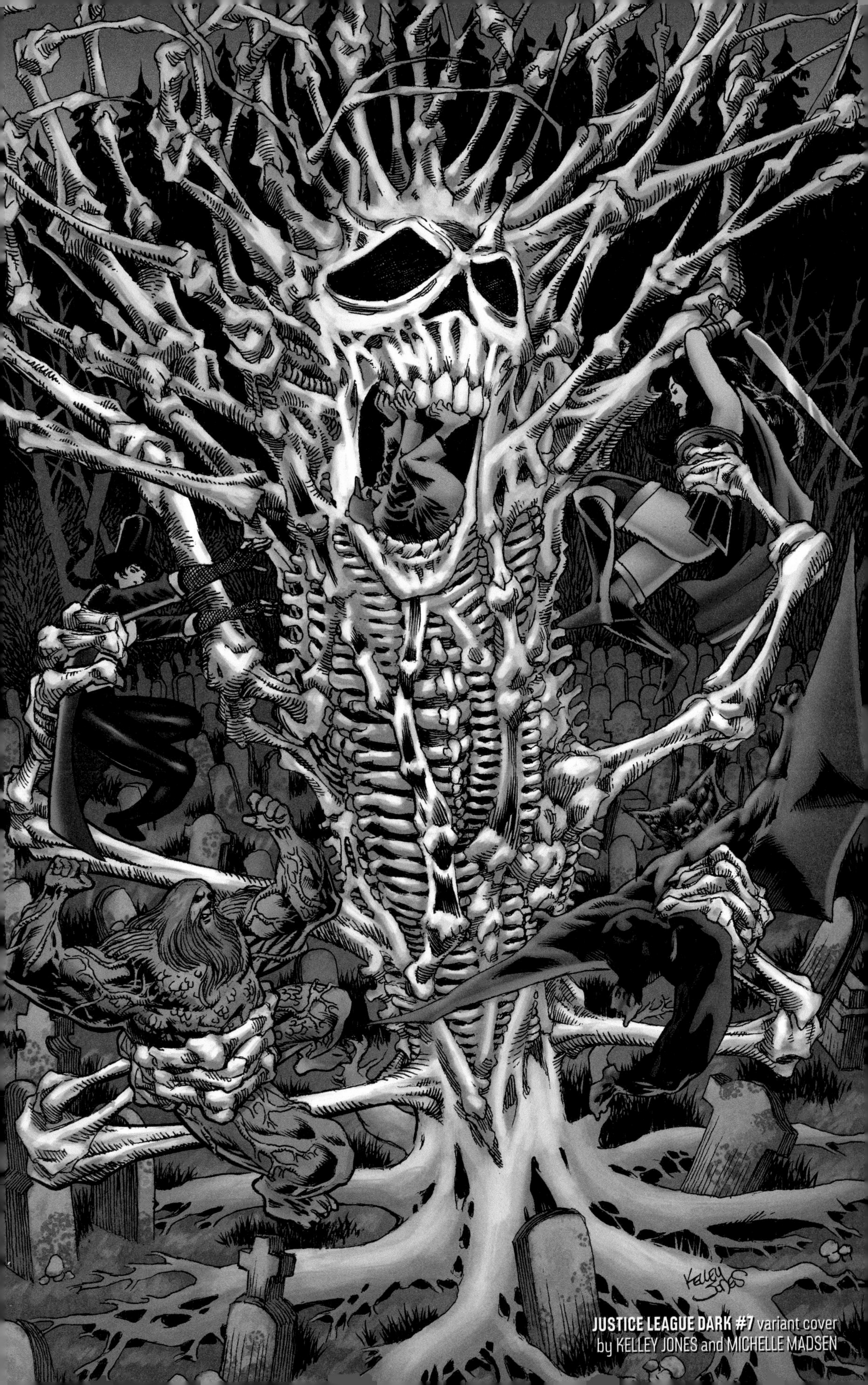

JUSTICE LEAGUE DARK #7 variant cover
by KELLEY JONES and MICHELLE MADSEN

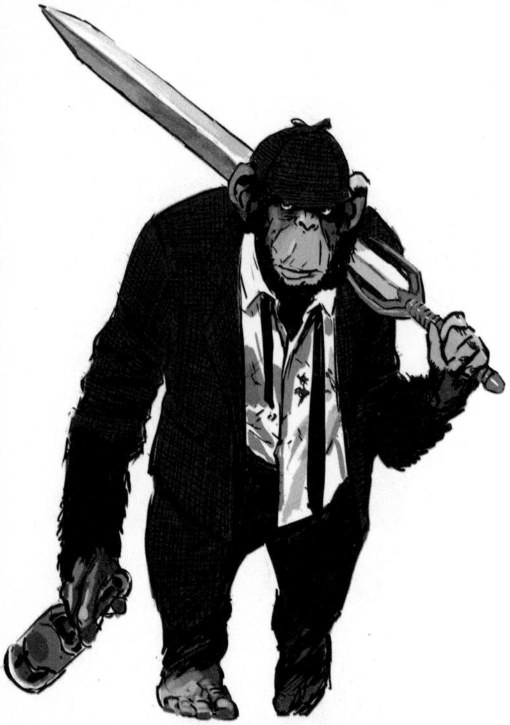

DETECTIVE CHIMP/JLD
BY ÁLVARO MARTÍNEZ

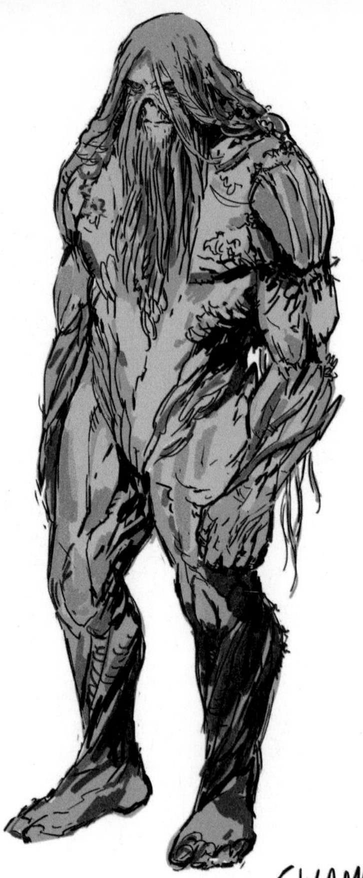

SWAMPTHING/JLD

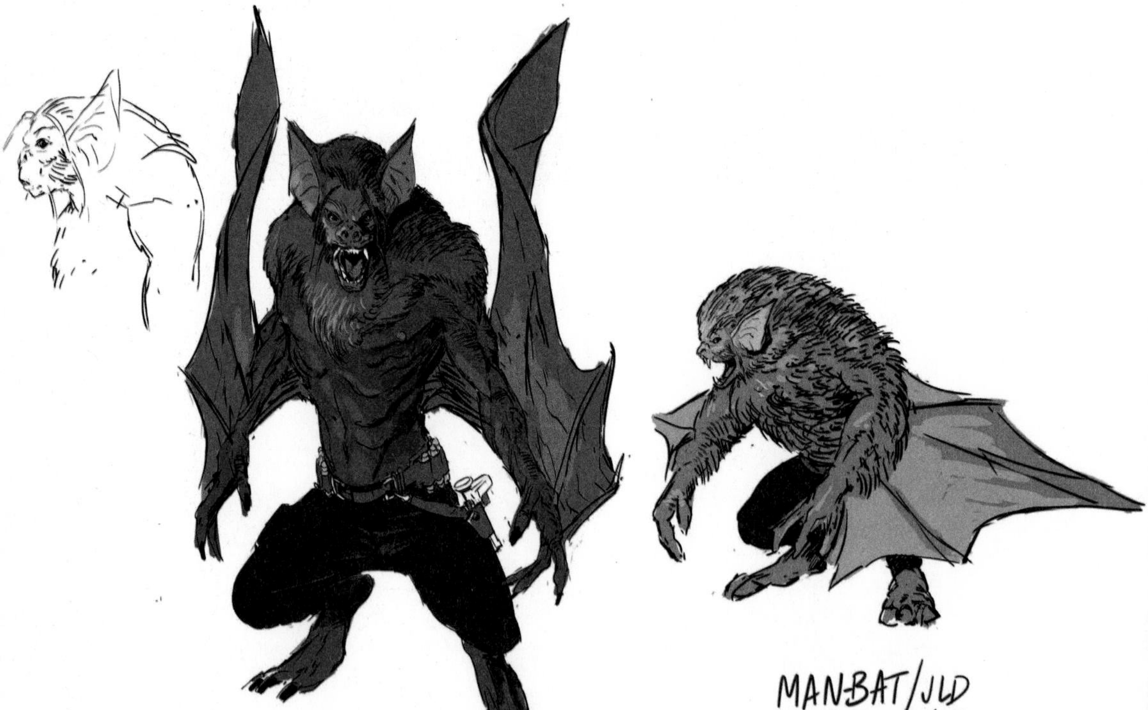

MAN-BAT/JLD
BY ÁLVARO MARTÍNEZ

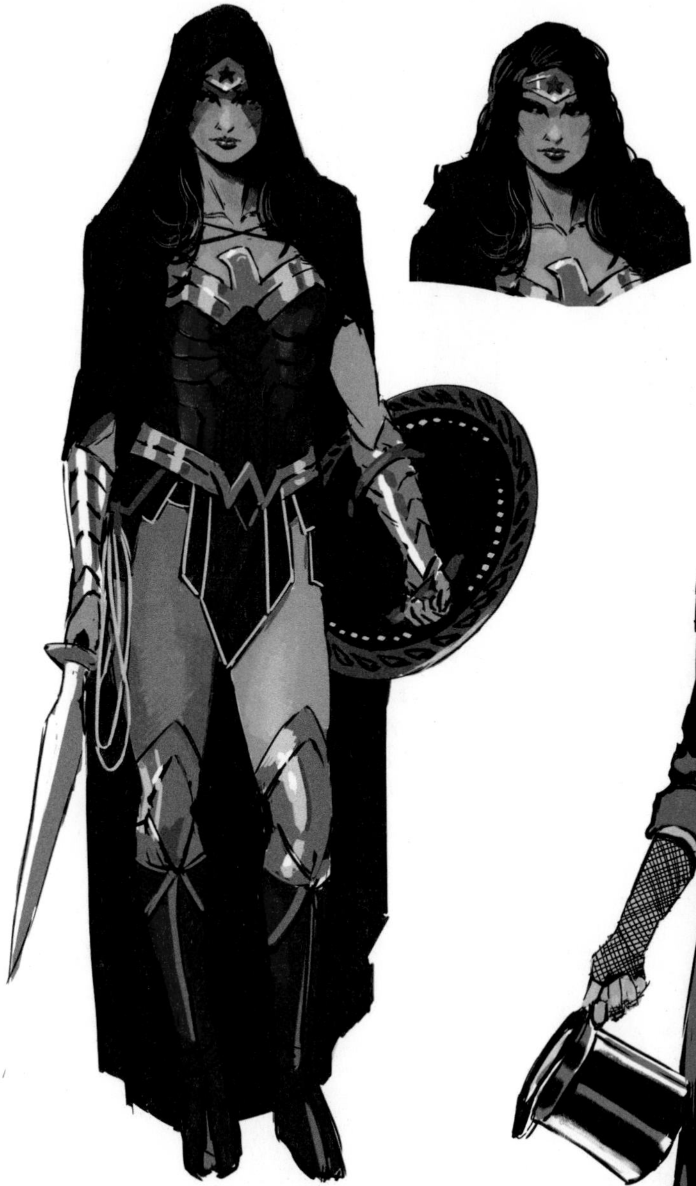

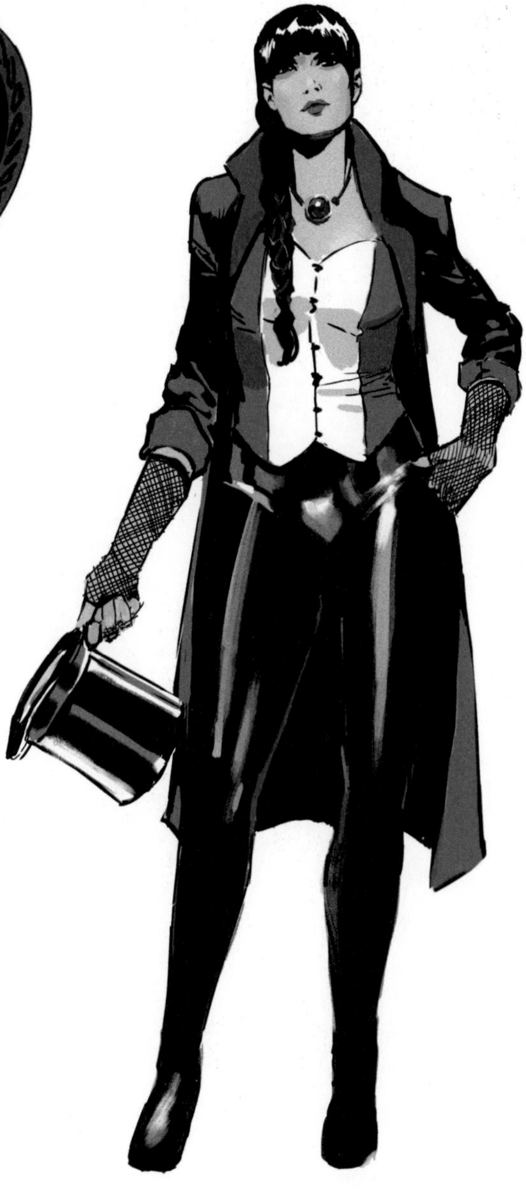

WONDER WOMAN/JLD
BY ÄLVARO MÄRTINEZ

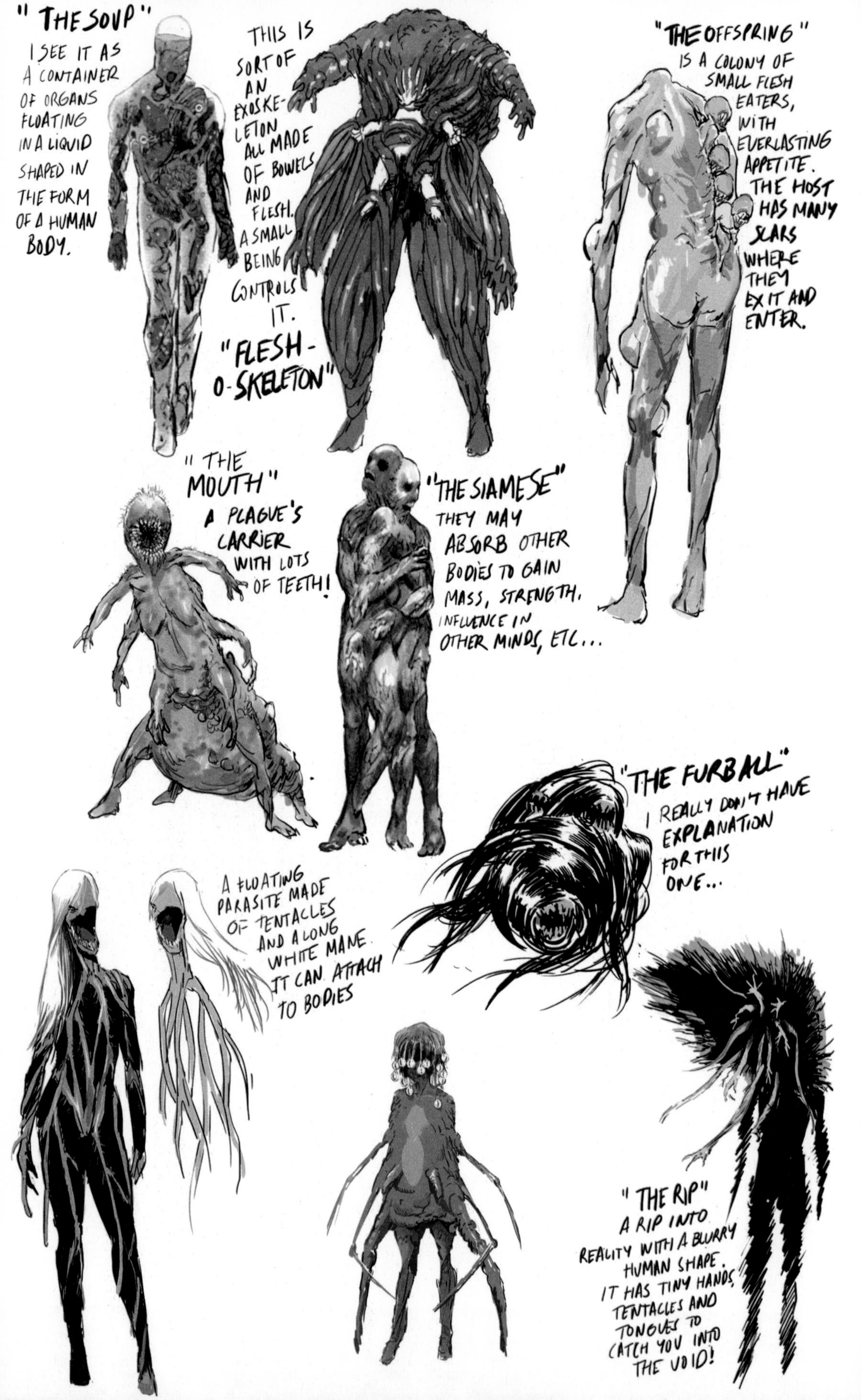

"THE SOUP"
I SEE IT AS A CONTAINER OF ORGANS FLOATING IN A LIQUID SHAPED IN THE FORM OF A HUMAN BODY.
THIS IS SORT OF AN EXOSKE-LETON ALL MADE OF BOWELS AND FLESH. A SMALL BEING CONTROLS IT.
"FLESH-O-SKELETON"
"THE OFFSPRING"
IS A COLONY OF SMALL FLESH EATERS, WITH EVERLASTING APPETITE. THE HOST HAS MANY SCARS WHERE THEY EXIT AND ENTER.
"THE MOUTH"
A PLAGUE'S CARRIER WITH LOTS OF TEETH!
"THE SIAMESE"
THEY MAY ABSORB OTHER BODIES TO GAIN MASS, STRENGTH, INFLUENCE IN OTHER MINDS, ETC...
"THE FURBALL"
I REALLY DON'T HAVE EXPLANATION FOR THIS ONE...
A FLOATING PARASITE MADE OF TENTACLES AND A LONG WHITE MANE. IT CAN ATTACH TO BODIES
"THE RIP"
A RIP INTO REALITY WITH A BLURRY HUMAN SHAPE. IT HAS TINY HANDS, TENTACLES AND TONGUES TO CATCH YOU INTO THE VOID!

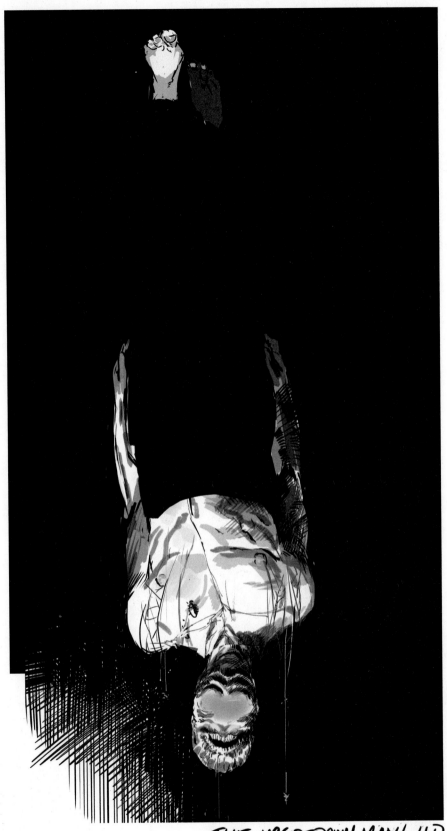

THE UPSIDEDOWN MAN/ JLD

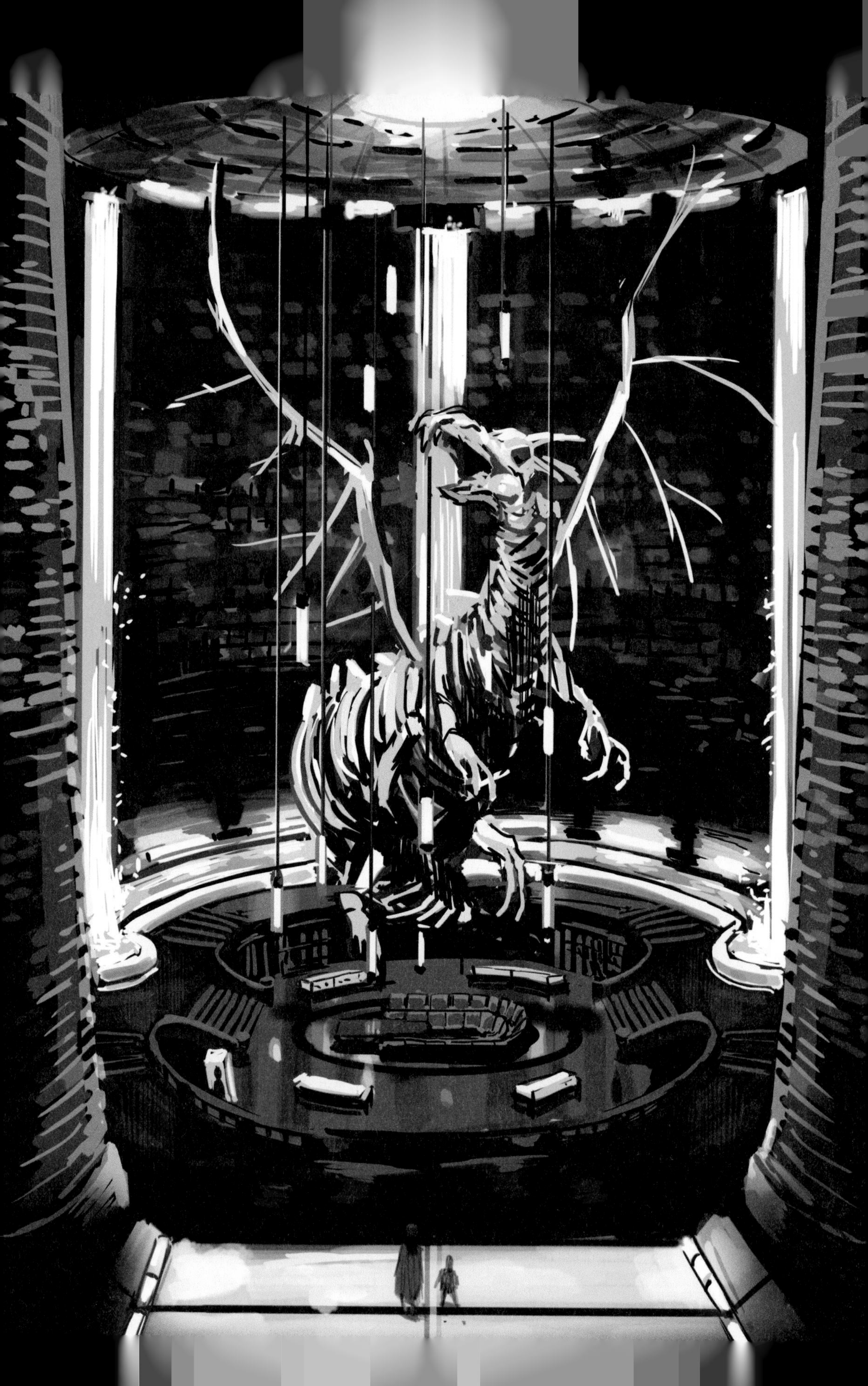